BOOKS BY MARIO PEI

All About Language
The Story of English
The Story of Language
Our National Heritage
Invitation to Linguistics
Glossary of Linguistic Terminology
How to Learn Languages and What Languages to Learn
Voices of Man
The Families of Words
Talking Your Way Around the World
Getting Along in Russian (with Fedor I. Nikanov)
Getting Along in French (with John Fisher)
Getting Along in German (with Robert Politzer)
Getting Along in Spanish (with Eloy Vaquero)
Getting Along in Italian
One Language for the World
Language for Everybody
Swords of Anjou
Our Names (with E. Lambert)
The Book of Place Names (with E. Lambert)
The Italian Language
The World's Chief Languages
Languages for War and Peace
*The Language of the Eighth-Century Texts in
Northern France*
First-Year French (with E. Méras)

THE STORY OF THE

English
Language

by Mario Pei

A TOUCHSTONE BOOK
PUBLISHED BY SIMON AND SCHUSTER

Acknowledgments

The author wishes to state his deep indebtedness to Professor Donald W. Lee, formerly of Columbia, now of the English Department of the University of Houston, Texas, who painstakingly read the entire manuscript of the original edition and offered many valuable suggestions and corrections; to the numerous authorities cited in the text, particularly Baugh, Jespersen and Robertson; and to the scores of newspaper writers and columnists who, by reason of their tireless reporting and creation of innovations, have so much to do with the growth of the English language of today and tomorrow.

M. P.

Contents

PART III THE FUTURE

PART ONE

The Past

Chapter One

THE PREHISTORY OF ENGLISH

*Pre-English Britain—The Mark of Rome—Early Teu-
tonic Legends and Languages—Near and Distant
Relatives of English—The Coming of the Anglo-Saxons*

Unless we choose to accept the doctrine of predestination, it is
chance that makes history. The panoramic future of men, nations,
races, religions, languages, often depends upon the cast of a die,
the turn of a card, the whim of a historical moment.

The fact that you are you, and not someone else, hinges upon
a series of concatenated events reaching back to the dawn of the
human race. Your parents had to meet, and their parents before
them, for countless generations.

It is the same with languages. If semi-legendary Hengist and
Horsa had been unable to overcome the resistance of the Romanized Britons and had been hurled back into the North Sea, this
language we today call English might have been as Romance as
French or as Celtic as Welsh, and might have been known by
another name besides. If the charge of Harold's men at Hastings
had not been broken by the showers of Norman arrows raining
from the skies, our tongue today might be as close to German as is
Dutch, or closer. Other events, before and since 1066, might have
led to our speaking an Indo-Iranian language, like Persian, or a
Semitic one, like Phoenician or Arabic. As late as the age of
Elizabeth, a victory on the part of the Spanish Armada might
conceivably have turned England and her possessions into
Spanish-speaking colonies.

The English we speak is not the fruit of a deliberate human

design. It is the sum total of a long series of historical accidents, behind which the only design that is perceptible is God's.

This is not to say we are to blame Divine Providence for whatever shortcomings we may discover in our speech, though we may thank it for our linguistic blessings. Many men, famous and obscure, have had a part in fashioning what goes into the tongue we speak and write. Few if any of them had any clear idea of what they were doing as they did it.

The mission of the linguist is to describe what has happened and is happening to a language rather than to philosophize upon it. The historical facts about the past rise and present progress of the English language make a fascinating tale—at least as absorbing as are our hopes and forebodings concerning the future development and status of the language that bears the message of our civilization throughout the globe. If a little geographical and political history gets intermingled with our linguistic discussion, let it be remembered that there is no divorcing language from other human activities.

Mist-shrouded Britain, rising sheer and white from the waves of the stormy North Sea, has always cast a spell over visitors approaching it from the European mainland. The visitors must have liked what they found, because often the visits turned into invasions or attempted invasions.

Anthropologists claim that Britain must have been inhabited for at least fifty thousand years, first by Paleolithic, then by Neolithic men. Earliest known inhabitants concerning whom there is any degree of assurance were short-statured, swarthy, long-skulled people, the progenitors perhaps of the ancient Picts of Scotland. Linguists with anthropological leanings like to speculate about the theory that they formed part of an early Mediterranean race, somehow connected with the Iberians of Spain, concerning whose language practically nothing is known.

Before the dawn of recorded history, however, the British Isles had been visited, overrun and conquered by two separate groups of Celtic invaders, speaking tongues which were the remote ancestors of present-day Gaelic and Welsh.

These ancient Celts were great wanderers and conquerors, as

evidenced by the fact that traces of their civilization are to be found in the valleys of the Rhine and Danube, the crest of the Alps, northwestern Spain, northern Italy, practically all of France, the Balkans and the kingdom of Galatia in Asia Minor. In Gaul their Druids used Greek letters, in Italy the Etruscan alphabet, at a time when the Romans had barely emerged from their rustic illiteracy. But there is not too much evidence that the high civilization of the continental Celts extended to their British kinsmen.

One of our earliest historical references to Britain is Herodotus' mention, in the fifth century B.C., of the "Tin Islands," but Herodotus hastens to add that he knows nothing about them. This statement is belied by the very name he gives them. Phoenician and Greek traders and navigators in the early Bronze Age knew the value of tin, and where to find it. About one century after Herodotus, Aristotle tells us that "beyond the Pillars of Hercules the ocean flows around the earth, and in it are two very large islands called British: Albion and Ierne, lying beyond the Keltoi." The allusion to Britain and Ireland is evident.

In those days, as today, geography served the purposes of power politics. The tin mines of Britain were probably known to Republican Rome even before the great city on the Tiber began its long career of conquest outside of peninsular Italy. Julius Caesar, conqueror of the Gauls, reconnoitered on British soil as early as 55 B.C., establishing friendly contacts with various British chieftains. The sphere of influence thus created led to outright conquest. Ninety-seven years later, during the reign of the Emperor Claudius, the Roman legions poured into Britain by way of the Straits of Dover, quickly seizing what is today Kent. In four years they had advanced up the Thames and even as far as Devon.

The Roman conquest of Britain was not completed till the time of the great general Agricola, over a century later, and it was marked by episodes of savage revolt, such as the brief war unleashed by Queen Boadicea in 61 A.D., and equally savage repression. But by the end of the first century of our era Celtic Britain had ceased to exist as a political entity, and Roman Britain had taken its place.

The completeness of the Roman cultural conquest is to some extent a matter of conjecture. Tacitus says that by Agricola's time (78-85 A.D.) the Britons were anxious to learn Latin, while Martial, in 96 A.D., states that his poems were read in Britain. The wealth of Roman ruins and remains on British soil would seem to indicate a thoroughgoing Romanization of the country, with at least a score of Roman cities, and the introduction of Christianity from the continent in the second and third centuries.

It is primarily the linguistic factor that leads us to doubt that the Romanization of Britain was as thorough as that of other Roman provinces, like Gaul and Iberia. The Gauls of France and the Iberians of Spain never went back to their ancestral tongues after Rome fell; the Britons did. The fact that today the Welsh speak a Celtic, not a Romance tongue, would seem to point to an incomplete process of linguistic and cultural absorption. Whether this reversion to type began as soon as the Romans withdrew, in 410 A.D., or was a gradual process that took place in the course of the Britons' long and bitter retreat before the later Anglo-Saxon invaders is something we shall probably never be quite sure of.

If the historical period from the third century B.C. to 400 A.D. is the Roman era, then the fifth century A.D. might well be described in history as the Germanic Century. During the course of those hundred fateful years Italy, along with Rome itself, fell to the Ostrogoths, Gaul to the Franks, Britain to the Angles, Saxons and Jutes, while Vandals and Visigoths swept over North Africa and Spain. The Roman world crumbled away, and the stage was set for the Teutonic Middle Ages.

The invading tribes had much in common in the way of race, customs and language. As far back as the days of Tacitus, at the end of the first century A.D., the *Germani* who dwelt beyond the Alps and the Rhine had been fully known to and feared by the Romans. Marius, almost two hundred years before Tacitus, had cut to pieces their vanguard as it tried to storm its way into the sunny Mediterranean lands. The would-be invaders had at that time been labeled "Cimbri" and "Teutones," and there seems to have been no consciousness in the minds of the Romans who defeated them that they were in any way different from the Celtic Gauls with whom Rome had fought since its foundation.

Caesar, in the course of his Gallic campaign, discovered the difference between the fierce men of Ariovistus who dwelt beyond the Rhine and the easier-going Gauls on the western bank of the great river, but he, too, with his superior strategy and equipment, had readily disposed of the Germans. Tacitus, over a century later, gives a full and precise account of the Germanic tribes, citing, among other things, a native Germanic poem which declares that the Germanic people are divided into three branches— Inguaeones, Hermiones and Istaeuones, each descended from one of the three sons of Mannus, who in turn is the son of Tuisco, son of Earth. A later Frankish document actually mentions the names of Mannus' three sons—Erminus, Inguo and Istio.

It would be of interest if we could connect up these three ancient branches of the Teutonic race with the three great branches of Teutonic languages, the eastern or Gothic, the northern or Scandinavian, and the western, to which English, German and Dutch belong. But proof is lacking.

Linguistically, all we can do is to reconstruct a proto-Germanic tongue from which our three known branches of Germanic languages stemmed. This proto-Teutonic was, like primitive Celtic, Latin, Greek and Slavic, itself a branch of a much vaster Indo-European linguistic system, extending in ancient times from Iceland and Ireland on the west to northern India on the east. This means that our West Germanic English is genetically related, more or less closely, with such widely diversified tongues as Celtic Welsh and Irish, Romance French and Spanish, Slavic Russian and Polish, Indo-Iranian Persian and Hindustani, as well as with Greek, Albanian, Armenian and Lithuanian. In addition, it is more closely related to kindred Germanic tongues of the northern branch, like Swedish, Norwegian, Danish and Icelandic, and most closely of all to the other West Germanic languages, German, Dutch, Flemish and Frisian.

The original speakers of the tongue from which English was born were Germanic dwellers on the continental North Sea coast, from Denmark to Holland. When they decided to move to Britain in the fifth century they took their language with them, leaving behind in the ancestral homeland the less venturesome members of the tribe, whose tongue in due course of time turned into Frisian, a language so close to English that the little rhyme

> *Brod, butter en grene chiese,*   (Bread, butter and green cheese,
> *En wat dat net sayse ken*   And who cannot say that
> *Is kin uprjuchte Friese.*   Is no upright Frisian.)

can still be understood, at least in part, by modern English speakers.

Who were the original Indo-European speakers, from whom the Germanic tribes, along with the Greeks, Romans, Celts, Slavs and other groups had stemmed? No one knows precisely, because at the time they flourished the art of writing either had not yet been invented or had not reached them. Their homeland is variously described as ranging from the shores of the Baltic to the Iranian plateau. From this, they are supposed to have wandered in successive migrations, either fanwise from north to south, or in westward-moving waves. Their original unified tongue became diversified as the various groups moved farther apart from one another, until it gave rise to a primitive Indo-Iranian, which later developed into Sanskrit and Old Persian; a primitive Balto-Slavic, later diversified into Lithuanian and kindred Baltic tongues on the one hand, Slavonic languages on the other; early Greek; early Italic, from which Latin came; early Celtic, which gave rise to the tongues of the Gauls, Britons and Irish; early Germanic; and other ancient tongues, which have since disappeared or become, like Albanian and Armenian, the languages of small ethnic groups.

Enough resemblance among these primitive Indo-European tongues has remained, however, to make it possible to trace their kinship. For one thing, the earliest Indo-European languages of which we have records display an identical grammatical structure. All are inflectional, with roots to which are added endings that indicate gender, number and case in nouns and adjectives, person, number, tense and mood in verbs. There appear in all of them identical fundamental words of the kind that are not likely to be picked up from the speakers of other languages in the course of migrations: words of family relationship, like *father, mother, sister, brother;* basic numerals (from one to ten, *hundred*); basic prepositions and adverbs; certain verbs, though with considerable shift of meaning at times (one Indo-European root, represented in English by "wit," "wot," means "to know" in Germanic and Sanskrit, "to see" in Latin and Slavic, and appears in Greek with both meanings).

On the basis of these vocabulary resemblances, some linguists have advanced the theory that the original Indo-European speakers knew snow and winter, but not the sea; that the trees they knew included the oak, beech, pine, birch and willow, while the animals that entered their common experience included the bear, wolf, rabbit, mouse, horse, ox, sheep, goat, pig, dog, eagle, hawk, snake, crab, ant and bee, but not the lion, tiger or elephant. Honey was apparently known to them. Since the beech does not grow east of Poland, and honey is not indigenous to southwestern Asia, these linguists incline to the belief that the original homeland of the Indo-Europeans was a European rather than an Asiatic one.

The Germanic invaders who overran the Roman Empire in the fifth century A.D. were therefore related to the Romans themselves, as well as to those other inhabitants of the Classical world, the Greeks and the Celts. Their tongues displayed the same structure as Latin, Greek and Celtic, with nouns and adjectives declined for gender, number and case, verbs showing by their endings person, number, tense and mood, and numerous related words, like the English "father" that corresponds to Latin *pater,* Greek *pater* and Sanskrit *pita,* or the "foot" that corresponds to Latin *ped-,* Greek *pod-* and Sanskrit *pad-.* It is evident, however, even from these few examples, that Germanic had undergone a special differentiation from the other tongues, consisting of the regular substitution of certain consonant sounds for other sounds of similar quality: *f* for *p, t* for *d,* etc. This transformation had already occurred when the first Germanic written records appeared. Another special Germanic characteristic was the division of verbs into two classes, strong and weak (the strong verb forms its past and participle by a vowel-change, the weak verb by an ending: compare English *write-wrote-written* with *love-loved-loved,* and further compare this two-class system with the Latin series of four separate conjugations: *amare-amavi-amatum, delere-delevi-deletum, regere-*

rexi-rectum, audire-audivi-auditum). A third Germanic characteristic, one that English possessed at the time of the Anglo-Saxon
occupation of Britain, but has since lost, was the double declen-
sion of adjectives (German still has it to a limited degree: *ein
guter Mann,* but *der gute Mann*). A fourth, which still rules
supreme in the Germanic languages, is initial accentuation, the
stress falling on the first syllable of the word, save in the case of
a few compounded prefixes (note, to this day, the tendency of
Germanic speakers to stress even foreign loan-words on the initial
syllable: English "plúmage" vs. French *plumáge,* English "véry"
vs. Old French *verái*).

By the time the Germanic tribes poured into the Roman
Empire, the original Germanic tongue which had stemmed from
Indo-European had itself become differentiated into three main
groups. The Ostrogoths who invaded Italy, the Visigoths who
settled in Spain, the Burgundians of southern Gaul, the Vandals
of North Africa belonged to an eastern Germanic group which
had already had extensive contacts with the Romans. Gothic
mercenaries had served in the Roman armies, and even helped
the Romans to turn back Attila and his Asiatic hordes at the
battle of Chalons. The Goths had been Christianized by their
own bishop Wulfilas in the fourth century, and had at the same
time received from him a system of writing which was largely
based upon the Greek alphabet. But this eastern or Gothic
Germanic branch, already Romanized and Christianized at the
time of its entrance into western Europe, was quickly diluted and
absorbed by the Latin-speaking populations it nominally conquered, so that within a brief period no trace of its language
remained save the fossilized loan-words that went to enrich the
Latin-Romance vocabulary. It has been established that vestiges
of the Gothic tongue survived in the Russian Crimea as late as
the sixteenth century (some say even later), but to all intents and
purposes the eastern branch of Germanic must be considered
extinct.

The northern, or Scandinavian, branch, fared better. Excluded
from contact with the Graeco-Roman world by its isolated
geographical position in the extreme north of Europe, the speakers of Old Norse gradually gave rise to speakers of Swedish, Nor-

wegian, Danish and Icelandic. They made, as we shall see, a considerable contribution to the growth of the English language. Their Runic inscriptions begin to appear in the third century A.D. Theirs was the language of the pagan Northmen who terrorized Europe in the ninth and tenth centuries, but were eventually absorbed by the populations among which they settled. The stay-at-homes among them gave rise to the modern Scandinavian languages, the differences among which become clearly perceptible in the eleventh century. Their early literary contributions are the Eddas and the Sagas, or prose epics. Among the characteristics peculiar to the Scandinavian branches which do not appear elsewhere in the Germanic world are the postposed article ("boy-the" instead of "the boy") and the development of a passive voice formed with the suffix -*s*, originally a reflexive form (Swedish *jag kallar*, "I call"; *jag kallas*, "I am called").

Third and most vital among the Germanic divisions was the western branch, including all the original inhabitants of what today is Germany, from the Rhine to the Elbe and from Jutland to the mountain passes of Switzerland. Franks, Alemanni, Longobards, Bavarians, Frisians, Angles, Saxons and Jutes all formed part of this array. But even within this relatively unified branch divergences began to appear at a comparatively early period. The Franks, overrunning northern Gaul, were in part absorbed by the Gallo-Roman speakers of Latin, in part remained Germanic-speaking. The West Germanic peoples living near the North Sea coast branched out eventually into Dutch, Flemish and Frisian speakers, but not before a large number of them had sailed off to the conquest of Britain. The Germanic speakers of the mountain districts developed, in the seventh and eighth centuries, special language peculiarities which set them off both from their brothers on the coast and from the emigrants to the British Isles. By a second sound-shift, they carried still further the consonant-substitutions that differentiate Germanic from other Indo-European languages. When we compare English, Dutch and Frisian "water" with German *Wasser,* English "dapper" with German *tapfer,* English "foot" with German *Fuss,* the general nature of these additional substitutions becomes evident. The second sound-shift of the High German speakers lies at the root of the main differences in sound between English and German today. But German, more given to consonant-changes than English, is far more conservative of early Germanic forms in vocabulary and inflectional endings.

The Angles, Saxons and Jutes who lived along the continental North Sea coast, speaking a Low German dialect or dialects, had undoubtedly raided the British shores even before the departure of the Romans in 410 A.D. But the crisis came with the withdrawal from Britain of the last Roman legions, summoned back to defend the tottering Italian homeland. Left to shift for themselves, the Britons seem to have quickly reverted to their ancestral pastime of fighting among themselves. Also, they were harried by the Picts from the north of the island, who had found in the originally-Irish Scots valid allies. According to one account, the first landing in force by Germanic tribes on British shores was made in 449, under the leadership of two quasi-mythical heroes, Hengist and Horsa. But the Venerable Bede, an Anglo-Saxon writer of the eighth century, relates in his *Ecclesiastical History of the English People* that the Jutes were first called in by a British king, Vortigern, to assist him in a local war, and that they settled, more or less peaceably, in Kent; that the Saxons didn't arrive till 477, settling down in Sussex and Wessex in 495; while the Angles did not reach Anglia until 547. The process of conquest and colonization went on until almost the end of the sixth century, with comparatively little intermingling between the newcomers and their Celtic predecessors, who retreated sullenly before the Germanic invaders, fighting every inch of the way, until they were relegated to the western mountain fastnesses of Wales and Cornwall.

It was during this century-long running battle that the new arrivals forged for their antagonists a new name, *Wealas* (or "foreigners"), which later became "Welsh" (the displaced Britons preferred for themselves their own native name of "Cymri," and use it to this day). Despite the fact that the Angles seem to have been the last of the three Germanic peoples to arrive on the scene, the names *Engle, Englisc* and *Angelcynn* became current to represent all three groups. In 601, Gregory calls Aethelbert *rex Anglorum,* and by the year 1000, the term *Englaland* is found applying to the country. "Anglo-Saxon," which had limited currency in Old English days, disappeared entirely from use after the Norman Conquest in 1066, but was revived in the sixteenth century. So far as the language is concerned, modern linguists prefer the term "Old English" to "Anglo-Saxon" to represent the mixture of dialects that gradually emerged out of the invasions from the mainland.

This language, or mixture of languages, will be more fully described later. The tongues spoken by Jutes, Saxons and Angles were very closely related, with the probability that there was full mutual understanding among their speakers.

Nevertheless, they gave rise to somewhat divergent Old English dialects. It is generally supposed that Jute and Saxon were the progenitors of Kentish and Southern English dialects, while Anglian split into a Mercian, or Midland, and a Northumbrian, or Northern form. Modern standard English is based upon the later mixture of Southern and Midland forms, with lesser contributions from Northern sources, which more largely enrich the Scots variety of English. If this is so, then all three groups, Jutes, Saxons and Angles, have contributed in approximately equal measure to the language we speak today.

For what concerns writing, the Germanic invaders brought in with them the Runic system, but shortly thereafter shifted over to the Roman alphabet. Ancestral Anglo-Saxon customs and traditions are perhaps best illustrated by the Easter festival, a survival of Germanic paganism even to the name, the Yule log, the mistletoe, and the names of the days of the week, which glorify the Teutonic, not the Graeco-Roman Olympus, save for Saturday. The story of Beowulf, possibly the earliest and assuredly the best of the Anglo-Saxon epics, though probably composed in the early eighth century on English soil, ranges for its locale over most of the Germanic world, but makes no allusion to England, while other Anglo-Saxon epic pieces, like the *Widsith*, or "Far Journey," make allusion to all the Germanic tribes on the continent.

The opening scene of the English language as a separate and distinct entity can therefore be placed in the great Germanic fifth century, but it was not until the beginning of the seventh that the language definitely emerged from the confusion and turmoil of the conquest of Britain and began to take its place among the nascent modern tongues of Europe. We shall see later what were the specific traits of this essentially characteristic tongue of the mighty West Germanic group. Its strength and its weaknesses, its complex grammatical structure and its hardy, earthy vocabulary, its harsh, rugged sounds and its unrefined, yet miraculously expressive syntax all go to form the backbone of the tongue we of America and Britain and the Commonwealth speak today. The skeletal structure of modern English is supplied practically in its entirety by the tongue the Jutes, Saxons and Angles brought with them as they followed the first invading waves of Hengist and Horsa onto the shores of Celto-Roman Britain.

Chapter Two

THE TONGUE OF THE ANGLO-SAXONS

Old English Dialectal Divisions—The Language of Beowulf, Alfred and Bede—Celtic and Latin Admixtures—Scandinavian Infiltrations—What Might Have Been

It is a peculiar and somewhat unfortunate characteristic of the human mind that remoteness in time, space or experience causes us to lump together what should be kept separate. This trait makes us view as a fairly unified period the thousand-year-long "Middle Ages," which were really a succession of distinct eras, in which the epoch of Charlemagne differed from that of Louis IX approximately as the eighteenth century did from the nineteenth; or to talk of "Oriental countries" and an "Oriental mind" as though Chinese, Indians and Arabs were one race, with a single set of beliefs, traditions and customs.

In like manner, people will speak of an "Anglo-Saxon period" as though it were a single entity, and of an "Old English language" as though a tongue that thrived for six centuries over a fairly extensive area displayed no differences in the course of its duration or geographical extent.

This, of course, is not true. No language is the same at its end as it was at its beginning, and no language is spoken in precisely the same form throughout its entire area. The rate of a language's diversification, in time and in space, varies with the strength of the cultural tradition and national feeling that bind the speakers together, and with the ease of their means of intercommunication.

The English language had its inception in three separate though closely related tribal groups, each moving to a different part of a new home, at a period when national unity was still a thing of the future and communications were in a very sketchy state. It was therefore bound to consist of different dialects, and these dialects naturally tended to evolve separately until an outside force bound them together. The theory has indeed been advanced, and by no less distinguished a linguist than Jespersen, that the Anglo-Saxon that has come down to us in written records is an artificially standardized language of poetry, different from that of prose, and representing a compromise among all the ancient spoken dialects. It may or may not be necessary to accept this hypothesis. Dialectal records of Old English are neither few nor doubtful. At the most, we may be forced to subscribe to the theory of a standard written tongue, differing from the oral forms, only for the period that follows the unification of the English kingdom and the settling of the Danes.

Our records, from the seventh century on, indicate four major dialectal areas for Old English: the Northumbrian and the Mercian, both stemming from Anglian; the West Saxon, coming from the language of the Saxons, the one that has by far the largest number of ancient manuscripts; and the Kentish, descended from the ancient language of the Jutes. England's major rivers are often the dialectal boundaries, with Northumbrian extending from the Forth to the Humber, Mercian from the Humber to the Thames, and West Saxon south of the Thames.

Political, religious and literary history are all interwoven with the development of the language. The seven separate kingdoms (sometimes more, sometimes fewer), or "Heptarchy," that arose out of the invasion, were very loosely connected by very shadowy bonds, and more often than not fighting among themselves. It took the new Danish invasions of the eighth and ninth centuries to unite them in a firmer mold under Alfred the Great of Wessex, toward the end of the ninth century. This served to shift to Wessex the vague cultural superiority that had at first been held by Northumbria, and was probably the cause of the ultimate triumph of many Southern and Midland forms over the Northern. At all events, it was not until after Alfred's time that we have such statements as that of Aethelstan, who in 934 calls himself *Ongol-Saxna cyning and Brytaenwalda eallaes thyses iglandes*

("King of the Anglo-Saxons and British ruler of all this island"), or that of Eadred, in 955, labeling himself *Angul-Seaxna cyning and casere totius Britanniae* ("King of the Anglo-Saxons and Caesar of all Britain"); the latter statement, beginning in Old English and ending in Latin, displays the Latin influence that had gradually crept into an originally pure Germanic tongue.

Once the storm and stress of the Anglo-Saxon invasion were over, the Christianization of the new inhabitants of Britain took place by precisely the same instrumentality that had served in the case of all other barbarians: Christian missionaries, coming either from Rome or from already converted countries. St. Columba, arriving from Christian Ireland, began the task in the second half of the sixth century, and St. Augustine, following the commands of Pope Gregory, who had fallen in love with the Angles in Rome and pronounced them to be "angels," carried it nearer completion toward the end of the same century. By the year 700, most of the Anglo-Saxons were Christians.

As in all cases where fierce Germanic barbarians were involved, there was a twofold menace to the new faith—direct backsliding into pagan ways, and new inroads by fresh and as yet unconverted barbarians. The Norse and Danish Vikings who struck at the eastern and southern British shores between 787 and 850 were difficult at first either to convert or to absorb, but thereafter their raids began to turn into settlements, and from that time on the process was simplified.

They still managed to capture both London and York, but in 878 Alfred halted their aggression, subsequently establishing for them the *Danelagh* or Danelaw, a section of England, including old Anglia and parts of Mercia, that ran east of a line from Chester to London. This was regarded as the Danes' own province, though, plenty of Angles and Saxons remained to mingle with the newcomers. In the course of the tenth century, Anglo-Saxons and Danes, closely related in appearance, language and customs, amalgamated, and by 1014 it was possible for England to be more or less peaceably ruled by a Danish king, Cnut, he who allegedly ordered the tide to stop but got his feet wet for his pains. Thereafter, in the brief half century that still remained before the Norman Conquest, Saxons and Danes inter-married, intermingled, and became one people.

The literary output of the Anglo-Saxon period, while fairly abundant and varied, is distinguished by its epic leanings. There were, to be sure, particularly from the ninth century on, prose and poetic works of many sorts and descriptions, including didactic labors, like the touching *Address of the Soul to the Body;* books of maxims and riddles; religious works (homilies, prophe-cies, ritual books, psalters); scientific or pseudo-scientific works on herbs, animals, leechcraft and astronomy; chronicles in Old English, like those of Winchester, Abingdon and Peterborough, and in Latin, like the *Book of Gildas* or the *Historia Ecclesiastica Gentis Anglorum* of the Venerable Bede, produced in the earlier half of the eighth century; and even attempts at English gram-mar, particularly by Bede. Translations from the Latin were numerous, especially under Alfred, whose avowed purpose it was "to render into the language we all know some of those books that are most necessary for men to know, so that all free-born youths in England may study and learn to read English books." The beginning of the English play, along with the word itself (*plega,* used to translate the Latin *ludus*), appears in Anglo-Saxon times, but the word is applied to dancing rather than dramatics.

It was, however, in the heroic epic that Old English literature most distinguished itself. This is not surprising. The epic form was the favorite of all Germanic peoples. The Goths are said to have had oral epics as early as the third century A.D., and the Scandinavian Eddas and Sagas were definitely of the epic variety. Anglo-Saxon literature at its outset is thoroughly pagan in in-spiration. *Beowulf,* which has come down to us in its entirety, outlines a Germanic hero's entire career, culminating in his vic-torious battle with the monster Grendel and his mother. It was probably composed in the earlier part of the eighth century in the Midland kingdom of Mercia, but reflects a non-Christian spirit that is at least two centuries earlier, though with a few Classical and Biblical influences.

Critics who do not like the *Beowulf* accuse it of being, like

Anglo-Saxon literature in general, naïve, unsophisticated, primitive, somber, cold, grim, narrow, and displaying little in the way of thought-progression. All this is probably true. Yet there is a certain fascination in the imagery of its metaphors, as when the sea is called the "road of whales" or the "playground of the winds," a sword the "light of battle," woman the "ornament of the home" or the "peace-weaver," and the harp the "glee-wood," while a king is "giver of rings," battle the "play of swords" and a boat "sea-wood." The alliterative element characteristic of most old Germanic verse leads to syntactical license and freedom of word-order (qualities that survive in modern English), as well as to repetitiousness and cloudiness.

Alliteration may be defined as initial rhyme. In most Old English lines of verse, the third stressed syllable begins with the same consonant or consonants, and occasionally the same vowel, as the first. This similarity of initial sounds sometimes extends to the second stressed syllable as well. It is as though one were to say in modern English:

> "*Pr*incess of *pr*imitive *pr*omise, awake!
> *Gl*adness and *gl*ory shall *gl*ow in thy cheeks!"

That this characteristic of Old English poetry did not disappear with the passing of the Anglo-Saxon era is proved by the fact that it was revived as late as the fourteenth century in West Midland verse, and Otto Jespersen claims that it is still quite alive today in such expressions as "busy bee," "part and parcel," "cool as a cucumber," "might and main," "labor of love," "friend and foe."

However we choose to interpret all this, there is little doubt that the interaction of language and literature in English begins with *Beowulf,* if not before, and that the tongue of the Anglo-Saxon *scops,* the bards who composed Old English verse, while drawn from the language of the people, contributed much to it in the way of fanciful imagery and rugged rhythm, figures of speech and freedom of syntax, as well as in ideas and thought-development.

*　　*　　*

For what concerns the language itself, as it has come down to us in numerous and varied documents, it can never be sufficiently stressed that our original English was a typical Indo-European and Germanic tongue, marked by vowels that could be long or short independently of the accent, which was regularly fixed on the initial syllable, and by an abundance of flectional endings.

The sounds of the language resembled those of modern German rather than those of modern English. Long vowels were for the most part pure, with no tendency to turn into diphthongs, as they do today. Old English long *a* was invariably the *a* of *father*. (In modern English, this sound has for the most part turned into so-called long *o*: *stān, hālig, hlāf* have become "stone," "holy," "loaf"). Long *o* and long *e* had the modern German rather than the modern English values (*fōt, mētan,* which have become "foot," "meet"). Long *i* was the *i* of *machine* (*līf,* which has become "life"). Long *u* was the *oo* of *food* (*hū, hlūd,* now "how," "loud"). In addition, Anglo-Saxon possessed the sound of modern French *u* or German *ü*, which English has since lost (*fȳr,* now "fire"). The written combination *æ* represented the sound of modern *a* in *bat*. The short vowels were closer to their modern English values.

Among the consonant-sounds of Anglo-Saxon, noteworthy was the *h*, more like the present-day German *ach*-sound than like the gentle modern English *h*. The Anglo-Saxon alphabet contained two symbols, *þ* and *ð*, which represented the sounds of modern *th* in *thin* and *this*. The letter *c* had in origin only a *k*-sound, but it later became palatalized before front vowels (*cēse*, previously borrowed from Latin *caseus*, to "cheese"), while *sc* came to have the sound of modern *sh* (*scēap* to "sheep"). The letters *j, q, v* were not used, but *f* served for the sounds of both *f* and *v* (*yfele*, "evil"). The letters *k, x* and *z* appeared only occasionally, in the later Anglo-Saxon period.

The grammatical forms of Old English were fully as inflected as are those of modern German. Nouns had four cases, nominative, genitive, dative and accusative, with an occasional instrumental, and there were many different declensional schemes. Adjectives were similarly declined, but in a double shift, the adjective taking so-called "weak" forms when preceded by another word, like a definite article, which itself bore a distinctive ending, but "strong" forms when not so preceded, a distinction that still appears in modern German. That all this wealth of endings is unnecessary for purposes of clear understanding is revealed by modern English, which has long since discarded all endings in the adjective, and retains very few in the noun (*stone, stone's, stones, stones'*).

The definite article itself was very strongly inflected. Our little word "the" could in Anglo-Saxon assume any one of twelve different forms, according to the gender, number and case of the noun it was used with.

Personal pronouns were much more in accord with modern English usage. We have lost the distinction between nominative and objective form in nouns, adjectives and articles, but still retain it in *I* and *me, he* and *him, she* and *her, they* and *them.* This conservatism of older distinctions where personal and other pronouns are concerned, curiously, appears also in many other western languages, both Germanic and Romance.

The Anglo-Saxon verb displays the customary Germanic strong and weak classes, which have passed down into modern English (*sing, sang, sung,* vs. *love, loved, loved*). In the Old English verb there were only two real tenses, present and past; but both had distinctive personal endings of which the only remaining trace is the *-s* of the third person singular in the present. Ancient Teutonic seems to have had both a future and a passive, but both were lost in Anglo-Saxon. The present generally served also as a future ("I go there tomorrow"), but there was an occasional use of *willan* and *sculan* ("will" and "shall") that foreshadowed future developments. One old Teutonic passive form that passed into Old English is *hātte,* the later "hight."

Old English normally used as an adverb the instrumental case of the adjective, which ended in *-e* (*wīde,* "widely" from *wīd,* "wide"). This adverb survives in some modern English forms ("hard," "fast," "far and wide"). Many Old English adjectives ended in *-līc* (*freondlīc,* "friendly"), and in the instrumental case they had the ending *-līce.* This ultimately became our widely used *-ly,* which in its older form is *-like.* A few genitive forms of adjectives survive as adverbs ("needs," "nights," "once," "a long ways").

In vocabulary, Old English was at first a typically Germanic tongue, with few borrowings. What one particularly misses in an Anglo-Saxon dictionary is the vast mass of Norman-French loan-words that have become such a standard part of our own English vocabulary. Conversely, many of the original Teutonic words dropped out of the language after the Norman Conquest, to such an extent that out of two thousand Anglo-Saxon words taken at random only 535 are found to survive in modern English. But among the survivors are those good, homely, mono-syllabic roots we could under no circumstances dispense with, many of them so little changed that it is not even worth while to translate them: *mann, wíf, cild, hūs, strang*. Many of the original Anglo-Saxon words, much as it will shock the advocates of mono-syllabism among us, were not monosyllabic then: *fugol*, now "fowl," did service for "bird" in general: *sawol, hagol, maga, nægel* were the dissyllabic progenitors of "soul," "hail," "maw," "nail."

Among these old, ancestral words are some to fit almost every form of human activity. *Horn*, quite unchanged, still serves the field of music, and with it went *hearpe* ("harp") and *fiðele* ("fiddle"). The shilling and penny appear as *scilling* and *pend-ing*, along with another coin, the *sceatt*, which still has a living relative in German *Schatz*. *Roc* (again surviving in German) has given way to "coat," but *brēc, hæt, gyrdel, hosa, scōh, glof, smoc* are still with us ("breeches," "hat," "girdle," "hose," "shoe," "glove," "smock"). *Heall* is our "hall," while the countryside is represented by *furhlang* ("furlong"), *geoc* ("yoke") and *girda* ("yard"). The military *here* has given way to Norman-French "army," but still survives in the verb "harry." The three Anglo-Saxon social classes, *eorlas, freomen* and *ceorlas*, have vanished as institutions, but survive as words ("earls," "freemen," "churls"). We no longer have the *witan* ("council," from the same root as "wit," "wot," to know), the *witanagemot* ("council-meeting") or the *wergild* ("man-money," the financial penalty for killing a man), but *ealdormann* (then "High Priest," now "alderman") is still with us. *Ylfe* ("elf") still testifies to ancestral superstitions, as do "warlock" (*wǣrloga,* "oath-breaker") and "weird" (*wyrd,* "fate").

The ingenuity of Anglo-Saxon in forming derivative words and compounds has often been stressed. It was probably no greater than that shown by Greek and Latin at an earlier period, or by German at the same or a slightly later epoch. What calls attention to it is the later disappearance of the Anglo-Saxon compounds when they were replaced by imported Norman-French or Latin words. At any rate, we have *dagung, frēondscipe, cyningdōm, cildhād* ("dawn," "friendship," "kingdom," "child-hood"), formed by means of the suffixes *-ung, -scipe, -dōm, -hād,* all of which come down to the present day. To mention one derivative word that did not survive, we have *giefolnes,* "liber-ality," from the root of *giefu,* "gift" ("giftfulness" would be the modern form if Norman-French had not intervened). A verb like *settan* comes down into modern English as "to set"; but in Anglo-Saxon it could assume various other meanings according to the prefixes used with it: *āsettan* meant "to place," *forsettan* "to obstruct," *foresettan* "to place before," *gesettan* "to popu-late," *tōsettan* "to dispose," *unsettan* "to put down," *wiþsettan* "to resist." Out of some fifty words having as a prefix *wiþ* ("against," "away"), only "withstand" survives today ("with-draw," "withhold" were created later).

A word like "medicine" was in Old English *lǣcecrǣft* ("leechcraft"), while "geometry" was *eorþcrǣft* ("earthcraft"); "gout" was *fōtadl* ("foot-pain"); "epilepsy" was *fiellesēocnes* ("falling-sickness"); "creation" was *frumweorc* ("beginning-work").

To illustrate the survival of some of these Anglo-Saxon com-pounds where one would hardly expect them, we have "lord" from *hlāf-weard* ("loaf-warden"), "hussy" from *hūswīf* ("house-wife"), "world" from *wereld* ("man-age"). Some linguists claim that the tendency of modern English to form such compounds as "runner-up," "hanger-on," etc. goes back to Anglo-Saxon, but this is hard to prove.

One might imagine that the Celtic of the original Britons would have supplied a fertile field for loan-words to the Anglo-

Saxons. Such is emphatically not the case. According to one source, there are in English, outside of place-names, only about a dozen Celtic words assimilated during the period of the Anglo-Saxon conquest, though many more crept in later. The reason for this seems to lie in the scantiness of social relations between the two races, the English considering the Celts as inferior and their own race and tongue as superior. Among these early borrowings from Celtic are words of geographical significance, like "crag," "dun" and "cumb" or "combe" (a deep valley), and a few religious words, like the "cross" said to have been imported among the English by Saint Columba ("rood" is the native English word, and "cross" itself came originally from Latin *crux*). The well-known Celtic words of English ("glen," "heather," "clan," "bard," "plaid," "slogan," "claymore," "dirk," "wraith," etc.) are later importations from Scots Gaelic, and many of them came into English by way of the Northumbrian dialect.

Celtic place-names, on the other hand, abound. Among them are Kent, Devon, York, London, Thames, Avon, the first part of Salisbury, Exeter, Gloucester and Worcester, Cumberland (land of the Cymri) and Cornwall (Cornubian Welsh).

The first large influx of foreign loan-words into English came with the Latin of the missionaries, as well as through cultural and trade relations with the continent. The latter give us "cheese" (Latin *caseus*), "mint" (Latin *moneta*), "bishop" (Anglo-Saxon *biscop,* from *episcopus,* originally Greek), "seal" (Anglo-Saxon *sigel,* from Latin *sigillum*), "street" (Latin *strata*), "kettle" (Anglo-Saxon *cytel,* from Latin *catillus*), "kitchen" (Latin *coquina*), "church" (*kyriakon,* a Greek word meaning "pertaining to the Lord"), and an assortment of words like "cup," "plum," "inch," "wine" and, probably, "butter." The missionaries, on the other hand, seem responsible for "abbot," "candle," "chapter," "minister," "noon," "nun," "offer," "priest," "shrive" (originally from *scribere,* "to write"), "cap," "silk," "sack," "pear," "cook," "box," "school," "master," "fever," "circle," "spend" and "turn." In the time of Alfred, such words as "cell," "prime," "accent," "paper," "term," "title" and "elm" entered English from Latin, and this despite the fact that Alfred himself says "few know Latin."

But several important facts must be noted concerning the Latin loan-words in Anglo-Saxon. The first is that Anglo-Saxon generally uses many Germanic words in religion, regardless of the missionaries. Cases in point are *hālig* ("holy"), *hādian* ("to ordain"), *gesomnung* ("congregation"), *thegnung* ("service"), *witega* ("prophet"), *thrōwere* ("martyr," from *thrōwian*, "to suffer"), *ealdormann* ("High Priest" or "Pharisee"), *taporberend* ("acolyte").

Secondly, there seems to have been a strong resistance to the importation of Latin words where an Anglo-Saxon term already existed: *God* and *godspell* ("Gospel"), *hlāford* ("Lord"), *Hālig Gāst* ("Holy Ghost"), *Dōmesday* ("Doomsday"), *synn* ("sin") are illustrations of the retention of such Anglo-Saxon words in the face of the Latin cultural invasion. Old English uses *lǣran* for "to teach," *bodian* for "to bring a message," *gebed* for "prayer." It admits *dēofol* ("devil," from *diabolus*), but also keeps *fēond* ("fiend"). "Cross" wins a hard-fought victory over *rōd* ("rood") only in later times. The Anglo-Saxon translation of the Bible has *mildheortnisse* (literally "mild-heartedness") for the Latin *misericordia* ("mercy" is a later importation from French), and *prynnes* ("threeness") for the later "Trinity." This hardy reluctance to abandon traditional Germanic roots persists far beyond the Anglo-Saxon period, as late as Cheke's sixteenth-century translation of the Gospel of Matthew, where "mooned" is used for "lunatic," "hundreder" for "centurion," "foresayer" for "prophet," "by-word" for "parable," and "gainrising" for "resurrection."

Thirdly, the Latin words that are accepted are fully assimilated. The noun *planta* gives rise to a verb *plantian*, and *martyr*, when finally naturalized, gives rise to *martyrdōm*.

Lastly, Anglo-Saxon words displaced from one meaning often continue to enjoy a hardy vitality elsewhere. Witness *tīd* (modern "tide") which at one time did grammatical work in the sense of "tense," from which it was displaced by Norman-French, but which retains its sphere of action in connection with the sea; or *dyppan*, no longer used for "baptize," but still existing as "dip"; or *handbōc*, killed by "manual" and "enchiridion," but restored to life in the nineteenth century and now in general use once more. *Biddan* no longer means "to pray," but what it has lost in the religious field it has gained in card games, auction sales and on the stock market.

It is estimated that about 450 Latin words came into Old English before the Norman Conquest. This is a surprisingly large total to those who think of the Anglo-Saxon era as the period of pure Germanism in the language. If to these words we add those that would normally have entered English from 1066 on, we see that even without the French cultural importations present-day English would not be altogether a simon-pure Germanic tongue.

One element entering the language in the Anglo-Saxon period is so akin to Old English itself that there is often confusion as to whether a word is Anglo-Saxon or Scandinavian. The fierce Danish and Norwegian pirates who struck at the east and south coasts of England in the eighth century were ultimately tamed, converted and absorbed, largely through the work of Alfred the Great. They brought with them dialects of the northern or Scandinavian branch of Germanic, which at that time was not as differentiated from the western Teutonic tongues as it is today.

There was between the Anglo-Saxons and the new invaders none of the bitter racial and linguistic animosity that had marked the earlier clash between Saxons and Britons. Though the Anglo-Saxons were Christianized and the Danes still pagans, the former were yet close enough to the ancestral Germanic tradition to feel a bond of kinship with the newcomers. This did not prevent them from fighting savagely, but history records no cases where all Danish prisoners taken by the English were put to death, a practice that seems to have been common in the wars with the Britons. While we ought not to underestimate the difficulties of amalgamation or the time-spread it required, amalgamation was at least possible. When we further consider that the *Danelagh,* established by Alfred, set apart nearly half of England as Danish territory, it will be easy to see how the Scandinavian influence on the growth of Old English was powerful indeed.

Some linguists claim that the process of inflectional decay that led to the death of Anglo-Saxon and the birth of Middle English was started not by the Normans, but by the Danes, and they point in proof to the fact that the Northern dialects, spoken in regions where the Scandinavian influence predominated, preceded the Southern ones into the great change by fully half a century. The explanation they give is ingenious, even if we hesitate to accept it. Old English had its inflectional endings, they say, and so had Old Norse. These endings were close, but not identical. In trying to understand one another, Saxons and Danes found the endings a hindrance rather than a help, since they aroused confusion by the fact that they were not the same. Hence, both Saxons and Danes tended to discard or merge their endings, and rely for mutual understanding upon vocabulary, which could be borrowed back and forth, and syntactical devices, such as word-order and the use of prepositions, which became more or less standardized.

Be this as it may, the fact remains that the contribution of Scandinavian to English was far vaster than is generally recognized by the layman, who is accustomed to think in terms of Anglo-Saxon and Norman-French alone.

At least 1,400 localities in England have Scandinavian names. The place-name suffixes include such popular ones as *-beck, -by, -dale, -fell, -how, -thorpe, -thwaite* and *-toft*. Scandinavian gave us the "law" that replaced Anglo-Saxon *æ* or *aew,* the *gain* of "ungainly," and the *stor* that appears in later Middle English side by side with "great." The *-son* of our family names is largely of Scandinavian origin (the Anglo-Saxon patronymic ending was *-ing,* and as far back as the days of Aethelred, son of Edgar, we find the king described by Norse writers as *Aðalraðr Játgeirsson*).

Steak, knife, birth, dirt, fellow, guess, leg, loan, seat, sister, slaughter, thrift, trust, want, window, flat, ill, loose, low, odd, tight, weak, call, die, egg, get, lift, rid, same, scare, though, till, both, husband, skin, hit, happy, rotten, ugly, wrong are illustrative of the words contributed by Scandinavian to English (a few more, like *fell* and *tarn,* came in later by way of Northern English dialects). The Scandinavian influx is responsible for the existence of such doublets as *no-nay, rear-raise, from-fro, shatter-scatter, shirt-skirt, ditch-dike, whole-hale,* where the first word is Saxon, the second Danish or Norse. *Shriek* and *screech* show a peculiar mixture, in which the typical Anglo-Saxon palatalization of *k* appears at the beginning of the first word and the end of the second, while Danish guttural *k* appears at the end of the first and the beginning of the second. *Bloom,* which means "ingot" in Anglo-Saxon (the word is still so used in the steel industry), means "flower" in Scandinavian, and it is the latter meaning that leads to the more popular use. Scandinavian "take" killed off Anglo-Saxon *niman* (note German *nehmen*); "cut" killed *sniðan* (note German *schneiden*); "sky" all but killed *wolcan,* which barely survives in "welkin." There are said to be over nine hundred Scandinavian words in English, plus thousands in the English dialects.

But the drive of Scandinavian is reflected in more than mere words. Grammatically significant forms such as *are, they, them, their* are included, along with phonetic processes like the retention of hard *g* in words like *give* and *gift,* which Anglo-Saxon normally turned into *y* (Chaucer, a southern Englishman, and therefore less subject to Scandinavian influence, used *yive* and *yift*). Occasionally a Scandinavian morphological feature gets into the language, as when we use "bask," which is a Scandinavian passive form in *-s* or *-sk* (*baða-sk,* "bathe oneself"), while among features of English syntax attributed to the Danes are the typical English omission of the relative pronoun and the conjunction "that" ("the man I saw," "I say you will go"), the regular use of "shall" and "will" to indicate the future, and even such use of auxiliary verbs as "could have done."

Naturally enough, the Scandinavization of the language appears strongest in the North of England and the Lowlands of Scotland, where the numerical preponderance of the invaders, and the fact that the earlier inhabitants spoke Anglian, the closest of the Anglo-Saxon dialects to Scandinavian, favored the process. It is reported that in parts of Scotland Norse continued to be spoken to the seventeenth century, and such typically Scottish and Scandinavian words as "braw" and "bairn" lend credence to this belief. The Shetland Islanders, descendants of the Vikings, still celebrate the ancient Norse festival of *Up-Helly-Aa,* while at St. Andrew's in Fifeshire a broad street is still called a "gate," after the Nordic *gade,* but just to show their impartiality in the matter of borrowings, the St. Andrew's Scots call a city gate a "port," which is French, as is also the "Bejan" which is the name bestowed upon a freshman (*bec jaune*, the "yellow beak" of a young chick), and a cold wind from the North Sea a "snell" wind, which is good Anglo-Saxon.

At the outset of the Old English period, the language was overwhelmingly Teutonic, and more specifically West Germanic. At the end, just before the coming of the Normans, it was a deft blend of West Germanic and Scandinavian, with the former still predominating, and a respectable amount of Latin-Greek borrowings, about half of them of a religious nature.

The grammatical structure was strongly Teutonic, with the transposed and inverted word-order so characteristic of modern German and so unfamiliar to modern English speakers that it is to this day flippantly satirized by our own writers (witness Mark Twain's "The Awful German Language").

For Anglo-Saxon in its religious and therefore more unchanging aspect throughout its duration, no better sample can be found than the Lord's Prayer. The translation given with it is not merely literal, but etymological:

> *Fæder ūre, þū þe eart on heofonum, si þin nama gahalgod.*
> (Father our, thou that art on heavens, be thy name hallowed.)
> *Tōbecume þin rīce.*
> (Become thy rich.)
> *Gewurþe ðīn willa on eorðan swā swā on heofonum.*
> (Worth thy will on earth so so on heavens.)
> *Ūrne gedæghwāmlīcan hlāf syle ūs tō dǣg.*
> (Our daily loaf sell us to-day.)
> *And forgyf ūs ūre gyltas, swā swā wē forgyfað ūrum gyltendum.*
> (And forgive us our guilts, so so we forgive our guiltings.)
> *And ne gelǣd þū ūs on costnunge*
> (And not lead thou us on temptation)
> *Ac ālȳs ūs of yfele. Sōþlīce.*
> (But free us of evil. Soothlike.)

As may be seen from the above passage, all the Anglo-Saxon words used in the Lord's Prayer, with three exceptions, have come down to us in one form or another. *Rīce* ("kingdom") no longer has that meaning, but survives in "rich"; *gewurþe*, corresponding to the German verb *werden*, "to become," is still to be seen in "worth" and "worthy"; the word for "those who sin against us" recognizably carries the root of "guilt." The exceptions are *costnunge,* which gave way to Norman-French *temptatiun;* *ālȳs,* which yielded to the imported *delivrer,* and *ac,* meaning "and," "but," which is perhaps related to the Scandinavian *och, og.*

What would the English language be like today if the Saxon axmen had succeeded in pushing William's archers back into the sea at Hastings?

The question is an idle one, as well as unanswerable. The links of the historical chain, unlike those of a physical chain, grow from one another. An Anglo-Saxon England unconquered in the eleventh century might have fallen an easy prey to another foreign invader in a subsequent century, and the language, kept pure of Norman-French influences, might have succumbed to changes from a different quarter.

Had England remained Anglo-Saxon throughout its entire history, it is our guess that the sound-pattern and grammatical structure would not be too widely different from what they are today, since both, despite the Conquest, are predominantly Germanic.

It is in the field of vocabulary that the main differences would be perceptible, though even here the Classical wave that engulfed western Europe at the time of the Renaissance would have made itself felt. But many individual words would have remained Germanic, as they did in German, Dutch and Scandinavian.

It is hardly necessary for us to attempt a reconstruction of a hypothetical modern English language shorn of alien influences, since Cheke did such an excellent job in his sixteenth-century Bible translation. But centuries before Cheke, a little book appeared whose title is a fair sample of Anglo-Saxon replacements of foreign words: *The Ayenbite of Ynwit,* or, as it would probably be spelled today, *The Againbite of Inwit.* How many will recognize it at once as "The Remorse of Conscience"?

Chapter Three

THE COMING OF THE NORMANS

*The Genesis of Old French—The Great Clash—The
Centuries of Symbiosis—The Anglo-Norman Period—
The Emergence of a National Tongue*

About the middle of the eleventh century, Anglo-Saxon England slumbered, fitfully if not peacefully, in much the same fashion that Celto-Roman Britain had slumbered before the coming of the Teutons in the early fifth century. Saxon and Dane had become one, and the saintly Edward the Confessor reigned. Fate was preparing a new master turn for the much-invaded island.

Let us for an instant leave England and shift the scene to her closest continental neighbor, France. The ancient Roman province of Gaul had yielded to the West Germanic Franks, closely related to the Anglo-Saxons, in the same fifth century that had seen Britain invaded by the hordes of Hengist and Horsa. Then the Franks had settled down. But unlike the Anglo-Saxons, they had seen fit to mingle and merge with the local Gallo-Roman population, giving rise to a new nation in which Latin, Celtic and Teutonic elements were freely and thoroughly blended. Again unlike the Anglo-Saxons, the Franks had accepted the language of the conquered populations along with the Christian religion, and the French tongue, conceived under the Merovingian dynasty, had finally been born during the reign of Charlemagne.

Then, in the middle of the ninth century, just as the Danes were coming to Britain, other fierce Scandinavian Vikings had struck at the coasts of continental Europe. Darting in their swift, shallow sailing vessels up the rivers of northern France, these pagan pirates from the north had brought death and devastation to the richest regions of Charlemagne's former realm.

But it was a compact national unit that received the impact of the Norse and Danish seafarers, who were fought to a standstill and driven back from the walls of embattled Paris. Still, the French kings had found it expedient to appease the newcomers by granting them the region centering about Rouen, in north-western France. Rollo (or Rolf), leader of the Norsemen, had accepted the offer and settled down with his followers in the new home. The Normans generally adopted Christianity, the language of the realm, and the institutions that had been elaborated by the collaboration of Teutonic Franks, Latin-speaking Gauls and descendants of the Roman legionaries.

The historical parallel between England and France is at first glance striking. Both were originally Celtic countries that had been Romanized. Both were seized by West Germanic invaders. Later both were reinvaded by Scandinavian pirates, who were placated in one case by the granting of the *Danelagh,* in the other by the offer of the Duchy of Normandy. In both cases the West Germanic invaders first, then the Scandinavians, were converted to Christianity.

But in the matter of language and customs there were fundamental differences. The Anglo-Saxons did not mingle with the earlier Celtic populations and rejected their languages, both Celtic and Latin, save for a number of individual loan-words. The later Scandinavian wave found in England a thoroughly Teutonic-speaking people with which to merge, and the language that ultimately resulted from the fusion was Germanic to a high degree. The Franks, blood-brothers of the Anglo-Saxons, not only merged with the earlier peoples, but gave up their Germanic tongue in favor of the Latin used by these peoples, while the Northmen who turned into Normans did the same when their turn came. There are reports that in some localities of Normandy Scandinavian continued to be spoken until long after the founding of Rollo's duchy, and we know for a certainty that Rollo's son, William Longsword, sent his own son William to Bayeux for the express purpose of learning Norse. But this fact in itself indicates how thoroughly the Scandinavian Normans had succumbed to the spell of the French language. The Norman prince, grandson of Rollo, could not learn his ancestral tongue at his own court of Rouen!

With the acceptance of the language came the inevitable acceptance of French customs, outlooks and ways of life, completely different from those of the primitive Teutonic tribes. Hence the Englishmen who, relying upon the racial origin of the Normans, were tempted to view William the Conqueror's invasion as just another Danish raid were in for a rude awakening.

William the Bastard, Duke of Normandy, descendant of Rollo and son of a tanner's daughter, when he conceived the ambitious plan of making himself master of the great island beyond the sea, did not minimize the difficulty of invasion. He knew that Anglo-Saxons and Danes had been forged into a united, hardy race by the wise policies of Alfred and Cnut, and that the armies of his opponent Harold were strong. Historians estimate that of the vast host gathered by William for the invasion of England only one-third was composed of native Normans. Under his banners served mercenaries from all parts of western Europe, including Germany, Aragon in far-off Spain and Apulia in southern Italy. These men were land-hungry. It was their expectation that in case of victory the lands of England would be wrested from their Anglo-Saxon owners and given to them. They were not disappointed, for William kept his promises.

When the Norman host disembarked at Hastings, Anglo-Saxon England was already, so to speak, carved up in advance. This Harold's men did not know. Fresh from a victory won against the king of Norway, supported by Harold's own brother, they may have thought, even while hoping for another victory, that in case of defeat their lot would be no worse than had been their ancestors' in the *Danelagh*. The Normans would be absorbed, Anglicized as to language and customs, and all would go on as before. In the final analysis they were perhaps right. But centuries had to elapse, and Anglo-Saxon civilization as they knew it to appear, before this would come to pass.

The tale of Hastings, the death of Harold, the quest of Edith Swan-Neck among the heaps of Saxon dead, are matters of historical record and poetic legend. The Norman victory was

complete. So was the Conquest. For five years after the fateful
day, the Saxon thegns and earls, forcibly deprived of their lands
and privileges by the insolent invaders, continued to rebel and
resist, while William and his mercenaries raged pitilessly through
the land, harrowing the Danish North of England in such
fashion that for centuries thereafter Yorkshire was almost a
desert. Then the resistance died away. Hereward le Wake,
partisan leader of the last band of Saxon fenmen, submitted. The
Saxon nobility, robbed of everything in favor of William's followers, sank sullenly to the level of their own peasantry, while
the ancient freemen of England, now undistinguished from the
churls, turned into villeins of the new seigneurs. Saxon England
was laid low. Norman England had replaced it.

Yet Saxon England was not quite dead. The new court, clergy
and nobility knew and spoke only French and Latin. But the
subject population lived on, and so did its language, a language
now scorned for literary purposes as the language of an inferior
race; a language shorn of all cultural pretensions; but a living,
powerfully throbbing language nevertheless.

Historians are not altogether agreed as to the precise state of
affairs in William's England after the Conquest. Some point to
the degradation of the English language in the two centuries that
followed and insist that there was complete linguistic divorcement between conquerors and conquered. Others recall the fact
that William tried, though unsuccessfully, to learn the language
of his new subjects at the age of forty-three, and that his charters
are written in Latin and English, not in French. They even go
so far as to claim that there were mutual respect, cooperation and
intermarriage between Saxons and Normans from the very beginning.

Other historians claim that so far as the language at least was
concerned, the speech of the conquered was banned from all
polite and official usage, that it was despised as the jargon of
peasants and practically ceased for a time to be a written
language.

Most obscure perhaps from the standpoint of linguistic history
is the twelfth century, during which the English language sank

to a very low ebb and its literary production all but disappeared. Noteworthy in that century is the continuation of the Anglo-Saxon Peterborough Chronicle, which went on by its own momentum until the year 1154. But what must be remembered is that the Norman conquerors replaced not only the English nobility, but also the English clergy with their own men. And since the clergy were largely responsible for what culture and literacy existed in that dark age, the replacement of Saxon abbots trained in the school of Bede with Norman clerics steeped in Latin and French could not but be reflected on the written tongue of England.

A flourishing literary production in French sprang up at the Anglo-Norman court. These were the days of the flowering of Old French epic and courtly poetry, and even if we reject the theory that the author of the deathless *Chanson de Roland* was Turoldus of Peterborough, an Anglo-Norman abbot of William's following, the fact nevertheless remains that much of the best and finest in Old French literature was produced on English soil. The Oxford manuscript of the *Song of Roland,* seemingly the oldest, as well as the *Pèlerinage de Charlemagne à Jérusalem,* was composed in England; so were the lovely lays of Marie de France and many of the Old French popular *fabliaux.* The romance of Tristan and Iseut, however grounded in ancient Celtic and Teutonic legends, was first elaborated by Anglo-Norman poets. The old myths of Merlin and Arthur came first from the pen of Geoffrey of Monmouth. Philippe de Thaün with his *Bestiaire,* Gaimar with his *History of the English,* Wace with his *Roman de Brut* and particularly his *Roman de Rou,* which celebrated the doughty deeds of Rollo and his descendants, were all part of this vast Anglo-Norman literary output which relegated the native language of England to temporary obscurity.

At the end of the eleventh century, the Domesday Book, a sort of census of national resources, makes a clear-cut if incidental distinction between English and French. During the obscure twelfth century there is not too much mention of matters linguistic. But it was precisely in the course of the twelfth century, when written English had sunk to an all-time low, that spoken English was making victorious inroads into the language of the conquerors. Gradually freeing itself from its burden of Teutonic declensions and flections, the peasant's dialect marched on, by an underground route, to a new freedom and vitality, symbolic, as Trevelyan remarks, "of the fate of the English race itself after Hastings, fallen to rise nobler, trodden under foot only to be trodden into shape."

Thus it is that the dawn of the thirteenth century finds a trilingual England, in which French, Latin and English live side by side, each for a different purpose and with a different function. The first was the literary and courtly tongue, the second the language of the church and the legal documents, the third the tongue of common intercourse.

With the loss of Normandy by King John in 1204, the English language received a mighty fillip. It is conceivable that up to that time many of England's new landed gentry thought of Normandy as "home," and of England as a colonial possession in which they held their major domains. Now there was no longer a "home" for them, save England. It is true that the new Gallic influx brought into England from Poitou in the early part of the thirteenth century by the Francophile Henry III served to strengthen and bolster the French language in England; but it is also true that it gave rise to a brand-new nationalism among the once Norman Barons, now turned into Englishman. They were, after all, the first arrivals, the rightful occupants of the land. The Frenchmen favored by Henry they considered aliens to the soil of England, now their own. For nearly one century, a political and cultural battle raged between the Anglicized descendants of William's followers and the continental Frenchmen, a battle marked by such episodes as the Council of Winchester, the Oxford Provisions and the Barons' War of 1258. By the time of Edward I, all Englishmen, whether of Saxon or Norman descent, were united, and in 1295 the King of England charged the French kings, among other crimes, with wanting to wipe out the English tongue.

Dialectal differences between the standard Francien of Paris and the Anglo-Norman French of England undoubtedly added to the fires of political and economic animosity. The attempts made in the course of the century to supersede the native Anglo-

French with Parisian French at the English court had the net result of throwing the speakers of the former more and more into the arms of English. As between the tongue of the overwhelming majority of their subjects and an alien, though related dialect, spoken with arrogance by the newcomers from the continent, they preferred the former.

So it is that by the end of the thirteenth century French had become almost a foreign tongue in England, though it was gaining influence and prestige on the continent, to such an extent that German barons had it taught to their children, that Brunetto Latini calls it "the speech that is most delectable and the most common to all people," and that Martino da Canale describes it as "current throughout the world, and most delightful to read and hear."

But so far as England was concerned, French was beginning to be taught out of manuals, as a cultural tongue, and even the children of the nobility learned it as a foreign language. A writer of the period says:

> *Lewede* [i.e., ignorant] *men cune* [know] *Ffrensch non,*
> *Among an hondryd vnneþis on* [scarcely one].

A petition to Parliament at this period had to be translated from French into Latin for the sake of those who knew no French. Henry III may have favored the French and their language, but his brother Richard was chosen Emperor of Germany because he "knew English, similar in sound to German."

In vain the scholars of the early fourteenth century tried to save the remnants of the French tongue in the churches and universities, decreeing, in 1325, that at Oxford "all conversation be in Latin, or in French," and in 1332, by an act of Parliament, that French be taught the children of the upper classes so they might know the tongue of the enemy. These measures simply indicate the low estate to which French had fallen as a popular spoken tongue in England.

About 1300 Robert of Gloucester states that it is well to know both English and French, but William of Nassyngton in 1325 replies:

Boþe lered and lewed, olde and ȝonge,
Alle vnderstonden english tonge.

Nevertheless, an Anglo-French fourteenth-century writer still describes French as the "loveliest and noblest speech, created by God to His own honor and praise, and comparable to that of the angels." It was the Hundred Years' War, with its bitter animosity against the French, and the Black Death of 1349-1350, leading to a rise in the importance of the laboring classes and their tongue, that gave the death-blow to French in England. In 1345 the chronicles of London were still written in French, and the same language was used in 1348 in a treaty between Oxford University and the town of Oxford. But in 1349 English was reinstated in the schools, in 1362 Parliament was reopened in English, and the same Parliament forbade the use of French in the law courts, on the ground that "French is much unknown." By 1385 English had penetrated the sacred precincts of the universities, with John Cornwall and Richard Pencrich teaching it at Oxford.

The court was probably the last English stronghold of French. In 1403 the Dean of Windsor, starting a letter to the King in French, according to protocol, suddenly switches to English in the middle of a sentence. This switch is symbolical. By the time of Henry V (1413) English is the official language of the court.

As to the nature of this medieval English language that all but disappeared from the world's literary scene in the late eleventh century only to stage a triumphal comeback in the late fourteenth, it must be admitted that there are spots in the course of the intervening centuries when its shape is actually obscure.

It is not quite exact to say that early Middle English was a non-literary language. There was, in the twelfth and more particularly in the thirteenth century, a literary output of sorts, mostly of a religious nature and devised for lower-class consumption. The trouble with it is that it subscribes to no standards. No one, least of all the Normans, attempted to interfere with the language of the English masses; but by that very token, the language was left to shift for itself and assume any form that the local dialect or the whim of the individual writer might care to give it. Hence, the twelfth and thirteenth centuries are dialectal centuries *par excellence*. In addition, the spoken dialects were evolving at a very rapid rate. The decay of flectional endings, already begun, particularly in the North, before the Norman Conquest, went on apace and unchecked. Often the progress of the language may be traced in a single work, like the Peterborough Chronicle, which begins in pure Old English, but by the middle of the twelfth century shows the approaching death of noun and adjective inflections.

The most we can say is that for approximately one hundred years after the invasion what literary records there are show an essential conservation of Old English forms. We must remember, however, that the harried North of England, which even before 1066 had shown signs of evolving toward a modern stage far beyond the South and Midlands, was an almost complete literary blank from the eleventh to the thirteenth century.

Then the transformation began. Vowels of final syllables, *a, o, u, e,* once distinctly pronounced, began to merge into an indefinite -*e,* so that Old English *stānas* became *stones* (pronounced, however, in two syllables; we must not forget, in this connection, that Anglo-Saxon *hatu, sello* and *tunga* had become *hate, selle* and *tunge* even before the Conquest). The final -*m* once distinctive of dative plurals became -*n,* then tended to fall. Only the -*s* of the genitive survived well. But at the same time that case distinctions became all but obliterated, there was a tendency for -*s* and -*es* plurals to become universal in the North, while -*n* and -*en* plurals were favored in the South. The ultimate triumph of the -*s* plural over the -*n* (*stones,* as against *oxen*) may perhaps have been favored by the presence of a flectional oblique plural -*s* in Old French and Anglo-Norman (note that in other Germanic languages that were not under French influence, like German and Scandinavian, the -*n* plural is quite in vogue, whereas in Dutch, another Germanic language which in its southern reaches was intermingled with French Walloon, -*s* plurals vie with -*n* plurals to the present day).

Adjective declensions, both strong and weak, were eliminated by what seems to be the triumph of nominative singular and

plural forms, *blinda* and *blindan* becoming *blinde* in accordance
with the phonetic trends described above.

Article forms like *sē* and *sēo* gave way to *the,* while the native
Anglo-Saxon *here* and *hem* still favored by Chaucer were replaced by the Danish *their* and *them* evolved in the North.

A verb like *drīfan* became *drīven,* then *drīve.* Many strong
verbs became weak, *burn, bow, climb, flee, flow, help, step, walk*
and *weep* among them, while new verbs admitted to the language were all placed in the weak division.

As for vocabulary, the Norman invasion acted like a bomb
that smashes a dike and lets loose a flood. The stream of French
words that began to enter English in 1066 is still unbroken today.
Yet it is well to note that up to 1250 no more than about one
thousand French words had entered the language, mostly of the
kind that the lower classes would naturally acquire from the
nobility, words like *baron, noble, dame, servant, messenger, feast,
story, rime* and *lay.*

The loss of Old English literary words from the language is
more surmised than proved, but their replacement by French
literary words is there for all to see. The upper classes, though
speaking English after 1250, could not be expected to grope for
English words that had all but vanished when the French equivalents were so easily available to them. *King* and *queen* remained,
but practically all the names of government and feudalism were
appropriated from French. Medieval "Law French," ejected only
by an act of Parliament in 1731 after Cromwell had vainly tried
to oust it, still gives us expressions in which the adjective follows
the noun, like *fee simple, attorney general, body politic, malice
aforethought.* Cooking terms are largely French: *sauce, boil, fry,
roast, toast, pastry, soup, jelly, dainty;* and remember also
Ivanhoe's French *beef, veal* and *pork* vs. Saxon *ox, calf* and *swine.*
Words of an exclamatory nature were freely borrowed: *alas,
certes, adieu;* Jespersen even calls attention to a thirteenth-
century *Deuleset* (*Dieu le sait*) which practically ousted the
native *Crist hit wat.* French and English words were crossed and
blended wherever there was the possibility; this happened to
Saxon *rice* and French *riche,* Saxon *choose* and French *choix,*
Saxon *iegland* and French *isle.* The outward parts of the body,
save for *face,* and most of the better-known inner organs were

untouched by the Normans (*arm, hand, finger, nose, eye, ear, skin, heart, brain, lung, kidney, liver, bone*); but *vein, nerve, stomach, artery, tendon* attest the foreign influence.

Perhaps one of the most notable results of the Norman-French invasion of the English language was the creation of the many synonyms that distinguish English to this day, giving it a firm foothold in both the Germanic and the Romance fields. As early as 1225 a devotional work shows such double forms as *cherite-luve, desperaunce-unhope, bigamie-twiewifing.* Chaucer speaks later of *cure* and *hele, poynaunt* and *sharp, lord* and *sire,* Caxton of *awreke* and *avenge, old* and *auncyent, glasse* or *mirrour,* and the Book of Common Prayer has to this day *acknowledge and confess, dissemble nor cloke, assemble and meet, pray and beseech, perceive and know, power and might.*

Jespersen aptly brings out the point that the heaviest borrowing from French took place not immediately after the Conquest, but between 1250 and 1400, at the period, that is, when French was definitely beginning to be felt as foreign and cultural, even by those whose ancestral language it had been. But this period was precisely the one that marked the rebirth of English as a literary tongue. The true fusion of French and native elements seemingly took place only after English had risen again from the thralldom to which William's Conquest had consigned it. As a slave tongue English sullenly kept to itself, refusing to have much to do with its rival and master. As the free tongue of independent men, English was more than willing to embrace French and take it to its heart.

At least three works of some literary note were composed in the thirteenth century that marked the resurgence of English. They are the *Ormulum,* a paraphrase of the Scriptures, from the year 1200 or thereabouts; the *Ancren Riwle,* a compendium of religious rules for anchoresses, or prospective nuns, of the year 1225; and Layamon's *Brut,* which is in part a semi-mythical account of the Brutus of antiquity, based on Wace's Anglo-Norman romance of the same name. None of them is of such a nature as to cast brilliant literary glory upon the language that serves them as a vehicle.

More in accord with the popular spirit of the period, and more typical of the transitional stage that ushers in the age of

the first great author of the English language, are two works,
both from the South of England. *The Owl and the Nightingale*
is from the early thirteenth century, and the excerpt given by
Baugh reflects a spirit not too far removed from Chaucer's:

Al so þu dost on þire side:	(All so thou dost on thy side:)
vor wanne snov liþ þicke & wide,	(for when snow lies thick and wide,)
an alle wiʒtes habbeþ sorʒe	(and all wights have sorrow)
þu singest from eve fort amorʒe	(thou singest from eve forth amorrow)
Ac ich alle blisse mid me bringe:	(And I all bliss with me bring:)
ech wiʒt is glad for mine þinge,	(each wight is glad for my thing,)
& blisseþ hit wanne ich kume,	(and blesses it when I come,)
& hiʒte aʒen mine kume.	(and hopes against my coming.)

The Kentish *Ayenbite of Inwyt* ("Remorse of Conscience") is
fully a century later (1340), but is in some ways more archaic and
closer to the Anglo-Saxon spirit:

Nou ich wille þet ye ywyte hou hit is y-went
(Now I will that ye know how it is gone)
þet þis boc is y-write mid engliss of Kent.
(That this book is written with English of Kent.)
þis boc is y-mad vor lewede men,
(This book is made for lewd [*i.e.* ignorant, simple] men,)
vor vader, and vor moder, and vor oþer ken,
(For father, and for mother, and for other kin,)
ham vor to berʒe vram alle manyere zen,
(Them for to shelter from all manner of sin,)
þet ine hare inwytte ne bleve no voul wen
(That in their conscience there may remain no foul wen)
"Huo ase god" is his name yzed
("Who as God" is his name said [*Michael* has that meaning in
Hebrew])
þet þis boc made god him yeve þet bread,
(That this book made God him give that bread,)
of angles of hevene and þerto his red
(Of angels of heaven and thereto His counsel)
and ondervonge his zaule huanne þet he is dyad.
(And receive his soul when that he is dead.)

The etymologist will note that both passages are completely free of Norman-French importations, save for the *manyere* of the *Ayenbite*. English, though a subject language, had developed freely and independently, scorning foreign support even when its fortunes were at their lowest ebb. But as we shall see, the latter part of the fourteenth century, as represented by Chaucer, spectacularly reverses this trend, and gives English the typically international flavor that distinguishes it today.

Chapter Four

THE CHAUCERIAN ERA

The Beginnings of Modern English—Latin and Italian Influences—Can We Read Chaucer?—The Tongue of London—Caxton and His Times

There are historical periods when language changes very rapidly, and others when language change is relatively slow. The first usually coincide with social upheavals, invasions, violent revolutions, while the latter are normally the mark of peace and domestic tranquillity.

The age ushered in by Geoffrey Chaucer is of the second variety, despite the Black Death and the Hundred Years' War. The plague could not, by its very nature, exert any powerful influence on the language, while the war, despite its distressing features, was fought abroad, on foreign soil, and did not disturb the now even linguistic progress of the English homeland.

As a matter of fact, if one seeks proof of the statement that only major upheavals bring about major language changes, such proof is to be found in English. The Anglo-Saxon invasion not merely changed, but replaced the Celtic and Latin of Roman Britain; the Norman landing, along with the previous Danish invasions, gave English an essentially modern guise, to such an extent that our understanding of the language of our ancestors may be said to date from the terminal point of the Norman period. Thereafter, there were no more successful invasions of England. Correspondingly, since that period the language has changed, but in orderly and continuous fashion, and without a break in its essential structure.

It might be added that the fundamental changes in language are the ones that involve morphology, or basic grammatical structure. Changes of sounds are in themselves noncommittal, save where they affect the grammar of the language. The North of England and the Lowlands of Scotland still to this day say *stane* instead of *stone,* as they did in Chaucer's day, but this does not mark them as possessing a different tongue from the common English of us all.

In like manner, individual words may come and go without marking a fundamental change. Chaucer used many words we no longer use, and perhaps the majority of the terms in use today would have been unintelligible to him. Yet he would say, listening to a modern Englishman or American, that the language was a dialect of his own. As for us, we cannot hear his tongue, but we can read it. At the most, we will need a glossary, similar to the ones that enable Britishers to understand American underworld speech; but we certainly do not need the kind of specialized grammatical study without which any attempt to read Anglo-Saxon is futile.

The latter half of the fourteenth century was an epoch of fruition from the linguistic standpoint. The vast stock of French words that had been clamoring for admission to a tongue once more grown literary had finally found their place. The cultured Englishman was no longer conscious of being a Saxon or a Norman, he was conscious only of being an Englishman. As such, he could appropriate and use, without fear or national prejudice, such words as the richer language of his French neighbors offered him. The situation has some points of resemblance to that of some of the immigrants to our modern American shores, who in the second generation are ashamed and afraid of their ancestral tongue lest it be interpreted as a sign of lukewarm Americanism, but whose descendants lose their inhibitions about studying and using German, Italian or Spanish, because they know their national feelings can no longer be questioned.

The very name of Geoffrey Chaucer is symbolic of this new state of affairs. His family name is without doubt French (*chalcier,* from Latin *calcearius,* "shoemaker"); but this need not indicate Norman origin; many Saxon families had Normanized their names during the period when Saxon was synonymous with peasant, and Norman with noble. His first name is likewise

French, but goes back to the Germanic substratum of the Franks (*Gottes Friede,* "God's peace," becoming Old French *Godefreit, Godefroy,* or, in a more advanced variant, *Geoffrey, Jeffrey*).

Chaucer was a Londoner, and the language he used in his writings was the East Midland dialect, combined with Southern admixtures, which was at that time the speech of London. This means that his language shows at times dialectal Southern forms which were later replaced by Northern ones (*hem* and *hiere* or *hire,* for "them" and "their," for instance, or *yive* for "give"). Other features of his speech remained in the standard tongue until much later (*his* as the possessive of *it,* which was not replaced by "its" until the seventeenth century).

The London East Midland dialect used by Chaucer was predestined to become standard English both for political-geographic and for linguistic reasons. It was the language of the capital; geographically, it occupied a position midway between the extreme North and the extreme South. Linguistically, it represented a compromise tongue that was comprehensible to both extremes. But at the time of Chaucer its predominance was far from fully established. That was to come later, when Caxton's printing presses gave it the indelible stamp of official recognition through the eye. In the days of Chaucer at least five major dialectal varieties were still easily recognizable: Northern, East Midland, West Midland, Southern, and Southeastern, or Kentish. Chaucer himself says: "and for ther is so gret diversite in Englissh, & in writyng of oure tonge." Earlier writers had described the dialect of Devon as "more archaic," and that of Yorkshire as "harsh and incomprehensible." Chaucer himself makes deliberate use of the Yorkshire dialect in his *Reeve's Tale,* putting it into the mouths of Cambridge students to lend local color to his work—the first deliberate use of dialect, perhaps, in English literature.

Some historians view Chaucer's influence upon the language as highly important. Others consider it problematical, pointing to the fact that the dialect of London, with or without Chaucer, would have taken the lead anyway, and further remarking that his language is more Southern than the standard English that ultimately resulted in the fifteenth century. The influence of

Oxford and Cambridge, they say, was more decisive in the fixing of standard modern English than the works of Chaucer.

But even if we favor this view, the fact remains that the work of Chaucer, quite aside from its literary merits, is of supreme interest to the linguist as an illustration of the trend of the language in the late fourteenth century.

Let us take an excerpt from his writings:

> Whan that Aprille with his shoures sote
> The droghte of Marche hath perced to the rote,
> And bathed every veyne in swich licour;
> (Of which vertu engendred is the flour);
> Whan Zephyrus eek with his swete breeth
> Inspired hath in every holt and heeth
> The tendre croppes, and the yonge sonne
> Hath in the Ram his halfe cours y-ronne,
> And smale fowles maken melodye,
> That slepen al the night with open yë,
> (So priketh hem nature in hir corages):
> Than longen folk to goon on pilgrimages
> (And palmers for to seken straunge strondes)
> To ferne halwes, couthe in sondry londes;
> And specially, from every shires ende
> Of Engelond, to Caunterbury they wende
> The holy blisful martir for to seke
> That hem hath holpen, whan that they were seke.

Here there is no question as to the comprehensibility of the language to a modern reader. Forms and spellings may strike us as strange and unfamiliar (many of them continue to do so down to the eighteenth century), but we can read Chaucer with an ease that finds no parallel in earlier writers.

Perhaps this is due in part to the free and easy way in which Chaucer makes use of the large stock of French words at his disposal. *Perced, veyne, licour, vertu, engendred, flour, inspired, tendre, cours, melodye, nature, corages, pilgrimages, palmers, straunge, specially,* are all words that existed in the language before Chaucer, but which earlier writers of English had at times hesitated to use. There is no such hesitation in Chaucer. He makes full use of the language's resources, both native and borrowed, and proves, perhaps for the first time, that English is sufficient unto itself.

Perhaps this is due to Chaucer's earlier background as a translator from the French. If so, it proves abundantly the advantages of bilingualism. But Chaucer also translated and adapted from the Italian (Boccaccio's *Filostrato* and *Teseide* and parts of the *Divine Comedy* appear in thin disguise or with no disguise at all in his many writings). Yet he seemingly refrained from importing Italian words into his English save as loan-translations (one remarkable error on his part occurs when he misunderstands Boccaccio's *navi bellatrici,* "fighting ships" as *navi ballatrici,* "dancing ships," and consequently uses in his Knight's Tale *shippes hoppesteres*).

The conclusion seems to be that Chaucer's use of the French words in the language was not due to a desire for linguistic innovation, but that he rather utilized to the full the resources of the tongue spoken about him, something which his predecessors had neglected to do, possibly because those resources were not yet sufficiently developed.

Chaucer's modernistic tendencies are revealed in other ways. His contemporary William Langland still makes use of the old Anglo-Saxon device of alliteration in his *Piers Plowman*. Chaucer, like many others, scorns it, and uses instead the sweet rhyme of Anglo-French; in one of his works, he has his character say that he is a Southerner, and consequently "cannot geste *rom, ram, ruf,*" thereby indicating that the alliterative survival is characteristic of the North. As for Anglo-French, which had enjoyed such literary vogue in earlier centuries, it had sunk to such low estate by Chaucer's day that the poet satirizes it through the mouth of his Prioress. The French of Stratford, he implies, is nothing but a bad dialect of Parisian French, which is in turn a foreign, even though cultural tongue.

The language of Chaucer's late fourteenth century and of the fifteenth that followed it are often described as Late Middle English. It could as well be called Early Modern English, save for the fact that a faint trace of inflections still remains. The numerous mute *e*'s that plague the would-be speller of English today were pronounced in that period, despite the fact that they were increasingly losing their power to mark distinctions of case, gender or number. As against an earlier *Him þuhte þæt his heorte wolde brecan,* we now have *Him thoughte that his herte wolde breke,* but *thoughte, herte, wolde* and *breke* were still pronounced in two full syllables. It was not until the end of the fifteenth century that these flectional vestiges disappeared or became what they are today—unless relics of the past.

Ich and *I* ran side by side in Chaucer's language, and the distinction between *ye* and *you* was still that of nominative versus accusative. Northern *they* had replaced the earlier Anglo-Saxon *hīe,* but *hem* was still alive (in fact, some linguists claim that modern colloquial *'em* in "I see 'em" is its lineal descendant). The Old English present participle in *-ende,* after having shifted to *-inde,* had joined forces with the verbal noun in *-ynge,* paving the way for our present *-ing* of many functions. The past participle still frequently bore a prefix *y-* or *i-* (*ydon, yclept, ironne*), which was the survivor of an earlier *ge-*.

Spellings were still based on French rather than on Latin models. Chaucer, for instance, uses *descrive, parfit, peynture,* as against the later Latinized *describe, perfect, picture,* while *equal, language, victuals* had not yet replaced the French *egal, langage, vittles. Reial* had not yet bifurcated into *real* and *royal,* and *gost* had not yet been influenced by Flemish *gheest* to take on a useless *h*.

The great change that marks Chaucer's era (1340-1400) and the following century is undoubtedly in vocabulary, and the great vocabulary change in turn is the wholesale admission of French words and, more remotely, of Latin words to the language, not merely of literature, but of common intercourse. Wyclif's translation of the Bible, composed in 1384, has such words as *generation* and *persecution,* which did not appear in the earlier Anglo-Saxon version. Anglo-Saxon compounds like *handbook* and *foreword* were unceremoniously dropped from the language in favor of the foreign *manual* and *preface* (many centuries later, they were reintroduced as neologisms, and objected to by purists unskilled in linguistic history). Even when words were borrowed directly from Latin, they were Gallicized in form.

The amazing part of all this is that it happened at the very time when French was being everywhere replaced as a spoken tongue, and to a large extent even as a written tongue. Few letters were written in English before 1400, French and Latin being viewed as the normal media of correspondence. But after 1450 this situation was reversed. Wills, town and guild records, the statutes of Parliament, all swung away from French and Latin and climbed on the English bandwagon in the course of the fifteenth century. It is no wonder that Caxton, at the close of that century, was able to say: "For the mooste quantyte of the people vnderstonde not latyn ne frensshe here in this noble royame of englond."

The role of Caxton, first of the great English printers to utilize Gutenberg's invention, is more important in the fixation than in the formation of the language. He it was who, from 1477 on, made the works of Chaucer, Gower, Lydgate and Malory accessible to the English reading public. He did not make the spoken language, and contributed relatively little to it. His great work lay in the standardization of spelling, which until his time had been largely arbitrary, and in the final choice of the East Midland dialect as the literary norm. Up to the fifteenth century, literary works almost invariably bear the stamp of one or another of the five great spoken dialects of England. After Caxton's time, it becomes almost impossible to judge the place of origin of a literary work by its linguistic form, save for a few works printed in the North. A fully established literary English language appears by 1485 in Malory's *Morte d' Arthur,* printed by Caxton.

The importance of this regularization of the English written tongue, semi-arbitrary though it was, is difficult to overestimate. The printed book addresses the mind through the eye, at the same time that it makes a mass appeal the old manuscripts could never achieve. The word seen in print is, as a rule, indelibly impressed upon the mind of the reader. But in addition, it places the stamp of social and cultural approval upon the form, both orthographic and dialectal, that the printer selects. Before Caxton's time, new writers felt justified in using both their own dialects and their own choice of spelling. After the fifteenth century, they felt increasingly constrained to use the forms that enjoyed the blessing of established tradition.

Nor should we minimize the influence that the written, printed form exerts upon the spoken tongue. A speaker who is also a reader may, if he chooses, use forms that diverge from the standard he meets in his reading. But he does it at the risk of constant correction from others, of constant detriment to his own intellectual prestige, of constant prickings from his own cultural conscience.

Whether this is good or bad, desirable or deplorable, is beyond the scope of this chapter. The fact remains that it happens, and, more specifically, that it occurred at the end of the fifteenth century.

From the time of Caxton on, English is not merely a series of related oral dialects, which are occasionally written. It is a full-blown cultural tongue, the equal, in its own fashion, of the Latin and Greek of Classical antiquity, a language with a numerous body of unified speakers and writers, or, to borrow a phrase from the field of trade, a language with a vast potential and actual market.

Though no longer in a completely fluid state, the Modern English that emerges from the era of Chaucer and Caxton is a tongue that still possesses vast possibilities of change, channeled in the direction of vocabulary rather than of sounds or grammatical structure. That this is so is abundantly proved by the linguistic history of the Elizabethan England for which the stage was set by the great printers of the late fifteenth and early sixteenth centuries.

Chapter Five

THE AGE OF ELIZABETH

The Language of the Reformation—Effect on English of the Rediscovery of Latin and Greek—The Role of Milton and Shakespeare—The Triumph of the Printers—King James and His Bible

In 1490, Caxton complained that when one said *egges,* after the fashion of London, he was likely to be misunderstood by one who used the Northern *eyren.* A compromise that would lead to general mutual understanding on the part of all English speakers was imperative, he added.

The nature of the compromise is revealed a little later by Puttenham in his *Arte of English Poesie:* "Ye shall, therefore, take the usual speach of the Court, and that of London and the shires lying about London within lx. myles, and not much above."

It goes without saying that this ideal compromise applied at first only to the literary tongue. The spoken dialects continued in existence; as a matter of fact, they blissfully endure to the present day.

But the great difference between pre- and post-Caxton times lies in the importance of the literary tongue for which a standard was developing. The invention of the press had led to a spreading of education, communications, and social consciousness such as Chaucer and his precursors would not have dreamed possible. In the latter half of the fifteenth century some thirty-five thousand books were printed in Europe as a whole. Between that time and 1640, over twenty thousand printed works appeared in English and on English soil. The impact of these works on popular culture and literacy can hardly be overestimated; neither can their effect on standardization and uniformity be minimized.

One far-reaching effect of a true linguistic standard is the freezing of grammatical forms. So long as there is no *point de repère,* no authority, real or fancied, for the language, the language continues to evolve in its basic feature, morphology. We have seen the evolution of Old English's four- or five-case system to the single form of today, with only the genitive in *'s* to act as a survivor of ancient flectional endings. Further innovations might well have crept into the language as time went on; the genitive in *'s* might have been lost; singular and plural might have developed into a single form, with distinction of number brought out by the use of added words only when necessary, as happens in a few cases (*one sheep, many sheep*). The spread of the printed word arrested this process of evolution, which some view as a deplorable decay from an earlier and nobler stage, others as a desirable progression toward ultimate analytical simplification. The distinctive grammatical forms we have today, relatively few in comparison with those of Anglo-Saxon or of conservative modern languages like German and Russian, are substantially the ones that were halted in their tracks by the work of Caxton and his fellow-printers.

But if the diffusion of the written word and its concomitant education and literacy have the effect of arresting certain phases of linguistic change, they also speed up, to an almost unbelievable degree, that other, more spiritual function and part of language which depends primarily not upon the blind working of the unconscious mind, but upon the deliberate functioning of the intellect. The growth of individual words, with their semantic burdens and endless possibilities of combination, is immeasurably spurred on by the activity of the conscious mind. This activity, in turn, is fostered and nourished by the printed form, and the reading and thinking that the printed form entails.

At the very moment when the evolution of English grammatical forms grinds slowly, not to a halt, for there is never a complete halt in language, but to a slower pace, the tempo of vocabulary growth begins to quicken to a throbbing, powerful rhythm, the speeding up of which through the successive centuries is one of the most astounding language phenomena the world has ever beheld. Words, new words, more words begin to pour into the language, at the same time that old words are changed and distorted into new meanings. From French, from Latin, from Greek, from Italian, from all of the world's distant languages comes the endless stream of words that enrich English in the sixteenth and subsequent centuries, while the language itself, intolerant of restraint upon its own boundless resources, coins, transforms, manufactures, shifts, creates out of thin air additional hordes of words. Quickened human activity calls new objects and concepts into being, and these, in turn, demand names. The names are duly registered in the great book of language's vital statistics, and once they are entered, thanks to the great invention of printing, it becomes exceedingly difficult to dislodge them.

It must be kept in mind that this new process of vocabulary enrichment is to some extent common to all the great western languages. To what degree English outstrips the others we shall consider later. The fact remains that while the West, until the invention of printing, had leaned heavily upon the great established language of tradition, Latin, and to a lesser degree upon the rediscovered Greek that swept Europe in the fifteenth century, it definitely began with the sixteenth century to rely upon its own living resources, and to use the Classical tongues not as literary and scholarly substitutes for the spoken vernaculars, but as storehouses and banks upon which it could draw at will whenever it felt at a loss for a word.

As customary in all periods when the new struggles against the old, there were controversies concerning the relative merits of the local tongues as against the tongues of tradition. Wyclif had carried the battle for English to the people by translating the Bible into their speech, but there is no clear-cut evidence of conscious linguistic nationalism on his part. The writers of the sixteenth century, on the contrary, were fully conscious of the issues involved. They knew perfectly well that they were in the process of deliberately appropriating something like one-fourth of the the Latin lexicon, and some of them not only acknowledged the fact, but gloried in it. Sir Thomas Browne, for instance, remarks that "one must learn Latin to understand

English," and Thomas Elyot uses, without apology, neologisms pilfered from both Latin and French, such as *education, dedicate, esteem, enterprise, endeavor, protest, reproach.* The popular demand for the fruits of the Renaissance led to innumerable translations from Latin, Greek and other languages. Among the authors who reappeared in English dress in the sixteenth century were Thucydides, Xenophon, Cæsar, Livy, Sallust, Tacitus, Plutarch, Plato, Aristotle, Cicero, Seneca, Marcus Aurelius, Virgil, Horace, Ovid, Homer, as well as St. Augustine, Boethius, Erasmus, Calvin and Luther. But the very translation process revealed the startling immaturity of the new linguistic medium, the woeful inadequacy of a tongue like English to render deep literary and philosophical concepts. Translators and writers were often forced to apologize for their own deficiencies and those of the language. More, they were compelled to resort to what someone derisively labeled "ink-horn terms," words plucked bodily out of the Latin lexicon, given a slight twist in their endings, and left to shift for themselves as English words. Such was the case with the words objected to by Thomas Wilson in 1553; today we think nothing of *expend, capacity, celebrate, extol, dexterity, fertile, native, confidence* or *relinquish,* but in his day they were the veriest of neologisms, incomprehensible to the majority of readers.

It is small wonder that Thomas Chaloner in 1549 wrote a treatise against the obscurity of the language of certain writers of his time, or that Thomas Cheke in 1561 composed a letter on behalf of the "purity" of the English language, supplementing it, by way of illustration, with a translation of part of the New Testament into pure Anglo-Saxon English.

The revolt against Classical importations reached its culmination around 1575, when Richard Carew, incensed at the constant charges of "barbarism" levelled against the ancestral language, wrote his *Excellency of the English Tongue.* Sir Philip Sidney, in 1583, spoke out even more definitely, claiming that English is equal to any other language, barring none, for the expression of common thought.

This revolt had not been without precursors on the continent, where similar controversies raged. In Italy, such writers as Alberti, Speroni and Bembo had extolled the vernacular (though without attacking the language from which that vernacular had sprung, something they could hardly have done, considering the lineal descent of Italian from Latin). In France, Du Bellay in 1549 had presented his masterly *Défense et Illustration de la langue française,* in which the latter was described as fully adequate for all literary purposes.

In his *Promessi Sposi,* Manzoni describes the sad plight of four live chickens, who, being transported to their doom with their feet tied together and their heads dangling, busy themselves pecking at one another, and reflects bitterly that often human beings who are partners in misery act the same way. Not too different was the attitude which the modern languages at this period assumed toward one another. Words aplenty had come from French into English, and from Italian into both. Here were three modern languages endeavoring to make their way in the world, and sharing common problems and difficulties. One might have expected them to collaborate in the solution of their troubles. Instead, we have Henri Etienne, in 1578, protesting volubly against the fact that the French tongue was "italianized and otherwise disguised." (He says among other things that the French courtiers who have borrowed war terms from Italian forget that in the future people will think the French had to learn the very art of fighting from the Italians.) So far as England is concerned, Gabriel Harvey deplores what he calls "Tuscanisms" in English literature, while another sixteenth-century writer states that English, having borrowed copiously from French, Italian and Latin, is now a "gallimansfray or hodgepodge of all other speches."

For this there was no remedy, nor is there any today. The Renaissance was on the march, and Renaissance meant, among other things, the curious phenomenon of nationalism and pride in the national tongue coupled with a thirst for international contacts and knowledge. It is a pity that English, in its extensive Italian borrowings, has overlooked a word, *campanilismo,* which, freely translated, means "the spirit of the belfry," that narrow parochialism which opposes what comes from abroad, but even more what comes from across the county or township line. The

Renaissance broke down the belfry spirit of the Middle Ages and caused Neapolitans, Sicilians, Florentines and Lombards to regard themselves culturally, if not politically, as Italians; Parisians, Burgundians, Poitevins and Normans to consider themselves Frenchmen; and Londoners, Yorkshiremen, Kentishmen and Midlanders to feel that they were primarily Englishmen. At the same time, it gave all of them a new breadth and depth of outlook and taught them that there was something beyond national borders which they could fight against, but from which they could also learn.

The Renaissance also had its share in freeing the language from its former dependence on political and military events and linking its course to that of cultural progress. During the Middle Ages every great language was molded into shape by invasions and wars. The latter continued after the Renaissance, as they unfortunately do to this day. But the cultural pattern established by the Renaissance froze the sphere of action of each language along with its primary grammatical forms. No matter who won or lost wars, the language patterns were now fixed in geographical as well as morphological terms, for what concerned the old continent. It was quite otherwise with the new, where languages closely followed the pattern of successful invasion, occupation and colonization. The reign of Elizabeth and her political doings wielded great influence upon the linguistic future of the American continent, but relatively little upon that of England.

One of the outstanding problems to beset the sixteenth century was the matter of spelling or, as it was called then, "right writing." It is true that along broad lines this question had been settled by Caxton and his successors, but endless problems remained. To cite but a few examples, we still find in that century the word *guest* in the following variants: *gest, geste, gueste, ghest, gheste*. *Peasant* also appears as *pesant* or *pezant; publicly* as *publikely* and *publiquely; straight* is rivalled by *strayt, limbs* by *limms, diverse* (or rather *diuerse*) by *dyvers*. *Tongue, townge* and *toung* appear, along with *swerd, sweard* and *sword,* and *yield, yeild, yielde* and *yilde*. In the works of a single writer we are faced with such inconsistencies as *featlye, neatlie, aptly,* or *been, beene* and *bin*. The conventional spelling was often finally set by printers, on a basis of line-and-letter economy or personal whim. But writers and scholars managed to make notable contributions along lines of etymology, as when they inserted a silent *b* in *debt* and *doubt,* on the ground that the original Latin forms have *b,* or of analogy, as when *delight* and *tight* were regaled with *gh* taken from *light* and *night.* Some of the spellings used by Cheke are reminiscent of Dutch vowel-combinations (*taak, maad, wijn, giv, belev, dai*). Mulcaster's *Elementarie* of 1582 attempts to codify current usage, which includes the addition of silent final *-e* to indicate a preceding "long" vowel (*made,* as against Cheke's *maad*). The recommended spelling for some seven thousand more commonly used words appears (*where,* for instance, is given preference over *wher, whear, wheare, were* and *whair*). But it is not until the middle of the seventeenth century that spelling begins to assume its crystallized, albeit highly illogical, present-day form.

The primary linguistic characteristic of this great period, in which Shakespeare and Spenser cast the foundations of modern English even while Elizabeth was laying the cornerstone of Britain's empire, may be described as that of conscious interest. People had at last become language-conscious through a process of increasing education, literacy, and literary output. This language-consciousness was reflected in the controversies about the relative merits of English and other tongues, about correct usage, about the literary standard. But the age was still plastic. It was not only spelling rules that were as yet not clearly defined. Pronunciation was in a transitory state. Grammatical forms were heading rapidly toward the ultimate crystallization that is in evidence today. Above all, vocabulary was rapidly evolving, in somewhat anarchical fashion, with the boundaries of the parts of speech even less set than they are today.

For what concerns sounds, English was completing what Jespersen calls the "great English vowel-shift," whereby practically all the long vowels of Chaucer's time rearranged themselves according to a new pattern. From the evidence at our disposal, which consists of spellings, rhymes, statements of writers of the period, and grammars of foreign languages, in which certain foreign sounds are equated with contemporary English sounds, it seems established that the long *i* of Chaucer's day, heading toward the modern English diphthong sound heard in *bite,* had reached an *ay*-stage, or perhaps the sound of *e* in unstressed *the* followed by *i* in *bit.* The *oo*-sound of earlier *hūs,* moving toward modern *house,* was at the stage where it was pronounced somewhat like the *oa* of *loan.* Chaucer's long *e* and long *o,* pronounced as in modern German, had already reached the modern sounds heard in *beet* and *boot.* The open long *e* of Chaucer's *beat,* pronounced like a prolonged *bet,* was approaching the modern sound, but had only reached a stage reflected in the present-day Irish pronunciation of *beat* (something akin to *bate*). The long open *o* of Chaucer's *boat,* resembling modern *bought,* had already achieved its present pronunciation, but the long *a* of *abate,* uttered by Chaucer with the *a* of *father,* was at the point where its sound resembled that of a prolonged *bet.* This means that present-day *bite, about, beet, boot, beat, boat* and *abate,* which in Chaucer's day had sounded respectively like *beet, aboot, bait, boat, bet* (prolonged), *bought* and *abaht,* were sounded in Shakespeare's day like *bait, aboat, beet, boot, bate, bote* and *abet* (prolonged). In addition, the vowel sounds of *brew, few, steward* and *rude,* which Chaucer kept separate in his pronunciation (*bray-oo, feh-oo, stee-ooard, rude* with French *u*), were converging toward the identical pronunciation they have today. The final unaccented *-e,* which Chaucer still sounded (*done,* pronounced in two syllables), was no longer heard in Shakespeare's day, save where it is heard today (*waited, houses,* etc.). Other minor changes included various vowel-shifts before *r* (*derke* to *dark, sterre* to *star*), the falling together in rhyme of *flirt* and *hurt* (though *assert* was still kept separate), the pronouncing of final *-ing* as *-in* (something that still goes on today in certain quarters, not all of them by any means American), the silencing of *l* in *should, would* under the influence of *coude* (which, however, added a silent *l* to its spelling in order to keep abreast of its companion auxiliaries), the silencing of *k* and *g* before *n* in words like *know* and *gnaw,* the arising of *sh, zh* and *j* sounds in words like *nation, mission, vision* and *soldier.*

Grammatical changes were comparatively few. There is

throughout the sixteenth century a struggle between Southern -*eth* and Northern -*s* in the third singular of verbs; the struggle ended with the victory of -*s*, probably because it saves a syllable in pronunciation (*makes,* as against *maketh*). The -*n* plural of verbs had vanished in the days of Caxton (*they saven* to *they save*), probably for the same reason. A few pronoun forms with -*n* were retained for euphony before a vowel (*an other, none other, mine own, thine own*).

For the rest, the progress of English grammar was no longer a question of morphology, but of syntax and word-order, and in these two fields unbridled license prevailed. Clearness and brevity were enshrined as gods, while "correctness" was consigned to oblivion. To cite but one division of word-order, this was the period when prepositions were most frequently put at the end of clauses and sentences, a usage tolerated today, on the ground that the alternatives are still more awkward, but strongly disapproved of in the intervening period. No less a writer than Shakespeare is responsible for expressions like "a world to hide virtues in," "a naughty night to swim in," "the meat it feeds on," "to point a finger at."

Analogical forms galore were created, with *wrote,* for instance, used as a participle ("I have wrote"), in imitation of *bound,* used both as the past and the participle of *bind.*

One of the most striking and far-reaching characteristics of this epoch is the quickening of the ancient process of functional change, whereby a given part of speech is used, without change in form, as any other part of speech that the speaker or writer may choose. This was a direct effect of the confusion caused by the loss of flectional endings. While these remained, it was difficult, not to say impossible, to confuse an adjective with a noun, or an adverb with a verb. But once the distinctive endings disappear, what is there to prevent a noun from being used as a verb? So we have in this period such gems as "to happy a friend," "to malice an enemy," "to act free," "a seldom pleasure." English was on its way to becoming a language like Chinese, where the same invariable word can be any part of speech, according to its position in the sentence. This tendency was partly repressed by the purists of the seventeenth and eighteenth centuries, but enough of it remains to permit us to "up someone ten dollars" or "undergo the ups and downs of life."

Above all else, this was an era of vocabulary growth, when writers and speakers reveled in the acquisition of new words, from whatever source—foreign and Classical borrowings, re-introduction of old Anglo-Saxon and Chaucerian expressions, compounding of new words from existing ones, giving old words new meanings, and downright, sheer creation. It has been estimated that at least ten thousand words were added to the language during the course of the Renaissance, and these words, far from remaining learned, were spread by the printing presses among the masses, so that they became part and parcel of the popular language.

Shakespeare, who is said to have used a vocabulary of about twenty thousand words, is one of the heaviest contributors to the language's vocabulary, though it is often difficult to distinguish between the words he merely accepted and gave currency to and those he personally coined. He seems to have been the first writer to use such words as *accommodation, apostrophe, dislocate, frugal, obscene, pedant, premeditated* and *reliance.* He gave us such compounds as *foam-girt, heartsick, needle-like, long-haired, ever-burning, lackluster, green-eyed, hot-blooded, hell-black.* He used certain words in their etymological sense, as *expect* in the meaning of *await, atone* for *reconcile, humorous* for *damp.* Despite his astounding acquaintance with both Classical and foreign sources, his vocabulary is about ninety per cent native, and it was he more than any of his contemporaries, with the possible exception of the compilers of the King James Bible, who gave the world a full realization of the boundless potentialities of the English language.

This does not mean that his contemporaries and immediate successors did not bear their share of the glorious burden. Spenser and Milton, more steeped perhaps in non-native elements, were nevertheless responsible for such new Anglo-Saxon formations as *askew, filch, flout* and *freak,* along with Chaucerian restorations like *astound, doom, natheless* and *mickle.* Spenser's *belli-bone* (possibly from French *belle et bonne*) for "fair maiden," *blatant, braggadocio, chirrup* and *squall,* his compounds of the type of *fire-spitting, heart-burning, rosy-fingered,* mostly live on to enrich the present-day language. Milton, who in his Latin works rejoiced in forming new Latin compounds which would have passed muster with Virgil (*olivifera, nimbifer, magniloquus, diversicoloris*), carried the practice into English, with the result that we have *smooth-shaven, sea-girt, thick-woven, deep-vaulted, earth-shaking, lovelorn, all-conquering.* Among other words entering the language at this period are *hapless, baneful, wolfish, bevy, belt, forthright, glee, glance, surly, endear, disrobe, enshrine, grovel, gaudy, gloomy, shady, wary* and *wakeful.*

Some of the language's most popular clichés originated at this period, or even earlier. W. B. Garrison brings out the fact that the expression "to go west" for "to die" was in current use by 1592; when Newgate prisoners were sentenced to death, they were led out of the prison by the western gate and conducted due west to Tyburn, where they were hanged. Even older is "to wash one's hands" of a matter, based on the Biblical precedent of Pontius Pilate, while "a far cry," with its now deceased counterpart "a near cry," is medieval and Scottish, and refers originally to couriers bearing distant or local messages.

No description of the Shakespearean age would be complete without reference to the King James Bible of 1611, which appeared when the Bard's lifework was drawing to a close. It has been estimated that less than six thousand words are used in this translation, and that fully ninety-four per cent of them are of native origin. Whether there is a direct connection between the high percentage of native words and the relative scantiness of the Biblical vocabulary remains yet to be determined, but the inference is difficult to avoid. The King James translators were apparently concerned, and with perfect justification, with reaching the masses in a language that would be thoroughly comprehensible to all, from the highest to the lowest. Hence it was up to them to eschew all words and expressions concerning the currency of which there could be the slightest question. The language of the King James Bible may be monotonous and repetitious (the word *and* alone appears 46,277 times), but it is unmistakably clear. To the linguist, the Bible represents a monument to the least common denominator in language at a given period and in a given area. We can be mathematically sure that if a word or construction appears in that great book, it was something with which all English speakers were acquainted.

By the same token, however, the language of the English Bible represents something less than perfection in the description of the linguistic usage of its times. The words and forms it first introduces are but a handful, and lend themselves to no particular study. Coverdale and Tyndale, who in their earlier translations had given us such memorable innovations as *noonday, loving-kindness, kind-hearted, peacemaker, long-suffering, stumbling-block, broken-hearted* and *beautiful,* are far more fruitful. The great contribution of the King James Bible lies rather in its style, at once majestic and simple. Shakespeare and Milton show us what can be done with many words. The Bible shows what English can accomplish with a few. It is perhaps small wonder that the favorite exercise of Basic English adepts is translation into their contrived language from the King James Bible, whose historical function is the crystallizing of the language into its fundamental pattern of clarity and simplicity, a pattern which three and a half centuries, with all their literary output, have not basically changed.

Chapter Six

THE DAWN OF PRESENT-DAY ENGLISH

*Restoration and Classicism—The Age of Dryden—The
Purists and the Spoken Tongue—The Victorian Age—
The Language Leaves its Shores*

When we say that the age of Shakespeare ushers in modern
English, the question arises whether that statement does not
bring the past history of the language to a close.

In one sense, it does. The sound-changes that have occurred
in standard English since Shakespeare's time are few and trifling
in quality, particularly when we compare them with the wholesale shifts that took place with the coming of William the Conqueror, or during and after the time of Chaucer. Changes in
grammatical structure since the seventeenth century are likewise
unimportant. The norms of syntax and style were set in Shakespeare's time. This leaves but one important division of language, vocabulary, to continue the great process of evolution of
which we have seen the beginnings.

But there was another preoccupation that beset the minds of
the seventeenth and eighteenth and nineteenth centuries, one
that has but lately subsided. This is the question of authority
and good usage, which may be described as uppermost in the
consciousness of English users since the first dictionary in the
modern sense of the word appeared in 1623.

That the English language existed had never been questioned,
not even by the conquering French-speaking Normans. That it
could be used not merely as a vernacular or series of vernaculars,
but as a full-blown literary medium had been proved by Chaucer
and those who followed him. That it possessed a literary standard
had been established by Caxton and his printers. The great lin-

guistic problem that now faced the men of the Roundhead interlude and the Restoration was the direction which that language should consciously take, the words it should admit to common usage, those it should discard, the grammatical forms that should serve it, the names that should be conferred upon such forms, the way in which words and phrases and clauses and sentences should be arranged so as to produce the clearest, most harmonious effect, with or without economy of voice and ink and time.

The story of the English language from the seventeenth century on therefore assumes the aspect of a deliberate controversy between purists and innovators, between grammarians and writers, between the philosophers of the language and its users. This aspect in large measure replaces the earlier picture of blind linguistic forces, rushing tumultuously into channels prepared by historical and social upheavals.

It was but natural that the countries of the European continent should have preceded England in the puristic attempt to force their national languages into literary strait jackets. The Italian Accademia della Crusca, founded in 1582, had for its avowed purpose to enhance the "purity" of the Italian language by sifting, as its name implies, the linguistic wheat from the chaff. Its major preoccupation was with the admission and rejection of words, and with the proper use of the words admitted. Richelieu's French Academy of 1635 had a similar purpose. England, with its liberal traditions, could never screw up enough authoritarian courage to launch upon a similar national enterprise, and in 1664 Dryden voiced the complaint that there was no Academy for the English tongue. The best that could be done was the creation, in 1572, of a Society of Antiquaries, to which no one paid the slightest attention, followed nearly a century later by a timid attempt on the part of the Royal Society to form a committee for the reform of English spelling. This abortive attempt at something faintly resembling the continental language academies was cautiously favored by such illustrious men as Defoe, Swift and Addison, but it was violently opposed by Johnson, Sheridan and Priestley, on the grounds that embalming the language would be tantamount to destroying liberty, and that there was only one way to fix language standards, and that was by popular appeal, a doctrine that is nothing if not democratic.

Yet it is noticeable that the very men who most bitterly opposed restriction on an organized official basis seldom hesitated to assert their own authority, even where it ran counter to the practices of the greatest writers. Dr. Johnson, who in his *Dictionary of the English Language* of 1755 refused to mark the full pronunciation of words because there was too much disagreement among the speakers, nevertheless had previously avowed his desire to "fix the pronunciation, preserve the purity, ascertain the use, and lengthen the duration of the English language."

Several movements, affecting the literature directly and the language indirectly, had either their inception or their culmination in the seventeenth century. One was Philip Sidney's Arcadianism. Another was the Euphuism of John Lyly, whereby clauses were paired for balance or contrast, with emphatic alliteration of the corresponding parts of speech in each clause. But these were primarily literary devices, and it is doubtful that they had much permanent effect on the spoken tongue. Of greater importance was the seventeenth-century puristic movement against ink-horn terms, overseas borrowings, and Chaucerisms. Words that had been in the language since the early sixteenth century, like *acceptance, anticipate, compatible, exact, exasperate, explain, fact, indifference, insinuate, monopoly* and *pretext,* used by Thomas Moore, or Elyot's *exhaust, irritate* and *modesty,* were looked at askance. In spite of this, the seventeenth century saw the admission to the language of words from scores of overseas tongues, particularly Italian. Some of the Italian words came straight into English, like *design, piazza, portico, stanza, violin, volcano;* others used French as an intermediary (*bankrupt, brusque, cavalcade, charlatan, gazette, infantry*). Transoceanic contacts with the great languages of colonization, Spanish and Portuguese, seem responsible for *alligator, anchovy, banana, cannibal, canoe, cocoa, desperado, hammock, hurricane, maize, mosquito, Negro, potato, tobacco,* and many others.

It is often asserted that John Dryden's *Of Dramatic Poesy,* published in 1668, marks the true emergence of modern English, with its qualities of clarity, accuracy and conciseness. Dryden may be regarded as a leader in the reaction against the excesses of seventeenth-century purism, and the discoverer of the fact that since Latin and Greek had grown and developed by borrowing from other languages, no stigma could attach to English for following in their footsteps. Dryden's ideas on language were perhaps over-reactionary. He cast some serious aspersions on the English language, which he labeled "barbarous," envying the regularity achieved by Italian and French, and asserting that he had to translate his ideas into Latin in order to express them properly in English. Nevertheless, his reaction was salutary, since it tended to confer upon English the international character that distinguishes it today. Gallicisms, Latinisms and Graecisms aplenty penetrated the language under his influence, and English acquired a sense of order, reason, logic and taste that placed it on a par with the great continental tongues he envied.

A little earlier, Ben Jonson had complained in his *Discoveries* that "a man coins not a new word without some peril and less fruit; for if it happen to be received, the praise is but moderate; if refused, the scorn is assured." This situation had not, of course, prevented Jonson's precursors and contemporaries from adding to the language. Dryden's crusade made it possible for new creations and borrowings to be offered with fewer inner qualms, and enhanced the importance of the individual as a "maker of English."

Yet the seventeenth century saw the disappearance of many Latin words that had succeeded in finding a foothold in the language. If we have any doubts on that score, we need only consult Samuel Johnson's 1755 *Dictionary,* which reveals a large number of words already obsolete or obsolescent in his day, words like *assation, ataraxy, clancular, dignotion, exolution,* which are dead today.

It is Samuel Johnson who dominates the linguistic picture of the eighteenth century, with his monumental dictionary and his exalted notion of the lexicographer as an *arbiter verborum.* He it was who defined *opera* as "an exotic and irrational entertainment," a *network* as "anything reticulated or decussated at equal distances, with interstices between the intersections," and a *cough*

as a "convulsion of the lungs, vellicated by some sharp serosity."
It is small wonder that Chesterfield compares him to a Roman
dictator.

But because of or in spite of purists and ink-horners, Drydens
and Johnsons, the English language marched on. Its greatest
eighteenth-century development was undoubtedly its full extension to overseas domains and the consequent differentiation that
ensued, of which more presently.

For what concerns the spoken language of the English homeland, little more need be said. The eighteenth and nineteenth
centuries are periods of continuation of the movements initiated
earlier. The floodgates opened by Dryden remain open, and
words continue to pour into the language from all quarters,
domestic as well as foreign. Specialized fields of activity develop
their own vocabularies, more and more incomprehensible to the
outsider. Borrowing, coinage and creation go on apace, speeded
by increasing literacy, floods of books, and the institution of the
daily press. Nineteenth-century Romanticism brings in exotic
words, which are looked upon with doubt and distrust, then embraced and granted the full privileges of citizenship. The Victorian Era is replete with literature, but makes no outstanding
contribution to the language, save the century-old one of new
vocabulary additions, continually opposed, to no avail, by the
purists (as late as 1864, there is objection to *commence, desirability, reliable, lengthy*). The last half of the nineteenth and
the first half of the twentieth centuries see the borrowing of
words like *chauffeur, confetti, bonanza, caracul, chop suey,* and
the forming of compounds like *lipstick, newsprint, streamline,
preview, delouse, stardom.*

Perhaps the greatest internal force that was exerted upon the
English language in the last two centuries, outside of the powerful
impact of colonization and the consequent growth of a new and
somehow different English language on non-English soil, was the
one that arose from the daily press. The creation of newspapers
leads to simplicity and clarity in the written form. The newspaper
is designed for mass consumption, not for an intellectual elite. It
must therefore bring itself down to the level of its readers and
imitate, within reason, their spoken form. The same principle

applies, though somewhat more remotely, to books. In an epoch when everybody reads, and literary success is measured by the number of copies sold, it is no longer possible for the written language to take the full initiative in linguistic development, as it often did in the earlier centuries. A book that is over the heads of its readers sells few copies and exercises scant influence, no matter how favorably it may be reviewed by the literary pundits. In a newspaper, the charge of over-intellectuality is even more deadly. Circulation drops, and the newspaper ceases to appear. This means that the literary market is no longer regulated by what an author wants to write, but by what the reading masses want to read. This in turn means that all but the rare writers must, consciously or unconsciously, exercise the greatest caution in the choice of their vocabulary and in making innovations, unless they do it with their tongues in their cheeks and with a deliberate view to seeking an effect. A writer can always play safe by using a limited and simple vocabulary, and constructions which are as close as possible to those of the spoken tongue. If innovations must be made, let them be those which have already appeared in speech, or which stand a good chance of being liked and adopted by the speakers.

Thus the linguistic initiative, which in the centuries of Chaucer and Shakespeare often rested with the written tongue, has largely passed to the spoken language. Writers' manuals on all sides insist that the writer for popular consumption must write as he speaks, must at all costs avoid stylistic or grammatical complexities and literary attitudes, use simple, short words (the more monosyllabic the better), colloquialisms, vulgarisms, even slang.

In part, this modern tendency is a problem for the future. Also, it is a problem which English shares with the other great languages of western civilization. Its effects upon the language have, however, been noticeable for some time, and cannot be overlooked in a discussion of the language's past.

Since both the tendency and the effects are perhaps more perceptible in one area of the English-speaking world than in others, a few words concerning the historical events leading up to this epoch-making division among English speakers and its earlier manifestations are now in order.

By far the most significant and far-reaching historical development of modern times for what concerns the English language was the migration of that language to remote shores. This movement, beginning in the early seventeenth century, achieved its culmination in the eighteenth, and its fruits are evident today in the fact that nearly four times as many speakers of English exist on non-European soil as live in the tight little islands.

Specific figures tell the imposing story. By the end of the eleventh century, shortly after the Norman Conquest, the total population of England seems to have been about one and a half million. In the year 1500, there were about five million speakers of English, as against ten million speakers of German, twelve million of French, eight and a half million of Spanish, nine and a half million of Italian. By 1700, the population of England stood at less than six million, but there were about eight million speakers of English. By the year 1790, when the first American census was taken, some four million persons were counted, ninety per cent of whom were of British stock. By 1900, the English population stood at thirty-two and a half million, but English speakers numbered 123 million, outstripping German with eighty, Russian with eighty-five, French with fifty-two, Spanish with fifty-eight, Italian with fifty-four.

The great eighteenth-century expansion of the British Empire had brought to a victorious close the mighty duel between England and France for the possession of overseas domains in India and America. Australia had proved to be a very satisfactory place for deporting criminals and other undesirables from England. New Zealand and South Africa later proved excellent havens for adventurous spirits from the home isles. But the English language, scattering itself to the four corners of the earth, found its most fruitful soil in the Western Hemisphere.

Today, the United States and Canada combined have over 200 million English speakers. True, at least twelve per cent of them are foreign-born or of foreign parentage, and they represent every race and color under the sun, from Negro to Scandinavian and from Italian to Chinese. But they all have one thing in common. They speak English, well, badly or indifferently. When their numbers are added to the fifty-odd million inhabitants of the British Isles, the English speakers of Australia and New Zealand and of the Union of South Africa, who total over fifteen million, and the people of Anglo-Saxon stock scattered in British and American possessions all over the globe, we reach the imposing total of over 300 million persons who speak English—approximately one out of every ten of the earth's inhabitants. To put it another way, English speakers, in point of numbers, are second only to speakers of Chinese, but they are far more evenly distributed over the earth's surface, and their technological and commercial achievements are such that no other body of speakers can rival them in those respects.

In the eighteenth century, a French scholar voiced regret over the fact that too few of his kind on the European continent could read English. Today, the scholar, scientist or man of letters in any country who does not have some acquaintance with the English language is rare.

All of this, it must be stressed, is due almost exclusively to the force of expansion of English speakers in the seventeenth and eighteenth centuries. Had this expansion not taken place, English would probably be today the speech of perhaps sixty or seventy million people living comfortably huddled together in the British Isles, rather than the world-wide, imperial, cultural language it is.

The diversity in speech to which this far-flung linguistic emigration has given rise will be discussed elsewhere. Suffice it here to say that while the English of Australia is largely Cockney in pronunciation, and that of South Africa a mixture of Cockney, Scots and Afrikaans, it is the American variety of English that most lends itself to description, partly because of the complexity of its origin and development, partly because American English speakers form an absolute majority of all speakers of the English tongue.

The American nasal twang of which Britishers complain was once satirized in the Puritans, who are also held accountable for the drawl and secondary stress of American. Most of the original Massachusetts immigrants came from East Anglia, the seat of

English Puritanism, and the theory is that these original New England speakers moved on to the West, being joined on the way by migrants from Pennsylvania and West Virginia, and gave rise to General American. Their place in New England, the theory continues, was gradually taken by new waves of immigrants from the southern English shires. Immigrants from the south of England are also said to have laid the foundation of our southern speech.

For what concerns the Middle Atlantic States, the picture is complicated by the presence of Dutch speakers and French Huguenots in New York, of Swedes in Delaware, of Germans and Welshmen in Pennsylvania. The South received French influences in South Carolina and Louisiana, Spanish overtones in Florida. Less easily demonstrated is the influence of African Negro languages in the South and of later immigrant groups such as the Irish, Germans and Scandinavians who came to America's shores during the latter half of the nineteenth century, and of the Southern Europeans who arrived in droves between 1890 and 1915.

All linguists seem agreed that archaism characterizes American English. They point to the strongly sounded *r* and the flat *a*, which British English lost in the eighteenth century, but which are retained by American English, particularly in its western variety. The pronunciation of *either* with an *ee*-sound, the use of *gotten* for *got,* of *mad* in the sense of *angry,* of *sick* for *ill,* of *Fall* for *Autumn,* of *rare* in connection with meat, of expressions like "I guess," are all archaisms that go back to the time of Shakespeare. But Professor Baugh makes the keen observation that the Northern English dialects are also very conservative, keeping in use words like *fortnight, porridge, heath* and *ironmonger,* and the question arises whether the archaic features in American English may not be due to the preponderance of Northern English elements in the American language.

The recognition of American as a separate linguistic entity came before the end of the eighteenth century. While one Englishman, Isaac Candler, remarked that American was close to educated Londonese, others deplored the "barbarism" of the American tongue. In 1756, Samuel Johnson, reviewing a book by an American author, denounced the "mixture of American dialect" as a "tract of corruption," while an annual of 1808 speaks of the "torrent of barbarous phraseology from America, threatening to destroy the purity of the English language," thus anticipating the later nineteenth-century strictures of Mrs. Trollope, Dickens, and Sir Richard Burton.

On our side of the ocean, one Princeton president, John Witherspoon, thought Americanisms were mere Scotticisms, but this view was contradicted by others. Proposals for an American Society of Language go back to the year 1774. Noah Webster, who stressed American rather than British usage in his American Spelling Book and American Dictionary, thought the new language would eventually differ materially from English. Actually, his 1828 dictionary is estimated to contain some 12,000 words that do not appear in Johnson's or any other British dictionary of the period.

The history of the British-American linguistic controversy appears elsewhere in this book. The generalization may here be made that for what concerns vocabulary, American is more prone to innovate than British, and that the major British criticism of the American language deals with reputed Americanisms which are often found to exist in English dialects (*in a jiffy, tip-top, whopper, gawky, glum, gumption, sappy* are cases in point). *Talented* and *scientist,* once attacked as American coinages, were found to have originated on English soil. The English normally wind up by accepting true Americanisms. Jefferson's *belittle* and Franklin's *colonize* and *unshakable* are current in Britain today. So are *advocate, antagonize, telephone, typewriter, prairie, caucus, graft, lynch, blizzard, joy-ride, stunt* and *highbrow,* not to mention those typically American words which America borrowed from sixteenth-century New Netherlands Dutch: *boss, snoop, spook, dominie, stoop, cookie, bluff* and *boodle.*

Also accepted are such American Indian words as John Smith's *raccoon* and *possum* of 1608 and 1610 (Smith spells them *rahaugcum* and *apossoun*); the almost contemporaneous *mus* or *moose* (Narragansett Indian for "he trims smooth"); the *skunk* that comes from *seganku,* the *woodchuck* that was originally *otchock;* and a flood of others (*papoose, powwow, pemmican, squaw, tepee, squash*); along with loan-translations like *war paint, peace pipe* and *Great White Father.* Lincoln Barnett, who has made a special study of the subject, claims that of the approximately 1700 American Indian words in our language, half were in by the end of the seventeenth century. Other American contributions of eighteenth- and very early nineteenth-century vintage are *bullfrog, catfish, katydid, mockingbird, sweet potato, whippoorwill, catbird, copperhead, cottonwood, watershed, water gap,* and *clearing. Freeholder,* a political term still current in New Jersey, dates back to 1665, when the Lords Proprietor, Berkeley and Carteret, called for the election of "Freeholders" to rule each county. American expressions criticized by Burton in 1860 and still rejected by the British include *neck of the woods, high old time, hanging up one's shingle, liquoring up,* the pronunciation *crik,* the use of *drink* for a body of water (with *big drink* reserved for the Mississippi River), and that untranslatable institution whose name is *doughnut.*

One trait of American English which was recognized almost as early as the language itself is its fundamental tendency toward unity. Fenimore Cooper in 1828 attributed this to the intelligence and activity of the population and the leveling of social differences, while some unfriendly critics have ascribed it to the American love of conformity and acceptance of authority. It is perhaps more likely that this unity is due to the ease of travel, trade and communications, which in America bring the speech-habits of one part of the population within easy reach of the others.

Without at this point going further into the question of the basic dualism of the English language, it may be remarked that the entire development of the past two centuries has been colored by a phenomenon which may be compared to the course of a river split by a rise of ground into two separate beds. There are now two currents where formerly there was one, and each of the two is affected by the nature of the soil it passes through and the tributaries it receives, to the point where the composition of the two streams materially differs. But once the narrow, elongated rise of ground subsides beneath the waves, the two streams are reunited, bringing to the renewed common current the diverse accumulations of water and silts they have gathered in the course of their separate travels.

In like manner, the two major English forms of speech, British and American, which began to diverge in the seventeenth century, and whose divergence became accentuated in the eighteenth and nineteenth, now tend to flow together once more. For this happy reunion there are many causes, material and psychological. Among the former are the rapidity and ease of twentieth-century means of transportation, bringing to one country the speech-habits and innovations of the other; increased travel and reading; purely mechanical devices, like the radio (or shall we say *wireless?*), the spoken film and transatlantic television, with their powerful mass appeal which few if any inhabitants of a country can now escape. Among the psychological factors are a common background of social, political and economic ideals; a common body of literature; a basic feeling of mutual respect and admiration, which squabbles and even wars have been unable to shake. Above all, perhaps, is that vague, undefinable something which may be described as a will to unity. Whatever the Americans, of many racial origins, may think of British policies, past and present, there are few of them who can escape the subconscious feeling that Britain is the fount, source and cradle of their own civilization. Conversely, when the British view America as "the former colonies," they can hardly forbear from mixing a tinge of paternal pride with their critical sourness or their resentment at America's ebullient success. "A scalliwag, but a chip from the old block!" they seem to say.

There is no denying that a common language is the greatest of the social factors that make for unity. Religion, race, color, political belief may fail, but language remains. While an American and an Englishman can understand each other without an interpreter, they will tend to gravitate together, no matter what else keeps them apart.

As we advance out of the past history of the English language into its present status and future prospects, it is this fundamental unity of the language and its speakers that we must keep in mind. Upon it is predicated much more than a series of episodes, of historical significance or of amusing import. On it depends, possibly, the future course of the world's civilization.

Chapter Seven

CHANGE AND RATE OF CHANGE

The Evolution of English Sounds—The Metamorphosis of English Grammar—Syntax and Word-Order—Putting Together What Man Has Sundered—The "Simplification" of English

Linguists are in the habit of dividing language into neat little compartments: phonology, or sounds; morphology, or grammatical forms; syntax, or the significant arrangement of words; and vocabulary, or the words themselves. That these compartments are far from watertight matters little. What is important is that language, in all its compartments, taken separately or collectively, is subject to perpetual change. We have already had an inkling of how this metamorphosis occurred, in each division of the English language, throughout its history. It may be of interest to review briefly the sources of our information concerning the changes, along with a few of the changes themselves.

In the absence of phonograph, tape, wire and other auditory records during the centuries preceding our own, it is obvious that our knowledge concerning the historical transformation of the language is primarily visual, in the form of written documents. These may seem at first glance quite satisfactory for studying the language's progress. Actually, they are quite the opposite. The first written appearance of a word or locution in a certain meaning by no means implies that it entered the language at the period when the document was composed; it may have existed for years and centuries before, and gone unrecorded in writings available to us. This may have been the result either of accident, because earlier documents in which the word or expression appeared were lost, or of design, because it was looked upon as coarse, slangy, and unworthy of a written form. So much for individual words. When we come to syntactical arrangements, the difference between spoken and written syntax is so well known that it need not be discussed. Written syntax, furthermore, often represents an archaic state of affairs, particularly in the case of literary and legal texts. Grammatical forms lend themselves somewhat better to study from written documents, but even here the danger of archaism is ever present.

When we come to sounds as reflected in writing, we stand on the most shifting of sands. Spelling always tends to remain traditional and conservative, and often reflects spoken-language conditions that antedate by centuries the text in which the spelling occurs. True, the authentic pronunciation sometimes pierces through the veil of official orthography, with the aid of rhymes and other poetic devices, puns, semi-literate spellings and the direct statements of writers who describe the sounds of their own or a foreign tongue. But even here there is no assurance. We are reasonably certain, for instance, that in Shakespeare's time the *ea* of *sea* and *clean* represented a sound close to the *a* of present-day *lane*, while *ee* in *deep* and *ie* in *field* had already assumed the modern pronunciation. The question is, precisely when did *ea* take on the same sound as *ee* and *ie?* We know that the Middle English spelling *oo* indicated a sound similar to that of *o* in present-day *bone*, but in some words the sound opened up into the *oo* of *blood*, in others it closed into the *oo* of *room* and later, in some cases, was shortened to the *oo* of *good*. When we find Shakespeare and even Dryden rhyming *good, mood* and *flood*, we can hardly assume that the sounds were still identical, and are forced to conclude that we are often faced with eye-rhymes rather than ear-rhymes. But this in turn tends to invalidate or weaken the evidence of rhymes in general. Shakespeare's coupling of *watch* and *match, wanting* and *granting, warm* and *harm*, Pope's rhyming of *join* and *divine, obey* and *tea, caprice* and *nice, glass* and *place, ear* and *repair, lost* and *boast, brow* and *grow*, are all somewhat open to suspicion.

Less uncertain is the evidence afforded by poetry as to accentuation, since rhythm is a more stable poetic feature than rhyme. We are thus informed that at various times *aspect, envy* and *welcome* were stressed on the last syllable, *character* on the second, *secure* on the first.

Despite all these difficulties, the progress of English sounds has been charted with reasonable accuracy from the Anglo-Saxon period to the present. Among the Old English long vowels, we have seen *ā* progressing to the modern *ō* (*stān* to *stone*); *ō* to modern *oo* (*fōt* to *foot*); *ē* to modern *ee* (*grēne* to *green*); *ī* and *ȳ* to modern *i* (*īs, fȳr* to *ice, fire*); *ū* to modern *ow, ou* (*hū, hlūd* to *how, loud*). Old English short vowels are generally far more conservative (*catte* to *cat, bedd* to *bed, scip* to *ship, pott* to *pot, sunne* to *sun, brycg* to *bridge*). It is interesting to note in this division that the short *o,* which in Britain retains its original quality, shifts in America to a more open sound, which could be phonetically represented by *a* (compare the British and American pronunciations of *God*); while the short *u,* which occasionally retains its original sound (as in *full*), more often assumes the indefinite sound heard in *sun, but, cut,* and occasionally, under Anglo-Norman influence, changes in spelling to *o* (*lufian* to *love*).

Most unstressed vowels, which in Old English had definite vocalic qualities, merge into the sound of *e* in unstressed *the* during the Middle English period, and often fall away in modern English, particularly when final (*oxa, wundor, lufu, heorte* to *ox, wonder, love, heart*). A notable exception is unstressed *i,* which retains a separate short *i* quality, as in the *-ing* of *making.*

Among Old English digraphs, *ǣ* and *æ* are worthy of special mention. The first normally becomes *ea,* the latter *a* (*dǣlan* to *deal, cræft* to *craft*).

Among consonants and consonant symbols, attention has been called to the fact that Old English *f* seems to have included both an *f* and a *v* sound, and *s* both *s* and *z*. Old English *þ* and *ð,* used indifferently to represent the separate sounds of *th* in *thing* and *this,* gave way to the spelling *th* under Anglo-Norman influence, which also accounts for the shift from *cw* to *qu* (*cwic* to *quick*). The palatalization of *c* (pronounced *k*) to *ch,* and of *sc* (pronounced *sk*) to *sh* before front vowels probably occurred before the Norman Conquest. Other noteworthy changes are *g* to *y* (*gēar* to *year, gīet* to *yet, gecleopod* to *yclept*), *cg* to *dg* (*ecg* to *edge*), *cn* to *kn,* with silent *k* (*cniht* to *knight*), *hl* and *hr* to *l* and *r* (*hlāf* to *loaf, hrōf* to *roof*). Among Anglo-Norman sounds, interest attaches particularly to the Norman-Picard variant *c* for the standard French *ch* (*cattle-chattel, catch-chase, caitiff* vs. French *chétif*).

If we were to select, from among these sound-changes and the many others we have overlooked, those which are most striking, our vote would go to the great English vowel-shift, whereby all the long stressed vowels were transformed, and to the palatalization which created the modern sounds of *ch, sh, j* and *y*. It was these two which, more than all the others, transformed the sound-pattern of the language. But if we were to be asked for the phonological phenomenon which had the most far-reaching consequences upon the structure of the language, we would be impelled to select the merging and fall of final vowels, which gave English its basically monosyllabic nature of today and was, in addition, the most potent factor in the elimination of flectional endings and the progress of English from a language of a predominantly morphological type to the predominantly syntactic and positional structure of modern times.

Most linguists are agreed that this important transition from a language of roots and endings to one of roots alone was due to the heavy initial stress that concentrated vocal energy on the roots and obliterated the endings. Perhaps this is an over-simplification of the facts, particularly since other Germanic languages, with what seems to have been the same stress-accent, merged or lost their endings only in part. It is possible that the Danish and Norman-French admixtures also had something to do with the death of inflectional endings, the first by turning English into a pidgin of common intercourse between Anglo-Saxons and Danes, the latter by preventing the establishment of a standard. What is certain is that from the Old English state of full inflections, running roughly from 450 to 1150, the language passes through a Middle English period of inflectional breakdown, which begins about 1150 and ends, roughly, around 1500. This process of "simplification," to all effects completed by Shakespeare's time, has been reduced to the vanishing point since the eighteenth century. Whether it has altogether run its course, or whether there is still more leveling to come, is a question that cannot be answered for the present. Another unanswerable question is whether English is better or worse off for the change. Some think there is something sacred about inflectional endings, while others believe there is something sacred about the lack of such endings. The sanest view seems to be that a language's historical development is its own justification.

Nouns, so thoroughly declined in Anglo-Saxon, appear today in a form where only singular and plural are distinguished, with an additional genitive form in 's. As we have seen, this transformation did not take place overnight, and many phenomena participated in it, notably the weakening and fall of final vowels, the change of final -m to -n, followed by the fall of the latter, and the analogical factor whereby nominative forms gradually supplanted other case-forms. The two most favored plural endings, -s and -n, one favored in the North, the other in the South, fought a hard battle until the end of the fourteenth century. But the triumph of -s did not quite mark the death of its rival. Sixteenth-century forms like *eyen, shoon, hosen, peasen* attest the vitality of the -n ending and even its encroachment upon other plural forms; so do the *oxen, kine, children* and *brethren* of today. Nor must we forget the "umlaut" plurals in which the vowel of the root is brought forward in the mouth in preparation for a front vowel in an ending later lost (*gōsiz* and *fōtiz,* hypothetical plurals of *gōs, fōt* in the parent Germanic language, turning to *gēs, fēt* in Anglo-Saxon, then into the *geese, feet* of today). Many umlauted plurals of Anglo-Saxon were leveled by analogy (*bōc,* plural *bēc,* for instance, should have given us *book,* plural *beek,* and *āc,* plural *ēc* should have turned into *oak,* plural *eek*). We need not discuss at length special borrowed plurals from Latin, Greek and other languages, like *data, insignia, phenomena, alumni, alumnae, illuminati,* or such linguistic freaks as the threefold plural of *octopus, octopuses, octopodes, octopi,* where the first is an attempt at an English plural, the second at a Greek, the third at a Latin.

The genitive or possessive in 's was originally characteristic of only one type of masculine noun (*stān,* genitive *stānes,* "stone," "stone's"). It was extended by imitation to other types of nouns. Interesting as an example of popular etymology is the fact that the -*es* genitive ending, often spelled and pronounced -*is* or -*ys* in early Middle English, was confused as early as the thirteenth century with *his*, the possessive of *he*, so that Shakespeare could later write "the count his galley," and even expressions like "my sister her watch" appeared. The apostrophe that ultimately developed to accompany the genitive -*s* is really in the nature of a compromise. Very occasionally we find today an old feminine genitive form without the -*s*, as in *Lady Day*.

The Old English grammatical gender system consisted of masculine, feminine and neuter, but it was not altogether based on natural gender. *Mægden, wīf, bearn, cild,* for instance, were neuter, and *wīfmann* was masculine. The logical gender process, however, begins early. In Aelfric's *Homilies* we read: "*Etað þisne hlāf; hit is mīn līchama* (eat this bread [masculine]; it [neuter] is my body)." It was powerfully helped along by the fall of declensional endings, which had tended to keep nouns in illogical gender categories. During the Middle English period gender assumed substantially the form it has today.

It is to the credit of English (though there probably was no deliberate intent on the part of the speakers) that adjectives lost both the strong and the weak declensional endings and assumed a single form for all genders and numbers. English alone among the Germanic languages has gone all the way in this matter, indicating only once what many other western languages indicate at least two or three times (compare Spanish *las muchachas bonitas,* where article, adjective and noun all carry distinctive feminine plural endings, with English *the pretty girls,* where number is shown only by the noun, and gender only by the meaning). This is supposed to represent a great economy of time, space and thought; actually, it is quite as natural for the Spanish speaker to make his agreements as it is unnatural for the modern English speaker to learn to make them.

The comparison of adjectives is one field in which English retains its Germanic heritage of endings. The -*er* and -*est* suffixes come straight down from Anglo-Saxon, and their replacement by the analytical *more* and *most* led to confusion at first. Shakespeare does not hesitate to use -er and -est with adjectives of more than one syllable ("honester," "violentest"), and occasionally mixes both forms ("more larger," "the most unkindest cut of all"). One curious development is that of today's *near, nearer, nearest;* in Old English it was *neah, nearra, niehst,* forms which carried down straight to the language of today give us *nigh, near, next.* This means that *near* is itself originally a comparative, and when we say *nearer* and *nearest* we are being, to put it mildly, redundant. Today's *nethermost* consists of a root *ne,* meaning "down," plus two comparative suffixes, *th* and *er,* plus two superlative suffixes, *m* and *ost.* It is forms like these that make us hesitate when we say that English is a language that has largely given up inflections.

The Old English adverb was originally the instrumental case of the adjective. The suffix *-ly* comes from the instrumental ending (*-līce*) of some adjectives ending in *-līc,* itself a suffix drawn from a root meaning "body." Hence, when we say "clearly" we are literally saying "with a clear body," paralleling to some extent the Romance speakers whose *clairement* and *claramente* mean "with a clear mind." That the *-ly* suffix is not limited to adverbial use is proved by such adjectives as *friendly, shapely, seemly;* that it is not applied to all adverbs is shown by *slow, hard, fast, much, far* and *wide.*

In much the same way as a much-inflected Anglo-Saxon definite article turned into the little word *the* which does service for all genders, numbers and cases, so the numeral *one* wore itself down to *a* or *an.* It may be remarked that the older language differed somewhat from the tongue of today in its use of the articles. Shakespeare, for instance, often omits the indefinite article in expressions like "with as big heart as thou," but uses the definite article in "at the length." There is one usage of the definite article over which controversy still rages, namely, with Celtic family names ("the McAlpin," "the O'Brian") to indicate the titular head of the clan. Certain Scottish clans would like to arrogate the use of the article to themselves alone. The contrast between English and other western languages, including even the Germanic, in the use of the definite article with family or first names is evident from the frequent use made of it in French and Italian (*la Boncour, il Petrarca, la Claretta*), as well as by the fact that English rejects the use of the article with abstract or generic nouns (*liberty, water,* vs. *die Freiheit, das Wasser*).

Among personal pronouns, the replacement of the Anglo-Saxon *hīe, here, hem* by the Scandinavian *they, their, them* is worthy of note. *Thou, thy, thine, thee* and *ye* fell into disuse in the sixteenth century, save as archaisms. But as far back as the fourteenth century there had been a tendency to confuse the nominative *ye* with the accusative *you,* and the confusion is reflected in Shakespeare's "throw us that you have about ye." *Its* as a possessive goes back to the end of the sixteenth century, *his* having done service earlier for the neuter as well as the masculine (Shakespeare's "how far that little candle throws his beams"). Until 1800, however, *its* was spelled with an apostrophe, a usage that still prevails today among those who are not too careful about grammatical prescriptions.

In Old English the relative pronoun was *sē* or *sē þe,* in Middle English it was *ðæt. Which,* originally only an interrogative, comes into use as a relative in the fifteenth century, while *who,* which in the form *hwā* had likewise been used only as an interrogative in Anglo-Saxon, gets into full relative use by the sixteenth century. Chaucer had at an earlier period used *whose* and *whom,* and Shakespeare's "who steals my purse steals trash" shows the use of *who* as a relative pronoun including its antecedent. The instrumental case of the Anglo-Saxon *hwā* was *hwȳ;* this turns into our interrogative *why,* which thus etymologically means "by whom" or "by what." Reflexive forms with *self* come into general use at a comparatively late date, the ordinary personal pronouns having been used also as reflexives down to the sixteenth century ("I dressed me").

The English verb, like all its Germanic cognates, is distinguished by the relative poverty of simple tenses and by the general division of the verbs into weak and strong. The strong verbs, far more characteristic than the weak, feature the ablaut change in the root vowel represented by *sing, sang, sung.* The story of ablaut (a German term, literally meaning "away-sound") is quite fascinating. In the original Indo-European parent-language, verbs had roots, suffixes, and frequently prefixes. The stress did not invariably fall on the root in all forms of the verb, and when it moved off to the prefix or suffix, the root-vowel, robbed of its stress, would weaken into a different vowel. *Sing* shows a reflection of the original root-vowel of this particular verb; the change to *sang* was caused by the shifting of the stress to a prefix indicating past time, and the change to *sung* by the shifting of the stress to a participial suffix. Both the prefix and the suffix to which the stress had moved were later lost, however, and the poor stress, having nowhere else to go, had to move back to the root; but by this time the effect upon the vowel of losing its stress was accomplished, and the change in the vowel remained as a perennial monument to what a shift in stress can do to a vowel. If we want an easy modern comparison with a Romance tongue, Spanish *dormir* will do; all the forms where the root is stressed (*duermo, duermes, duerme*) have *ue;* but where the stress falls on the ending (*dormir, dormimos, dormía*), the root-vowel is *o.*

As against verbs with this ablaut vowel-shift, called strong, because they have within themselves the resources to indicate a change of tense without recourse to an ending, the Germanic languages have weak verbs, in which the root-vowel never changes, but endings are added to form the past and past participle (*love, loved, loved*). From the very outset, there is in English a struggle between strong and weak forms, with the latter more often winning because they are more regular and easier to remember. Today *help* and *fare* are weak verbs (*help, helped, helped; fare, fared, fared*), but in Anglo-Saxon they were strong (*helpan, healp, holpen; faran, fōr, faren*). Fully half of the Old English strong verbs have turned weak. Many changed in the thirteenth century, *help, burn, flee* and *step* among them. Dryden still uses *clomb* as the past of *climb,* and in the sixteenth century we find *low* as the past of *laugh* and *yold* as the past of *yield.* But the trend was sometimes reversed. *Blew* and *knew* had a hard time winning over *blowed* and *knowed.* We still have double forms like *cleft-clove, heaved-hove,* and a few originally weak verbs became strong, among them *strive, dive, wear, spit, stick* and *dig.* Is it any wonder that some of our illiterates still use *drug* as the past of *drag* or *clumb* as the past of *climb?*

The present and past tenses in Old English bore distinctive personal endings. All that remains of them today is the *-es* or *-s* of the third person singular. This comes from an earlier *-eth*, which was universally used by Chaucer, and is very frequent in the King James Bible and Shakespeare ("it blesseth him that gives and him that takes"). The *-s* or *-es* form is a Northern one that spread southward in the fifteenth century. In Southern Old English, the *-th* or *-eth* ending indicated the third plural (the Midland dialects used *-en,* the Northern ones *-es*). By Chaucer's time the Midland *-en,* often abbreviated to *-e,* had spread; the fall of *-e* left the third plural in its endingless present-day state. Shakespeare, interestingly, sometimes uses the Northern *-s* ("troubled minds that wakes").

Today a strong verb can have, at the most, five distinctive forms (*speak, speaks, spoke, speaking, spoken*), a weak one only four (*love, loves, loving, loved*). But this simplification of endings is attended by a terrific complication of auxiliaries.

First, there is the use of compound tenses with *have,* permissible in Old English only with transitive verbs. A form like "I have been" does not come into use until around 1200. Next is the new future with *will* and *shall,* used only occasionally in Anglo-Saxon, probably under Scandinavian influence (the most normal way to indicate futurity in Anglo-Saxon is to use the present tense). The progressive forms of which modern English is so fond are likewise scarce in Anglo-Saxon (*he wæs lærende*), and still rare in Middle English (but Chaucer says *"syngynge he was"*). Even Shakespeare prefers "goes the king hence?" The present participle which is such an indispensable adjunct to the progressive originally had the form *-ande, -ende* or *-inde,* the first more characteristic of the North, the second of the Midlands, the third of the South. The *-ing* we use today was at first *-ung,* a noun ending. It seems probable that *-ing* was formed by blending the Southern *-inde* participial ending with *-ung,* at first only for weak verbs, later for strong ones as well. It is only in the sixteenth century that we get such combinations as "having written" or "being seen," and a progressive passive like "the house is being burned" appears only in the eighteenth century, along with the use of *do* as an auxiliary ("does he speak?," "he does not speak"). Another latecomer among verbal constructions is the passive with *get* ("he got hurt"), which does not put in an appearance until the seventeenth century. The older language, on the other hand, made greater use of impersonal constructions like "it yearns him."

While this is hardly the chapter for personal opinions, it may be remarked that the present-day English verb, despite its lack of flectional endings, is a redoubtable thing for one who must approach it from abroad. Its almost endless array of possible auxiliaries, each carrying a different shade of meaning (*have* and *had, shall* and *will, should* and *would, may* and *might, ought* and *must*); its tricky progressive conjugation, offering such monstrosities as *I should have been learning;* its use of *do* as a negative and interrogative auxiliary as well as an intensifier, more than make up for its lack of flections. The English verb is a precision tool that calls for the handling of an expert. Foreigners mistreat it, but so do natives when they write "I should of went." How simple everything would have been if we had retained the old Anglo-Saxon conjugation, with a present to do service for the future, and a past to take care of all past connotations! Man sometimes complicates as he "simplifies," and no finer example of this truth can be offered than the English verb.

In the syntactical division, two outstanding facts should be noted. The first is that the historical development of English shows us practically all the "errors" that the school manuals warn us against. The split infinitive has been in vogue since the fourteenth century, and Burns proudly says "who dared to nobly stem." Shakespeare offers such horripilating triple negatives as "nor understood none neither." Dryden criticizes the preposition at the end of the sentence, but uses it himself. Both the Bible and Shakespeare have a singular verb with a compound subject ("hostility and civil tumult reigns"). Group genitives like "the King of England's influence," "someone else's property" have been the vogue for a long time. The Fowlers, in *The King's English*, claim that a southern Englishman still knows how to use *shall* and *will* correctly, but few others do, and the convenient abbreviation *'ll* in *I'll, they'll* is almost universally used in the spoken tongue. Then there is the King James Bible's "Whom

do men say that I am?" This list could be extended almost in-
definitely.

Secondly, Robertson makes the keen observation that some of
our most common errors ("it is me" for "it is I," "who did you
see?" for "whom did you see?") illustrate the paramount importance that word-order has assumed in English. Insofar as there
is a distinction between a nominative and an objective form,
whatever precedes the verb is automatically assumed to be the
subject, whatever follows the verb to be the object. Whether or
not he is correct in his assumption, the two errors just listed have
a long and venerable past history. "It is I" goes back to a Middle
English *hit am I,* which in turn stems from Old English *ic hit
eom* ("I it am").

The higher, literary syntax of English, of course, goes back in
large measure to French and Latin models. But the tongue of the
people seldom comes out in the form of complex-compound
sentences. The popular syntax is dominated by the simple clause,
and this in turn by the subject-verb-object order, rendered necessary by the lack of distinctive case-endings. In true Germanic
fashion, the modifier precedes the modified; adjective before
noun, adverb before verb was the regular order in Anglo-Saxon
and is still the regular order today. A greater use of prepositions
is made necessary by the disappearance of case-endings, but the
retention of a separate genitive gives English the advantage of
variety over some other languages ("the king's crown," "the
crown of the king"). For the old dative, we can use *to,* but we can
also use a word-order convention whereby if two objects are
expressed without a preposition, the first is taken to be indirect
("I gave the boy the book"). These alternative ways of expressing
the genitive and dative relations give English a foothold in two
linguistic families, the Germanic and the Romance, and add to
our international flavor.

Word-formation properly pertains to the field of vocabulary,
but in some respects it has points of contact with grammatical
endings.

We have seen that Old English had the power to form new

words by means of prefixes and suffixes to the same extent as its kindred languages, Latin and Greek. Had it not been for the Norman Conquest and the consequent importation of foreign loanwords of a learned type, English today would have approximately the same appearance as German. The prefixes *for-*, *with-* and *un-* were particularly productive, and the older language shows such compounds as *forhang, forcleave, forshake* (Chaucer's *forweped* and *forwaked*), *withsay, withspeak, withset;* Middle English has *unpossible, unpatient, unfirm,* with the Germanic *un-* prefixed to Latin roots. Even today we have *forbid, forget, withdraw, withhold;* but the foreign *renounce, contradict, resist* have replaced the *with*-compounds named above.

Among the most productive native suffixes for the formation of abstract nouns are the *-ness* of *kindness* and *baldness,* the *-lock* of *wedlock,* the *-red* of *hatred* and *kindred,* the *-dom* of *wisdom* and *kingdom,* the *-hood* of *girlhood* and *womanhood,* the *-ship* of *friendship* and *worship.* The interchange among these suffixes has been heavy. *Richdom* and *falsedom,* for instance, have given way to *richness* and *falsehood.*

Adjectives from nouns are formed largely by means of the suffixes *-ful, -less, -some, -ish.* The last was originally *-isc,* and was used only for national names (*englisc, francisc; childish* and *boorish* are later developments). Old English used *-ster* as a feminine noun suffix to denote the doer of an action, but the feminine connotation was soon lost; today we have not only *spinster,* but also *youngster, gangster, huckster, teamster.*

Two suffixes, one denoting manner, the other direction, are so close to case-suffixes in their effects that they may almost be said to confer upon English a manner-case and a limit-of-motion-case. They are the *-wise* of *crosswise, likewise* (even *percentagewise* and *centurywise*), and the *-ward* of *upward, backward, homeward, skyward.* The second is more legitimately used, in the sense that it seldom appears save where there is true limit of motion. The *-wise* suffix, on the other hand, lends itself to serious abuses. From "in the manner of," it has gradually extended itself to cover the meaning "so far as something is concerned." This is the way in which it appears in such recent combinations as *taxwise, curriculumwise, housingwise, calorie-*

wise. So far as grammatical terminology is concerned (or should we say *terminologywise?*), the ablative of manner has become an ablative of specification as well. It is properly satirized in the admonition given by the head of a weather bureau to one of his acolytes: "Wordwise, 'weatherwise' unwise."

One extremely productive suffix in modern times comes from abroad. This is the French *-ee* of *consignee, payee, standee.* In the original French, *-ée* is the *feminine* past participle ending, and there is something ludicrous about its use in forms like *draftee, trainee.* Perhaps it should be cut down to *-e,* as occurs sometimes in *employe.* Its native counterpart is, of course, *-ed.* When we compare *hunter* and *hunted* with *employer* and *employee,* even those of us who are not linguistically trained perceive that there is something more indigenous about the former pair.

The tendency to combine a verb and a preposition into a noun (*mark-up, hook-up, hangout, line-up, show-off, slow-down*) is relatively modern and still deplored in certain quarters. It has not yet been definitely established whether hyphens should be used or not in these compounds, or whether each of them should be a law unto itself.

For compounds formed of two nouns, Jespersen reminds us that the older ones among them are definitely stressed on the first syllable (*footstep, grandson*), to such an extent that their pronunciation is often changed by the stress (*weskit* from *waistcoat, hussy* from *housewife*); the recent ones, on the contrary, distribute the stress evenly (*toothbrush, snowball*).

One might well philosophize about these compounds, the majority of which are of pure Anglo-Saxon origin. English is a language that tends to monosyllabism. At the same time, the compound-forming tendency restores the polysyllabic balance. No sooner have we achieved a word of one syllable by getting rid of inflectional endings and prefixes than we go to work and combine the monosyllabic root thus achieved with other roots and suffixes and prefixes to form new long words. Was it worth while to get rid of the final pronounced vowel-sound in the ancient *wīde* (instrumental of *wīd,* and used as an adverb with the meaning of *widely*), when later we added *-ly* to the shortened form and attained a new dissyllabism? Perhaps not. But this long historical process establishes three points: (a) that language is always dynamic, never static; (b) that language processes are, or at least have been up to the present time, highly irrational and not at all logical; (c) that there is no such thing as a completely analytical or completely synthetic language; the two processes, that of breaking up a language concept into its component elements, and that of putting the component elements back again into a single concept, alternate in seemingly endless succession. English may and probably will go further along the road toward monosyllabism. But it may also, astonishingly, retrace its steps and become again a language of long words and inflections.

Chapter Eight

BUILDING THE WORLD'S MOST EXTENSIVE VOCABULARY (1)

*Our Million Words—The Native Stock—Early Loans—
The World's Heaviest Borrower—The Riches of the
Language*

A comprehensive dictionary of Anglo-Saxon falls short of fifty thousand words. Even granting that half the words in the spoken language failed to find their way into records accessible to us, we can safely assert that Anglo-Saxon was a tongue of not over one hundred thousand words.

The most comprehensive dictionaries of modern English at our disposal reveal a total vocabulary of well over one million words. Even granting that three-quarters of them belong to specialized fields like medicine and technology, or to trade jargons, or to slang, the fact remains that the English word-stock has, in the course of less than a thousand years, multiplied tenfold.

Before we try to ascertain whence comes the increase, let us recall a few hard facts about vocabulary in general. The average adult is said to have a use-and-recognition vocabulary of between thirty thousand and sixty thousand words. A highly literate adult is not likely to go much beyond one hundred thousand. This means that nine out of ten words recognized by the present-day official language are as strange to him as though they formed part of a foreign tongue. Fortunately, he seldom if ever misses them. They are, as we have said, words from special fields with which he has no contact. He can get along without them.

Jespersen estimates that Shakespeare used only about twenty thousand words in his works. He finds fewer than six thousand in the King James Bible. Other great books and authors, domestic and foreign, are equally sparing in their use of the total resources at their command. Milton is said to have used eleven thousand, Homer nine thousand, Victor Hugo twenty thousand. This might indicate that the use of a large vocabulary is not necessary even for lofty literary purposes. But a linguist reminds us that such figures, even if accurate, do not mean too much, because we do not know how many additional words authors like Shakespeare and Milton may have considered and decided not to use.

If we return for an instant to the historic consideration of the English vocabulary, we are struck by the fact that a relatively poor language like Anglo-Saxon had already developed about as many words as can be conveniently recognized or used by a present-day cultured English speaker. The additional nine hundred thousand that have come in since the Norman Conquest have gone either to replace original words that dropped out, or to convey new concepts that had not yet arisen by 1066, or to swell specialized lists that are not generally within the public domain.

The first attempt to list all the words in the language was Nathaniel Bailey's *Universal Etymological English Dictionary* of 1721. Mulcaster had urged one as far back as 1582, but the only immediate fruit of his suggestion was a *Table Alphabeticall of Hard Words* (about three thousand of them) published in 1604 by Robert Cawdrey. Our complete dictionaries of today, which will be more fully described later, indicate that the total number of words in the language runs past the one-million mark (this figure had already been tentatively advanced by Dr. Charles Funk in 1942, and the intervening years have brought us many thousands of innovations).

Robertson estimates that only about twenty thousand words are in full use today, and if this estimate is correct, it brings us up to Shakespeare's total. Of these, one-fifth, or about four thousand, are said to be of Anglo-Saxon origin, three-fifths, or about twelve thousand, of Latin, Greek and French origin. This, of course, does not mean that foreign words predominate in our tongue of common intercourse. The words most frequently used are native. Robertson estimates that one-fourth of all our spoken language consists of repetitions of the words *and, be, have, it, of, the, to, will, you, I, a, on, that* and *is.* Another analysis of five million words written by adults reveals that our ten most frequently used words are *I, the, and, to, of, in, we, for, you* and *a*. Both lists consist, without exception, of native words. *Very* is the only foreign word, as well as the only word of more than one syllable, to break into the highest-frequency category. If we go into literary usage, we find that words of the Bible are ninety-four per cent native, Shakespeare's ninety per cent, Tennyson's eighty-eight per cent, Milton's eighty-one per cent, Samuel Johnson's seventy-two per cent. Only in present-day technical writings do we find the foreign element climbing to forty per cent.

From a practical standpoint, therefore, the situation has not changed too drastically. Still, the one-million-word figure appearing in our most comprehensive dictionaries is such as to give us pause. How, when and for what reasons has the language managed to effect such a growth? Is this situation peculiar to English, or do the other modern languages show a similar state of affairs?

Answering the second question first, we may hasten to assure the reader that English is by no means alone in its phenomenal vocabulary growth. The vocabularies of French, Spanish and Italian compare with that of their ancestral Latin in pretty much the same way. The reason why words have multiplied lies in the multiplication of human activities and concepts. There are more things, more qualities, more actions in the modern world than there were in the ancient, and the number of nouns, adjectives and verbs has accordingly increased. Some of the things, qualities and actions of the ancients have become obsolete and have vanished, but for each such effacement there have been at least ten innovations during the last thousand, and particularly the last hundred, years. It's as simple as that. The prospect for the future is that things, activities and concepts will continue to multiply, and the vocabulary with them. Only a reversal to barbarism or savagery, the sort of thing that might quite possibly attend full-scale atomic warfare, could lead to a new impoverishment of the vocabulary by reason of the dropping out of human activities.

The original vocabulary of English is, of course, Anglo-Saxon. We have seen that within this once limited vocabulary there existed a thoroughly developed machinery for increase from within, by the process of combining roots with prefixes and suffixes or with other roots. This machinery has never stopped operating. It functions day and night, time and overtime, through the centuries. But it is far from being the sole factor in vocabulary growth. Innumerable words from the outside, with their own processes of combination, come to its aid. Then there is the process of spontaneous creation, usually anonymous, of words that have no previous root in the language. There is the process of analogy, whereby words are coined in imitation of other words already in existence. There is the process of functional change, whereby a word that exists, say, as a noun, gets to be used as an adjective or verb. There is the process of semantic change, whereby a word used in one meaning takes on other acceptances. The sum total of all these factors far offsets the process of obsolescence and decay, whereby words once used are dropped out of the language. Let us examine these processes in turn.

The Germanic, and particularly the Anglo-Saxon, element is basic in our vocabulary. Verbs like *live* and *die, come* and *go, do* and *make, give* and *take, eat* and *drink, work* and *play, walk* and *run* are either Anglo-Saxon or derived from the kindred Scandinavian. *Home, house, room, window, door, floor, roof, hearth* indicate that our housing is fundamentally Germanic. *Flesh, meat, bread, corn* (or *wheat*), *fish, milk, beer* formed the main staples of our ancestors' nourishment, and are Germanic in origin. Outward, visible parts of the body, like *hand, finger, thumb, head, mouth, nose, ear, eye, arm, leg* and *foot* go back to our Teutonic heritage.

Anglo-Saxon transmits to us a certain number of naturalized words which it had borrowed from Latin or other sources, like *street* from *strata, cheese* from *caseus,* and *cheap* from the verb *ceapian,* which goes back to Latin *caupo,* "merchant." Other Anglo-Saxon words of Latin origin gave way to new French importations after the Conquest; *cirs* and *persoc,* from *cerasia* and *persica,* were supplanted by *cherry* and *peach,* which were taken from French, and which French had developed from precisely the same Latin sources.

The Anglo-Saxon ability to form compounds leads to expressions in which the original elements are almost unidentifiable (*good-by* from "God be with you," or *daisy* from *dæges eage,* "day's eye," or *worship* from *worth-ship,* or *not* from *naught,* from *no whit,* from *no wight*). It also gives rise to successful or attempted replacements of foreign words (*handbook* and *foreword* for *manual* and *preface; folkwain* and *steadholder* for *omnibus* and *lieutenant*).

Derived words from Anglo-Saxon roots combined with prefixes and suffixes also lead to the language's enrichment. A prefix like *be-,* once felt to be somewhat derogatory (*befog, bewilder, befuddle*), quickly lost that connotation (*bedeck, behoove, believe*). A suffix like the *-th* of *wealth, health, strength* led to strange Elizabethan compounds, which have since disappeared (*lowth, illth, greenth, coolth*).

A relatively modern development is the verb-adverb combination, which gives English a distinctive flavor, but also contributes to the bewilderment of foreigners who have to learn the delicate meaning-machinery of loose compounds like *set out, bring about, catch on, give out, put up with, lay off, hold over, size up* (note that the verbs in these combinations, while almost invariably monosyllabic, are not necessarily Germanic: *catch* and *size* are both from the French). Many of these groups are of colloquial or even slang origin (*cough up, dish out, shut up, crack down on*). Baugh claims that twenty of our simplest verbs enter into 155 different combinations leading to over 600 distinct meanings or uses. While foreigners regularly find these combinations distasteful, English speakers seldom object to them until they pass out of their category and get to be used as nouns; *pushover, know-how* and similar forms were once frowned upon.

It is fashionable among etymologists to point out the picturesque original meanings of Latin and French words. Saxon words are more often slighted, possibly on the score that their meaning is too literal. Yet the picturesque element is just as present there. *Spider,* for instance, is a "spinner," *wasp* a "weaver," and *beetle* a "biter." According to one account, *farm* comes from French *ferme,* which in turn goes back to Latin *firma,* "firm"; but another possible derivation is from Saxon *feorh,* "life," which seems to come from the same Indo-European root as the *par-* of Latin *pario,* from which we get *parent,* or "life-giver"; this *feorh* led to *feorm,* a "living," or the most common source of an honest livelihood in those agricultural days. *Poll,* from which we get the *poll tax,* is the Middle English word for *head;* the tax was at first unconnected with voting, but was simply levied on heads, or the individual's right to exist.

Anglo-Saxon, and Germanic before that, are the names of the days of the week, with the exception of *Saturday,* which the Germanic tribes borrowed from the Romans' Saturn. *Sunday* and *Monday* are the days of the sun and moon, *Tuesday* is from a Germanic *Tiw* cognate to the Latin *Diu* in *Diupiter* or *Jupiter, Wednesday* comes from Woden (Wotan, Odin), *Thursday* from Thor, *Friday* from Frigga.

Of paramount importance in any language are the brief connecting words, prepositions like *of, to, by, for, from, in, at, on, under,* conjunctions like *and, but, if, then, too,* adverbs like *here, there, where, when, how.* The constant repetition of these words, which are almost without exception Anglo-Saxon, continues to impart to the English language a characteristic Germanic flavor, which hundreds of thousands of less frequently used borrowed words cannot dispel.

Yet the English language would be a poor thing indeed if those hundreds of thousands of borrowed words were eliminated from it. We have seen the poverty of the language before the time of Chaucer. Its scanty use as a literary medium may have been at once the cause and the effect of that poverty. It is only when the full, rich stream of French, Latin, Greek and the other great western languages joins the eddying current of English that our tongue begins to assume the majestic aspect of a great river flowing tranquilly toward the sea.

Anglo-Saxon, with its original Classical borrowings and with the Scandinavian additions brought in by the Danes, might in course of time have developed from its own internal resources all the words that a great modern language must have. But there was no need for it to do so, since the treasure-house of Classical culture was thrown open to it by the events that followed the Norman invasion.

Let us first look at the vast stock of French words that came into the language between the time of William the Conqueror and that of Chaucer. Here we find in first line the government words, terms like *crown, state, reign, royal, sovereign, court, council, parliament, assembly, tax, office, mayor;* the terminology of feudalism, *prince, duke, count, marquis, squire, page, sir, manor, vassal, peasant,* replacing to some extent, but not altogether displacing the *lord, lady, thane, earl, yeoman, churl* of an older day. *Oppress, rebel, treason* and *exile* remind us of the dark days that followed the Conquest.

Words of religious faith came in aplenty in the days when the Saxon hierarchy of Bede gave way to Norman clerics: *sermon, penance, pray, lesson, clerk, dean, pastor, virgin, saint, faith, mercy, preach, convert* are all of this kind; but note the survival of the earlier *rood* or *cross, church* and *minister, God* and *Gospel.*

In the legal field the triumph of French was well-nigh complete; *equity* replaced the native *gerihte, judgment* displaced *dōm* (but only as a legal term; *doom* lives on); *crime* took the place of *synn* and *gylt,* both of which nevertheless survive. *Bar, summons, proof, bail, fine, prison, arrest, accuse, pardon, trespass, arson, larceny, fraud, estate, tenant, heir, justice* are only a few of the many French terms that crowd our law courts today. It may be mentioned *en passant* that more of these terms than is generally realized were of Germanic origin, having formed part of the ancestral Teutonic heritage of the Franks who incorporated them into their Salic laws and capitularies. This is particular true of *felon* and *felony, seize* and *pledge.*

In the military division, French gives us *army, navy* and *host, peace, enemy* (but not *foe*), *arms* and *armor* (but not *weapons*), *battle* (but not *slaughter*), *siege, sortie* and *sally, defense, soldier* and *guard, spy, sergeant, lieutenant, lance* (but not *spear*), *archer* (but neither *bow* nor *arrow*), *moat, array* and *rank, vanquish* and *conquer.* Here again we must recall that many of these words are Germanic in origin: *spy, guard, rank* fall into this category.

The social graces imported by the French give us words like *fashion, dress, gown, robe, coat, collar, garter, boot, fur, jewel,* while in the household, where basic words are Anglo-Saxon, French imports include *curtain, chair, screen, towel, basin, parlor, closet* and *pantry,* as well as *palace, chamber, ceiling, cellar, chimney* and *porch.* The *stable* and *kennel* are French. So are some of the oldest known inhabitants of the kennel, the *levrier* (whose Saxon name is *greyhound*), the *mastiff*, whose name, curiously enough, seems to go back to Latin *mansuetus*, "tame," and the *kennet,* a medieval ancestor of the modern spaniel. The *forest* and *park* are French, but the *woods* are Saxon.

Amusement, leisure, dancing, art, painting, sculpture, beauty, color, all come from French. So do *poetry, prose, study, grammar, title, volume, paper, pen, copy* and *noun. Medicine* (but not *illness*), *pain* (but not *well-being*), *grief* and *joy* (but not *sorrow* or *gladness*), *marriage* (but not *wedlock*), *error* (but not *mistake*), *flower* (but not *bloom* or *blossom*), *city* and *village* (but not *town*), *labor* (but not *work*), *power* (but not *might*), *rage* (but not *anger*), *river* (but not *stream*), *season* (but no names of seasons except *Autumn*) come from the medieval French.

People often think that short words of common use are necessarily Anglo-Saxon. This is not at all so. In the sentence that begins this paragraph, *people* and *use* are French. Among hearty monosyllables that are forever on the lips of the masses and are nevertheless French are words like *air, cost, fault, noise, pair, piece, sound, seem, chief, firm, large, nice, poor, real, safe, sure, change, close, cry, move, please, pass, pay, push, quit, rob, wait.* Longer, but still very popular French words are *double, eager, easy, gentle, honest, perfect, precious, second, single, special, sudden, usual, allow, carry, complain, cover, enjoy, excuse, marry, obey, remember, satisfy, suppose, travel.*

The ease with which these French words and hundreds of others like them were assimilated into the language is proved by the freedom with which they blended with Anglo-Saxon suffixes. *Gentleman, faithful, faintly,* even *battle-axe* had all come into use by 1400.

Many of the Saxon words that were displaced by the newcomers have very recognizable cognates in modern German. French *uncle* replaced *ēam* (*eme* is still to be found in comprehensive dictionaries); *anda* gave way to *envy, æthele* and *ætheling* to *noble* and *nobleman, dryhten* to *prince, leod* to *people, dēma* to *judge* (but *deem* remains), *sibb* to *peace, ieldu* to *age* (but *eld* is still with us), *lof* to *praise, lyft* to *air, wlite* to *beauty.* The Anglo-Saxon words that refused to be displaced and stayed on side by side with the newcomers give English its rich array of synonyms and near-synonyms: *doom* and *judgment, hearty,* or *heartfelt* and *cordial, smell* and *odor, ask* and *demand, shun, eschew, avoid* and *evade, seethe* and *boil, wish* and *desire.* Jespersen aptly brings out the advantage that English derives from *kingly, royal* and *regal,* where French has only the last two.

Forty per cent of all French words in English, Baugh estimates, came between 1250 and 1400, coinciding with the adoption of English by the upper crust of English society. The conclusion is obvious that as these higher levels adopted the new language they transferred to it the words for which it had no precise equivalents, or with which they were more familiar.

From the fifteenth century on the borrowing is of a more literary nature, with words like *harangue, sumptuous* and *furtive;* or the *brunette, ballet, canteen, champagne, coterie, dentist, publicity, patrol, routine* and *syndicate* to some of which objections were raised by Defoe, Dryden and Addison; or the *cadet, grimace, prestige, trait* and *foyer* concerning whose pronunciation in English there is still a question; or the nineteenth-century *chauffeur, garage, chaperone, rouge* and *automobile;* or the words and expressions still printed in italics and for which a French pronunciation is used or attempted: *par excellence, comme il faut, belles lettres, qui vive, de rigueur.*

The French suffixes which have had the greatest impact on English are the *-age* of *voyage, garage,* etc., and the *-ee* which is claimed to have been even more prolific in English than in French (*trustee, referee, draftee, evacuee; cursee* and *laughee* had been used by Carlyle, in the sense of the recipient of curses and laughter).

One English category in which French reigns supreme is undoubtedly the realm of cookery. Old French gave us *dinner, supper, taste, mackerel, oyster, venison, beef, veal, mutton, pork, gravy, toast, biscuit, cream, salad, fruit, grape, cherry, pastry, jelly, roast, boil, stew, fry, saucer, plate.* The medieval *salver* (taster for poison), *charger* (the servant who brought in the joint), *trencher* (the one who carved the same) and *voider* (the cleaner-up of remnants) were all French, at least in name. So is the *butler* (*bouteillier,* or "bottle-keeper"); but not the *steward,* who is an

Anglo-Saxon *stywarden*. Cutlery has nothing to do with *cut*, but comes from French *coutelier*, "knife-maker," from *couteau*, "knife." The *dessert* is from *desservir*, "to clear the table." The French tradition continues today with relatively modern borrowings like *menu, sauté, omelette* (originally *lamelette*, "little blade"), *casserole, hors d'œuvre, vol au vent, pièce de résistance* and dozens of other semi-naturalized terms which make our *cuisine* a tributary of the French.

French are some of the curious terms of square dancing. *Sashay* is an original *chassez* ("chase" or "drive"). The caller's *balansay* is, of course, *balancez*. His *do-si-do* (also spelled *dozey-doe* and *dough-see-dough*) is *dos à dos*, "back to back." But these terms are normally used without any knowledge of their source or true meaning.

Quite definite and clear, on the other hand, are the terms used in the ballet: *cedez, terre à terre, en l'air, serré*. Art, in all its forms, comes in with *objet d'art, dada, bizarrerie, art nouveau, collage,* and that interesting form of optical illusion in painting known as *trompe l'œil*, "deceive the eye." The stage and entertainment world have their *entrée, succès d'estime, fugue, motet, soubrette, ingénue, Grand Guignol, dénouement,* right down to *discothèque* and *à gogo. Vers de société* and *roman à clef* pertain to literature, *idiot savant* and *couvade* to the social sciences, *cadre, Jour J, force de frappe* and *force de dissuasion* to the military (the last three represent French versions, often used in English, of the more familiar *D-Day, striking force, deterrent force*).

Entering English by way of America are *butte, coulée, levée, portage, prairie, praline, picayune, buccaneer.* But going directly into the slang of the London teen-agers is *wuzzy* for a girl, taken bodily from French *oiseau*, "bird."

Many loan-words from the French have a picturesque history. *Dandelion* is *dents de lion,* or "lion's teeth," from the notching that appears on the leaves of the plant. *Coffin* is an Old French *cofin*, "basket," though it in turn goes back to a Graeco-Latin *cophinus,* which means "coffer" or "casket"; the medieval Englishmen applied this word to their piecrusts. *Challenge* is from an Old French verb which goes back to Latin *calumniari,* "to slander" or "attack with false accusations." *Invoice* has nothing to do with *voice*, but comes from Old French *envois*, things sent or forwarded. *Chamberlain* is from *chambre* (originally Greek *camera*) with a Germanic suffix *-ling*, and literally means a "chamber attendant."

Anglo-Irish *gossoon* is merely the French *garçon*. *La crosse* is an American borrowing from the French of the early explorers, who thought the stick used in the Indian game of *baggataway* resembled a bishop's crozier. A borrowing that takes a highly naturalized form is the distress signal *Mayday*, from the French *m'aidez*, "help me." There are also peculiar loan-translations, like William Buckley, Jr.'s "No enemies on the left" (French *pas d'ennemi à gauche;* any leftist nation or individual can do what it or he wants, and get away with it, but right-wingers are by definition hostile). *Vive la différence!* is more often used untranslated when circumstances warrant.

Enough has been said to prove two things. One is that French, next to Anglo-Saxon, is the greatest purveyor to English of words in common use. The other is that a majority of the French words in English have had a way of insinuating themselves into the language that is not duplicated by any other imported stock, save perhaps the Scandinavian. Structurally, English is Germanic, but when it comes to vocabulary, English, thanks to its disguised and naturalized French words, may be said to be half-Romance. The French element has added grace and expressiveness to our language; but above all, it has made that language relatively easy for the hundreds of millions of Romance speakers, who meet at every step words akin to their own; this quite apart from the general stock of Graeco-Latin words that are common to all or most European tongues. The implications of this fact are important to the future of the English language, as will be seen later.

Classical (i.e., Latin and Greek) borrowings constitute perhaps an absolute majority of all the words in our language. Most of them are infrequently used, and a great many of them belong to professional jargons; but many are ordinary, everyday words, appearing in the conversation of any literate person. Who has not, at some time, used *alibi, bonus, exit, extra, item, (omni)bus, propa-*

ganda? Who has not read, in accounts of political happenings, of *deficits, agenda, quorums* and *vetos?*

There are many shadowy border lines in Classical borrowings. For one thing, it might be claimed that most of the French words discussed in the preceding section are Classical borrowings, since French developed them out of Latin, which had in turn taken many of them from Greek; such are *basilica* and *coma,* both in the medical and in the astronomical sense.

Secondly, among Classical borrowings which did not come from French, or which French itself took from the Classical lexicons during the Renaissance, a distinction must be made between those words which are genuinely Latin and Greek, having been used in Classical times with somewhat the same meaning they have today, and those which, though based on Latin and Greek roots, prefixes and suffixes, were never used by the ancients, and would have struck them as barbarisms if they had heard them. When fourteenth- and fifteenth-century English takes from Latin such terms as *gesture, interrupt, lunatic, nervous, picture, polite, prevent, submit,* we have a borrowing process pure and simple. Some of these words retain without change the Latin form and general meaning (*census, censor, genius, inferior, minor, stupor*). Others merely drop a Latin ending, or replace it with an English ending itself derived from Latin (*quiet, reject, suppress, ulcer, legal, contempt, history, include, popular, individual, necessary*). But in addition, we have nineteenth- and twentieth-century scientific creations of the type laughingly described as "Schenectady Greek," a term that refers more specifically to electrical terminology, though the process by which it is applied in other sciences is the same: *dynatron, cyclotron, allergy, protein, hormones, orthopedic, antibiotic, stratosphere, deltiology,* or "postcard collecting," from *deltos,* "writing-tablet." These expressions really would have stumped the ancients. To these Greek terms could be added scientific Latin ones: *quantum, relativity, radioactive, introvert, facsimile, suicide;* and even Graeco-Latin hybrids, like *nihilist, sociology* and *television.* Words like *Protestant, undine, inertia, dynamics, transcendental* are based on Classical roots, but were created in modern times (the first dates from 1539, the second from 1657, the third was coined by Kepler, the fourth by Leibniz, the last by Kant). *Patina* and *corona, umbra* and *nova, nebula, abscissa, integer, simplex, libido, superego,* are only a few samples of the way Latin is used in the physical, mathematical and social sciences. The political *caucus* may sound like an American Indian word, but it is really the Greek *kaukos,* "drinking cup."

The treasure-house of Classical roots is what gives English and the other western languages an inexhaustible supply of words, adapted for all uses. It is also the chief element that the great modern languages hold in common. To the extent that its use increases (as it has been increasing at headlong rate in the last fifty years) the languages become mutually comprehensible. This vast body of international scientific words, based on Greek and Latin roots, has led many scientists to dream of an international language that would really become practical and universal. Standing four-square against this dream are the high-frequency words of ordinary everyday use, words like *bread* and *water, of* and *from, the* and *and.* But more of that later.

The number of productive Latin and Greek prefixes and suffixes that came in with the Renaissance is such as to dwarf even the native contingent. As against the Anglo-Saxon *fore-* and *with-, -ness* and *-dom* and *-hood,* consider the words beginning with *pre-* and *pro-, sub-* and *super-, hypo-* and *hyper-, anti-* and *amphi-,* or ending with *-al* and *-ous, -ty* and *-ble, -ate* and *-ism, -tion* and *-ize, -ic* and *-ist.* They are often used with Saxon roots, forming such lovely hybrids as Dryden's *witticism,* Meredith's *womanize,* or the *remacadamized* which is Latin-Celtic-Hebrew-Greek-English.

Latin and Greek words compete not only with the native stock, but also with their own French descendants. *Fantasy* and *fancy, regal* and *royal* (or *real*), *candelabra* and *chandelier* sometimes provide us with the *embarras du choix,* but more often with near synonyms or remote cognates whereby we can bring out whatever shade of meaning we choose. Some of the original French words gave way before the Latin form, as was the case with Caxton's *confisk,* replaced by *confiscate.* But in our linguistic history deaths are few, and births are many. The Saxon-French-Classical trinity often endows us with three words for approximately the same meaning, one of which is popular, the second literary, the third downright learned; such is the case with *end-finish-conclude, rise-*

mount-ascend, goodness-virtue-probity, time-age-epoch (or *era*),
ask-question-interrogate.

The picturesque story of Latin and Greek words has often been
told, but people never seem to tire of it. There is, for example,
that peculiar word *autarchy* which gathers in itself the widely
different meanings of Greek *autarkeia* ("self-sufficiency") and *au-
tarchia* ("act of ruling by oneself," "absolute sovereignty," "des-
potism"); having once been requested to write about the "Fascist
autarchy," a writer composed a lengthy piece about the measures
which Mussolini's government was taking to make Italy economically self-sufficient, only to discover that what the editors wanted
was an article about Mussolini's concept of absolutism.

English *commonplace* is a Latin-French loan-translation from
Greek *koinoi topoi,* a medieval rhetorical term meaning "stock
expressions," "metaphors," "familiar tricks of form"; the Greek
word directly gives us *topic* and *topical.*

Hybrid is in Latin the offspring of a tame sow and a wild boar;
but the word goes back to an Aeschylian Greek *hybris,* "arrogance," "unbridled pride," "ruthlessness," "wanton violence,"
qualities which the Romans, apparently, felt to be characteristic
of a wild boar's offspring.

Cosmetic is from Greek *kosmos,* which means "universe," "harmony," "order" and lastly, by logical semantic progression,
"adornment," that which leads to order and harmony in attire.

Muscle is Latin *musculus,* "little mouse"; *uvula* is "little grape";
and *tonsil,* from the root of *tondere,* "to shear," seems to fore-
shadow the modern operation known as tonsillectomy.

If Anglo-Saxon and Scandinavian combined account for about
one-fifth of our vocabulary, and French, Latin and Greek for
another three-fifths, what about the last fifth of our language? It
comes from all over the globe. Once English had acquired the
borrowing habit in connection with French and the Classical languages, it lost all inhibitions about picking up anything suitable
that came along. Celtic, which had contributed little in Anglo-
Saxon times, now came in with its offer of Irish, Scottish and
Welsh words. Most people know about *colleen, blarney* and *shil-
lelagh, pibroch* and *slogan, plaid* and *eisteddfod.* It is not generally known that *flannel* is Welsh, that *bug* is Celtic for "ghost"

or "goblin," that *ferret, ass* and *bin* are probably from Celtic sources. There are those curious pseudo-Celtic words, which are not Celtic at all, but Anglo-Saxon, Scandinavian, or even French, and which were reimported from Scotland into England about the time of the Reformation: *auld, lang, bairn, bonnie, braw, dinna, syne, unco.*

Next to French, the greatest continental influence upon English was exerted by Italian. So great was it in Shakespeare's time that *Signior* was used in addressing all sorts of persons, not Italians alone. In the sixteenth century several writers objected to the Italian element in the language. This element is in part purely musical, artistic and literary (*tempo, aria, alto, piano, crescendo, staccato, torso, stanza, tondo, passacaglia, ritornello, portico, chiaroscuro, cello,* which is really only an Italian diminutive suffix, the full word being *violoncello*). In part it is Gallicized (*burlesque, vogue, campaign, intrigue, artisan, serenade*). Some of it is very Italian in appearance (*vista, incognito, gala, malaria, manifesto, cameo, trombone, zucchini, broccoli,* and the very recently imported *credenza* and *marina*). Some of it is disguised almost beyond recognition (*kohl rabi* from *cavoli rape,* or *wig* from *periwig* from *perruque* from *parrucca*). Some of it is mispelled, mispronounced, or otherwise mishandled (*regatta* for *regata, banditti* for *banditi, Sienna* for *Siena, Boloney* for *Bologna; spaghetti* and *ravioli,* which are already plural, further pluralized by the addition of an English *-s; confetti,* which are hard candy, used for paper favors, something that led to bruises when American movie directors insisted that Italian extras pelt the leading characters with "confetti"; *Punch,* derived from an English corruption, *Punchinello,* of an original *Pulcinella*). *Del credere* and *tale quale* are used in the world of finance, *Dolce Vita* and *Cosa Nostra* in connection with questionable activities. *Commedia dell'Arte* and *dolce far niente* are relatively ancient, but *mano a mano* ("little by little") is recent, like *palestra,* a general Italian word for "gymnasium," which is the title of a Philadelphia sports arena.

As is the case with French words, more Italian words than people suppose have been so Anglicized and are so generally in use that it occurs to no one but an etymologist to question their native citizenship (*cash, deposit, partisan, sentinel, radish, chicory, costume, pilot, medal, gallop, carnival, escort, barrack, canteen, cartoon, laundry, manage, group, gallery, gulf, pants, garb*). Others are, strangely enough, accepted in full popular use despite their obvious Italian appearance (*influenza, studio, trio, presto, solo, motto, ghetto, buffalo, opera*). A few are even used in jargon and slang (*Rialto* for "Broadway," *ducat* for "admission ticket," *bambino* for Babe Ruth). A few other of our Italian acquisitions taken at random are *concert, infuriate, attack, reprisal, cannon, compliment, improvise, caricature, parasol* and, of course, *italicize*.

Spanish and Portuguese give us *rodeo, sombrero, bonanza* (literally "calm weather"), *cockroach* (from *cucaracha*), *cargo, cork, mosquito, sherry, stampede, tornado, gringo, molasses, pimento, commando*. *Alligator* is *el lagarto*, "the lizard." *Bienes* ("possessions," "assets") appears in financial writings, and *aficionado* for "fan" in our sporting pages. But the great stock of our Spanish words comes out of the Southwest. Here we have *canyon, mesa, sierra, Eldorado, placer, adobe, patio, plaza*, the *chaps* that are a cut-down version of *chaparrejos*, the *lariat* that represents *la reata*, the *buckaroo, vamoose, calaboose* and *hoosegow* that are bad pronunciations of *vaquero* ("cowboy"), *vamos* ("let's go"), *calabazo* and *juzgado* (both roughly meaning "jail"). *Poncho, desperado, alfalfa, bronco, burro, corral, peón, pinto* appear unchanged, but *incommunicado* has acquired an extra *m*, *cinch* has lost a final *e*, *ranch* a final *o*, and *mustang* can be regarded only as a corruption of *mesteño*. Foods and drinks include *frijoles, tortilla, tamale, bonito, pompano*, originally Indian *chile, mescal* and *tequila*, and now the cooling *sangria*, or wine-fruit-and-sparkling water punch, that is becoming popular in New York restaurants. *Carioca, samba* and *conga* are from Brazilian Portuguese, but the last two are of African Negro origin.

Dutch-Flemish, closest of all Germanic national languages to English, has made abundant contributions, particularly in the fourteenth and sixteenth centuries, when commercial relations between England and the Low Countries were at their peak. But since the Dutch words, by their very nature, blend easily with English, they are often unrecognized as foreign borrowings. The English speaker who uses *yacht* or *schooner* may suspect something from the spelling; if he uses *trek* or *veld* he knows he is dealing with South Africa and the originally Dutch Boers; but *boor, drawl, deck, boom, cruiser, furlough, onslaught, nap, gin, landscape, pack, tub, scum, spool, stripe, freight, leak, pump, dock, jeer, snap, switch, toy, brandy, uproar, cole slaw, cranberry, cruller, dumb* (in the sense of "stupid"), *pit* (of a fruit), *Santa Claus, scow, sleigh, waffle,* even *dollar,* will arouse no suspicion whatsoever in him. *Yankee* is said to come from *Jan Kees,* "John Cheese," a Dutch derisive nickname for the English; but there is an opposing theory that it is an Indian mispronunciation of *English.* Modern Scandinavian gives us *floe, ski, slalom, geyser* and, among mountain climbers, *glögg,* the name of a Swedish punch. The same mountain climbers attribute Scandinavian ancestry to *glorp,* an energy food composed of raisins, nuts, cereal and chocolate, ground into bars.

German is responsible for *swindler, carouse* (from *gar aus trinken*), *halt, plunder, sauerkraut, sleazy* (from Silesian cloth), *stroll, kindergarten, poodle, yodel, poker* (from *pochen,* "to brag"). Even more numerous perhaps than the German words we have borrowed are the loan-translations we have made: *masterpiece* from *Meisterstück, homesickness* from *Heimweh, sharpshooter* from *Scharfschütze, standpoint* from *Standpunkt, swan song* from *Schwanenlied, chain-smoker* from *Kettenraucher, winebibber* from *Weinsäufer* (this is Martin Luther's creation; his *Romanist* and *Papist* came into England unchanged in the early sixteenth century). *Mailed fist* is Wilhelm II's *gepanzerte Faust; environment* is Carlyle's rendering of *Umgebung; storm and stress* is Goethe's *Sturm und Drang,* and *eternal feminine* his *Ewig-Weibliche. Superman* is Shaw's final rendering of Nietzsche's *Uebermensch,* for which earlier translations had been *beyond-man* and *overman.* One German term for which all suggested translations have failed is *Festschrift; homage-volume, anniversary-volume, jubilee-volume* have all fallen by the wayside. *Weltanschauung, Weltschmerz, Sehnsucht, Gemütlichkeit* are other literary terms that are hard to translate, judging by their use in the American daily press. We could perhaps do better with *Lied, Stimmtausch, Sprechstimme, Gestalt* and *Einstellung.* The bearded vulture of Africa continues to be *lammergeyer.* German dialectal *kitsch,* "to scrape up mud," has penetrated our intellectual circles to represent work, artistic or literary, that is slammed together.

German words brought to English by two World Wars are *Blitz, Führer, Bund, ersatz, Lebensraum, Reichswehr, Luftwaffe, Wehrmacht, Gestapo. Panzer,* the German word for tank, is a Renaissance borrowing by German from Italian *panciera,* "breastplate." Less warlike and more graceful among recent borrowings is *Dirndl.*

Slavic words, especially of late, have been numerous. The old *tsar, vodka, balalaika, troika* (repopularized by Khrushchev as a political term), *steppe, knut, pogrom* and *duma* have been joined by *bolshevik, tovarishch, kulak,* and several words that Russian borrowed from the West, like *commissar* and *intelligentsia.* Highly productive has been the *-nik* suffix of *sputnik,* as witnessed by *beatnik, lunik, spacenik,* even *Vietnik* and *peacenik. Cravat* and *chetnik* are Serbo-Croatian, *robot* is Czech, *polka* and *mazurka* are Polish.

Among Oriental languages, first place goes to Arabic and Persian. *Algebra, alkali, alcohol, assassin* (originally the plural of *hashishī,* or "hashish-eater"), *syrup, divan, sofa, mattress, magazine, safari* are well known; astronomy's *almucantar* and zoology's *marabou* (stork) and *bulbul* (bird) slightly less so. Also well known are Persian *bazaar, caravan, crimson, jackal, jungle, khaki, scimitar, shawl, van* (a cut-down form of *caravan*); less well known is the fact that a good many familiar Greek terms came into the language from ancient Persian: *asparagus, magic, paradise, peacock, rice, rose, tape, tapestry* and *tiger* belong to this class. Medieval Persian-Arabic are *azure, candy, check, lemon, lilac, orange, scarlet, spinach* and *sugar. Tulip* and *turban* are Turkish contributions.

From Hebrew come many old words, like *camel, ebony, sapphire, seraph, cherub, kabal, rabbi;* and a few modern ones, like *kibbutz* and *sabra* (a Palestinian native Israeli, as distinguished from an immigrant; the term originally described a type of cactus indigenous to Israel). *Loot, pundit, rajah, punch, mahatma, coolie, bandanna, bungalow, calico, cot, polo, thug* come from India, along with *veranda, chintz, gunny, jute, seersucker, dungaree, dharma.* Chinese gives us *tea, tycoon, kow-tow, fantan, yen, tong, kaolin.* Japanese, whose older contributions include *kimono* and *samurai,* later gave us *kamikaze, Nisei, Bushido, kabuki, haiku, bunraku* (the Japanese classical puppet theater) and *Zen.* Malay gives us *caddy.* African languages offer *gorilla, guinea, voodoo, zebra, hoodoo, jazz;* American Indian languages *moccasin, totem, tomahawk, terrapin, hominy, mackinaw, pone* and *potlatch,* with those of Mexico specifically responsible for *chocolate, tomato* and *coyote,* those of the West Indies for *mahogany, barbecue, hurricane, cannibal, maize, potato* and *tobacco* (and, more recently, *maraca*), those of South America for *quinine, llama, pampa, jaguar* and *tapioca. Hubbub,* according to the National Geographic Society, comes from the shouts of "Hub-hub-hub" that accompanied an American Indian dice-like game. Australian languages give us *boomerang* and *kangaroo,* those of the South Sea islands *lei, atoll, tattoo, boondock, muumuu, mana* and *taboo. Coffee,* which Francis Bacon described in 1624 as "*caffa,* a drink black as soot and of a strong scent, that comforteth the brain and heart and helpeth digestion," comes through the Arabic from the name of the Ethiopian province of Kaffa.

One final word of caution must be spoken in connection with borrowed words. When we say a word comes to us from a certain language, there is no guarantee that that language did not get it from a third tongue; in fact, that is what usually has happened. "French" words are in origin Latin, or Greek, or Germanic and, in turn, Indo-European. "Greek" words are often from the Persian. The situation resembles that of a double or triple play on the baseball field. Italian gives us *bank, violin* and *lumber.* But if we investigate the history of the Italian words we find that *banco* comes from Germanic, having probably been brought to Italy by the Ostrogoths; we have an Anglo-Saxon cognate for it in *bench. Lumber* is from *Lombard,* and reminds us that in medieval England Lombard merchants often dealt in old household stuff; but the earlier form of *Lombard* is *Longobard,* drawn from *Lang Bart* or *Longbeard. Violin* is a diminutive form of *viola;* this is the descendant of a medieval instrument called *vidula,* a name which came from the Germanic and is akin to English *fiddle. Kaput* is a word which our G.I.'s borrowed from the Germans;

but the German word seems to come from the French expression *faire capote*, "to make an overcoat," a slang term similar in meaning to our "kicking the bucket"; *capote* in turn comes from Latin *cappa*, "cloak," from which we directly draw *cape*. *Kraal*, appearing in South African stories, is taken by many to be either a Boer or a Zulu word; it is neither, but comes from Portuguese *curral*, the same word as Spanish *corral*, so much used in our own western stories. *Bistro* has of late appeared in our newspapers as the synonym of *saloon, bar* or *dive*. It comes from French, but is apparently of Russian origin, with the original meaning of "quick" (a fast drink).

The Greek *pepon* ("ripe"), turning into Latin *pepo*, becomes French *pepon* and *pompon*, then English *pompion, pumpion*, and, finally, *pumpkin*. The *ñape* ("bonus," "gift") of the Quechua-speaking South American Indians receives the Spanish feminine definite article and becomes *la ñape*, then is adopted by French, and ultimately by English, as *lagniappe*.

These rich word-histories, far from detracting from the fascination of our immense stock of loan-words, prove the internationality of language in general and of the English language in particular. Even if it could be achieved, nothing would be more monotonous and poorer than a language restricted to its own native stock of words. Let us give thanks that our enlightened, though unconscious, linguistic policy has made our language the richest on earth.

Chapter Nine

BUILDING THE WORLD'S MOST
EXTENSIVE VOCABULARY (2)

Spontaneous Creation and Lack of Restraint—Functional Change—The Semantics of English—The Coinage of Expressions—Word-Casualties

In all languages there exist words for which the etymologist is at a loss. He can find neither a satisfactory derivation nor a suitable history for them. All he can say is that at a certain moment a particular word began to appear. This situation occurs frequently in the case of the Classical languages, where certain Greek and Latin words cannot be traced to a definite Indo-European root, and evidence is lacking that they were borrowed from the non-Indo-European languages of antiquity. In the early Middle Ages the same state of affairs appears. Many Vulgar Latin words which give rise to Romance and English descendants are difficult to account for, though plausible hypotheses may be advanced. Such is the case with *brave, bronze, baron, zinc.*

There is little doubt that in many cases such words are the creation of an individual, but the individual remains anonymous. If the historical records were not at our disposal, many of the creations we definitely ascribe to certain writers would be just as anonymous and mysterious. As matters stand, we can seldom be certain that the writer who first introduced a word was its coiner.

English has probably a larger number of such words than other languages. They may have been initiated as slang, have found favor, and remained in the language. In the thirteenth century we meet for the first time *bad, big, lad* and *lass*, in the fifteenth *blab, tot* and *chat*, in the sixteenth *dad, jump* and *bet*, in the seventeenth *job, fun* and *chum*, in the eighteenth *fuss*, in the nineteenth *slum*. Other mystery words are *boy, girl, cut, fit, fog, put*. Specific American English creations are *bogus, blizzard, jitney, sundae*. Imitation of natural noises is held responsible for *zip, zing, oomph* (the last is said to come from the call of a mating bull).

The process of vocabulary growth whereby prefixes and suffixes are added to a root has already been mentioned, and English holds it in common with other Indo-European languages (one such coinage reported from Russian is *kukuruzhnik*, "hayseed," "corny person," from *kukuruzh*, "corn," indicating that Russian and American minds can on occasion run in the same channel). In the same class are *paratrooper, telecaster, countdown, feedback, whirlybird*, even *picketeer* and *zillionaire*. *Dismerger* appears in a CAB report; *Luce-tongued*, descriptive of one given to untimely invective, was coined by Representative Udall of Arizona, and *re-Morse-less comment* by Representative Coffin of Maine.

By this process of adding suffixes, we get *containerization* (a new system of trash collection at Columbia University; Vice-Presidential candidate William Miller's *categoring* (based on *category;* he could have used *categorizing*); the verbs *to orbitize* and *to delethalize* (aircraft), used by the Air Force; and even a *framization* based on *fram*, itself an anagram for "Fleet Rehabilitation and Modernization."

There are also coined phrases, of the type of *double-talk, hot rod, skin diver, summit meeting, disk jockey, cover girl, glamor puss, rat race*, where it is difficult to tell from the component parts what the meaning of the complete expression may be.

A less general process, though occasionally known to other tongues, is what linguists call back formation or, to use the original German term, *Rückbildung*. Here the suffix is cut off, leaving what looks like, but need not necessarily be, an original root, used in a different function from the original word. Such are *edit* from *editor, peddle* from *peddler, burgle* from *burglar, buttle* from *butler, jell* from *jelly, enthuse* from *enthusiasm, orate* from *orator, reminisce* from *reminiscence, peeve* from *peevish, gloom* from *gloomy, greed* from *greedy*. A theatrical reviewer once offered *grue* from *gruesome* ("We have so long been exposed to the gruesome that we simply don't grue any more"), while a Senatorial candi–

date from Utah is held responsible for "I prefer a polygamist who doesn't polyg to a monogamist who doesn't monog."

Closely related to this process is that of abbreviation *(pub* from *public house, pup* from *puppy, props* from *properties, caps* from *capitals, cad* from *cadet,* more recently the Army's *to attrit* from *attrition.*

The great process peculiar to English among the western languages, and one which makes English reminiscent of Chinese, is that of functional change, whereby a noun turns into a verb or an adjective into a noun, without the addition or subtraction of any suffix. To this class belong such words as *eye, elbow, hand, skin, stomach, requisition, service* used as verbs, or *show, hit, shave, smoke, find* used as nouns. The adjective *green* becomes a noun when we speak of *greens. Better* is originally an adjective, but when one speaks of one's "betters" it becomes a noun, and when one says "to better existing conditions" it turns into a verb, all this without the addition of any distinctive suffix. *Chin* is a noun, but it becomes a verb in "to chin the bar." The adjective *idle* becomes an intransitive verb when we speak of engines that idle, and a transitive one when a newspaper reports that workers have been idled by a shutdown. The functional change process has been going on in our language for centuries, yet every time it is repeated it draws fire. *Cod-liver oil* and *mystery man,* where the nouns *cod, liver* and *mystery* are used as adjectives, shocked the purists at first. Later the shock was administered by *contact* used as a verb. *Cavalier* in *cavalier treatment* or *cavalier attitude* shows a noun not only used as an adjective, but also wrenched from its original semantic connotation. To *rat* and *ratting* (or *to fink* and *finking*) are samples from the labor field, but "he messaged Roosevelt" is from the *New York Times.* Another newspaper has "Expected Change in Wave-Length Will Not Obsolete Zenith Television," and still another has "Allen May Emcee Video Show," which is the height of something or other, considering that *emcee* stands for *M. C.,* which in turn abbreviates *Master of Ceremonies.* A headline gem is "Police Police Police Poll." *To satellite* comes from outer space enthusiasts; *to TV,* used as a verb, comes from Texas; *towarding,* in the sense of "to move toward," has been noted; and we have even heard *catter* in the sense of "more like a cat" (not *cattier*). Functional change is at once the delight and the despair of foreign students of English.

Analogy is a process whereby words are created in imitation of other words. It is illustrated by *motorcade* and *aquacade,* created on the model of *cavalcade; valeteria* coined after *cafeteria, cashomatic* after *automatic,* *litterbug* after *jitterbug, cheeseburger* after *hamburger, telethon* and even *talkathon* after *marathon.* One elegant and literary sample of analogy is *parajournalism,* used by Dwight Macdonald to describe the form of writing that exploits both the factual authority of journalism and the atmospheric license of fiction, aiming at entertainment rather than information. Another such literate example is *infraliterature,* coined originally in Spanish, to describe the study, for literary purposes, of westerns and sex novels. The Ku Klux Klan offers an entire series of analogically coined titles: *klaliff, klokard, kludd, kligrapp, klabee, kladd.* In much the same style are *aqualung, astronaut, bloodmobile, beatnik, payola,* finance's *duopoly* (a monopoly held by two corporations) and *globopoly* (a world-wide monopoly; both terms were used in testimony at a Washington hearing), *aquabelle, convertiplane,* and the *pornovisual* which is the New York D.A.'s office's description of certain spectacles.

In this connection, there is what the linguists call an index of productivity. Certain suffixes are more likely to be productive than others. The *-acious* of *audacious, pugnacious,* goes on with a minor spelling change to produce *curvaceous, predaceous;* the *-tel* of *hotel,* after having given rise to *motel,* goes on to *boatel,* and even to a Japanese *ryotel,* which combines the suffix with the first part of the native *ryokan* ("inn"). From *photogenic* and *eugenic* we pass on by easy stages to *videogenic* and even *leg-o-genic.* *Univac* inspires a *New York Times* writer to coin *Unifink,* described as a computer that checks on other computers and reports their errors, while Winchell contributes the ingenious *Age of Chiselry.*

Akin to analogic creations are the portmanteau words, like *flaunt,* produced by combining *flout* and *vaunt; twirl,* from *twist* and *whirl; squash,* from *squeeze* and *crash; smog,* from *smoke* and *fog.* *Jeepney,* a vehicle used in Manila, is from the combination of *jeep* and *jitney*. There are many humorous coinages of the type of *anecdotage, shamateur, soaperatic, alcoholiday, booboisie, blotterature, socialite* and *jingle-bellegance,* but as can be seen from the list, not too many are in widespread use. Clare Boothe Luce's *globaloney* was one of the most successful of this kind. Combinations of legitimate and slang words occasionally appear, like the *beerstro* which unites *beer* and *bistro.* A highly intellectual combination, appearing in Arthur Krock's column, is the "political *quidnuncs*" (*quid nunc?* is Latin for "what now?").

Portmanteaus are popularly supposed to have originated with Lewis Carroll, but *gingerly* goes all the way back to *ginger* crossed with Middle English *gentior,* akin to *gentle* and *genteel.* The portmanteau word is having quite a vogue. The weather bureau supplies *humiture* (a composite index of humidity and temperature); agriculture has given us *zumpkin* (zucchini crossed with pumpkin); from California comes *smust* (smoke plus dust); an educationist offers *pompetent* (pompous but competent); *humanation* is the process of keying human resources to the demands of automation. *Goldwaterloo* was coined after the 1964 election. France holds out *monokini* (described as the two-piece-minus-one swimsuit; but as alternative terms France also offers "illusion destroyer," "anti-mystery" and "demystificator"). *Sexplosion* appears on our side of the Atlantic. The *-roni* ending of macaroni is used to coin *beef-a-roni, noodle-roni* and even *rice-a-roni;* while a writer for the movies is described as a *movelist.* A Michigan rabbi has coined *ignostic* to describe one who holds there is a way of knowing the truth, but without empiric proof. The Parsipanny high school has a *cafetorium* which is a combination cafeteria and auditorium, while Sukarno has coined a *necolim* which combines neo-colonialism, colonialism and imperialism.

Dictionaries, save for the most comprehensive, seldom devote enough attention to the growth of two- or three-word expressions, as distinguished from individual words. Such expressions usually bridge the gap between word-creation and semantic change, since they normally consist of words which taken by themselves have a specific and easily traceable meaning, but in combination acquire a very special connotation. Take, for example, *white elephant,* an

unwanted gift; Siamese kings once sent white elephants to courtiers whose fortunes they wished to destroy, since the white elephant needs very special care. Or take *Gin Rickey*, partly named
after one of the constituent elements plus the name of the inven-
tor, but also crossed with *jinrick'sha*, the man-drawn vehicle of
the Far East. "Bee" in *spelling bee*, *husking bee*, etc., seems to
refer to the swarming of neighbors, friends or pupils to cooperate
on a project, like bees issuing from a hive (*examen*, the Latin word
from which we get *examination* and *exam*, was originally a farm-
ing term for "swarm of bees," too). *Free lance* refers to the medieval and Renaissance *condottieri*, who placed their mercenary
bands at the service of the highest bidder. *Drawing room* is in
origin *withdrawing room*, to which the ladies would retire from
the dining room where the men stayed on to smoke, drink port
and tell naughty stories. *Career man* is etymologically a highway-
man, since *career* is the Low Latin *carraria*, "road suitable for
vehicles," later becoming the road chosen for one's life-work. *Fel-
low-traveller* is, appropriately, a loan-translation from the Russian
poputchik, "one who travels the same road"; it gained currency
in the early days of the Soviet Union, when a few sympathizing
non-Communists were given government posts to create the impression of broad popular support. *Pin money* goes back to the
days when English husbands gave their wives on New Year's Day
money with which to buy pins for the whole year.

A noun like *lurch* is hardly ever used save in connection with
to leave in. It comes from an Old French game called *lourche*,
where if a player's pieces failed to advance across the board he
was left stranded.

Many of our word-combinations are of recent military origin.
Some have advanced to the composition stage, where they are
spelled as one word (*blackout*, *dogfight*, *flattop*, *blockbuster*, *over-
learn*, *overkill*), others are still felt as separate words (*scorched
earth*, *lend-lease*, *walkie talkie*, *swing shift*, *hate-monger*).

In these expressions, many separate linguistic processes can be
observed working at once: functional change, analogy, composition, and, above all, semantic shift.

Semantic shift is a process that is easy to define, but hard to
describe. Basically, it means that a word changes its meaning. But

this change, the causes of which are often obscure, may be attended by varying circumstances; the original meaning may disappear, or it may survive side by side with the new meaning, in which case the language is enriched or impoverished, as we care to view it. Also, the meaning may be extended, restricted, enhanced, or it may degenerate.

Politician is used in Britain in its literal sense only, and Macmillan or Wilson would not be at all offended at hearing themselves so described. In the United States the word, while retaining its original meaning, has also assumed a slightly malodorous connotation. One speaks scathingly of the way the city is run by the politicians, and one may even divorce the word from the political field and speak of a man who is clever at getting others to do what he wants as a "smart politician." There is an extension of meaning in the common use of *lovely* and *awful* (not to mention the slangy *lousy* and *swell*); a restriction of meaning when we limit *doctor* to an M.D. Meaning has both degenerated and been restricted in the British use of *bug* ("bedbug") and *sick* ("nauseated"). General degeneration appears in *harlot* ("servant" in Chaucer's day), and in *wanton* and *lewd,* which once meant merely "untaught," "ignorant"; in *wench* (once "protégée"), in *boor* and *churl* (once equivalent to "peasant"), in *notorious* (once merely "well-known"). There is, on the other hand, enhancement in *governor* (once "pilot"), *fond* and *nice* (once "foolish"). *Female* and *woman* have exchanged places within the last century, the former having once been the regular designation for a member of the gentler sex (it is still used that way in legal parlance), while the latter was at one time considered somewhat vulgar.

But semantic changes need not be attended by any of these processes. In Shakespeare's days, *rheumatism* meant a cold in the head (French *rhume* and *enrhumé* still preserve that meaning); *bonnet* was a man's hat; *charm* equalled "magic." In the language of the King James Bible, *admire* and *admiration* refer simply to wonder or astonishment (Thomas Fuller, in 1639, still says: "Admirable how Mohammedanism should gain so much ground on Christianity"); the phrase "respecter of persons" is best interpreted as "acceptor of an actor's mask, or outward appearances," "one who takes another at face value"; St. Paul's "better marry than burn" refers not to the flames of hell, but those of passion;

base, high-minded, naughty, prevent, have, respectively, the older meanings not of "vile," but of "lowly"; not of "noble," but of "proud," "haughty"; not of moderately wicked, but of really evil; not of hindering, but of preceding ("I prevented the dawning of the morning" in the Psalms). Even *even* means not "even," but "that is," "namely." In the eighteenth century, a *smock* was part of a woman's underwear; it has since been assigned another function, and was replaced successively by *shift, chemise, combination, step-in. Tabloid,* before it became a newspaper format, was a drug dispensed in tablet form. The glue, mucilage or stickum on stamps was at first described as *cement.* A *spout* in Elizabethan days was a rope-drawn lift, *to prove* was to test, *to cater* to cut diagonally. The use of *Latin* in the sense of "Latin-American," fostered by the Latin-Americans themselves (*bodega latina* and kindred signs) is fairly general, but a headline like "Resort Wear Goes Latin" still deceives me into thinking of Roman togas.

A study of the semantic count of common words, like that made by Professor Lorge, establishes certain astounding facts that seem to point to poverty of words rather than the opposite. The word *run,* for instance, is found to be used with 829 distinct meanings, of which the primary, as might be expected, is "to go fast." Perhaps Dr. Lorge was splitting hairs, but the fact remains that Funk & Wagnall's *New College Standard Dictionary* gives no less than thirty-nine definitions of *run* as a verb, eighteen as a noun, four as an adjective, and eight idiomatic phrases in which the verb or noun *run* is used. This is a distressing situation in a language boasting of over one million words, and shows how overworked some of those words are, for lack of substitutes as yet uncoined. It reminds us of another acute pronouncement made by Robertson, to the effect that primitive groups use specific, but not generic, terms (e.g., *cypress, ash, beech* but not *tree*). This places the primitive languages at a distinct disadvantage, which is in some ways paralleled by our own language's use of the same word in an excessive number of connotations. The use of the right word rather than the right argument is advocated by Joseph Conrad for those who wish to persuade others, but how can the right word be used when it conveys dozens of different meanings?

This carries us off to another and far more popular subdivision of semantics and semantic change, that dealing with the deliberate use of certain words in certain meanings for purposes of persuasion or propaganda, whether commercial, political, military, religious or social.

Here it is Hayakawa who warns us to demand a precise definition of every word used in such contexts if we wish to avoid semantic pitfalls. The advice would be good were it not for the fact that in attempting to follow it we would spend our entire lives seeking definitions and nothing else.

"How old is *antique?*" innocently queries a would-be collector. The reply (from U.S. Customs authorities) is disconcertingly direct, if somewhat arbitrary: "1830 fixes the dividing line between antique and modern." Not long ago a Boston organization changed its name from Institute of Modern Art to Institute of Contemporary Art, purely to escape the connotation conveyed by *modern* used in juxtaposition with *art.*

The number of words and expressions which of late have been laden with special semantic charges runs all the way from *formalistic* in art (equivalent terms in the minds of Soviet reviewers are *capitalistic, Western, cosmopolitan, bourgeois* and *decadent*) to the *capitulationist* with which the Chinese Communists describe their Russian brethren and the *dogmatist* which is the Russians' retort. On our side of the fence, "Big Business," alarmed at the semantic odium heaped upon it, suggests "Big Labor" and "Big Government" for its rivals. The use of the term *free* in advertising is challenged by the Federal Trade Commission so long as any obligation to purchase is involved. *Academic,* once suggestive of ivy-covered collegiate cloisters, has now come to be, in the words of a professor-author, "a sort of critical bludgeon wielded by newspaper reviewers against books by professors." He suggests that the distinction between *academic* and *pedantic* (or downright *dull*) be revived.

Blasts have been leveled on semantic grounds at such words as *motivational research, evaluate* and *challenge, underprivileged, maladjusted, insecure,* (socially) *disadvantaged, culturally deprived, emotionally unstable,* even *Education for Leadership,* in the Teachers' College sense, for which someone has suggested a counterpart for the 1984 society we are rapidly approaching, *Edu-*

cation for Followship. There is a whole range of "weasel words," ranging from *American heritage, spiraling inflation, creeping Socialism* on the right to *lunatic fringe, consensus, mainstream, moderate* on the left. The last of these terms has been compared to the *temperance* of the old Prohibition days, a term which served as a convenient cover-up for extremists better described as *teetotalers.* Today, a *happening* is getting to be used in the sense of any event that cannot be precisely or instantly categorized; the *anchor man* now so frequently used on TV programs to describe the announcer who imparts unity to the program has in the Third Edition of Webster (1961) only the meaning of "the member of a team who competes last"; the *escalation* whose use draws thunderbolts from press and radio in connection with war-like activities has in that same 1961 Webster a definition that applies only to rising prices on the market.

Solidarity is a good all-purpose word that can range from labor unions to leftist groups. Government and military circles have brought us such semantically charged words and word-groups as *population explosion, nuclear holocaust, restricted* (or, better yet, *classified*). *Senior citizen* is a rank euphemism that has elicited the suggestion that we label our babies *junior Americans.*

Semantics goes hand in hand with politics, both national and international. "Welfare State" has so undermined *welfare* that the outright abolition of the word is urged in connection with the Department of Welfare and even of Welfare Island. But since "Welfare State" sounded as good to some as it was unpleasant to others, *statism* was brought in to pinch hit, despite the fact that its dictionary definitions are for the most part harmless. *Progressive, liberal,* and even *independent,* have been, in the words of columnist Robert Ruark, "termited by scabrous innuendo and wrecked by frequency modulation." Actually, the odoriferous connotations of *liberal* had already led former Governor Arnall of Georgia to apply to himself the term *libertarian;* someone else suggested *eclectic,* but that word is too much tied up with philosophy to work well in politics. Previously, semantic charges had attached themselves to *reactionary, conservative, decontrol, reconversion, directive, operation something-or-other, capital gains, deductible.* Among semantically charged expressions listed by a financial writer are "marshalling public opinion" (lobbying performed by government bureaus); "selfish interests" (utilities that resist public ownership); "social justice" (unions seeking economic advantages); "gluttons of privilege" (corporations seeking ditto).

On the international side, we have had the practical disappearance of *comrade* because of its use among Communists. The terminology used by Soviet writers in referring to the West has already been alluded to. *Imperialist, warmonger, racialist, fascistic, exploiters, people's democracy* are part of the paraphernalia of propaganda. We retaliate with *Iron Curtain, puppet, satellite, totalitarian, free enterprise,* and similar well-chosen gems.

This brings us to the most melancholy portion of our chapter, that dealing with the death of words. The obituary will be brief, because few words die in comparison with those that survive. Still, a bird's-eye view shows us quite an imposing cemetery, dotted with the printer's little black crosses. Upon the graves we read not *R. I. P.,* but *obs.* or *arch.*

The first row of graves consists of all those Anglo-Saxon words which found it impossible to survive the Danish and Norman invasions; of these many examples have already been given. Next comes the Middle English array of words which disappeared in the fifteenth century, words like *mizzle* ("drizzle") and *toom* ("empty"). Medieval English knew money-lenders as *Kauersyns,* from the city of Cahors in France, a banking center. It knew long, pointed shoes as *crackowes* or *poleynes,* from the fact that they had originated in the Polish city of Crackow. The sixteenth century offers words like *pingle* ("fight"), *yuke* ("itch"), *begeck* ("cheat"), *whirlicote* ("carriage"). A little later, we find the "aureate" terms which actually began with Chaucer, but ran amuck in the writings of the Scottish Chaucerians, particularly James I and Dunbar. A *Ballad of Our Lady* by the latter author begins: "Hodiern, modern, sempitern, Angelicall regyne," and John Metham contemptuously labels it "halff chongyd Latyne." But some of the aureate terms survive, among them Chaucer's *laureate, prolixity, meditation* and *oriental.*

There are words which today sound quaint, but saw service in their time. *Skrimshander* is still locally used to denote the dying handicraft of New England sailors, making *scrimshaw* out of whale's teeth. *Gardaloo* was once used as the equivalent of a "Bronx cheer"; actually, it came down from the good medieval custom of emptying slop-jars from windows onto the streets, at which time considerate householders were supposed to cry out *"Gardez l'eau!"* ("Watch out for the water!") to passers-by below. In the same class are *bonaroba* (Italian for "good stuff," used in Tudor England to describe a semi-prostitute), "chirk as a chitterdiddle on a pokeweed" ("cheerful as a lark"), *hunca munca!* (the rough equivalent of the modern "tripe!" or "boloney!"), *hoodledasher* ("deadhead," "sap"). One good sample of a word that has become altogether literary is *ere* for *before;* it is also, incidentally, a good sample of the proposition that the speakers do not invariably go for the shorter of two synonymous words.

Numerous other words lead a touch-and-go existence for years and centuries before they are finally consigned to oblivion and desuetude. Among them are *anacephalize* ("recapitulate"), *deruncinate* ("eradicate"), *demit* ("dismiss"), *eximious* (used by Browning in the sense of "distinguished"), *mansuetude,* the use of which extends from Chaucer to Browning, *suppeditate* ("supply"). Baugh points out that in the days of Shakespeare five adjectives from the root of *effect* were used side by side: *effectual, effective, effectuous, effectful, effectuating;* only two of them live on today.

Of particular interest are the nonce-words, or words that are labeled such. By definition, a nonce-word is used on one occasion, or in one connection, then falls out. Among words labeled as nonce-words by no less eminent authorities than the Fowlers in *The King's English* are not only *rectitudinous, brisken, insuccess* and *unquiet,* but also, startlingly, *forceful, racial, intellectuals, Minneapolis* and *Pennsylvania* (just how a place name can be a nonce-word they fail to explain).

The process of obsolescence goes on today, and not merely in the field of slang, where the mortality is heavy. A miniature kerosene lamp placed in a living-room was called a *sparking light* in the last century. Today, the term has disappeared with the object, which is, of course, the normal way for words to disappear. Clark reminds us, however, that the obsolescence of words need not be attended by the vanishing of the object they denote. A slight change in model may bring about a new terminology, as when *station-wagon* and *convertible* replace the *runabout* and *touring car* of our younger days. The more legitimate *train* has now replaced the *cars* of the turn of the century. *Dear* in one of its meanings was to all intents replaced, first by *costly*, then by *expensive*. The European-sounding *conscript* was replaced in America by a series of euphemisms (first *draftee*, then *selectee*).

There is little reason to suppose, so long as the material aspects of our civilization continue to grow at a miraculous pace, that our vocabulary will not continue to keep pace with them. In the field of words, few die, none resign, and many are born. Yet the fear expressed by some writers that one day our words will rise above our neckline and swallow us up seems groundless. The same human genius that permits millions to crowd within the space of a few square miles in a state of congestion that our forefathers would have found intolerable will also save us from the evil effects of the existence of too many words.

To begin with, there is little doubt that the average man's vocabulary is expanding. With present-day literacy and education, we may expect that elastic word-container to expand still further. The day may not be distant when a use-and-recognition vocabulary of over one hundred thousand words will be the common possession of us all, instead of the prerogative of an intellectual few.

Secondly, the expansion of vocabulary is, as it always has been, most noticeable in specialized fields, where it affects the specialist directly, and the non-specialist only indirectly. It is not at all necessary that the engineer know the complicated terminology of medicine, or that the physician be acquainted with the words of the automotive industry. What is desirable is that all these terminologies be made accessible to us in case of need, and this is the function of our numerous and excellent comprehensive dictionaries, encyclopedias and other works of reference.

At the most, an appeal may be directed at the specialist not to over-complicate his terminology when he is addressing the layman. It is undeniable that there is a tendency on the part of all specialists to create new and often unnecessary terms, which are sometimes confusing even to their own kind. Controls might properly be placed over these tendencies, but they will have to be created and administered by the specialists themselves. An effective way to attain this goal is to deride the complicated and unneeded coinages of their fellows instead of accepting them with gaping mouths like unsophisticated country yokels.

Above all, we must equip ourselves to live with our expanding vocabulary in the same manner that we have trained ourselves to live with an ever-increasing number of our fellow human beings. It is irksome to find our places of dwelling, work and amusement and our means of transportation overcrowded, but there are compensations in the closer cooperation that over-crowding begets. In a sparsely settled community houses often burn down before the firemen can be gathered together and gotten to the scene of the fire; in a crowded city the fire-engines are right around the corner and ready at a minute's notice.

It is the same with words. There may be advantages to floundering about in search of a word, as yet uncoined, that will precisely express our thought; there are greater advantages to having at one's disposal numerous words, each one capable of doing the job.

The vocabulary of a language is the measuring-rod of the sum total of the activities of that language's speakers. But human activity is in turn the material index of civilization. Plunge us back into barbarism or savagery, and the sum total of our activities will drastically decline, and the vocabulary with it.

Chapter Ten

THE SAGA OF PROPER NAMES

Place-Names and Their Mysteries—The Evolution of Personal Names—What Lies Behind Family Appellations—Nicknames and Pet Names—Personalizing the Inanimate Object

Some linguists hold that place-names are a better index to a nation's history than history itself, but this historical criterion needs to be applied with caution. The trouble with most "English" place-names is that they are not English at all. This is perhaps even more true of Britain than it is of America, and is due in part to the tenacity with which ancient designations for localities survive invasions and conquests, in part to the ease with which place-names are bestowed by every visitor to a given land.

The roots, though not the endings, of British place-names very often go back either to the Celtic of the Britons or to the hypothetical language of the aboriginal (Iberian?) inhabitants. They first begin to appear in Latinized forms in the works of Roman writers from the second century on. York, for example, is Eboracum, Lincoln is Lindum (*colonia* was later added to produce the modern form), Manchester is Mancunium, Gloucester is Glevum, Colchester is Camulodunum, Exeter is Isca, London is Londinium. The *-dunum* suffix, very frequent in British and Gaulish place-names, is from a Celtic word meaning "hill"; it later becomes *-down* and *-don*. The *-chester, -caster, -cester* endings are Latin, and represent *castrum*, "encampment" or "fort." Most of Britain's rivers, the Dee, Trent, Thames and Severn among them, are of Celtic origin.

The Saxons bring in numerous suffixes which get added to existing names. Such are *-burg, -borough, -bury,* from Old English *burh*, "fortified town"; *-bourne, -borne, -burn,* from *burne,* "stream"; *-ey, -ea, -y,* from *ig,* "island"; *-ham,* from *hām,* "home," or *hamm,* "enclosure"; *-hurst,* from *hyrst,* "wood"; *-sted, -stead,* from *stede,* "place"; *-ton* from *tūn,* "enclosure"; *-wich, -wick,* from *wīc,* "dwelling"; to these we may add others that are self-explanatory, like *-bridge, -church, -ford, -hall, -head, -hill, -land, -minster, -mouth, -stone, -tree* (or *-try*), *-well.*

Scandinavian suffixes are *-beck,* "stream"; *-by,* "town"; *-fell,* "mountain"; *-holm,* "island"; *-how,* "hill"; *-thorpe,* "village"; *-thwaite,* "piece of land"; *-toft,* "green knoll"; *-with,* "wood"; and *-dale.*

Norman contributions are surprisingly few, though we find a scattering of straight French and combinations (Beaulieu, Thorpe Mandeville, Chapel-en-le-Frith, Alsop-en-le-Dale, Barnoldby-le-Beck, Barford St. Martin). Sussex place-names, however, often end in *Quarter,* which is the French *quartier* (Peening Quarter, March Quarter). Charing Cross is so called because here Edward I erected a cross to the memory of his beloved queen (*chère reine*) Eleanor, who died in 1290.

Few Englishmen realize what the force of combination is in place-names. Near Plymouth rises a ridge called Torpenhow Hill. *Tor* is Saxon for "hill"; *pen* is the Celtic word for "head" or "hill," added later, when the force of *Tor* was lost; *how* is the Scandinavian *haugr,* which also means "hill" or "height." Last came Middle English speakers on whom the force of the earlier words was spent. Their final contribution makes the name Hillhillhill Hill!

English place-names often have peculiar connotations. Motorists in Britain report Great Heck and Little Heck, Nether Wallop, Kidsty Pike and Isle of Muck. There is in York a Whip-ma-Whop-ma Gate, said to be derived from the former presence in that spot of a whipping-post. London has not only a Ha Ha Road, but also a Sly Street, a Matrimony Place, a Haunch of Venison Yard, a Remnant Street, a Rotten Row and a Cold Blow Lane. There is a Barking and a Tooting, a Cat Hill and an Angel Station.

There is also change aplenty in the history and form of British place-names. Birmingham has gone through an estimated one hundred changes, from a supposed Latin Bremenium, largely discounted by today's historians, through Bromwycham, Bruma-gem and Bermingham, to its present form, while the Yorkshire Burlington that is the ancestor of our towns by the same name in New Jersey, Vermont and Iowa, to name only three, seems to have had Bridlington as its medieval variant.

The place-names of America are equally varied and pictur-esque, and display precisely the same linguistic and historical processes as those of the ancestral country. To begin with, there is that mass of names from the little-known languages of the Indians. It is these names that cause the biggest headache to that bureau of the Department of the Interior which is charged with toponymy, because the Indian languages are many and varied, and several of them are extinct or nearly so. Massachusetts, Connecticut, Minnesota, Mississippi, Missouri, Kansas, Okla-homa, Nebraska, Ohio and others of our States derive their names from this source. Wyoming, said to be from the Delaware Indian *Maugh-wau-wa-me,* or "Great Plains," appeared in the East before it did in the West. Kentucky, according to one etymology, is "the dark and bloody ground," but another derives it from *Kentahten,* "land of tomorrow." The East has the most copious supply of Indian place-names, probably because the earliest settlers followed the customary linguistic pattern of adopting the place-names of the earlier inhabitants, while the western pioneers preferred to display their bouncing indi-viduality. Canandaigua, most westerly of New York's Five Finger Lakes, is "the chosen spot." Shenandoah is the poetic "daughter of the skies," and Onteora, Indian name for the Catskills, "land in the sky." North Carolina's Kitty Hawk, is from *Chickahauk,* but the original meaning is lost. Mooselookmeguntic, Maine, is said to be the longest postoffice name in the the United States, but Buzzard's Bay, on the Massachusetts coast, gives us a series of island runners-up: Chappaquiddick, Sippiwisset, Cotochesset, Squibnocket and several other tongue-twisters: offsetting these are other island names which remind one of French, Italian or Latin: Cotuit, Uncatena and Que Quam Quisset.

New Jersey in particular abounds in Indian place names. Mahwah, once the residence of Joyce Kilmer, means "meeting-place." Rockaway is "place of sands," Kittatinny "great hills," Matawan, or Mechawanienk, "path" or "trail," Hohokus "cleft in the rocks" or, according to another derivation, "red cedars." The Indian Kelikonikan ("sumac") was turned into Calico, a more familiar word, while Chaqusitt, "upland," became the Cheesequake that arouses the curiosity of all who traverse it. For some of the names, like La-Ha-Way, there is not even a theory as to the meaning; but the general area of New Jersey itself was once Sheyebchi, "land by the long water."

The West's Indian names are complicated, too, with an occasional loan-translation, like the Dakota Bad Lands, from *Mako Sica*. Peoria is a "place of fat beasts," and Chicago a "place of skunk smells." The tale is told of an eastern motorist in Washington State who was requested by his wife to find out the names of the last three towns they had driven through; he was told: "Cathlamet, Skamokawa, Wahkiakum"; he reported that none of the people he had asked could speak English.

The Dutch who first settled New York were somewhat less inclined than the New England settlers to accept Indian place-names. As a result we have Kinderhook, so named by Hendryk Hudson because Indian children greeted his *Half Moon* at that spot; Breukelen, Haarlem and Rustdorp (later Jamaica), named after Dutch cities; the Bouwerie, or "Farm," the Heere Graft (now Beaver Street); Maagde Paetje, or Maiden's Lane, so called because young laundresses bleached white Dutch shirts in the brook that flowed into the East River; Kloch or Kalch Pond, later Collect Pond; Heer Deutal's Bay, which was misconstrued as Turtle Bay. Wall Street was the Dutch Maginot Line against the Indians, and the Bronx was the estate of Jonas Bronck, a Swedish immigrant who purchased five hundred acres of New York's most intellectual borough from the Indians. Staten Island was named after the Dutch States General, and Coney Island was 't Coneyn Eylandt, or "the Rabbit Island."

With the coming of the English to Nieuw Amsterdam, burgomeisters, *schous* and *schepens* gave way to governors, sheriffs and justices of the peace. At the same time, the English-speaking tide began to wash away the Dutch place-names. Breukelen became Brookland, then Brooklyn; Boswyck turned into Bushwick; the

Waalboght turned into Wallabout, and 't Vlacke-Bos, or "the Flat Wood," became Flatbush. Breederweg turned into Broadway, while other picturesque street-names sprang up, both before and after the Revolution: Featherbed Lane, Pomander Walk, Shinbone Alley, Republican Alley, and even that peculiar street entitled from Tom Paine's *Age of Reason,* which was cut down to Reason Street, then to Raisin Street, then vanished. Special sections of the city, which gave trouble to the police, were named Jacob's Ladder, Gates of Hell and Brickbat Mansions.

The English and American mania for picturesque place-names is proved by thousands of examples. There is a Water Proof in Louisiana and a Frost Proof in Florida, a Rough and Ready in California (named after Zachary Taylor) and a Baseball, Ohio, formed by the linguistic and geographical fusion of two smaller townships, Basil and Baltimore. Railroad, Pennsylvania, is located on the Pennsy Line, but boasts no station. Loving, Texas, and Romance, West Virginia, sound idyllic, but are actually named after individuals. Nameless, Georgia, is due to the fact that the city fathers could not agree on a name. There is a Money in Mississippi, an Old Trap in North Carolina, and a Kill Devil Hill in the same state. There are Paradises in half a dozen States, but seemingly only one Hell, located in Michigan (there is, however, a Bumpass Hell in California, which is the site of hot springs). The only Earth recorded is in Texas, and it permits the local rodeo to advertise itself as "Earth's Biggest Rodeo."

The city of Washington, boasting of fifteen hundred byways and not to be outdone by New York, has such street names as Goat Alley, Shad Row, Porksteak Alley, Barefoot Alley, Fighting Alley, Temperance Alley, Moonshine Alley and Tin Cup Alley. Baltimore sports Necessity Alley, and Port Arthur has Mistreating Alley. Western mines bear such tell-tale names as Whynot, Ready Cash, Second Chance and Miser's Dream.

Nome, Alaska, may be described as an "accidental" place-name. On an early map what is now Cape Nome was marked simply "? Name," to indicate that a name should be conferred upon the locality. But the *a* looked like an *o,* and the misreading stuck.

Americans are ready to fight over their place-names. Among the disputes that have arisen are the one over Ardsley-, Croton- and Hastings-on-Hudson (with or without hyphens?), and the one over the *h* in *-burgh* in such names as Middleburg(h), Plattsburg(h) and Newburg(h). Our neighbors to the north have their own difficulties over the question of abbreviating New-foundland to Newland and Newfoundlanders to Newfies, at least for headline purposes.

Not all American place-names are new creations, as evidenced by New York, New Jersey, Maine and New Hampshire. Thirty-seven place-names in the United States are called Berlin, twenty-one Rome, nineteen Vienna. There are Moscows and St. Peters-burgs, Paris and Vincennes, Athens, Sparta, Syracuse, Utica and Ithaca. There is Phoenix, Arizona, so named by an Englishman because it was rising from the ashes of an aboriginal civilization. But what American pronunciation does to continental European names is weird. Berlin is made to sound like Merlin, Calais rhymes with palace, Rheims with screams, Pierre with deer, Versailles with curtails, Prague with plague, Bolivar with Oliver. Mikado in Michigan is "My-kay-dough," and North Carolina's Vade Mecum is "Vaid Meekum." Maine's Vienna is "Vye-enny." Strangely, even English names are mispronounced—Quincey as Quinzy in Massachusetts, while Elgin has a soft g in Illinois and a hard one in Texas. Under the circumstances, it is hardly odd that Americans are great mispronouncers of foreign place-names, particularly now when the trend in geographies and atlases is to give them in native form (Livorno and Napoli rather than Leg-horn and Naples).

The question of what to call people from certain areas has always troubled English speakers. The English are burdened with such concoctions as Mancunian (inhabitant of Manchester), Liverpudlian (Liverpool), Glaswegian (Glasgow), Brummagen (Birmingham), Scillonian (Scilly Islands), Dundonian (Dundee), Cantabrigian (Cambridge), Exonian (Exeter). We have our an-noyances with Minneapolitan, Orleanian, Angeleño, Barbareño and Phoenician, while the Canadians are plagued with Hali-gonian and Gaspesian. Best of all are the Louisiana Cajuns, in whose name it is difficult to recognize the Evangelinian Acadians.

Nicknames for places and their inhabitants form a division of toponymy worthy of serious study. Who first inflicted *Hoosiers* on the people of Indiana, or *Sooners* on those of Oklahoma, or *Tarheels* on those of North Carolina? Legends abound (*Hoosier*, for instance, is traced back to Saxon *hoozer*, "hill dweller"), but they are legends. "City of Brotherly Love," "Windy City," "Smoky City," "Baghdad on the Subway" are perhaps literary terms. And let us not forget that foreigners sometimes coin their own nicknames for our cities. Italians have been known to refer to Chicago as the *Porcopolis* of America.

The other great division of proper names consists of names of persons, both given and family. Here the English-speaking world displays its individuality in several different ways. We have, of course, mainly as a heritage from the days when the Christian Church was one, the old array of Saints' names. There are said to be in the United States six million Marys and four million Johns, while James, George, Charles and William account for twenty million more of our male population. But a very recent listing of first-name popularity drawn up by a Chicago psychologist seems to indicate Robert, Mark and Stephen as currently most popular names for boys, Linda, Sandra (or Sandy) and Susan for girls.

Biblical names from the Old Testament came into vogue with the rise of Protestantism. They were especially favored by the Puritans, and the Noahs, Obadiahs, Ezekiels and Mordecais accordingly predominate among the more Anglo-Saxon portion of our population. So far as America is concerned, there is a sprinkling of native names left among the remnants of our aboriginal population, even if only in loan-translation form. Pay checks have to be made out to Apache and Navaho extras on Hollywood sets in such names as Yellow Left Hand, Little Children, Many Whiskers, Jack Owl, Dog Tired and Sam Skunk. Other Indian names come to us in both forms (Fus-Hut-Ge-Ha-Jo, Intoxicated Bird, or No-Kos-Fixico, Bear Without a Heart). Occasionally the Indian names stray from the red race; Tallulah is said to be "Terrible" in an American Indian dialect. Our American Negroes, who centuries ago gave up their African nomenclature in favor of Christian and Biblical names, in small part went over to a new system under the leadership of Father Divine; True Love, not otherwise qualified, was the payee on a check once seen by the writer. There is no tendency, however, to adopt such ultramodern names as have become popular in Africa among the native tribes: Radar, Beer, Airplane, Plutonium, Stop Light, Five Roses, Inch by Inch.

Personal-name peculiarities among English speakers abound. There is, for instance, the Scottish custom of giving unborn children masculine names, which are turned into feminines by the addition of -ina if circumstances warrant it, with the result that Thomasinas, Georginas and Jamesinas abound in Scotland. There is the ambivalent name, particularly in the southern United States, which does duty for both sexes (Beverly, Leslie, Lynn, Dana). There are the strange religious names bestowed by the Pilgrim Fathers upon their offspring—Humility, Elected, Kill Sin, with the culmination reached in If-Christ-Had-Not-Died-For-Thee-Thou-Hadst-Been-Damned Barebone, later cut for the sake of convenience to Damned Barebone. Their modern, secular counterparts are to be found in first names that commemorate historical events—Manila Bay, Free Kansas, Iwo Jima, Bastogne, Pearl Harbor, Invasia, Points and Dee Day. Breech Loading Cannon fought in the Revolution, and Genuine English Tweed at the battle of New Orleans. Historic names sometimes embarrass their possessors, as when Abraham Lincoln Harris asked that his name be changed to Al Harris.

Regional preferences in first names are described by some researchers. The South goes in heavily for feminine double names, like Mary Lou and Bessie Sue, and for supposedly abbreviated forms like Cindy, Jody and Purly, while the Midwest, as already pointed out by Mencken, has the choicest collection of name-inventions to be found anywhere. Here we meet not only Jurvie, Jewel, Inga and Darleen, but also Covadonga, Duphemia, Earthel, Townzella, Ureatha and Suvada. Two that have recently come to our notice from the Ohio Valley are Iciephine and Sweupta Belle. A St. Louis consulting internist has the appropriate name of Dr. Safety R. First. One Oklahoma family named its six children Tonsilitis, Appendicitis, Meningitis,

Peritonitis, Phlebitis and Jakeitis, the last-named being a disease that medical men may fail to recognize. But the prize for Anglo-Saxon inventiveness goes to a Floridian whose thirteen children with their double names represent the twenty-six letters of the alphabet, ranging from Audie Bryant and Curtis Drue to Wilson Xava and Yon Zircle.

The middle name so often sported by English speakers offers a problem by reason of the same speakers' tendency to abbreviate names to initials, like "Jay Bee" for John Bernard. "Watch out for embarrassing combinations, like S. O. S., S. A. P. or H. O. G." says the National Baby Institute. But to offset this, there is the popular superstition to the effect that you will be lucky if your three initials spell out a word. Then there is our thirty-sixth president's family of L.B.J.'s; and one West Virginia family boasts of nothing but L. J.'s, from Laymond Joyce to Lammy Jack. Our *Sr., Jr.* and *Third* have been known to arouse wonderment in non-English-speaking countries, despite the fact that antiquity records Senior and Junior series in Plinies and Catos.

The story of family names has so often been told that it is useless to repeat it here in great detail. The three great sources of family names are the patronymic, which instead of being changed each generation becomes crystallized (Johnson, "son of John"; Bevan, originally the Welsh Ap Evan, "son of Evan"; the Celtic Mac or Mc, meaning "son"); the transferred place-name (London, Berlin, Frankfurter, Atford, Hearst, originally "wooded hill"); and the fossilized trade name or nickname (Baker, Brewer, Taylor, Doolittle, Longfellow, Cruikshanks).

Mightiest among the occupational names of the Anglo-Saxon world is Smith. This fact may or may not be a tribute to the mechanical leanings of English speakers. At any rate, in Britain, among contributors to the National Savings Scheme, 290,000 Smiths were counted, to 200,000 Joneses, 150,000 Browns and 130,000 Williamses. In the United States, among 24 million names card-indexed in the Veterans Administration, the Smiths predominate, with 217,000 to 130,000 for the Joneses and 100,000 for the Browns. Not even Smith, however, comes up to the three million total shown for García in the most recent census from Spain, a nation of only 30 million inhabitants.

Among significant family names brought to America by the early English settlers we find Styffchyne, Stenchefoote, Spendlove, Calvesnose and Wrigglenecke, but they do not seem to have survived.

It has already been pointed out that many Anglo-American family names have perfect counterparts in other languages. Miller, for example, began with Latin Molinarius; its German form is Müller, the French is Meunier, the Italian Molinari, the Hungarian Molnar, the Czech Mlinar. Truman goes back through Trewman to an originally French Tremayne (three-handed, one handy with his hands), which came to England with William the Conqueror. One theory about Shakespeare is that the first part is connected with Gaelic *seac*, "hawk," and the Shakespeare coat-of-arms seems to lend it some credence.

Legal changes of family names in line with Americanization have been discussed at length by Mencken, who offers Matoushek to Matthews, Podlesnik to Underwood, Ionescu to Jones, Esbjörn to Osborne, Casalegno to Woodhouse, Pulkkinen to Polk, Chisefsky to Chase. Some of these changes are based upon similarity of sound, others upon literal translation, as in the case of the Pole who sifted from Gwozdz to Nail.

A poster seen as you approach Chicago on the Pennsylvania Railroad suggests that the advertiser's name, Czerwiec, be pronounced, more or less phonetically, as Sir-wick. This is in line with earlier English practice whereby originally Norman-French Beaulieu and Beauchamp are pronounced Beuly and Beecham, and even occasionally spelled that way.

"Appropriate" names reported from Britain include B. Quick for a tax collector; Work for a technical advisor in the Ministry of Labour; Ken Scotland for the captain of the Scottish rugby team; and Susan England for Miss England in a beauty contest.

Nowhere does the name-creating craze of the Anglo-Saxon world display itself to better advantage than in the bestowing of nicknames upon persons, animals and things. Why "Bing" Crosby? From childhood mock warfare, or from addiction to a comic strip called "The Bingville Bugle"? Both versions are current. George Ruth was the "Babe" or "Bambino," but this was a study in contrasts. "Mahatma" and "Redhead" were names bestowed upon two baseball club officials. The second is self-explanatory, but what about the first? Capone was "Scarface," and Guzick "Greasy Thumb." Both Disraeli and ball-player Dean were known as "Dizzy."

This has nothing to do with wartime code names, based on secrecy, but they are equally portentous. How many know today that General Eisenhower, in wartime code, was "Duckpin," and General Marshall "Fourfold"? Truman was "Kilting," Stettinius "Collodion," Byrnes "Ice-blink," and Harry Hopkins "Knee-piece." No significance was supposed to be attached to these names, but it is nevertheless significant that Stalin's code name was "Glyptic," and that the Russians were collectively known as "Alibaba." On the other hand, the United States was "Inferno."

Dogs, cats and horses come in for their innings. It has been statistically determined on the basis of license applications that New York's favorite names for dogs are Skipper, Queenie, Brownie and Blackie. Runners-up include Fluff, Buster, Pal, Pee Wee, Scrappy, Bubbles, Cuddles, Yawn and Trouble. But these are the proletarians of dogdom. The aristocrats sport such monikers as Aristo von Marienlust, Ch. Cartlane Once, and Foxbank Entertainer of Harham.

For cats there are, side by side with Tom, Tabbie and Mehitabel, glamour-puss or villainous names like Sinbad, Robin Hood, Glowlyter, Busstopper, Shimble-Shanks and Old Deuteronomy.

The Siamese feline (called in his own ancestral land *sisawat*, "light-stone-colored," or just *vee-lah,* "cat") normally bears lucky names like Sahp, "wealth"; Kah-oo, "gem"; Tong Dang, "red gold"; Tong Lung, "yellow gold"; Ngun, "silver"; Tup Tim, "ruby."

Horses, of the racing variety, bear similar names in both Britain and the United States. The former offers a sprinkling of Fancy and Loose, Fast Minx, Chaste and Fair; the latter gives us Idle Dell, Shut Out, Sand Lot, Discovery, Seabiscuit, Twenty

Grand, One Hitter, Questionnaire, Monday Lunch, Hasty Wedding, Swing and Sway.

When it comes to places and inanimate objects, imagination runs riot. There is a Citrus Junior College in California and a Western Union College in Iowa (now renamed Westmar to end the clash between the academic and the communicational). West Virginia boasts of schools with the suggestive names of Long Sought, Murder Hollow, Goose Neck, Hob Knob, Big Stick, Odd, West Droop, Red Mud, and Unexpected. Ships range from the poetic *Sea Witch* and *Herald of the Morning* to the publicitarian *Pure Woco Pep* and *Standard Portland Cement,* and the disguised understatement *Slo-Mo-Shun.* Railroad lines known by their initials succumb to the mordant wit of their commuters, with the result that the Middletown and Unionville becomes the Miserable and Useless, the St. Johnsbury and Lake Champlain turns into the St. Jesus and Late Coming, The Maryland and Pennsylvania is popularly known as Ma and Pa, D. L. & W. (for Delaware, Lackawanna and Western) are misread as Delay, Linger and Wait; G. & F. for Georgia and Florida become God Forgot; and N. C. & O. for Nevada, California and Oregon give Narrow, Crooked and Ornery.

Baugh claims that there are in English over five hundred common nouns derived from proper ones. This is probably an understatement, when we consider the vast number of place-names, personal names and nicknames that appear today as names of objects. A few of the better known ones are *macadam, derrick, hansom, shrapnel, silhouette* (Etienne de Silhouette, French minister of finance in 1750, passed drastic measures for government economy with the result that his name became synonymous with *outline,* slender at first, later of any description); *lynch, boycott, pasteurize, mercerize, mesmerize, fletcherize, spoonerism, pander* (from Pandarus, in Chaucer's *Troilus*), *lilliputian, tabasco* (a Mexican state, home of the condiment), *Charleston* (the dance, from the name of its place of origin). A *mausoleum* is a perennial monument to the memory of Mausolus of Caria, whose inconsolable widow built the first memorial of that name about 350 B.C. The *cardigan* is named after James

Thomas Brudenell, seventh Earl of Cardigan, who led the Charge of the Light Brigade. *Ammonia* first came from the site of the temple of Jupiter Ammon in Egypt. *Artesian* wells are so called from Artesium, now Artois, in France. The *sequins* sewed onto women's dresses are not synonymous with the medieval coins of Arabic origin, but are named after the shining artificial flowers invented by a chemist named Sequin in 1802. *Bedlam* is a corruption of *Bethlehem,* the name of a London madhouse. *Canter* comes from Canterbury, and *saunter* is from *Sainte Terre,* or Holy Land; both are places whither pilgrims traveled by slow and easy stages. *Tawdry* is from St. Audrey's Fair, where cheap objects were sold. *Demijohn* is neither half nor John, but comes from the name of the Persian city of Damghan, renowned for its pottery. *Worsted* is from the English city of Worstead, *lisle* from the French city of Lille, *calico* from the Indian city of Calicut, *millinery* from the Italian city of Milan.

Enough has been said to indicate the important role played by proper names in the building up of our language. In part, this movement runs parallel to that of other languages, in part it is specifically our own. Place-names, personal names, family names, even nicknames offer a fascinating insight into the past and present history of the language, and this chapter has not even begun to scratch the surface of a topic that yields rich harvests to those who are willing to delve into it further.

Chapter Eleven

ENGLISH LANGUAGE AND ENGLISH LITERATURE

*What the Language Has Given the Literature—What
the Literature Has Given the Language—Popular and
Learned Vocabulary—Proverbs, Sayings and Slogans—
Euphuism and Euphemism—The Language of Poetry
and the Language of Prose*

The interaction of language and literature is a question that
has long agitated linguists, causing them to divide into two more
or less well-defined camps.

Should language be viewed primarily as a speaking activity,
and the written, literary language be considered ancillary to
speech? Or should the two be equally important in the linguist's
consideration? This looks at first glance like a harmless academic
problem, but its practical implications and applications are
many and important.

If you believe in the linguistic importance of the written and
literary language, you will be likely to take it as your standard,
all the more since it is obviously far more stable than the spoken
tongue. This in turn will lead you to make all sorts of pronouncements on what is and is not "correct." It will color your language-
learning method, to the extent that you will use as a base the
codified, standardized written language rather than the shifting,
uncertain oral form. In extreme cases, it will lead to a puristic,
pedantic attitude, a worship of the literary, and an aristocratic
contempt both for the slang and dialects of established languages
and for the languages of groups that have not achieved literary
eminence.

If you view the spoken tongue as all-important, and the
written language as a secondary offshoot, you will scoff at grammatical "correctness." Your language-learning process will start

from the ear rather than from the eye. In extreme cases, you will acquire a disregard for the written language, a veneration for oral forms, however vulgar, substandard and dialectal, and an equalitarian attitude toward all languages, both those which have served and are serving as vehicles of advanced civilizations and those which have no claim or pretension beyond that of serving as media of oral communication.

It is, of course, possible to reconcile both views, to accept language as being historically and fundamentally an oral means of semantic transfer, and to recognize that all languages hold within themselves the same possibilities of development, the same potential ability to serve as mouthpieces of advanced cultures, while at the same time recognizing that this has not yet happened in fact, that some languages have, as a result of chance, not of divine choice, exploited their own possibilities to a far fuller degree than others. This exploitation normally assumes a written-language form, and the highest development of the written-language form is the literary.

A comparison between English and Zulu is perfectly possible and feasible on the purely linguistic, oral level. Both languages possess a machinery for effecting the transfer of meaning, and within both lie the means for developing this machinery to the full. But while English has already effected this transformation, Zulu has not. English has acquired a written form and a literary style; Zulu has barely, and very recently, acquired the first. English is a highly polished diamond of many shining facets; Zulu is a similar diamond in the rough. We may not even ascribe the polish of English and the roughness of Zulu to an intrinsic superiority of the speakers of the one over the speakers of the other, since the historical conditions under which the two have developed are completely dissimilar. The temporary superiority of one language over another as a means of communication and expression does not negate the basic equality of languages, any more than the emergence of a cultured, refined individual from a semi-literate and ignorant mass negates the fundamental equality among human beings.

At the same time, it is ridiculous to deny that the temporary inequality exists. To treat the languages of civilization in the same fashion in which we handle the oral forms of darkest Africa and the jungles of New Guinea is tantamount to issuing identical treatment to the cultured, refined individual and to the savage. It is ignoring history, historical development, and the reality of the given moment. The classless society, in languages as in human beings, is a figment of the imagination, and the advocates of the classless society are the first to recognize this in practice. True equality is only of the spirit and in the eyes of God. The best we can achieve under material, earthly conditions is equality of opportunity.

But even equality of opportunity is a recent historical development. What we have had since the dawn of history is inequality of opportunity, and this has applied in equal measure to men and languages.

English has been among the favored, privileged languages, by reason of its geographical situation, its cultural development, and the tendencies of its speakers. Accordingly, it has grown into a mighty, imperial language on the one hand, holding dominion over palm and pine; on the other, it has developed into a highly refined literary tongue, capable of expressing, in written as well as in oral form, the most delicate nuances of thought and emotion. To overlook this historical, literary development of English in connection with the language itself, to forget the interaction of language and literature, to place the language on a purely oral basis, is a grievous error. Throughout its history, the spoken English language has acted upon and been acted upon by the written, literary form. The tongue we speak today, like all the major civilized tongues, is not merely the product of mysterious, unconscious sound-changes and spoken-language analogies; it is also the product, in approximately equal measure, of the deliberate efforts at cultivation, refinement and self-expression conducted by our "best minds" throughout the ages, from Beowulf to T. S. Eliot.

After all that has been said in connection with the various periods of the historical development of the English language, repetition would be boresome. The writers of the days of King Alfred naturally used the language they heard spoken around them. At the same time, there is little doubt that they exerted their influence upon that language, coining and composing words that had not previously existed and giving them currency in the spoken tongue, regularizing a grammatical system upon which all sorts of centrifugal forces were being exercised, hammering out a style and syntax where none had existed previously. What Layamon, Chaucer, Langland, Caxton, Wyclif did for the language in the way of adding to its store of words, normalizing its forms, refining its word-order has been seen. The popularity given by Shakespeare to words and expressions of his day (*occupy* and *activity,* to mention two of them) that would otherwise have died a natural death is among the greatest merits of the Bard. Later writers, though not exercising upon the linguistic structure the same influence as their predecessors, nevertheless set the vogue for thousands and tens of thousands of words in current use today, not merely in literary documents, but in the spoken tongue of us all.

Robertson has carefully collated long lists of words and expressions introduced by various writers. Many are of the kind that properly belong to the literary, or at least the written-language sphere (*loving-kindness* from Coverdale, *elfin* from Spenser, *pandemonium* from Milton, *evil-starred* from Tennyson, *quodlibetically* from Browne; *irascibility* from Johnson, *persiflage* from Chesterton, *exhaustive* from Bentham, *Philistine* in the sense of "graceless," "boorish" from Carlyle, *anesthesia* from Oliver Wendell Holmes, *infracaninophile* from Christopher Morley). But others are so much in the mouths of English speakers that we wonder they could at any time have been literary creations; Coverdale first gave us *kind-hearted* and *noonday;* Tyndale is responsible for *broken-hearted* and *beautiful;* Shakespeare for *dwindle* and *lonely;* Burns for *croon;* Tennyson for *moonlit;* Byron for *bored;* Scott for *raid, gruesome, glamour, slogan, blackmail;* Carlyle for *self-help;* Noah Webster for *demoralize;* A. Roberts for *spoof;* Gelett Burgess for *blurb;* W. E. Woodward for *debunking.* It was Teddy Roosevelt who popularized *pussyfooting, weasel words, lunatic fringe, hat in the ring.*

Jespersen reminds us that the so-called archaic words of the poets are often nothing but sympathy-arousing devices, selected because they sound novel, yet familiar; *eve* and *morn* are cases in point, while *e'er* and *o'er,* which were once condemned as vulgarisms in prose, are other examples.

Under the circumstances, how is one to draw the line between the oral and the literary, the popular and the intellectual? The language is one, whether it be spoken or written. The once popular word ceases to be spoken and turns literary, at the same time that the literary coinage waxes popular and goes into general spoken use.

This does not mean that we do not have extensive areas of our language which are almost exclusively literary, and others in which the literary origin is self-evident. Words coined out of literary proper names, or the characters of literature themselves, often supply entire pages of literary history. "Man Friday" takes us back to *Robinson Crusoe,* but it has even been popularly transformed into "Girl Friday." "Frankenstein" is Mary Shelley's constructor of a monster by whom he is eventually destroyed, but the word is often quite popularly used to refer to the destroying monster itself. *Malapropism* is from the literary Mrs. Malaprop, whose name was artfully constructed on the basis of French *mal à propos,* "out of order," in the parliamentary sense. We speak of *masochism,* from the name of an Austrian writer, and *sadism,* from that of a French one. We speak of *bowdlerizing* the language, from the name of a self-appointed censor. *Rabelaisian* or *Pantagruelian* humor celebrates the author, or his work. *Epicurean* and *stoic* are philosophical terms, but with literary overtones. *Solon* applied to a statesman is historical, with similar shadings.

Typical among purely literary coinages that are beginning to penetrate the popular language is Horace Walpole's *serendipity,* the quality of wandering about happily and aimlessly in search of adventure and discovering things one is not seeking; it is based upon Serendip, an old Arabic name for Ceylon (Sindhala-wipa, "Lion Island"), among whose princes this amiable inclination is supposed to have once prevailed.

From the individual literary word one moves on by easy stages to the cliché, or stock expression, the kind of thing most of us use without ever wondering where it comes from. Fowler, in *Modern English Usage,* describes the cliché as a hackneyed phrase serving a purpose in a special context, but used even where plain speech would be better. Hayakawa calls it "meaning-less noise," and Bergen Evans, apostle of usage that he is, thunders against it. Only Theodore Bernstein advises us not to avoid the cliché, but rather to use it discriminatingly. Actually the cliché has an ancestry, and the ancestry is nine times out of ten literary, even though the cliché may have entered the universal spoken language.

Chaucer is responsible for some early clichés; to him we owe *a verray parfit gentil knight* and *fresh as is the month of May.* The King James Bible and Shakespeare are probably the most fruitful sources of clichés for the English-speaking world. The former gives us *house divided, light under a bushel, wars and rumors of wars, powers that be, still small voice, killing the fatted calf, whited sepulchers, holy of holies.* The Bard, in *Hamlet* alone, gives us *flaming youth, not a mouse stirring, brevity the soul of wit, there's the rub, something rotten in the state of Denmark, method to one's madness, to smell to heaven.* In *Julius Caesar* he contributes *dish for the gods, it's Greek to me, the most unkindest cut of all, itching palm, lean and hungry look, live-long day.* From other assorted Shakespeare plays come *heart of gold, to give the devil his due, too much of a good thing, the naked truth, foregone conclusion, single blessedness, to break the ice, to cudgel one's brains, to breathe one's last, the course of true love never runs smooth, to tell the world, strange bedfellows, all that glitters is not gold, to wear one's heart on one's sleeve, the milk of human kindness, to eat out of house and home, more sinned against than sinning, to paint the lily.* He may not have coined all of them, but he certainly made them popular.

Milton contributes *fallen upon evil days* and *confusion worse confounded,* but these are still predominantly literary. So is Keats' *alien corn. Without benefit of clergy,* usually assigned to Kipling, was used before his time; he does, however, seem to be directly responsible for *snug as a bug in a rug.* A thoroughly American cliché is Washington Irving's *almighty dollar.*

Political clichés often run into slogans, but at least they have the merit of advertising their origin. Bryan's *cross of gold,* Theodore Roosevelt's *big stick, strenuous life* and *malefactors of great wealth,* Wilson's *self-determination* and *safe for democracy,* Harding's *return to normalcy,* Franklin D. Roosevelt's *New Deal,* Truman's *Fair Deal,* Kennedy's *New Frontier* and *Alliance for Progress,* Johnson's *Great Society* and *War on Poverty* (not to mention *Unconditional Negotiations*) illustrate the twentieth-century tendency to govern by slogan and catchphrase, but also offer the advantage of definite authorship. This is not true of *Iron Curtain,* popularly ascribed to Churchill, but apparently coined in 1904 by H. G. Wells, or of *Tell it to the marines!,* which, according to one authority, has been traced back to General Sherman, and according to another, goes much farther back in history. *One man one vote* is at least based on a Supreme Court decision, but *ability to pay* and *regressive tax* as a basis for taxation appear to be anonymous.

Commercial clichés may be described as literary to the extent that most of them originate in written form. Under this heading come *You're a man, aren't you?; You got a good thing going!; Double your pleasure, double your fun!; Takes you out of the kitchen fast!* They occasionally backfire, like *Twenty-four per cent fewer cavities* and *But don't take it out on them!*

Some modern clichés of which we have some sort of satisfactory account include *no sirree* and *yes indeedy,* which are attributed to Irish influence. *Take it easy* is said to spring from an earlier *easy does it,* which is English rather than American. *Putting on the dog* is traced to the *nouveaux riches* after the Civil War, whose wives displayed their wealth, among other ways, by having expensive lap-dogs. *Hard-boiled* comes from the excessive use of starch on shirts by pioneers' wives (note in this connection W. B. Garrison's *boiled* [or *biled*] *shirt*). No one seems to know how the *now* became attached to *good-by* to form *good-by now* (although it is possibly a shortened form of the earlier *good-by for now*).

A comparison of clichés over a hundred-year period involves an 1860 Vermont scrapbook which lists such expressions as *poor as a church mouse, rough as a gale, bright as sixpence, pure as an angel, bright as a steel trap, ugly as sin, proud as a peacock,*

mad as a March hare, strong as an ox. What modern times have
to offer includes *it's the bomb* (already slightly *passé*), *you can't
do this to me,* and *that's life* (said, however, to be a loan-
translation of French *c'est la vie*).

One major difference between a cliché and a proverb or
popular saying is that the former can usually be traced to a
definite author, while the latter is just as often anonymous,
being, as Cervantes calls it, "a short sentence based on long
experience." *Calling a spade a spade* is shrouded in mystery, but
minding one's P's and Q's has been tracked down to an old
English alehouse custom; in the pubs books were kept for each
customer, with *P* for pints and *Q* for quarts.

There is a definite literary flavor about many of the proverbs,
sayings and popular clichés of the Anglo-Saxon world, even when
we cannot put our finger on the original document. "One man's
meat is another man's poison," "Silence is assent," "Clothes make
the man," "A word to the wise is sufficient" seem to have this
literary flavor. On the other hand, "fly in the ointment," "Don't
bite off more than you can chew," "hitting a nail on the head"
sound popular, while "The worm is wrong when it argues with
the hen," "When luck gets to running your way, sawdust is as
good as brains," " 'Mean to' don't pick no cotton," are not only
popular, but regional. Counter to the general anonymity of the
proverb is Dizzy Dean's "Lots of people who don't say ain't ain't
eatin'." English is not as much given to turning old bromides
into jokes as are other languages, notably Italian (*slow but sure,
and you never get there* or *silence is assent, but if you keep your
mouth shut you're not saying anything*). Here, however, are two
that make the grade: "Too many broths spoil the cook"; "Half
a wit is better than none."

Taboos are words which may not be pronounced (in our
civilization, they more often may not appear in writing), and
euphemisms are supposedly less offensive words used to replace
them. It is difficult to find a field in which the literary influence
is more powerfully exerted upon the spoken tongue. Left to
themselves, the speakers would probably use the tabooed words,

but spoken words must generally also appear in print, and this creates a mighty urge toward the replacement of the obnoxious ones among them. The fact that in recent time the current has been reversed and that popular writers use once-forbidden expressions in their so-called literary works does not contradict the basic proposition. A general with no literary pretensions recently went on record in an interview as saying that if the Americans had attempted to bring an armored convoy into Berlin at the time of the air-lift, they "would have got their *derrières* shot off," adding that he had never been known to use the word *derrière* in ordinary speech. This incident is a perfect illustration of both the taboo and the euphemism, as well as of the literary or written-language motivation for the latter. Some modern novelists make it a practice to shock their readers through the use of "four-letter words" (this expression, by the way, is peculiar to the Anglo-Saxon world), and apparently achieve tangible results thereby. Whether their writings will be recognized as worth while once the shock has worn off is another matter.

The history of the euphemism is an ancient one. Typical of medieval formations is *king's evil,* for a loathsome disease, though here is also involved the superstition that a king's touch could cure it. Typical of modern euphemisms are expressions like *Jiminy Crickets,* or the British *serviette* and *paying guest* for *napkin* and *boarder. Denture* for false teeth, *mouton* and *Hudson seal* for sheep and rabbit fur are interesting samples from the commercial world. *Pregnant* has given rise to an entire series of euphemisms, from the French *enceinte* and the Italian loan-translation *in an interesting condition* to the native *expectant mother. Saloon* has passed through the *bar* stage and is now a *cocktail lounge.* A *spanking* or *licking* is known in educational circles as *aggressive punishment. Juvenile delinquent* for *bad boy* and *underprivileged* for *poor* are attacked by Ivor Brown as forms of the "barnacular," a lingo that clings like a barnacle to our vernacular. *Bra* is in the nature of a double euphemism, being a euphemistic abbreviation of *brassière,* which in the original French was coined not from the word for "breast" or "bosom," but from that for "arm."

Intoxicated for *drunk* is a characteristic Anglo-Saxon euphemism (the word etymologically means "poisoned," and no other language uses it to describe one under the influence of liquor). It is, however, a fact that Benjamin Franklin collected as many as 228 euphemisms for *drunk* current in his day. Among them are many that survive to the present time (*mellow, tipsy*), but also many that have gone down the drain (*cherry-merry, been to Barbados, nimtopsical, seeing two moons, in his altitudes, half-seas over*). Later creations include *slewed, sprung, blotto, corked, embalmed, stewed, stoned, atomized, pie-eyed, three sheets to the wind, higher than a kite.*

Other random euphemisms are *Congressional liaison officer* (for lobbyist), *home manager* or *domestic engineer* (for housewife), *mixologist* (for bartender), *spiritual advisor* (for fortune-teller), *ecdysiast* (for strip-teaser), *naturist* (for nudist), *custodian* (for janitor), *archivist* (for library attendant). One of the sweetest euphemisms reported comes from Japan, but could be recommended for American use. If a student has failed his college exams, the telegram he receives from the university office reads: "The cherry blossoms are falling."

Taboos and euphemisms are most in vogue where censorship is most aggressively exercised. Thus it is that in the movies both titles and lines are often recast after careful scrutiny.

In the face of euphemism and its widespread penetration of the popular spoken tongue, the euphuism common in Shakespeare's day, the style characterized by antitheses and similes, cannot be said to have exerted a similar lasting influence. Shakespeare is acclaimed by Mark Van Doren as the greatest master of rhetoric, with at least two hundred figures of speech at his command, and the claim is advanced that most of these were also well known to his contemporaries. But then came the era of the worship of the prosaic life and the language of clerks and bankers, with the magic of the spoken word cheapening in the eighteenth century and almost vanishing in the nineteenth. It is only with Christopher Fry, in recent years, that this magic has returned to the stage, but whether it will again penetrate the everyday or even the literary language is a moot question.

Much is said today of "writing as you talk," comparatively little of "talking as you write." Rudolf Flesch, author of *The Art of Readable Writing*, urges us to use contractions, repetitions, loosely strung sentences with prepositions often coming at the end, in imitation of the spoken language. But there is more: a set, or almost set number of words per sentence, of syllables per hundred words, of "personal" words and sentences; all this to be accompanied by "color" and "human touches." Priestley, who does not always practise what he preaches, urges us to make our writing "simple."

Fortunately, there is another school of thought, represented by T. S. Eliot, who warns us that "an *identical* spoken and written language would be practically intolerable," since no one would listen to the first or read the second; that they must be neither too close together nor too far apart. He is joined by E. A. Mowrer, whose pronouncement is that "American society might start producing a new class of mandarins, pledged to cultivation of forceful, subtle and expressive speech and writing."

A British writer with no literary or commercial axe to grind, Eric Partridge, sums up the situation as between language and literature in the last fifty years. The poetic language as apart from the language of prose, he claims, is fast disappearing. Even the language of written prose now comes close to everyday speech, as witnessed by Shaw's rhetoric. The literary English of today is less pretentious, polysyllabic, abstract, stiff, allegorical, artificial, ponderous, pompous, didactic and circumlocutious, and correspondingly more direct, simple, clear and vigorous than of yore. All this on the credit side. On the debit side are "jungle, invertebrate, elephantine English"; journalese, commercialese, officialese, "fellow-travelers in the sinister contemporary sense of that once companionable term"; the perverse art of the headline; the distortion in meaning of short words for typographical convenience; the increase in the use of "vogue" words; the development of a "snappy" style which is often intolerably jerky. His final conclusion is that "English" is merging with the vernacular to give rise to a single variety of language, in which the differences between the literary, the non-literary and the colloquial will be more or less ironed out.

These conclusions may be generally accepted, but with a word of caution. It has never happened in the history of any language that such a merger as Partridge describes has failed to be followed by a new fracturing of the language into brand-new literary, non-literary and colloquial varieties. By the time all the vulgarisms, substandard forms, obscenities and improprieties of the spoken tongue have been fully accepted by the written language and passed on to the literary language (a process we see going on under our eyes today—witness Salinger, Genet, Henry Miller *et al.*), there is no guarantee whatsoever that the spoken tongue will not have developed new vulgarisms, new obscenities, new four-letter words and combinations thereof. Whereupon we shall have a new vernacular and a new language of literature, with new possibilities of two- and three- and fourfold development. For in a language we often reach the point of no return, but never the point of crystallization, save when the language and all its speakers and writers have uttered their last gasp.

One more possibility needs to be noted. In view of spreading literacy and education, accompanied by an expanding vocabulary for the masses, there is a remote chance that Eric Partridge's pessimistic previsions may not be realized, and that the movement of the language as a whole may be upward rather than downward, with the literary language becoming to an increasing degree the property of all the speakers. The final result, ironically, will be the same. A segment of the popularized literary tongue will set itself apart to fulfill a colloquial or even a slang role. Classes in language, as in society, are hard to eradicate.

PART TWO

The Present

Chapter One

THE GEOGRAPHY OF ENGLISH

Territorial Extent and Distribution—Speaking Population—Dialectal Divisions—The King's English—The Tongues of the Commonwealth

The English language, spoken by over 300 million of the earth's inhabitants, is numerically the second of the world's leading tongues. Only Chinese, with its estimated 700 million speakers, surpasses it. But while Chinese is concentrated in eastern Asia, with relatively few and small speaking groups outside the home country, English has spread to the far corners of the globe, so that only French among the world's great languages shows comparable distributional features; French, however, has fewer than one hundred million speakers. Hindustani and Russian, the world's third and fourth most widely spoken tongues, do not approach English numerically (Hindustani has between 180 and 200 million speakers, Russian about 160 million), and they share with Chinese the feature of concentration in a single area, however extensive. Spanish, with its estimated 150 million speakers, over three-fourths of them in the Western Hemisphere, is the only other language that definitely passes the 100-million mark. German, Japanese, Portuguese, Italian, Malay-Indonesian, Arabic, Bengali, all hover between 50 and 100 million. No other of the world's 3,000 or so spoken languages approaches the 50-million mark.

The English language, spoken by one out of every ten of the world's people, combines all the features that make a language great—a vast body of speakers, widespread distribution over the earth's surface, cultural, commercial, scientific and political achievement. Its speakers range all the way from English, Scottish, Irish and Welsh whites of Germanic and Celtic extraction to African Negroes of Liberia and Nigeria. In between are gradations of every race and color under the sun—brown East Indians, red American Indians, yellow Nisei, Caucasians of Semitic, Latin, Slavic, Greek, Scandinavian and German stock. There are among them representatives of all the world's greatest faiths—Catholic, Protestant, Jewish, Moslem, Buddhist, Hindu, even Fetishist. The speakers of English are as composite and variegated as is the English language itself.

All this was not accomplished in a day. We have seen how a tongue that had about one and a half million speakers at the end of the eleventh century grew to about eight and a half by 1700, when it was still outranked by French, Russian, German, Italian and Spanish, then, in the course of two great centuries of emigration and colonization, to a total of 123 million in 1900, when it already outstripped all its western rivals.

Today, approximate figures show English spoken by almost 200 million in the United States, fifty-eight million in Great Britain and Ireland, seventeen million in Canada, eleven million in Australia, three million in New Zealand, over two million in South Africa. At least twenty million more, represented by English speakers in British and American possessions, the countries of continental Europe, Asia, Africa, South and Central America, round out the estimated 300 million, which is a rather conservative figure, considering that some linguists hold that at least twenty-five million in India and Pakistan alone assimilated English during the long British rule.

It will be noted that this estimate involves the question of bilingualism. But there is no good reason why a French Canadian, a New York Puerto Rican, a Welshman, an inhabitant of India or Pakistan, a Nigerian native who has gone to school, or a cultivated Frenchman, Hollander, Japanese or Turk should not be included in the English-speaking total, if he has assimilated English as a tongue secondary to his own and speaks it well.

Actually, this matter of bilingualism is a tribute to the power of expansion of the English language. In Wales, in 1891, thirty per cent of the population knew no English and spoke only Welsh;

in 1921, monoglottal Welsh speakers constituted only six per cent of the population; and today it is doubtful if more than a handful of Welshmen persist who know no English.

In the Western Hemisphere, the continental United States, Canada, Newfoundland, Labrador, the Bermudas and Bahamas, Jamaica, the Leeward and Windward Islands and Guyana (formerly British Guiana) recognize English as their national and official tongue. In British Honduras, the Canal Zone, Puerto Rico and the Virgin Islands English is official, and in the Spanish, Portuguese and French-speaking lands of Latin America English is widely taught and spoken.

In Europe, outside the British Isles, English is official in Gibraltar and Malta, and it is estimated that at least five million continental Europeans speak it.

In Asia, outside of British possessions and former possessions like Burma, Ceylon, Cyprus, Malaya, Hong Kong, India, Pakistan, Israel, where the estimates vary from fifteen to thirty million English speakers, there are claimed to be over one million Japanese and perhaps two million Chinese who are acquainted with English. For the African continent, the total number of English speakers runs to nearly five million, of whom two million are in the Union of South Africa, while in Oceania, outside of English-speaking Australia and New Zealand, control is exerted by the United States and Great Britain over native populations of nearly three million, exclusive of Hawaii's seven hundred thousand, most of whom speak English, and the Philippines' thirty-one million, of whom over one-fourth can be reached with English.

One need not, therefore, be a political imperialist to claim that the English language exerts a form of spiritual empire over extensive areas of the globe, molding its speakers to the viewpoints and ways of life and thought that are characteristic of the two great national groups to which English is native, the British Commonwealth and the American Union. The English language is necessarily the conveyor of Anglo-American thought (it would indeed be strange if it were not). There is consequently plenty of justification for those proponents of other political systems and modes of life who view the spreading of the English language with growing alarm.

As is invariably the case with all tongues, great and small, English has succumbed to the inherent centrifugal tendency of language to break up into local varieties or dialects. This tendency was responsible for the original fractionalizing of Indo-European into its various groups (Germanic, Celtic, Slavic, Italic, Greek, Indo-Iranian, etc.). Continuing to operate uninterruptedly, it led to the division of Germanic into Gothic, Scandinavian and West Germanic, the last of which ultimately split up into German, Dutch and English. We have already seen that Anglo-Saxon showed dialectal divisions into Northumbrian, Mercian, Kentish and West Saxon, and that Middle English continued this dialectal division with a Northern, a Southern, and two Midland forms.

Today the dialectal divisions of English continue in part these traditional splits on English soil. But new varieties have sprung up, owing to the departure of the language from its homeland. English speakers from different or the same dialect areas, moving to new lands in the Western Hemisphere, Australia, New Zealand and South Africa, have in the course of time differentiated themselves from those who remained on the British Isles, with the result that one may speak of a "British" English, subdivided into various dialects; of an "American" English, which in the course of three brief centuries has nevertheless had time to evolve varieties of its own; of "Australian," "New Zealand" and "South African" English, in which local dialectal forms are not yet outstanding; and of an entire series of English sub-varieties and Pidgins, born of the attempt on the part of native colonial populations to adapt Imperial or Federal English to their own speech-habits.

There are on British soil at least twenty-four separately identifiable local varieties of speech, most of which are far more divergent among themselves than are corresponding varieties of American speech. To a large extent the English dialects still group themselves around the traditional Middle English divisions (North, South, East Midland, West Midland), with the addition of Scottish, Welsh and Irish adaptations. To some degree, the British dialects are matters of intonation. As one extremely keen American observer, writing for the *Christian Science Monitor,* puts it, "In the west country, you will hear a rich and leisurely burr; in Wales, a melodious attack in the speech, which lends itself to singing; in London, a sharp-witted staccato Cockney; in East Anglia, an odd, almost shy lilt; in the Midlands, a deliberate down-to-earth quality which matches the great central plain; in the North, a hard, vigorous utterance full of dialectal words; in the Northeast, surprisingly, a tongue as soft and gracious as a southern wine; in Scotland and Ireland, a dozen associated accents and dialects, so marked and evocative that you will probably remember them long after the sights that went with them have faded from the mind."

But grammar and vocabulary come in for their innings, too, as a few random examples will show. One Scottish dialect uses *lippen* for "believe," *aboon* for "about," and *till* for "to." Ulster says *yon* and *thon* for "that" and "those," the North has *thee* and *thir* for "these" and "those." Yorkshire has *han, liven* and *shan* for "have," "live" and "shall," and *till* for "while" (this little linguistic peculiarity led to disastrous results when a Yorkshire foreman directed his southern English helper not to build a fire under the boiler "till" it was empty). The Midlands *chilt, ged* and *wod* for "child," "get" and "what" are matters of phonology, but Sussex brings in imagery when it calls big clouds *Hastings ladies,* and sunny weather *a butterfly day.* Equally poetic are Ireland's greeting *a soft mornin' this mornin'* and *to have a long finger* for "to be slow in getting things done."

Of particular interest among Britain's dialects is London's Cockney (the name is said to have originated from the "land of Cockaigne," an imaginary country where the streets were paved with sausages and roast geese). Eric Partridge brings out the interesting fact that south of the Thames the London Cockney dialect is of Kentish origin, while north of the river it stems from the Midland variety of English. Various sixteenth-century spellings show Cockney already in existence at that time (*bylyffe* for "bailiff," *towle* for "toll," *stallyd* for "installed"). He also reminds us that during Britain's three major wars within recent times there has been considerable penetration of the standard language by the dialects, particularly Glasgow and Cockney.

Aside from purely dialectal forms, there exists on the British Isles an object of awe and reverence to its speakers known as the King's English. This linguistic form, favored by all the cultured classes of Britain, is a constant source of wonderment, occasionally mixed with some amusement, to Americans. Along with the American Language, it constitutes perhaps the greatest stumbling-block to Anglo-American unity, for English speakers on both sides of the Atlantic have, in general, deep-seated respect for one another's institutions, in all fields but the linguistic.

The King's (or Queen's) English is based neither on the affected Oxford pronunciation, which many Britishers deplore, nor on the Cockney of London's lower classes. Rather is it the sublimated Londonese of the English aristocracy and upper bourgeoisie, a tongue fashioned out of a mixture of Southern and East Midlands dialects, and refined by centuries of court usage. Though Americans occasionally find it difficult to understand, there is something pleasantly soothing to the ear in its modulated rise and fall and its clipped, incisive, staccato enunciation. Phonetically, its outstanding characteristics are the broad *a* in words like *laugh, dance, vase;* the open *o* of *pot* and *lot;* the *ow*-quality of so-called "long *o*" in words like *bone, stone;* the explosive quality of final consonants, particularly *-t;* and the disappearance of *r* before consonants and in final position. In personal and place-names, the British tendency to drop unstressed syllables occasionally produces astonishing results (*Gloucester* into *Gloster, Auchinlek* into *Afleck*). Differences in the pronunciation of individual words also distinguish it from American English (*clerk* pronounced *clark, been* pronounced as spelled, *leisure* as *lesure, schedule* as *shedule*); so do differences of stress (*nécessary* and *nécessraly, papá, primarily, fináncier, labóratory*), and of spelling (*labour, connexion, defence, gaol, waggon, kerb, programme, tyre, cheque*). Words which in America are more commonly spelled with *-ter* (*theater, center*) in Britain more usually have *-tre* (*theatre, centre*). Characteristically, a *Punch* cartoon reprinted in the *New York Times,* purporting to be a letter from the UN to Brezhnev, shows two spelling differences in fewer than thirty words: *Organisation* and *pretence.*

Grammatical differences are relatively few, save for the fact that the British are normally more careful about their grammar than we are. To cite one or two divergences, the British often prefer a plural verb with a singular collective subject (*Her Majesty's Government are in favour of this measure*); Britishers generally use *do* before *have* only when the action or status is habitual (*Does he have blue eyes?* but *Has he the book?*). The British are far more careful in distinguishing between the past and the present perfect than we are. A phrase like "I just ate" would be interpreted in Britain as "I only ate," with the further implication "I didn't do anything else."

It is in the use of individual words that the most marked differences occur. H. W. Horwill, in his *An Anglo-American Interpreter,* has collected a fairly complete list of the outstanding divergences, and it may be repetitious to cite expressions like *goods waggon* (for freight train), *lines* or *metals* (for tracks), *wage packet* (pay envelope), *hoarding* (sign), *chemist's* (druggist's,) *joint* (roast), *sweet* (dessert). *Shoes* usually mean slippers in Britain, where *boots* mean shoes. A *press cutting agency* is our clipping bureau.

It was recently brought out that motoring in Britain means that you travel on a "dual carriage-way," where the signs say "Halt" instead of "Stop," "Lay-by" for "Recessed space for emergency repairs," "No waiting" for "No stopping," "No overtaking" for "No passing." Other interesting phraseologies are "Road works" (or "diversion") "ahead," "Dead slow" and the grim "You have been warned!"

But there is far, far more. A private garage is a *lock-up garage,* a sharp turn is a *hairpin bend,* a truck trailer is a *transporter,* grounding a wire is *earthing* it, a rental car is a *self-drive hire car,* and a town map is a *street gazetteer.* A *patrolman* is not a policeman on his rounds, but a uniformed official of the R.A.C. (Royal Automobile Club, the equivalent of our A.A.A.) who patrols the roads to render assistance to the stranded motorist. The latter, if he has not made a reservation, may be able to get hotel or motel accommodations *on spec* (for "speculation"). A *full lock* means a full turn of the steering wheel, a *coach tour* our bus tour, a *clean licence* (note the spelling) means no driving offense (or should we spell it *offence?*) on your record, and a taxi driver *plies for hire. Aubergine* means eggplant, *vegetable marrows* are squashes, *chips* are French fries, and *crisps* are our potato chips. A list of British dishes would puzzle the American housewife or restaurant diner: *gooseberry fool, treacle tart, October cobble, drop scones, fidget pie, roastit-bubbly-jock* (this is turkey roasted in a special way), *savoury, banger* (a type of sausage), and, surprisingly, *American salad,* which is described as having among its ingredients sweet corn, pimento, peas, salami, anchovies and mayonnaise.

There are words and expressions for which no proper equivalent exists in American English because the object is not in use. Everyone knows that the British *pub* is only in part the equivalent of our bar, saloon, or cocktail lounge. *Mild and bitter, shandy, stone ginger* are common enough words in British pubs, but they do not mean too much to an American. The British *bob, quid* and *guinea,* being monetary units, have to be translated into dollars and cents; but the British also speak colloquially of a *pony* (25 pounds) and a *monkey* (500 pounds), in much the same way that we refer to a thousand dollars as a *grand.*

As one might well expect, it is in the field of the colloquial, bordering on slang, that many of the most startling differences between the two English languages appear. In Britain a *bouncer* is a *chucker-out,* a *bookie* is a *turf accountant.* In a British *public school* (which is a private school) a professor does not flunk his students, but *ploughs* them. The most common British equivalent for *O. K.* is *righto,* but the British also use *tiggerty-boo,* sometimes given as *tickety-boo,* which comes from Hindustani *teega* and is said to have been introduced to Britain by Lord Mountbatten. Another imported slang word is the Arabic *bint,* "girl," but the native *knitting* is used to denote the feminine sex as a whole; a lively party is called a *snake* in Britain, and *snake charmers* are members of the dance band. *Teed-up* means "all set to start," and a *shaky-do* is an occurrence that has serious consequences. A *poodle-faker* is a gigolo, *to flannel* is "to soft-soap," and what is a "rube" or "hick" to Americans is a *Hodge* to the British. The equivalent of our "scram" is *hop it,* pronounced, however, *'up it!*

In British colloquial, a *punter* is a gambler, and a *stiffener* is a bore. The British equivalent of our hamburger is more often called a *wimpy,* while *Freddies* are hot dogs, and *gob-stoppers* are jawbreakers. To a British juvenile, a *frat* is a girl date. The *Teddy* (or *Elephant*) *boys* of the recent past have been replaced by *Mods* and *Rockers,* with *Stylists* as their feminine auxiliaries. Colloquially, a *fag* is a pal, *jakes* is the rest room, *subtopia* are the suburbs, a *doorstep* is a thick slice of bread. The movies are *flicks,* girls are, among other things, *cookies,* and our all-purpose *guy* is replaced by *show, type,* or *chap. Dust bin* is our ashcan, and *dustman* our garbage collector. Our *ad* is more commonly an *advert,* and "I'll ring you" does service for "I'll call you." N.B.C.'s newscaster is B.B.C.'s *newsreader,* and B.B.C. is often affectionately referred to as *Auntie.*

Among more legitimate expressions that trouble the would-be speaker of a unified English tongue are terms like *fee,* often used in Britain with the meaning of "tip"; *compassionate leave* (our "emergency leave"; members of the American Armed Forces regularly satirize the British expression into *passionate leave*). One of the strangest cases of linguistic misunderstanding across the ocean took place when an American theatrical producer received a wire after the opening night in London, "Posting notices tomorrow." This was despairingly interpreted to mean that the show was closing. But his British partner merely meant that he was mailing some rave reviews! The American director of a show, incidentally, is the British *producer;* while the American producer is the British *manager.*

Lastly, there is that subtle area of word choice. "Keep America clean!" is paralleled by "Keep Britain tidy!"; "Let's go, boys!" becomes "Let's go, lads!"; "I'm on vacation" turns into "I'm on holiday." It isn't as though we didn't have *tidy, lad,* and *holiday* in our vocabulary, or the British didn't have *clean, boy* and *vacation* in theirs; it's simply that we (and they) are accustomed to using different common words in certain set phrases. This can make a Britisher (or an American) just as readily identifiable from his speech as from his spelling, even if the omnipresent distinctive accent were not there to guide us.

But enough of differences. What of the similarities? When one reads of crime in the newspapers, he is unconsciously tempted to think that at least half of all people are criminals. Newspaper accounts do not glorify the millions who lead honest, decent lives; their achievements, socially beneficial as they are, are of scant news value. In like manner, the differences between British and American English, with their appeal to the imagination, are apt to be overstressed. People forget about the thousands of words, sounds, grammatical forms, syntactical constructions to which notice is not drawn because they are exactly alike in both countries. Yet these areas of contact constitute over ninety per cent of both languages. The written tongue is one, though with a few minor spelling divergences; the literature is common to all English-speaking lands; even the spoken tongue differs in only a few particulars.

Furthermore, at the same time that the lexical and grammatical idiosyncrasies of one division have been made abundantly known to the other through the medium of constant reiteration in books and in the press, radio, spoken film and Telstar have brought the speaking habits of Britain within the range of the common American ear, and vice versa.

Let us therefore accent the positive and stress the fundamental unity of the English language, that marvelously resilient tongue that spans oceans and takes mountains and continents in its stride, carrying everywhere it goes the gospel of individual initiative and individual rights, the spirit of fair play and the doctrine of respect for one's fellow-man.

The countries of the British Commonwealth speak each its own tongue, a tongue which is in all cases a direct offshoot from the language and dialects of Britain. In Canada, the American influence is strong, both because Canada was at least partly settled from what is now the United States and because of geographical proximity and ease of communications across an unguarded frontier. In South Africa (now no longer a member of the Commonwealth) the local variety of English has received admixtures not only from the native African Negro languages, but also from the Afrikaans Dutch of the Boers. Australian and New Zealand English have grown up by themselves, uninfluenced save by the native tongues and, of course, the language of the mother country.

Partridge and his associates remind us that the two primary immigrant streams that led to the formation of Canada's English-speaking population came from Scotland and the United States (the latter stream, incidentally, consisted in large measure of American Tories who preferred to continue under British sovereignty when the American colonies seceded from the Empire). Today, the English of Canada is quite homogeneous, and there is a stock linguistic joke to the effect that a Canadian get mistaken for an American in Britain and for an Englishman in the United States. The first portion of this pronouncement impresses us as more truthful than the second. In a British-compiled *Dictionary of Canadianisms* containing approximately one thousand terms, only about three dozen are found which are not common to the United States as well, and the majority of these are jocular localisms concerning the land and people across the border or across the ocean (*gridiron* for the American flag, *Rebel Picnic* for the Fourth of July, *improved Britisher* for an English resident of long standing, *new chum* for a recent arrival; the last is common also to other British Dominions). In spelling, Canada joins America in such words as *tire* and *wagon*, but Britain in *woollen* and *honour*. All in all, Canada, while forming a part of the British Commonwealth, belongs linguistically to the American division of English.

The South African accent is described by Baugh as a mixture of Cockney, Scots and Afrikaans, with a higher pitch than either British or American, unaccented syllables more distinctly pronounced than in Britain, and a few phonetic variants like *pen* for *pin, keb* for *cab,* and *gite, pile, trine* for *gait, pale, train.* Partridge's South African collaborator regretfully informs us that Afrikaans is scoring gains over English, and cites a number of local expressions, some of which are loan-translations from Afrikaans (*Are you coming with?; Shall we sit on the stoop so long?*), while others are straight borrowings, like *apartheid,* the local variety of racial segregation. As in the case of other Commonwealth tongues, many picturesque expressions of South African English, borrowed from Afrikaans, Zulu or other sources, have found their way into literary English. Such is the case with *lager, trek, veld, baas, kraal, sjambok, mealy-meal.* In addition, there are the inevitable localisms, based on custom. Juveniles, for instance, are described as *ducktails* if they are white, *skollys* if "colored" (in South Africa, this means of East Indian or mixed ancestry), *tsotsies* if black.

Australian English is without doubt the most picturesque of the Commonwealth varieties, and the one that has had the best press in the United States. Partridge tentatively advances the theory that the high pitch of Australian may be due to the climate. It may also, however, be an indication of predominantly Cockney ancestry, as indicated also by the universal "long *i*" for "long *a*" (as in *lidy* for *lady*). This phonological characteristic affects what is known as Educated Australian as well as Broad Australian.

The Australian Language Centre of the University of Sydney has compiled a long list of early nineteenth-century Australianisms. These include the well-known *brush* and *bush-ranger*, the use of *paddock* for field and *station* for ranch, the *wallabee*, *wallaroo* and *wayrang* (all kangaroo varieties); nearly sixty other animal, bird and fish names (*dingo, koala, kookaburra, wombat* among them); nearly eighty plant names (including the fruit known as *jibbong*); many terms descriptive of native customs, dwellings and weapons (*corroboree, bunyip, humpy, wurley, woomera*) as well as *rainmaker* (mouth organ), *sneaky Pete* (red wine), *tin* (money), and, of course, *jumbuck* and *Matilda*.

The Australian mind is linguistically creative, like the American. Hence slang terms abound, side by side with native borrowings. *Outback* for frontier, *swagman* for hobo, *sheila* for girl, *shikkered* (originally Yiddish) for plastered, *cobber* for pal, *oscar* for money, *shake* for steal are a few scattered examples of this highly imaginative slang. *'Roo* and *Joey* are the affectionate nicknames bestowed upon the kangaroo, which is the nation's zoological symbol, and its young. Nor must we forget the borrowings from native and foreign languages with which songs and literature have made us acquainted: *billabong, boomerang, cooee, cow* (for which the closest American equivalent is the slang *lousy;* it is possible that this is a loan-translation from French *vache*, similarly used).

To the imaginative Australian mind, a soda fountain is a *milk bar*, a banjo is a *frying-pan*, drowned is *baptized*, a Bronx cheer is a *barrack*, a redhead is a *bushfire blonde*, a schoolteacher *chalk and talker.* There is *cop shop* for police station, *happy returns* for retching, *inked* for drunk, *jam* for affection, *poor wet* for poor dope, *beano* for blowout, *curling the moe* or *dinkum* for on the up and up.

Many of these expressions are shared by New Zealand, which has perhaps a greater proclivity to borrow from the native Maori (*kapai* for atta boy, *paheka* for stranger, *mana* for prestige, *tenakoe* for hello, *kia ora* for good luck). There are Maori names for local dishes: *toheroa, paua* soup, made with shellfish, *tekoteko,* even *Maori skewer.* Expressions like *to be on one's muttons* (on one's guard), *bushwhacked* (beaten), *a bit crook* (somewhat ill), *skite* (brag), *up stick* (move house), *be pie on* (be good at) seem locally developed, though some of them may be found to exist in the British Islands or in Australia. Peculiarities of New Zealand pronunciation include lengthening of final and initial syllables in words like *citee, likelee, eeleven, beefore;* shortening of long *o*-sound in *toll,* and of the *au* in *auction;* and *utt uzz* for "it is."

One consideration offered by Partridge in connection with the tongues of the Commonwealth nations and non-English portions of Britain is that while linguistic nationalism is strong in Ireland, Scotland and Australia, it is little in evidence in Canada, New Zealand and South Africa, and this despite the fact that Canada has dropped "Dominion" from its title, while South Africa has withdrawn from the Commonwealth entirely. We wonder, however, whether linguistic nationalism is not too strong a term to describe a conscious desire for linguistic individuality. Both Irish and Scots can, if they wish, retreat to the mountain fastnesses of their ancestral Gaelic. The fact that they show very little inclination to do so would seem to point to a mere token resistance on their part. As for the Australians, their slangy exuberance is hardly to be interpreted as the forerunner of a separatist movement. Rather is it something on the same order as that great and successful rival of the King's English, the American Language.

Chapter Two

THE AMERICAN LANGUAGE

The Rise of American English—Its Acceptance by the British—Its Dialectal Varieties—The Language of Empire

The arising of American English as a unit has already been described, and the controversies concerning the King's English and the American Language are reserved for a later chapter. Suffice it here to remind our readers that according to most current linguistic theories General American, as current in the Midwest, is supposed to have stemmed from the speech of the North of England, but the current speech-forms of New England (particularly Bostonese) and the South from the southern English shires.

The divergence of American from British English was first noticed around 1750, and by 1800 the first acrimonious discussions had arisen. There were half-hearted attempts on both sides of the ocean to make the divorcement between the two speech-forms complete, but they were, luckily, dismal failures. As late as 1933 the *Shorter Oxford Dictionary* specifically disclaims making allowance for dialectal, colonial or "American" pronunciations, reflecting the uncompromising stand of speakers of the King's English in this matter. Our own older dictionaries, on the other hand, mostly favor a New England pronunciation, which is closest to that of England.

In matters of phonology, it may be remarked that American generally preserves more of a spelling-pronunciation than does English (the influence, perhaps, of schoolmarms and spelling bees). It neglects the obscuring of unstressed vowels and the drastic lopping off of unstressed syllables which is characteristic of British speech. As a by-product, we have secondary stress in long words where the British have none (*interèsting* vs. *int'rest-ing, législàtive* vs. *législative, dictionàry* vs. *dictionary*). This may offend British ears, but it is less disconcerting than pro-nouncing *Cholmondeley* as *Chumley, Beauchamp* as *Beecham,* and *Leicester* as *Lester.* It also, incidentally, proves the power of the written language over the spoken.

The British may not approve of our pronunciation, but they usually subscribe to our vocabulary innovations, perhaps to a greater degree than we subscribe to theirs. It was in vain that the Fowlers, in their *The King's English,* protested against such rank Americanisms as *back of, anyway, standpoint, right along* and *just,* for the British now use them too, as indicated by the more recent Gowers manual. Protests, however, still appear in the *Birmingham Mail* against such American usages as *Oh, yeah?* (meaning "No") and *Come again!* (meaning "Explain yourself"). On the other hand, the list of Americanisms seemingly cleared for British colloquial usage includes not only *sidewalk, hoodlum, Jim Crow, gasoline, G-man* and *josh,* but *hornswoggle, craps, hooch, gat,* and even, in their slang acceptance, *drag, cool, kinky, hot rod, beat, cat* and *bird* (for "girl"; in fact, the British have gone on to translate it into French: *oiseau,* which comes out as *wuzzy*).

It is probable, though not proved, that more vocabulary in-novations have come into the language from American than from British sources in the course of the last three centuries. Baugh, in a long list of American words, gives us the key to this phenomenon. On the one hand, new physical conditions in a new continent call for new words (*clearing, underbrush, garter snake, groundhog, land office, apple butter, sidewalk, hitch-hike, low-down, have an axe to grind, fly off the handle, bury the hatchet*). On the other hand, Americans were in contact with foreign languages more than their British cousins during the period of colonization and wholesale immigration. The Indians gave us *porgy, succotash, wampum, wigwam, sachem,* and such loan-translations as *warpath, paleface* and *medicine man.* From the French we got *portage, chowder, cache, bayou, levee;* from the Dutch *cole slaw, cookie, boss* and *scow;* from the Germans *noodle, pretzel* and *sauerkraut;* from the Negroes *banjo, hoodoo, jazz,* from the Chinese *kowtow, fantan, tong* and *yen;* from the

Jews *kosher* and *mazuma*. Our own coinage gave us *nickels* and *dimes* and *dollars* and *eagles* after eighteenth-century *marks* and *quints* had disappeared. M. M. Mathews, who has gathered in his *Dictionary of Americanisms* no less than fifty thousand words and terms, has traced the history of most of those American contributions to the common language, showing, among other things, that Admiralty Island Indians (Hutsnuwus tribe) gave rise to a crude firewater called, after them, *kootznehoo,* and later *hooch;* that *appendicitis* and *moron* were born on American soil; and that we too, despite the briefness of our national history, can render words obsolete. Many reputed Americanisms, when tracked down, have been found to be of British origin. Mathews, for example, discovered that the term *cracker* as applied to poor whites in the South has the original meaning of "boaster," "braggart," which is a Scottish usage. *Ain't,* of course, is found on English soil at least as far back as Shakespeare, and the same applies to *without* for *unless.*

More recently, a long list of idioms coined on American soil (many accepted and adopted by the British) includes *shotgun wedding, to make a bee-line, mad as a hornet, to play possum, to work like a beaver, to bark up the wrong tree, chip on one's shoulder, cross as a bear, to settle someone's hash, horse sense, stag party, to pull up stakes, to do a land-office business, dead beat, corn belt, stamping ground, hired hand, to talk turkey, to kick like a steer, to hold one's horses, boom and bust, assembly line, trouble-shooter, sweat-shop, lockout, cooling-off period, take-home pay, white collar, priming the pump, pork barrel, to slice a melon, dark horse, favorite son, lame duck, to sit on the fence, landslide.* A similar list of individual words, starting with forms that have achieved full and undisputed respectability (*reliable, talented, influential, lengthy*), goes on to *bulldoze, caboodle, cantankerous, highfalutin, rambunctious, splendiferous, spondulicks,* and finishes off with *boondoggling, gobbledegook,* and Truman's 1952 *snollygoster.* There can be no question concerning the creativity of Americans.

Intriguing as are the dialects of Old World English, those of American are at least as fascinating. Twenty-four major varieties have been listed, and Linguaphone recordings of them have been duly made under the direction of Columbia University phoneticians. (These recordings are said to be of special practical value to traveling salesmen.) The scientific study of American dialects began in 1889 with the American Dialect Society, and its principal milestones are Mencken's *American Language* of 1919, the quarterly *American Speech,* G. P. Krapp's monumental *English Language in America* of 1925, the University of Chicago's *Historical Dictionary of American English,* and the *Linguistic Atlas of the United States,* directed by Hans Kurath and numerous associates.

Insofar as it is possible to condense the mass of findings accumulated by these scholars, it may be said that American speech-forms have three major groupings, an Eastern, a Southern and a Midwestern or General American (more recent maps, based on indefatigable field work, show as many as ten major regional dialect areas); but within each group variations are numerous and profound, and large cities like New York, Boston and Philadelphia have developed many local peculiarities.

The work of the *Linguistic Atlas* in particular has revealed interesting by-facts, such as the migration routes of our earliest settlers, and the existence of focal or "prestige" areas whose speech is admired and imitated in the surrounding country. Characteristic of the first is the cattle-call *chay,* used around Williamsburg, South Carolina, and duplicated only in County Antrim, Ireland, from which the original Williamsburg settlers must have come; the *pavement* (sidewalk) of Philadelphia, betraying the conservatism of that city in keeping the British word; the *smearcase* of Pennsylvania (from the German *Schmierkäse*) as opposed to the Hudson Valley *potcheese* (from Dutch *potkaas*), and the western New England *Dutch cheese,* an evident coinage.

Both New England and the South drop final *-r,* which the West retains. This parallels the development of the Southern British dialects as against the North of England, and would seem to fit the area migration theory. Clark, however, advances the possibility that final *-r* may at one time have been universal in American speech, and that the South and East, being in touch with Southern England, may have dropped it in imitation of the official pronunciation of the home country, while the Midwest, which had lost its overseas contacts, firmly retained the -r. New England, however, inserts a parasitic r in such expressions as *I sawr 'im,* which the South generally does not do. The open sound of *o* appears in the New England pronunciation of *fog, hot, coffee, long,* the broad *a*-sound in *ask, grass, bath,* the short sound of *u* in *proof.* The South, on the other hand, tends to drop final consonants in words like *find* and *kept,* and to diphthongize open *e* (*fin', kep', yais, aigg*). Other vowel distinctions separate the West from both East and South (typical key words are *wash, fog, daughter, house, bird,* and the now notorious *merry, Mary, marry,* where a threefold distinction prevails east of the Alleghanies, but not to the west).

But the main American dialectal distinctions are in vocabulary. An extreme case reported by the *Linguistic Atlas* is the name of the insect generally known as a "dragon-fly"; in New England it is a *devil's darning needle,* in parts of New Jersey a *spindle,* in the Pennsylvania German country a *snake waiter,* in the Appalachians a *snake feeder,* while in other parts of the South it is a *snake doctor* or *mosquito hawk. Closet, outhouse, bull* are words to be avoided in certain areas of the United States; for the last, there is an entire series of euphemisms: *he-brute, stock cow,* even *gentleman cow* and *preacher cow. Evening* is synonymous with *afternoon* in some Southern rural districts. Imaginative are *chicken hollerin' time* for early morning and *greenup time* for Spring. Sections of New Jersey use *blickey* for "bucket." The differences between *bag, sack,* and *poke* are geographical; so are those between *carry* and *tote,* (city) *block* and *square, calling up* and *phoning up.* In South Dakota, you *don't belong to get up* till 9 A.M. A grocery-store sign advertising *mangoes* in the Midwest does not imply an offer of tropical fruit, but only of green peppers. A heavy rain is a *gully-washer, frog-strangler* or *chunk floater,* depending on your location, and Midwestern weather bureaus have been known to speak of "slow and gentle *sizzle-sozzle*" instead of "drizzle" (the South would probably call it *falling weather*). Oklahoma requests you not to "*cabbage on* to me every time I pass," and Philadelphia restaurants and food-stores have a widely advertised *hoagy* which on investigation turns out to be a real he-man sandwich (*hero sandwich* or *submarine sandwich* in New York). *Get shut of* and *jin* are still occasionally heard in the Midwest for "get rid of" and "do odd jobs." West Virginia describes a Ph.D. as a *"teach-doctor,* not a real doctor."

In connection with the American dialects, the less said about grammar the better. One grammatical feature of general interest is the so-called "generous plural," represented in the South by *you-all* (for which there is Biblical precedent in Job 17:10), in eastern cities by *youse,* with an intermediate *you-uns,* and a localized *mongst-ye* heard on Albemarle Sound and in Norfolk. The humorous features of American dialectal grammar are illustrated by Uncle Remus' "You er what you is, en you can't be no is-er"; by the spurious weather report "It blew and snew and then it thew, and now, by jing, it's friz"; and by the seemingly authentic apology of a farmer who was being chided for driving past a friend on the highway without any sign of recognition: "If I'd knowed it wuz you, I'd a retch out an' wove!" More seriously, the Center for Applied Linguistics brings out the semantic difference between Negro dialect *he sick* (temporary condition) and *he be sick* (chronic illness).

The Linguaphone Institute once conducted a poll to ascertain where, from the standpoint of diction, the best English in America is spoken. The three winners were Washington, Nashville and Boston, with New York proudly holding last place.

This naturally leads us to a discussion of the linguistic situation in the nation's greatest metropolis, and particularly in its most picturesque and best-beloved borough, Brooklyn. To begin with, Brooklynites are accused of sharing with County Kerry Irishmen the characteristic of never answering a question directly, but only by asking another ("Do you think the Mets will win the pennant?" "Why shouldn't they?"; "What do you think of the Vietnam situation?" "What am I, a TV commentator?").

The three major criticisms levelled against untutored Brooklyn phonology are: 1) the double substitution of *er* for *oi* and *oi* for *er,* as in *Soiving the Erster,* or *Let us adjoin to the adjerning room;* 2) the intrusion of a parasitic hard *g* after *ng* and

before a vowel, as in *Long Guyland,* or *getting gout;* 3) the substitution of *d* for the *t* and voiced *th* sounds in *city, little, the,
them,* etc., and of *t* for unvoiced *th* in *threw, third.* In grammar,
there are such triple negatives as "an' I don' never git no
breaks." It may be remarked that these features are by no means
restricted to Brooklyn, or even to Greater New York.

These and similar characteristics have led a Representative
from Texas to remark that New York "isn't an English-speaking
place," a statement which drew not merely hot retorts from New
York language authorities, but also a jocular *Voyager's Language
Guide* containing such expressions as *Pahrmee* (described as a
translation from the French *pardonnez-moi*), *lemeawf* (an expression said to be often helpful in debarkation from the subway) and *aniainfoolin* (interpreted as "This, I want you to understand, is an order.").

Defenders of the New York speech and its Brooklyn sub-variety
were at pains to point out that *goil* is a better rendering than
the *gel* or *gairl* of Britain, that an "ultimate *r*" gets added to the
Oxford and Harvard as well as to the Brooklyn pronunciation
of *India* and *law,* and that Brooklyn contractions of the type of
gumnt and *jeet* for *government* and *did you eat* go *pari passu*
with Britain's syncopated *Chumley* and *Lester.*

"Brooklynese," said Dr. Bender, "is no upstart. It has a fine
tradition going back to the early Dutch burghers. Despite its
age, it is still virile and is spreading." Former Bronx Borough
President Lyons, riding forth gallantly to the defense of the New
York-Brooklyn speech, charged that "some Texans speak a language no one understands."

But this, too, is an exaggeration. Practically all Americans
understand one another, even if, according to the Linguaphone
survey, "their speech-patterns are typical of the lazy South," as in
Atlanta, or "they sound as though they are being chased by
gangsters," as in Chicago; or "they speak as if they had hot
potatoes in their mouths," as in Los Angeles.

What is more, they generally manage to understand their
British, Canadian, Australian, South African and New Zealand
cousins. The English language is fundamentally one, and one it
will remain while the institutions of the English-speaking world

stand. The language is one of empire—not the empire of physical domination and brute force, but the empire of individual freedom and achievement, of tolerance and consideration for others; in brief, of what a great political leader has chosen to call "the Empire of the Mind."

Chapter Three

USES AND ABUSES ABROAD

The Spawn of English—Foreign Influences, Cultured and Uncultured—What English Does to Foreigners—What Foreigners Do to the Language—English Abroad and Its Vagaries

When pidgin English is mentioned, one's thoughts run immediately to the uncouth Melanesian variety that was so widely publicized during the Solomons campaigns of World War II. In reality, there are as many varieties of pidgin as there are localities where a compromise language had to be evolved between English-speaking settlers, colonizers, traders or missionaries and a foreign-speaking native population. The word *pidgin* is a Cantonese corruption of English "business," and the term originated in the South China trade ports. Pidgin is English adapted to other habits of thought, syntax and pronunciation; but these are far from the same everywhere, and the same applies to pidgin.

We may note at this point that there are numerous pidgins of other tongues as well as of English: the pidgin or "bazaar" Malay of Indonesia and Malaya, the *petit nègre* of the French-speaking West African countries, the Portuguese pidgins of India and Africa, the Spanish-Tagalog pidgin of the Philippines, the Papiamento of Curaçao, the French Creole of Haiti and Mauritius, all fall to some extent under the pidgin classification. But there are probably more varieties of English pidgin than of any other pidginized tongue.

Chinese-English pidgin often reflects Chinese syntax combined with an English vocabulary: *larn-pidgin* for "apprentice," *top-side* for "chief," *two piecee* for "two," referring to objects; *two fella* for "two," referring to persons.

From China, the pidgin habit spread quickly to the South

Seas, giving rise to the pidgin *par excellence,* the variety current
in the Melanesian Islands. In some localities this linguistic form
has become fully standardized, and rules of grammar and syntax
have been devised for it. Here we find expressions like *put clothes
belong-a table* (set the table); *what for you kinkenau knife belong
me?* (why did you swipe my knife?).

New Guinea, with its two million primitives and hundreds
of native languages, has its own variety of pidgin, represented by
kiranki cuss-cuss (irritable office-worker), *long long along drink*
(drunk). So have the Blackfellows of Australia, with their *sing-
'im-along-dark-fella* (mosquito), *kill-'im-stink-fella* (disinfectant);
think-fella-too-much (intellectual), *big-fella-talk-talk-watch-'im-
that-one* (high-pressure salesman). The Tahiti and Samoa vari-
ties (Bêche-la-Mer, Sandalwood English) have expressions like
water-belong-stink for perfume and *belly-belong-me-walk-about-
too-much* (I have a stomach-ache).

But one must not think that the natives of Melanesia, New
Guinea and Australia all use pidgin. Some are fairly well educated. Here is an excerpt from a letter written by Papuan natives
to an Australian official: "Oh dear, dear, please Mr. Woodward
the labor boys want £½ a week because no rations are received.
If you pay up we stay. Otherwise look out." Official English could
be a lot worse.

In West African pidgin, a man who has been to Britain is
known as a *been to;* one who owns his own car or refrigerator is
a *carful* or *fridgeful.* Nigeria, which goes a little further, has
coined the combination *bintojaguarfridgeful* for the lucky person
who combines all these attributes. Being education-conscious, it
also has *megotbuk* for a man who has finished grade school and
bigbigbuk for a college graduate. Sierra Leone has actually produced a pidgin called Krio, spoken by perhaps 25,000 people,
which has an English base, overtones from French and Portuguese, and admixtures from at least seventeen native languages,
which have even contributed their significant tones. Since Krio
is used as a semi-official tongue, a dictionary is being prepared
by a linguistic commission.

American insular possessions have embraced English in a big,
generous way. A Samoan chief recently deplored the increasing

corruption of the native tongue in the mouths of younger generation Samoans, who have adopted American slang and colloquialisms, thereby discrediting Samoan dignity. The state of Hawaii, which boasts of an English that is almost pure, nevertheless inserts native expressions like *kamaaina* (old-timer), *malihini* (greenhorn), *wahini* (woman), *pilikia* (trouble), *wikiwiki* (quick) and, of course, the inevitable *aloha, lei, luau* and *hukilau*.

In parts of southeastern Asia and the islands of Indonesia, a form of English pidgin has been evolved whereby canapés are known as *short eats,* and certain nouns take the common Malay suffix *-lah* ("I like noodles-lah"). A more authentic pidgin is that spoken on Norfolk Island, off the coast of Australia, by Pitcairn Islanders who were resettled on Norfolk. While the majority of them speak fairly good Australian English, they reserve for use among themselves a form of rural English argot which their ancestors brought to Pitcairn, mixed with a good deal of Tahitian.

In India, where the language question is at all times acute, there is, in addition to the Hobson-Jobson (or Anglo-Indian dialect) interspersed in the English of the colonizers, a form of Indian English which has had the honor of a debate in the *India Times,* and which S. P. K. Gupta has defended as a distinctive variety of English, similar to the American. Typical of this *babu* English are expressions such as *you-all,* leading to *this-all, a fun, rupees ten, to marry with, to travel sixty miles as the cock crows, as if* (used where American would use a sarcastic "That's what *you* think!"). An aunt is referred to as a *cousin mother.* Other choice expressions are "What is your good name?"; "Don't blame my name"; "Why did you come here, simply?"; "I know him only personally" (by sight); "I'm not empty now" (I'm busy).

Western Hemisphere varieties of pidgin English include the Ningre-Tongo (or Talkie-Talkie) of Surinam, in the Dutch West Indies, the blend of English and French used on the island of St. Lucia, and, most interesting to Americans, the Gullah used by some twenty-five thousand speakers of the South Carolina coast. This dialect, containing over four thousand African words, is a blend of English with two Liberian languages brought to the

South by the earliest slaves. Many words from Gullah have penetrated the standard American speech, among them *goober*
(Liberian *guba*), *biddy-biddy* for chick (a general name for bird
in Congolese), *jigger* (from *jiga*), *juke* ("wild time" in Senegalese),
tote, etc.

It is perhaps unfair to refer to the language of Trinidad and
Jamaica as a pidgin, since cultured natives of those islands not
only speak a highly cultivated English, but compose in it their
inimitable calypsos. But the names of some of the instruments
in their steel bands (*tock-tock, shac-shac, boom, ping-pong*) may
have been imported from Africa, and some of the natives themselves occasionally come out with linguistic creations like *freeness*
(liberality), and *don't worry with me.* Interestingly, the Trinidad
calypso was originally a French *patois,* which only gradually
turned into English. As late as 1890, the words of a calypso
sample run: "Captain Gaba 'bas moi un passage souplay / Pour
montrer you qui la roi moi ay."

Chinook Jargon, an Indian-English pidgin formerly current in
the Northwest, is perhaps the best known of our continental
pidgins. But in a sense, all our traders and settlers who com-
municated with the Indians on the basis of *heap big chief, fire
water, squaw, papoose, paleface* and *plentum* were definitely
using a brand of pidgin. The Chinook variety, once widely
spoken from Oregon to Alaska, grew up around the trading posts
of the Hudson Bay Company, being used especially in communication between English, French and Indian speakers. A few of its
expressions still survive: *chee-cha-ko,* "newcomer," "greenhorn";
skukum, "strong" (still used as the name of a brand of apples);
Siwash, "Indian" ("old Siwash," the name of an imaginary Alma
Mater). In Chinook, *wawa* is "to speak"; *tum tum* is "heart," but
also "to think"; *naika tilicum* is "our people" or "friends";
klakauya is a common greeting; French influence is betrayed by
lelang, "language" and *lema,* "hand"; while *alki* means "after
a while," but if the first syllable is prolonged, "after a long
while."

Some wish to see a social significance in pidgin. Others go so
far as to prophesy that pidgin English is a vehicle of communication for the future. To our mind, pidgin is a natural linguistic

phenomenon, not at all peculiar to English, which proves nothing, save that the English language has gotten around in the past. It is not likely that pidgin will spread further. Rather, with the spreading of literacy and education, it is probable that the speakers of the various forms of pidgin will go on to assimilate good English, or a reasonable facsimile thereof.

Meanwhile, the use of English in pidgin form adds an undetermined number of marginal speakers to the vast English-speaking population—perhaps as few as ten million, perhaps as many as thirty million.

Historical episodes of resistance to the English language on the part of foreign speakers exist. William the Conqueror, who vainly tried to learn the tongue of his new conquest, George I, who ruled Britain for three years without learning to speak or write the language, and George III, who preferred his ancestral German, are examples. But these are exceptions that prove the rule. Foreigners who are introduced to the English language normally wax enthusiastic about it and love to use it.

It is a fact, established by abundant observation, that when two foreigners in America attempt to communicate with each other, they habitually do so in English; this is true, surprisingly, not only when they know each other's national language, but even when they come from the same country but from different dialect areas. English seems to provide an ideal means of international intercourse.

It has also been noted that foreigners who learn English well frequently either forget their own language or handle it in such a way that it no longer sounds native to their fellow-countrymen.

There are other ways in which the English language does things to foreigners—untranslatable expressions, like the "What's cooking?" that troubled foreign UN delegates who thought they spoke perfect English, or words like *supermarket, smog* and *bebop,* for the proper translation of which a specialized Spanish Copywriters' Association has sprung up.

In a survey conducted at one time at Washington Irving High School in New York it was discovered that less than forty-four per cent of the four thousand four hundred students had native-born fathers. Sixty-six separate nations beyond America's continental borders were found to have contributed to the school's population. Among the more unexpected were Albania, Cyprus, the Dodecanese Islands, Gibraltar, Malta, New Zealand, South Africa and Tasmania, while the students' home languages ranged all the way from Italian, Spanish, French, Chinese, German, Greek, Polish, Russian and Yiddish to Gaelic, Arabic, Bulgarian, Hindustani, Latvian and Rumanian. This will serve to give some indication of the extent of the language problem that has been troubling the United States since colonial days.

But Britain is far from free from the same language problem. In a British census, the questionnaires had to be printed in English, Welsh, Polish, German, French and Italian.

The question therefore legitimately arises: "What do the foreigners do to our language?" Do they exert upon it the sort of influence that was wielded by the Danes and the Normans in medieval times? Or is their contribution limited to individual words which we borrow from them, plus a number of immigrant "dialects" which disappear in two or three generations, supplying vaudeville humor and little else while they endure?

There are numerous theories concerning the influence of the Dutch in the Brooklyn interchange of *oi* and *er,* that of the African Negroes in the formation of the sounds of our southern speech, that of Italian immigrants in the creation of such cut-down forms as *delish* or *ambish*. But they are largely unproved. Under the pressure of English-language schooling and the desire for social prestige and economic advancement, the immigrant tongues seem to vanish with little or no trace, save in localities where the immigrants are in such absolute majorities as to be able to retain their native tongues. But even under these circumstances there seems to be a transitional stage, a form of pidgin which eventually debouches into standard English.

There is, for example, on the Mexican border a linguistic form known as *pochismo* (from the Spanish *pocho,* "discolored"), in which Spanish is interlarded with such English borrowings as *bebi* (baby), *yaque* (jack), *lonche* (lunch), *pene* (penitentiary), *traque* (track) and *huachar* (to watch). In certain of our mountain states reside communities of Basque sheepherders who are said to have created a new language based on English words adapted to Basque flections. Our so-called Pennsylvania Dutch (really a Pennsylvania German, since its speakers came originally from the Palatinate) is a mixture of German and English. But these pidgins are eventually destined to go the way of all pidgins, and their American-born speakers to become speakers of American English pure and simple.

H. L. Mencken, in his *American Language,* has given an excellent description of the immigrant pidgins of his generation, fluctuating, unstable languages that resulted from the attempt of foreign speakers to compromise between the sounds, words and grammatical forms of their native tongues and those of English.

For what concerns sounds, it seems established that it is the two *th-* sounds of English, as heard in *thing* and *this,* that cause most trouble to continental Europeans, since they do not exist in most continental languages. The nearest approximation to the voiced *th* is either *z* (*zees, zat*) or *d* (*dees, dat*), while unvoiced *th* is generally rendered as a dental *t* (*ting*).

Next in difficulty come the short vowels of English, particularly the *i* of *bit* (confused with *beet*), the *oo* of *good* (given the sound of *food*), and the *u* of *cut* (pronounced as open *o;* continental Europeans are normally unable to differentiate between *hall* and *hull*). Speakers of languages where the majority of words end in vowels find our consonant endings difficult, and insert a glide-vowel.

The difficulties encountered with English by foreign speakers (particularly of Romance tongues) are best illustrated by three episodes. A Havana newspaper, endeavoring to teach English songs to its readers, gave the following transcription of the pronunciation of one of them: "Iu most rimembar dis, e kis is stil e kis; e saig is chost e saig; di fondamental zings aplai es taim gos bai." A French singer at the British Court wrote out for himself the following reminder of English pronunciation: "Si-ted ouan dei at dhi or-ganne; Ai ouaz oui-ri an dil ah tiz; ahnd mai fin-gerz, ouann-der daid-li-o-vaire dhi no-izi kis." Lastly, here is an Italianized version of *Jack and the Beanstalk:* "Uans apanne taim uasa boi neime Giacche. I uorche anne fam, milche di cause, fidde cichense—itse toffe laif."

Loan-translations from foreign tongues account for much immigrant humor. The French-born professor who inquired whether his voice reached the students "in the bottom of the room," the Italian who complained that he was being made to pay "perfumed prices," the French Canadian who lamented that he was "unbuttoned" (found out), and that "this was another pair of shoes" (a horse of another color) are always good for a laugh.

What about grammar and syntax? Here are two samples culled on the subway: "Is enough he's making after all a living," and "So he's my boss, so what he's my boss? It gives him a right he should talk that way?"

One of the earliest examples of cultured perpetrations upon the English language, antedating by centuries France's *Malbrough* for Marlborough, occurs in Canto X of Ariosto's *Orlando Furioso,* which describes the English barons about to set forth for the Crusade. Their names are given in detail, but it is doubtful if any English speaker outside of a literary expert would recognize them. Lancaster becomes *Lincastro* in the Italian poet's language, Warwick is *Varvecia,* Kent is *Cancia,* Northumberland *Norbelandia.* Berkeley (this one is almost phonetically transcribed) is *Berclei,* but *Battonia* for Bath, *Sormosedia* for Somerset, *Burgenia* for Abergavenny, *Croisberia* for Shrewsbury and *Angoscia* (which in Italian means "anguish") for Angus are beyond the pale of understanding.

Since that time, the English language has constantly been the victim of similar attempts. In the late eighteenth century there is the case of the Dutch-speaking minister of six collegiate churches in Brooklyn whose English was so imperfectly assimilated that when he once attempted the marriage service in English, instead of saying, "I pronounce you man and wife and one flesh," he came out with, "I pronounce you two to be one beef."

In more modern times, and further down the educational ladder, a Canary Islander engages in a bout with the tongue of Shakespeare that leaves a shambles of dangling participles and ruptured infinitives in its wake. To quote from his communication: "I have the honour of direct to you for the medium of the present for petition of favor of that I believe I shall be please . . .

and I desire unite to this the of the great ss of your worthy direction." This is only the beginning of trouble for Spanish speakers of English. A hotel in Colombia announces: "The price of one day with all services of rigour is $4. The other expenses are separate count"; while a Mexican grocer in Cuernavaca replied to the inquiry whether some eggs were available: "No smeggs today." An Italian book reviewer writes in English: "He is very delighted of being so. The author not always keep himself into well defined limits." The announcement of an Italian scientific publication says in part: "We have much pleasure in informing you of the publication of the second volume. The first volume dealt with the reviviscence of heroic ideal within the sphere of Humanism." The boat landing at Stresa announces: "Departure all 30 minutes," while a sign on the Venice-Milan *autostrada* warns the English-speaking motorist: "Cars are forbidden to invert direction" (we would say, more briefly: "No U-turn"). Paris signs announce: "Car reput in condition to be driven," "Corn Flak" and "Frieds Eggs," and a Parisian love letter reads in part: "Since our meeting, do you forget yourself of me, or think to me a few?" A similar letter, composed by a Czech, says: "Today, my heart is really fulfilled with joy . . . and with freed, renuvelated energy I shall serve there, where I shall be asked to do it." A Paris liquor ad states: "You are allowed a case of 5 bottles per person inclusive the babies." A French Cajun speaker once declared solemnly: "You can work us as fifty by ourselves, but never one in a bunch."

Japan advertises "Sudden Service" and notifies motorists "Right turn toward immediate outside," "May parking and stopping," "Press the breaking of the feet as you reel around the corner." Calcutta says: "Come in and be homely"; a Bangkok newspaper advertises: "The news of English we tell the latest; do a mighty chief die we publish it and in borders of somber." A Baghdad hotel has the signs: "Entrance In"; "Entrance Out." A Thursday Island laundry announces: "We most cleanly and carefully wash our customers with cheap prices as under." A Greek guerrilla leader once informed his British allies: "We are resolved to die till one." A Liberian paper has it: "This is not for pleasuring" and "They threw a vex."

What really hurts is to see our language mangled by kindred Germanic speakers. Both these excerpts are from letters written to the *New York Herald-Tribune,* by a German and a Dane, respectively. The first says in part: "We took us a map from America and we bethout ourselves a fine plan for a yourney . . . we hope our wishes become on this wise true." The second runs: "It is my plan to brake enny Record there ever is made by small segelbowts . . . I'm a Dane and Blacksmith of trade, 50 years all, and I've never seglet a segelbowt before over 20 miles."

But why go further with this dreary tale of murder and rape done by supposedly cultured people to a harmless language? Consider this passage from the English translation of Hindemith's *Marienleben,* and *ab uno disce omnes:* "Later it came to her how she him in upon his way had closed; for was he not now very wonder-doer?"

There is a serious counterpart to all this authentic tomfoolery, and it consists of that portion of the English vocabulary which has in recent years penetrated the various tongues with which it has come in contact. Part of it stems from cultured influences, part from sports, part from commercialism, part from the tongue of the G.I.'s in their world travels.

Even before the war, the languages of Europe and Asia had borrowed copiously from English. French, for instance, had adopted *baby, bridge, club, sandwich, film, wagon,* while *boxe* and *bouledogue* had undergone spelling modifications. A popular French cigarette of the first decade of the century was called *High-Life* (pronounced, however, *Heeg-Leaf*). Then came such words as *gangster, steak* (used in the place of the older loan-word *bifteck*), *des shorts, le bebop, un bikini, starlette, boyfriend, les yeux swing* ("swing eyes" whatever that may mean), *nioulouque* ("new look" to you), *bestseller, groggy, racket, covergirl.*

The most recent waves of French borrowings from English, however, show three processes that betoken thinking that is at least in part independent: phonetic adaptation, recombination of elements, and loan-translation instead of straight borrowing. Typical of the first are *teuf, sexi, rimèque, trilleur* ("tough," "sexy," "remake," "thriller"). The second is indicated by *jazz hot, restoroute, libre-service, télé-spectateur* (the last three are part borrowings from road restaurant, self-service, TV viewer). There are also the Parisian so-called *ye-ye* magazines, devoted to rock-and-roll (the title of one of them is *Salut les Copains!*, which may be freely retranslated as "Hi, Pals!"). The last is in part illustrated by the new baseball terminology: *un but, deux buts, but sur balles, arrêt-court, cambrioler, blanchissage* (one base, two bases, base on balls, shortstop, to steal, shut-out, though the literal meaning is "laundering"). The same loan-translation process appears in Italian (*rubata, tiro pazzo, doppio incontro, raccattamazza* for steal, wild throw, double-header, batboy); and by Spanish (*incogible*, literally "uncatchable," for hit; *jardinero corto*, literally "short gardener," for shortstop; *guardabosque*, literally "forest warden," for fielder). In this connection, Japanese prefers word-borrowing with phonetic adaptation (*picha, boru, purete, batta, hitto, suturaiku*, for pitcher, ball, plate, batter, hit, strike; remember that a medial or final *u*, while it appears in transcription, is practically inaudible in spoken Japanese, so that *suturaiku* sounds far more like "strike" than its appearance would indicate).

Germany speaks today of *ice creme* (kept distinct from the native *Eis*); *party*, in the festive sense; *drink* (*ich möchte ein Drink haben*). Curious are the wanderings of *frankfurter* and *hamburger*, once brought into English from German, now returned to Germany, where they usurp the place held by *Wiener Wurst* and *Fleischpflänzchen*. German civilians working for the American occupation forces no longer described themselves as *eingestellt* or *entlassen*, but as *ge-hired* and *ge-fired*, and their conversation with G.I.'s swarmed with such phrases as "Macht" (or "mox") "nix to me!" ("It makes no difference to me!"), "That's for bestimmt!" ("That's for sure!"), "Get raus!" ("Get out!") and "Let's go essen!" ("Let's go eat!"). German musical pieces are replete with expressions like *boogie woogie* and *hillbilly*, and German sporting pages with *team* and *comeback*. *Job, lift, jeep, hitchhike* have become part of the German vocabulary.

Italy had already rendered *cold cream* and *football* by *colcrem* and *futbol* before the war. The American occupation of Italy brought about an Italo-American pidgin in which Italian verbs were used invariably in the infinitive, but some English verbs were taken over and given the Italian infinitive ending (*brekkare,* "to break"; *spiccare,* "to speak"; *gangsterare,* "to run a black market"). *Tegedizi* and *tumorro* represented "take it easy" and "tomorrow," but the latter was used by the Italians as an adjective to mean "lazy," "slow" ("*È il funzionario più tumorro di tutto l'accampamento.*" "He is the laziest official in the whole camp"). More recent Italian appropriations are *buki buki* (boogie woogie), *pulova* (pull-over), and *gomma americana* (bubble gum, as distinguished from ordinary gum, which is *ciuinga*). But Italian has developed the elegant *autostoppista* for "hitchhiker."

A study of issues of the Japanese daily *Asahi* reveals the following recent borrowings, among others: *disuku jokii* (disc jockey), *surogan* (slogan), *kosto, sumogu* (smog), *baransu* (balance), *semento* (cement), *pama* (permanent), *sutereo* (stereo), *depaato* (department store), *supiido* (speed), *misairu* (missile), *supu pauda* (soup powder), *teirumu* (tearoom), *niyu sutairu* (new style). There are *gohe* (go ahead), *orai* (all right), *bakapu* (back up). There is the charming blend *jazu kichigai* (jazz crazy). But not all Japanese innovations come from English. *Arubeito* (German *Arbeit,* "work") does duty for "side job." *Abekku,* "date," is French *avec,* "with." Also French are *kokuuru* (*concours,* "contest") and *bakansu* (*vacances,* "vacation"). In addition, Japanese is Japanizing the names of some sports: golf, which used to be *gorafu,* is now *zokyu* (literally "strike ball"), and rugby, once *ragubi,* has become *yakyu,* "fight ball." Two charming transcriptions are *kurosu wurudo pasaru* (cross-word puzzle) and the widely advertised *007-Sandaboru,* our "Thunderball."

Spanish had many English words such as *líder,* for "political chief." The Mexican variety had added *coctel* (cocktail), *lleñeral* (ginger ale), *te y ponque* (tea and pound cake), *brecas* (brakes), *sandwich spred*. The Chinese, in pre-Mao days and on Formosa, have been known to use *p'u k'e* for poker, *yu meh* for humor, *te lu feng* for telephone; but on the continent they have switched to the native *hsiao hwa* ("laugh talk") and *tien hwa* ("lightning talk") for the last two. Swedish has borrowed *petting,* Hindi has taken "damn cheap" and turned it into *dam chee*. Even Russian calls a beauty shop *amerikanka* (literally "American woman").

In the days immediately following World War II, the two English words that appeared in practically all languages were "O.K." and "nylon." The latter had even become a sort of synonym of "superfine" in Greek and Turkish. Barnett, who has made a special study of the English words most used in foreign lands, gives us a list which still includes "O.K.," but excludes "nylon." Other words, arranged alphabetically rather than by preference, are: *baby-sitter, bar, beefsteak* (but this is an old favorite, long antedating the war), *best seller, boy-friend, bridge, bus, cocktail, cover girl, cowboy, gangster, goddam, hamburger, holdup, hot dog, ice cream, jazz, jeep, juice, knockout, night-club, party, pinup, pipeline, racket, sandwich, sex appeal, shorts, strip-tease, week-end, whiskey.*

This list lends itself to the melancholy reflection that other nations seem to have taken the worst and most materialistic aspects of our life to their hearts. It also lends itself to the anti-English movement of which the standard-bearer is Etiemble, the fiery French writer who has raised the standard of anti-English revolt in his *Parlez-vous franglais?,* a book in which he unmercifully castigates those Frenchmen (and Frenchwomen) who seem inclined to turn the French-speaking world into an Anglo-American colony more abject, perhaps, than the old colonial African and Asian possessions of European powers, because it is based squarely on the cultural element. It is a pity that this book has not to date found an English or American publisher, because from it we would learn precisely what it is that foreigners object to in us and our influence. The objections have been repeated, in more dignified fashion, by Spain's venerable writer and scholar Ramón Menéndez-Pidal, and *Franglais* has been parodied into *Pinglish* in Israel and *Panglish* in Oriental areas where the institution of the *pang pang girl* exists.

From these charges of cultural imperialism we defend ourselves as best we can. If French, Spanish, Italian, German and Japanese are becoming surfeited with English borrowings, it is well to remind our critics, particularly the French, that at an earlier historical period they, too, invaded the premises of the English language and left their mark. When a writer complained in a letter to the *New York Times* that too many Frenchmen were becoming deeply concerned over the growing number of English words creeping into their language, I composed the following letter, which also found its way into the *Times* pages:

"Monsieur le Redacteur:

M. Wechsberg has a thousand times reason! In effect, sans the Normands, we would still be waxing sore wroth at the bouleversement inflicted upon the English language, instead of turning very enraged at the above-said bouleversement; And we would still be telling out geld in lieu of paying money to maintain Les Nations Unies, is it not?

"I pray you, M. the Editor, to want well to agree the expression of my sentiments the most respectful."

It would be easy to predicate extravagant conclusions upon facts such as the ones outlined above. In reality, they mean little so far as the English language itself is concerned, though they have considerable significance with regard to language in general.

A language whose speakers move from place to place, bearing with them their commercial, scientific, cultural, political and military prestige, is bound to give rise to pidgin forms. It is bound to be assimilated, often imperfectly, by speakers of foreign tongues, and be consequently mishandled. It is bound to borrow copiously from the tongues with which it comes in contact, and in turn to contribute abundantly to those tongues. In the case of foreign speakers who come to its home, there are bound to be immigrant dialects at first, but these are naturally submerged as their speakers beget new generations which are able to distinguish between the linguistic conglomeration that arouses only ridicule and the standard language that carries prestige and preferment. We can agree with the late columnist Robert Ruark when he deplores the passing of Jewish, blackface and other "dialects" from the vaudeville stage, but we can hardly agree with his contention that this passing is due to greater sensitivity on the part of minority groups in our midst; rather is it due to the gradual disappearance of the "dialects" themselves.

The significance to be found in the abuses of English by foreign speakers is to the effect that English is a great, powerful and influential tongue, one that people want to learn and handle to the best of their ability. Latin must have been similarly mishandled when it became a language of empire, bus just as Latin remained a fundamentally united tongue while the Empire lasted, so will English stand united while its speakers and their countries flourish.

Chapter Four

USES AND ABUSES AT HOME

*The Underworld of Slang—The Slang of the Under-
world—The Tongue of Teen-Agers—The Jargon of
the Services—The Talk of the Trades*

If we are going to resent the abuse of our language by alien
speakers of other tongues, immigrants to our midst, and poor,
benighted heathen users of pidgin, what shall we say of our own
native abusers, who bring down the language to the level of slang,
cant, and jargon?

Webster, in 1828, defined slang as "low, vulgar, unmeaning language." Granted that there may be some justification for the first
two epithets, we must certainly balk at the third. Slang is anything but "unmeaning." On the contrary, it deliberately tries to
be too meaningful, creating words and figures of speech that
sparkle and dazzle, bringing to light delicate semantic nuances
for which the standard tongue has no mode of expression, giving
full vent to the power of popular imagery and imagination.

The Concise Oxford Dictionary of 1911 defines slang as "language of highly colloquial type, below the level of standard educated speech, and consisting either of new words, or of current
words employed in some special sense." This is far more reasonable, and Baugh rounds out the Oxford definition with a discussion of the levels of speech usage. Words and forms current on
one social and educational level may be scorned by another (this
scorn, by the way, extends upward as well as downward; the language of the intellectuals may arouse as much ridicule among the
semi-literate as "swell" and "lousy" do among educators).

Slang has probably always existed and probably always will
exist, in all languages and at all times. It seeps upward from be-

neath. Thousands of its creations recede and vanish, but others sweep on to submerge the standard tongue and subject it to the will of the lower orders of society, turn it into new directions, and eventually create a new standard tongue. In a sense, slang is the vengeance of the anonymous masses for the linguistic thralldom imposed upon them by the educated classes.

This is not to say that all slang is of anonymous or illiterate creation—far from it. From Chaucer, who first used *bones* in the sense of "dice," to Walter Winchell, who is credited with *making whoopee,* the history of our own and other languages is replete with slang creations by famous names. All we need do to prove this assertion is to remind the reader that Shakespeare fathered (or fostered, or foisted, as the case may be) *beat it, done me wrong, fall for it, not so hot, tell the world,* and that Browning gave us *what a man!*

But the fact remains that slang is (it would perhaps be more exact to say "has been in the past") more usually than not of anonymous origin. We are not so naïve as to believe, as do many of our contemporaries, in the "popular" origin of either language or literature, a term that logically implies cooperation on the part of an entire community for purposes of linguistic or literary creation. When we say "anonymous," we mean nothing more or less than "anonymous." The creation has a name but the author is unknown. This does not mean that he did not exist as an individual—only that his name did not come down to us. As to the slang creator's desire to revenge himself, personally, upon the pundits and schoolmasters for their irksome restrictions, or his avowed intention to express the spirit of the obscure multitudes to which he belongs, that is something to be inferred rather than proved.

One insidious quality of slang is its tendency to seep up into the standard language until it becomes the standard language itself. Who would suspect today that *methinks, encroach, purport, subject-matter, drive a bargain, handle a subject, workmanship, man-of-war, until, self-same, devoid, nowadays, downfall, furthermore, wherewithal,* were once "slang," and attacked as such? Yet that is definitely the case.

It is a fairly common misconception in foreign lands, that all

English slang is American, and that the British tongue is simon-pure. This belief is indirectly fostered by the British, who often come out with extraordinary glossaries of Americanisms (one such glossary, cited by Robertson, defines *to crack wise* as "to speak knowingly," *flivver* as "cheap motor-car of delicate build," *heck* as "familiar for Hecuba, a New England deity," *roughneck* as "the antithesis of highbrow"). But slang often travels the other way, coming to America from Britain. It is again Robertson who reminds us that *swank, spoof, click, wind up, tell off* are of British origin.

In fact, slang is a very ancient phenomenon in Britain, and the literature on the subject goes back to the sixteenth century. Selecting one term at random, we find that in the days of Queen Anne the hoop skirts worn by the court ladies, with their series of five iron rings, made such creaking noises when their stately wearers walked that the term *screeches* was applied to them.

In relatively recent times, the London lexicon has regaled us with such choice terms for the work-shy as *spivs, drones, eels, butterflies, limpets* and *wide boys*. *Spiv* was at first thought to be *vips* in reverse, or perhaps a back formation from *spiffy*, but one racing expert insisted that the term had been used for forty years in the sense of "bookmaker's helper," another claimed it was a police abbreviation for "suspected persons and itinerant vagrants," and a scholar produced a reference from 1690 referring to "gypsies and spivics." *Spove* was created for the feminine of the species. On a lower level, we find the Cockney rhyming language (*brass tacks* for "facts"; *trouble and strife* for "wife"; *plates of meat* for "feet"; *apples and pears* for "stairs"). The story goes that the Cockney rhyming language, originating in London in the days of Queen Victoria, spread through England, Scotland, Wales and Ireland, then moved overseas to Australia and San Francisco. It tends to abbreviation, as where *china* (without the original *plate*) does service for *mate*. In the 1830's, the Dublin and Belfast Irish gave it their own humorous admixture, with such expressions as *Iron Duke* for "fluke," *holy friar* for "liar," *flowery dell* for "cell," *skin and blister* for "sister." California, in the 1850's, added *alligator* for "see you later" and *soup and gravy* for "Navy."

Some criticism against current slang in England has been directed at such "ugly" words as *eats, snooty, all wet* and *tinker's cuss,* as well as the harmless *mum* for "mother," and the not so harmless *kinkies* for "perverts."

On a somewhat higher level are *to cod* (to kid along), *to box clever* (to use one's brains), *steam* (work hard), *stiffener* (bore), *toffee-nosed* (stuck-up). One may say that these terms represent the English vernacular rather than English slang; but slang infiltrates the vernacular to approximately the same extent that the vernacular penetrates the standard language. Eric Partridge, that indefatigable researcher in the recesses of British slang and vernacular, prophesies with a blend of melancholy and resignation that it is only a question of time before the vernacular becomes the English language pure and simple. If he is correct, much slang will move in with it.

On our own side of the ocean, it is possible to divide up slang into several categories, with the preliminary remark that slang is best defined as that portion of substandard language which is common to, or at least understood by, the majority of the population; this sets slang apart from dialect, which is a local speech-form; from cant, which is specifically the language of the underworld; and from jargon, which is the language of a certain calling or class. These boundaries are often vague, and there is a large measure of interchange among slang, dialect, cant and jargon. It must also be remembered that not only social groups, but even age-groups (teen-agers, for example) and sexes have their own terminologies. One columnist, for instance, deplores the expression "trim your tummy" in a health hint addressed to men, on the ground that *tummy,* along with *pantie, nightie, hankie, deary, sweetie* and *yummy,* forms part of the feminine vocabulary.

There is, to begin with, an entire series of slang usages which originate with a known creator, often from the sporting or motion picture world. Sam Goldwyn is credited with "include me out." Dizzy Dean's linguistic outrages, mostly perpetrated with tongue in cheek, are too numerous to mention. Fight promoter Joe Jacobs seems responsible for *we wuz robbed* and *I should of stood in bed.* Vince Foster gets credit for *I wisht they had of let it went,* Rocky Graziano for *they trut me good,* Red Barber for *I have skum the surface.*

Next we have pithy, expressive words, generally of unknown origin, which strive for legitimacy and often make it: *scuttlebutt, poker-face, dead-pan, yammer, juice joint;* a noun and an adjective descriptive of feminine pulchritude, *gam* for "leg" (could this come from Italian *gamba?*) and *leggy.* The adverb *so* at the beginning of a sentence ("So I'll pay for it!"), probably of Yiddish origin, recurs frequently in conversation. *Corny* and *loaded* are two all-purpose adjectives.

It is difficult to determine to what extent the jive-joint language has penetrated the popular slang. Expressions like *get lost* become general to the extent that they lend themselves to ready understanding. This example is fairly obvious, even if one has not heard it before. A glance at *The Lingo of Tin Pan Alley* arouses alarm. Here we find *schtickel* and *schlump, potchky* and *trumbenick,* which sound downright foreign; *big one* replaces the earlier *grand* ($1000), while *bill* does for a hundred-spot, *pound* for a fiver, despite British devaluation, and *tear* for single dollar; *biscuit* is a girl, *chutzbah* is gall, *cornball, peasant, cube, square* or *matzoth ball* is one who "does not know the score." *Grunt, hot* or *third rail* may be used to designate a restaurant or nightclub check. *The end* is the absolute superlative.

Some slang phrases have penetrated the general colloquial to such an extent that they can hardly be called slang any more (*having a ball, to have had it, let's face it,* or, on a slightly lower plane, *leave us face it, get with it, be with it;* the last has climbed so high that a TV ad for the staid *New York Times* says: "If you're not with it, you're without it").

On the border line between slang and colloquialisms are expressions like *eager beaver, bats in the belfry, big mouth, bigwig, dim-wit, hit the road, squelch, take a gander, screwy, what's cooking?, I couldn't care less, you're so right, are you kidding?, be my guest, how horrible can you get?* A little lower in the social scale are *make with the mouth, clock the kid, do the mother bit.* There are abbreviations, like *natch* and *def.* There are names of dances, or what passes for such: *watusi, swim, frug, hitch hike, hully gully, elephant.* There are Yiddish influxes, like *schmeetings* and *shtup* (the last means to pressure or pester). There are Negro influences, like *ofay, Mister Charley, them* (all referring to the whites); *Uncle Tom, Aunt Thomasina, Doctor Thomas, honorary white boy* (all referring to Negroes who believe in racial collaboration), *head rollers* and *Charley Goons* (the police), *Mau Mau* (the Black Muslims), *fox* (a pretty girl); *waste* (to beat up). There are items from the borderland of the theatrical world, where a girl is a *hat* and *star-dusting* means going steady, where shoes may go by the name of *kicks, bottoms, stompers* or *ends,* and a car may be known as *go-it-all, rubber, short* or *wheels.* In this jargon, *to bring down* is the opposite of *to send* (in the slang sense of "This sends me"); *clock the action* is to understand; a cigarette may be a *bonfire, slim* or *weed,* while a cigar is a *four-alarmer;* the older *lay an egg* has become *lay a bomb;* dark glasses, fists and a toupee are described respectively as *shadows, folded fives* and *funny top; you have eyes to cool it* if you feel like relaxing, but if you're going down South you're going *behind the Cotton Curtain.* To the question "What's new?", the answer is "You got it all." It is not definitely determined whether the *-ville* craze (*Lootville, Feelsville, Soulville,* the latter applied especially to Harlem) originated in Harlem or on Broadway.

Some slang expressions are of very ancient vintage. *Wolf,* for example, was first traced back to Bulwer-Lytton, who in 1858 used the term as synonymous with "professional seducer," then to Perrault's fable of Red Riding-Hood of 1679, and finally to Abelard's *Historia Calamitatum* ("to entrust a tender lamb to the care of a hungry wolf").

Others are very recent. *Yoot* for "juvenile delinquent" seems to be the creation of a foreign-born grocer. *Jerk* (unpopular person) finally received the sanction of Funk and Wagnalls, on the ground that it was at least as important as *chiseler.*

Dr. Louise Pound, world-renowned expert on American English, in her foreword to Berrey and Van den Bark's *The American Thesaurus of Slang,* informs us that one of the largest group of slang terms consists of words expressing personal disparagement, which far outweigh terms of encomium; that derisive terms for women and girls loom large in the slang vocabulary; and that the descriptive terms for intoxication are so numerous that they occupy five pages.

The only thing that saves the language from being swallowed up by slang is the high mortality rate of slang terms. Consider, for example, the fate of *scram* (along with the earlier *twenty-three skidoo*), *nuts* (or the more elegant *nerts*), *stacked, Howling Horace* (for sirens), *ersatz, Hun* of the First World War, the *evacuee, quisling, Kraut* of the Second. But even though the ratio of quick and sudden deaths to survivals is ten to one, the survivors are numerous enough to give the language a peculiar flavor that changes from generation to generation. This need not be cause for undue alarm to the speakers of the English language. Slang, vulgarisms, colloquialisms, innovations, neologisms are part of a spoken tongue's own living machinery whereby to keep alive. While there is English slang, there will be an English language.

The cant of the underworld, like its speakers, has many contacts. It borders on universal slang when its terms are picked up and generally adopted by the community. It often crosses the frontier of teen-talk. It is a trade jargon, or rather a series of trade jargons, to the extent that each branch of crime sports its own terminology. Its international network is such that there is a variety of what might be styled "criminal Esperanto." Lastly, it has its roots fastened deep in the history of the past, so that it can be chronologically traced to Elizabethan days and beyond.

In 1567 Thomas Harman composed a book entitled *A Caveat or Warning for Common Cursetors, Vulgarly Called Vagabones*, in which he describes various practices or "disorders" still in use today. *Hookers* or *anglers* were the ancestors of our modern pickpockets. The forging of licenses was left to *jarkmen* or *patricoes*. *Freshwater mariners* or *whip-jacks* posed as shipwrecked sailors. *Priggers* (or *prancers*) antedated our horse-thieves, and *demanders for glimmer* pretended that their homes had been burned.

From the middle of the nineteenth century comes a poem which runs in part:

And where the swag so bleakly [prettily] pinched,
A hundred stretches [years] hence?
The thimbles [watches], slangs [chains] and danglers [bunches of
  seals] filched,
A hundred stretches hence?
The chips, the fawneys [rings], chatty-feeders [spoons],

The bugs [breast pins], the boungs [purses], the well-filled
   readers [pocket-books],
And where the fence and snoozing ken [bawdy house],
With all the prigs and lushing men,
A hundred stretches hence?

It will be noted that while some of the words require a translation, others do not (*swag, pinch, filch, chips, fence, prig, lush*).
This is characteristic of slang in general and of criminal cant in
particular. Some of François Villon's *jobelyn* is still good Paris
cant today, though most of it is quite incomprehensible.

The rhyming argot mentioned under Cockney slang is also
known as *Australian argot* among criminals, though it is well established that it originated in Britain. Characteristic are expressions like *bees and honey* (money), *clink and blank* (bank), *gay
and frisky* (whiskey), *kick and prance* (dance), *seldom seen* (lim-
ousine).

There is, however, also a reputed Australian criminal slang,
publicized in a *Dictionary of "Flash,"* as early as 1819, before
any similar works had appeared in America, by one James Hardy
Vaux, a New South Wales convict. But it seems to be mostly
English.

Canada, too, has its gangster slang, much influenced by the
wealth of cant across the border. The Toronto police glossary
includes *hardrock* (tough guy), *soup caper* (safe-blowing), *mouse-
feet* (rubber-soled shoes), *bluebeetles* (cops).

The modern British criminal world offers *lagging* (three-year
stretch) and *old lag* (habitual criminal), *squeaker* or *copper's nark*
(stool-pigeon), *dabs* (finger-prints), and *climber* (second-story man).

One word that has come recently to the American underworld
is of definitely foreign origin. It is *don*, a title used by the Mafia,
and means, approximately, "big shot"; legitimately, *don*, from the
Latin *dominus*, "lord," "master," is a title of respect used in Italy
and Spain before a man's first name (*Don Luigi, Don Manuel*);
but in American usage, the name is dropped ("he is a don").

It was recently brought out that criminal slang is marked by
dialectal, or at least geographical, differences within the United
States. A bribe to a public official by racketeers, for instance, is
juice in California, but *ice* in Florida (note that *ice* is also used

for "diamonds"). Then there are other local names, such as *cumshaw, palm oil, the difference, sugar, schmier, scratch, payola*.

Each branch of the underworld has its own specific lingo. Automobile thieves, for instance, speak of *lookers* (browsers in used-car lots), *ups* (prospective customers for stolen cars), *tramps* or *junkers* or *crates* (broken-down cars), *cream puffs* (good cars), *originals* (cars with their first paint job), *roughs, slicks* and *sharps* (cars in various states of disrepair).

Illegal "numbers" gamblers know their occupation under the various names of *clearing house, butter and eggs, the bug*. A *drop* is the store where you place your bet; a *runner* is the man who takes it. But race-track gambling has a slightly different vocabulary; here we have *nits* (small-time bookmakers). Reno and Las Vegas gamblers have their own lingo. *To go south* is to steal a card during play. *Eyes in the sky* are the gambling-house guards, stationed on the balconies. Various types of cheats are known as *crossroaders, muckers, pressers, pushers, coolers* and *daubers*.

Dope-peddlers speak of *junk* (dope in general), and *junkie, hophead, cokie* or *snowbird* (addict). A dope-seller is a *pusher* or *mule*. Heroin is *H* (but also *horse, smack* or *schmeck*), with *snow* more commonly reserved for cocaine. Opium is *black stuff* or *mud*. Marijuana is *weed tea* or *pot*. The place where one gets an injection is the *shooting gallery*.

From the pickpockets' lingo come *moll buzzing* (stealing from a woman), *softy* (victim), *creeper* (woman who works on drunks), *breech-bridge* (side pocket), *shorts* (trolleys or buses), *hole* (subway), *fagin* (pickpocket trainer; right out of Dickens). Practitioners of the art are pursued by a *fuzz* (detective) who effects a *sneeze* (arrest).

Safe-crackers are *petermen, boxmen, rippers* or *blow men* (but the ripper rips the safe open, while the blow man uses *soup*, or nitroglycerin).

The hold-up man is a *heister*, usury is *shylocking* (again a literary reminiscence, this time from Shakespeare). A female shoplifter is a *bloomer girl* or *booster*, a prostitute is a *hooker* (but *hooked* more commonly refers to one who has acquired the drug habit), a night burglar is a *Dutch house man*. If you land in jail (*pen, can, stir, cage*, with *Big House* reserved for Sing Sing), you are in contact with *screws* (keepers), but you can write *kites* (letters entrusted to fellow-prisoners about to be released); you can also *pitch a doozie* (stage a tantrum), and there may *be a breeze,* or you may be able to *hang it on a bush* (break out).

There is even a police slang, which in part reflects that of the underworld, and, as is customary for slang, has a wealth of synonyms. What is euphemistically known as an "abnormal" may be any of these things to the police: *cracker, spook, head case, half, psycho, lily waver;* "arrested" can be translated by *canned, joyed, salted, brigged* or *bucketed;* the police station may be referred to as *house, night-club, salt mine, bullhouse* or *cop shop.* A veteran cop is *hairbag, old sweat* or *grumpy.* The official salute is *highball, one-two, heaver, five-throw;* the uniform is *bag, blues, monkey suit, formal, sports suit;* the shield is *patsy, tin plate, five-point, buzzer, flasher;* an arrest is a *pinch, bust, sneeze, feel his collar, claim, habeas grabbus.* But only *composite gun* is given for illegal abortion. *N.Y.U. grad* is police slang for a member of the New York underworld.

The extent to which the slang of the underworld infiltrates the underworld of slang and even the literate vernacular may be gauged by the following list of words, all of criminal origin; none of them requires an explanation or translation: *take a powder, rap, well heeled, clip joint, mug, take for a ride, throw the book at, hot stuff, fix, hot seat, stiff, rub out, blow one's top, muscle in, hatchet man, punk, frisk, mobster, case the joint, scram, gat.*

On the other hand, there is a whole series of creations with which the general public is not as yet acquainted. Here are a few, culled from the *Dictionary of American Underworld Lingo: blath* (underworld), *cannon* (pickpocket trade), *cruller* (head), *five-and-fifty-five* (single blow followed by rapid cuffs with the back of the hand, as you see in the movies), *gullion* (jewelry), *ghee* (guy), *putting the clown to bed* (following a small-town cop home before committing a crime), *shlub* (fool), *scoff joint* (restaurant), *specker* (jail term), *tumuler* (rough criminal), *zex* (exclamation of warning).

It is difficult to classify the lingo of the teen-agers, which has at least three distinct ramifications: a connection with underworld slang, a common frontier with the world of popular music, and a mystery-vocabulary born of a desire to be unintelligible to the elder generation.

Characteristic of the first are the incredible names assumed by teen-age gangs: *Slacksters* and *Socialistic Dukes, Happy Knights* and *Shangri-La Debs, Nits* and *Stompers;* also expressions such as *punk, caper, rumble* (this is a fight to the finish between two gangs), and the now universal *chicken,* replacing the *yellow* of our youth (note that in this expression, *chicken* becomes a pure adjective, and is never pluralized: "they are chicken").

Gone are the *trolleyriding* (for going steady), the *bubble* or *moroff* (for drip), the *pouter pigeon* (for hard-to-please girl) of a generation ago. The teen-agers of the simpering sixties use *cowboy* or *squirrel* (or even *space happy*) for a reckless driver, *bur* for hair (which, as everyone knows, may be *weird, tatty* or *grotty*). A *frat* (youth who conforms to decent standards) is no longer told to *scram,* but to *blast off.* To *snow* is to kid along, and a homosexual is now a *flit.* The boy friend is known as a *flutter bum* by the *Nike* (girl who gets her man). The former *square* is either a *yo-yo* or a *party-pooper.* Expressions of disgust are *duh, wuzza wuzza, queer, fag, fink* (but *funky* means indifferent, and *George* means good). *Blurpy* has replaced *cool, to browse* has replaced *to rat, to gas* is to discuss. A *pazazz* or *p'zazz car* (and note that *pazazz* did not even manage to find its way into Webster III) has already been changed to *gook wagon. The Action* has replaced *The Who* as the top teen group, whose motto is "No more long hair or dirt." In Britain, the *Teddy* or *Elephant Boys* who gave way to *Mods* and *Rockers* are already being displaced by *Greasers* (those who tend their own motorcycles) and *Thicks* (these are the real tough eggs).

There is one variety of language which borders on both slang and trade jargon. It is the tongue of the G.I.'s, a tongue that runs all the way from the absolutely unprintable to the harmless creations of the Big Brass.

There is also what might be described as an elegant military jargon, used by the very top echelons. Here we have *confrontation, conventional* (as applied to weapons), *overkill, tacnuk, um-*

brella, pace, fail-safe, unacceptable damage (what a nation can't take in the way of atom bombing) and *city-bargaining* (you spare New York and we'll spare Moscow). Older terms have new acceptances. *A Dear John Letter* is now a notice of retirement. *To bolo* and *pasear a bucket of blood,* both going back to the days of fighting in the Philippines, mean "to mess up" and "to go out for a drink."

Missilese is a weird military tongue devised by our guided missiles experts, or *missiliers*. Its terminology includes *beeper* (the individual who flies a pilotless aircraft by remote control); *brennschluss* (perfect German; the time at which a rocket ceases to burn); *dither* (radio signal that quivers a valve in the missile mechanism); *drone* (remote control aircraft); *monocoque* (type of fuselage); *nolo flight* (flight of pilotless aircraft); *payload* (warhead); *glide bomb* (winged missile powered by gravity).

Military requirements have given rise to two other different types of language. One is a working vocabulary of the five thousand words most clearly heard and understood when a speaker is surrounded by the noises of combat planes. The other is a technical jargon composed of English, French, German and Italian, to be used by Atlantic Pact forces; but this is still in the discussion stage, though there is a precedent in the Swiss Air Force's trilingual jargon. It is estimated, incidentally, that it takes about three months of combined military and language training to impart the language of command to a recruit with no previous knowledge of it.

The jargons of the various occupations are as numerous and varied as the occupations themselves. Some, by reason of contact with the outside world, or constant representation in literature, manage to make themselves so popular as to pass into the standard tongue. This is particularly true of navigation, which has contributed to the common language expressions like *windfall, under way, keeping on an even keel, knowing the ropes, keeping one's weather eye open, giving plenty of leeway, falling afoul of disaster.* But navigation also has its private jargon, something made up of *skivvies* (sailors' underwear, from the *skivaclothes,* or "crazyclothes" originally applied to skin-tight sailors' pants), *battle the watch* (a phrase of encouragement), *bricklayer's clerk* (inefficient seaman), *donkey's breakfast* (a straw mattress in a sailor's bunk), *mud hook* (anchor), *soojie-moojie* (washing soda).

The flying fraternity, which has given the language *buzzing,* in the sense of flying so low as to skim the rooftops, also makes use of abbreviations like *Fido* (from the initials of *fog, intensive, dispersal of*), *Cavu* (ceiling and visibility unlimited) and *forat* (flight orders at later time). To the commercial pilot a *noshow* is a passenger who fails to show up after making a reservation, and a *go show* is the one who turns up without a reservation; *pulpit* is the pilot's cockpit, *glidepath* in a radio beam, and *fizz job,* or *stovepipe,* a jet plane.

The other and more traditional transportation industries, railroading and trucking, have elaborate jargons of long and honorable standing. A stationmaster is an *ornament,* while *deadhead* is an employe on a pass, an empty train, or a lone engine. The switchman is a *reptile,* a tracklayer a *rust-eater,* a section hand a *donkey. Smart Aleck* for conductor, *tarpot* for fireman, *pinhead* for brakeman are other choice railroad terms. The passengers are *fish.* Truckese includes such expressions as *eating gravel* for "to detour," and *sold out to the Yankees* for a wrecked car; a *boom wagon* is a truck with explosives, a *tap dancer* a retail delivery driver, a *spook* an insurance company observer. In the higher echelons, we have *containerization, piggyback* and even *fishyback* (for cars accompanying their owners on board ships).

The extent to which labor parlance has entered the general language is indicated by *check-off, featherbedding, fink, rat* (also *ratting* and *to rat*), *lackey,* (or *yes-yes*), *goon, swing shift, graveyard shift, third trick, wildcat strike.*

Automobile manufacturers speak of *sergeant stripes* (the bright trimming on the sides of a car), *hockey sticks* and *egg crate* (grill parts and grill assembly), *bananas* (chrome fender louvres). The world of fashions (and possibly some of our female readers) are acquainted with *guimpe, gusset, gigot sleeves, bellows pockets, godet, plastron.* Interior decorators thrive on *bombé, burl, case goods* (wooden furniture), *crazing* (cracks on china surfaces), *clerestory, distressed* (this is a deliberately worn-looking finish), *dowel, flock paper, marquetry* and *shoji* (Japanese-style sliding doors), along with *aubergine, banquette, bobeche, cartouche, cheval glass, coirboully* and *epergene*. Builders have changed the old *skylight* to *roof window*, while fishmongers have changed *catfish, dogfish* and *coalfish* to *rockfish, flake* and *saithe,* respectively.

Heard in the retailing world are such terms as *P.M.* (premium money, a bonus for selling hard-to-sell items); *skig* (a slow mover); *end sizes* (biggest and smallest); *size lining* (grouping merchandise by size). Culled from the field of construction are such interesting terms as *buckerup, air-leg drill, cherry picker, creeper traveler, dolly, ginniwink, gin pole, grizzly, scalper, scarifier, sky hook, sheepsfoot roller, shoo-fly track, snatch block, spider* and *spud.* Plane pilots give us *blowtorch* and *stovepipe* (both in connection with jets), *goods* (*cargo* is never used for merchandise transported by air), *trip circle, open-jaw, voice reflector.*

There is in existence a *Dictionary of Occupational Titles* with well over forty thousand entries. Some of them are unheard-of by the general public. A *kiss-machine operator,* for instance, runs the machine that wraps chocolate kisses; a *horser-up* hangs hides over saw-horses; a *pulpit man* works in a rolling mill in an enclosure known as a *pulpit;* and an *end man,* unconnected with football, works in the iron and steel industry. *Chiefing* is the unique profession of looking like an Indian chief to draw tourists to souvenir shops (the occupation is now restricted by law to authentic Redskins). The expression *drumming up trade* and the use of *drummer* for salesman go back to the days when Punch and Judy shows and patent medicine displays at fairs were staffed by trumpeters and drummers as well as high-pressure barkers.

The special jargons of collectors contribute strange words. *Goofies* are ordinary plastic buttons to button collectors, who also know certain types of glass buttons as *old lacy* and *clam broth;* a *rockhound* is a hobby-hunter of semi-precious stones; *royal flashes, thirty-strikers* and *midgets* come from the language of match-cover gatherers; while the field of antiques offers *neo, quasi* and *wantiquest.*

Taken all together, slang, cant, jargon, dialect are examples of the language's creative power. To repress them is impossible. Better by far to accept, utilize and enjoy them—if you can.

Chapter Five

ENGLISH AS A CLASS TOOL (1)

*The Speech of the Intelligentsia—The Classes and the
Masses—The Language of Politics—In Legal Parlance—
American Officialese and King's Gobbledegook—The
Language of Faith*

"Class jargons," said Josef Stalin in his famous *Pravda* article
of June 20, 1950, "are not languages. They may develop individual words, but have to depend on the common grammar and
vocabulary. Furthermore, they do not serve the entire community."

This pronouncement, intended to correct the errors of N. Y.
Marr, who chose to view language as a series of class suprastruc-
tures using society as a base, is thoroughly in accord both with
the dictates of reason and with the findings of linguistic science.

At the same time, it needs to be carefully interpreted. It is quite
true that a trade jargon or the language of a given social class
cannot exist by itself, but must utilize the grammatical structure
and vocabulary of the whole community, particularly the former.
But it is also true that while the entire community generally
shares a common set of sounds and a common grammar, it does
not necessarily share a common vocabulary, save for those basic
words (a few thousands at the most) which are used by scholars
and illiterates alike.

Beyond that fundamental word-stock common to all speakers,
the most astounding variations and divergences may occur. It has
already been pointed out that few indeed of the speakers of English are acquainted with more than one out of ten words in the
language, or one hundred thousand out of a possible one million
words. What of the other nine hundred thousand words and ex-

pressions in the dictionaries? The best definition that can be given of them is that they constitute either localisms and dialectal terms, or else professional, occupational and trade jargons—in other words, class languages.

Thus it is that while sounds, grammar and basic words go to make up the common language of us all, the majority of words, over three-fourths of the language's total word-stock, belong to individual "classes," in the broadest acceptance of that term.

This fact cannot be overlooked. Neither should it be overemphasized. It would be as unreasonable to deny the existence of class vocabularies as it would be to assert that they constitute the "language."

If these class vocabularies never crossed the threshold of the common tongue, one could perhaps ignore them. But this is emphatically not the case. Just as regional and dialectal expressions often travel far beyond their original geographical frontier, so we find the class languages turning up where we least expect them. Seldom do their possessors shrink modestly into the background, hugging their creations to their bosoms. Far more often they flaunt them openly, defiantly, even hopefully in the face of the rest of the world, expecting some of them to be adopted by the community and to contribute to the prestige, enhancement and preferment of the group that has devised them.

Propaganda, of one sort or another, for one purpose or another, rides on the wings of class words. This makes the tongues of the classes socially significant and linguistically important—not to the point of overshadowing the common tongue, but certainly to the point of calling for a detailed examination.

Without invalidating the proposition that there is a main stream of language, more or less common to all the speakers of a given community, which must always be kept in view, a survey of the specialized vocabularies of art, politics, law, government, religion, finance, commerce, science, education, stage, screen, radio, press and sports will be rewarding. It will show to what extent the common tongue is infiltrated, deliberately or accidentally, by each of these activities, most of which are of a predominantly intellectual nature, and therefore peculiarly qualified to influence our outlook, opinions and behavior, and, eventually, our common tongue itself.

A magazine article once discussed the terminology that one must use in order to be the Life of the Intellectual Cocktail Party. "The argot is the thing!" proclaimed the author, although argot alone does not suffice unless it is combined with the proper subject-matter.

There is a set of recommended phrases to be memorized and used when the right occasion arises—a phraseology that will mark you as a connoisseur and esthete, and set you apart forever from the lowly mob that talks in terms of baseball scores and jockey recordings.

For a musical discussion, the judicious use of *calculated dissonances* and *sonorous acerbities,* coupled perhaps with one or two importations of the type of *comprimario* (a singer's part which is not quite the leading role) will set you up as an expert. If the discussion turns to modern art, by all means try something like "free-flowing form and evocative symbol," or "subtly tinted mists and blots across which dart swift linear lightnings," or, better yet, "suprematist painting" and "Paranoiac-Astral Image" (the title of a Dali painting). "Latent subject" will help, too. The *-isms* of modern art, all abstract and non-objective, run to a total of at least thirty: *Constructivism, Neo-Plasticism, Dadaism, Proto-Surrealism, Orphism-Simultaneism, Fauvism,* and, of course, the original *Cubism* and *Futurism.* For the dance, the recommended nouns are *virility* and *plasticity,* while favored adjectives include *fluid, sculptured* and *kinesthetic.* In describing furniture, one may use *biomorphic,* if the articles in question are of the modern body-fitting variety, or, in the case of antiques, fall back upon the *-ana* suffix which originated in seventeenth-century France and does service for literature and history as well. The cinema may be said to be *faced* with the usual *insoluble dichotomy,* while for literature there are available such terms as *lettrism* (a theory of poetry as rhythmic architecture, with emphasis on the sounds of letters) and *sensorialism* (which claims that nothing is valid except experience of the senses, with sexual experience as the most intense and valid). *Existentialism* is now almost *passé;* but one can still speak of *stream of consciousness, vers de société, roman à clef,* and that new but somewhat hazy quality known as *camp.*

In addition to all this, there are terms that straddle the various topics, and may be used on almost any occasion (*intimate, intuitive, delightfully non-objective, precious, gracious, over-designed, abstract, organic, functional*), as well as complete clichés like "to herald a trend" and "lacks un je ne sais quoi." *Creative* is an all-purpose word.

That all this represents a class language there is very little doubt. These expressions, used by an intellectual or pseudo-intellectual elite, set you apart from the general body of speakers just as much as the cant of the underworld.

There is, of course, a legitimate jargon of music, poetry, art and the dance, terms which are clearly defined and definable and must be used by the experts for the sake of clarity and precision, even if they are not always fully meaningful to the layman. *Campanile, quoin* and *soffit* to the architect, *hocket, quodlibet* and *melisma* to the musician, *collage, chiaroscuro* and *sculptural assemblage* to the artist, *allongé, épaulement* and *coup de pied* to the ballet dancer, all have precise meanings. There are even semi-slangy abbreviations, like the *pop* in *pop concert* and the *op* in *op art,* replacing a more impressive *kineto-optical,* which tend to clarify issues to the layman. They also tend to spread a gospel, but for that there is no help.

The transition from this tongue of the artistically inclined classes to the lingo of politics is represented by the use made in Soviet and pro-Soviet circles of terms like *formalism, objectivism, traditionalism* and *bourgeois art.* But both Reds and Pinks have evolved their own general vocabulary, which they would like to impose upon the world as a language of the proletarian masses. Beside the customary invectives (*warmongers, imperialists, fascists, reactionaries, cannibals,* etc.) are new terms like *diversionist* or *deviationist* (a party member who has fallen into bourgeois ways), *revisionist, lèse democracy* (based on *lèse majesté,* and ironically applied to those acts which displease believers in western democracy). Then there is a whole series of terms of approval: *progressive* for one who wants to take you back into the Dark Ages, *collectivism* for Communism, *pacification* for the extermination of class enemies, *people's democracy* for a regime under which the people are never consulted, *peaceful coexistence* for what is more properly known as *cold war*.

There is no good reason to keep the Marxist and Socialistic terminology separate from the general political parlance which English speakers have evolved over the centuries. Political terms have always carried a semantic charge far exceeding that of most other words.

A political dictionary of the past reveals completely forgotten terms which in their day were fraught with meaning: *Goose Question* (slavery question), *Silver Greys* or *Woolly Heads* (Whigs), *Democraws* (British term applied to the French Revolutionists), *Barnburners* and *Loco-Focos, Pewter Muggers* (Tammany rebels) and *Horsmandering* (a term that could profitably be revived: Daniel Horsmander, an eighteenth-century judge, was one of the first public servants to use his records of a public experience as the basis of a full-length book).

The same dictionary will reveal a host of terms still in use today, though their original connotation has vanished or been distorted: *mugwump* and *scalawag, logrolling* and *filibuster, stalwart Republican* (coined by Blaine to designate the group that refused to abandon the party's remnant in the South) and *lame duck* (originally an English financial term to designate the bankrupt). British political usage involves terms which to us are meaningless, like *front-benchers* (the Cabinet Ministers and their aides, and the leading Opposition members) and *back-benchers* (the rest of the M. P.'s), *strangers* (non-members of Parliament), and the practice of *naming* (reproaching a member for unparliamentary conduct).

Political creations of the present day are almost infinite in their variety. Foreign policy has given us *Sinologist* and *Kremlinologist, brinkmanship* and *positions of strength, escalations* and *summit conferences, hawks* and *doves, peaceniks* and *Vietniks*. From the Civil Rights movement come *backlash* and *frontlash*, *freedom riders* and *tokenism, teach-ins, sit-ins* and *creative conflict* (the last a super-euphemism for the already euphemistic *peaceful demonstration*). The jargon of ordinary politics contributes *reorienting* and *senior citizen, mainstreams* and *moderates, one man one vote* and *the ability to pay.*

The mania for classification of documents on the part of both military and non-military government bureaus has led to the use not only of *restricted, confidential, classified, secret* and *top secret,* but, as absolute superlatives, of *cosmic* and *eyes only.*

The press of Washington affairs has led to the expressions *top-drawer worrier, ulcer fodder* and *Potomac fever.* Then there are the humorous nonce-words and nonce-uses the authenticity of which may be questioned: the case of the Senator, for instance, who, bewildered by economic talk and pressed to take a stand, solemnly replied: "I'm not for inflation; I'm not for deflation; I'm for only *flation!";* or the slurring definition of "Upper House" said to have been given by a Lower House member: "We pass an appropriation bill and send it to the Senate, and they up her!"

Since the beginning of organized society, a battle, sometimes silent but more often vocal, has been waged between the individual and the state. The will of the state is expressed in laws, and laws require interpretation, which is supplied (and occasionally withheld) by lawyers and judges. This august class has developed a special terminology, coupled with a parlance all its own, against which the uninitiate strive in vain.

The study of Anglo-American law, based for the most part on legal precedent rather than on code, is in full truth a historical pursuit. Our legal terminology comes in small part from the Saxon forebears, but is largely a conglomeration of French and Latin evolved by the Normans and their descendants. Take, for example, our various writs, pleas and other legal instruments and terms: *mandamus, habeas corpus, certiorari, nolo contendere, subpoena, affidavit, onus probandi, in rem, lis pendens,* even the *posse (comitatus)* of the Wild West; however they may be mangled in the mouths of modern American lawyers to whom the study of Latin is no longer a necessity, their meaning is still clear to one Classically trained, obscure to the products of so-called

"modern" education. In Florida, not too long ago, precinct officials refused to allow the wife of a high-school principal to vote
in a school trustee election because they did not know the meaning of *et ux.* after the principal's name on his tax receipt.

Then there are all those quaint French terms which carry with
them a history that few know. Why is a *coroner* so called, considering that the term means *crowner?* In the Middle Ages the
coroner's task was not so much to keep watch over corpses as over
crown property. What are the *dine* and *poulage* which still prevail on the Isle of Sark? The former is a levy of one-tenth on all
cereals grown on the island, and comes, appropriately enough,
from Latin *decima* and Old French *disme,* "tenth," from which
we in America get *dime; poulage* is, as the name implies, a
chicken tax imposed at the rate of one chicken per year per house
chimney. *Embracery* is not an attempt to embrace one of the opposite sex, but an attempt to corrupt a jury.

But there are terms which are not at all foreign-sounding, and
yet carry very special legal meanings. The layman is accustomed
to think of a *slanderous* letter, but the law normally reserves
slander for what goes by word of mouth; *libel* is the proper legal
term for what appears in writing. *Assault* would be defined by
most as an act of violence; legally, it is only an unlawful offer or
attempt to do hurt to another; *battery* is the actual doing of the
hurt. *Savings* means something definite to you; but in its legal
acceptance, the word could not, until recently, be coupled with
account save in an extremely restricted sense, so that commercial
banks were forced to fall back on such synonyms as *compound
interest account, special interest account, thrift account,* etc.

Have you ever heard of *adverse possession,* or of *constructive
eviction?* The first is the ownership right which a squatter acquires after a number of years of continuous and uncontested
possession; the second is serious interference on the part of the
landlord with the use of rented space (erecting a wall in front of
windows so as to cut off the light, for instance), whereupon the
lessee must consider himself evicted and vacate the premises.
There is *tenancy by entirety* (as against *tenancy in common,* or
joint tenancy) for a husband and wife who own a house under
the provision that if either dies the property shall pass directly,

not by inheritance, into the sole possession of the other. There is even a legal definition for that elusive entity which crops up so frequently in real estate advertising, the *half room:* a kitchen with an area less than sixty square feet, or a dining alcove more than forty-five square feet and having separate outside light. For a clear, precise legal definition, we favor that which a British court gave of a "plunging neckline": "a cut which tends to show rather more of the bosom than is usually shown."

It is said that lawyers sometimes "murder" English, in proof whereof the following gems have been garnered from the Newark court records: "That in a kernel is the gist of what this case is concerning," and "In these cases such as these, insofar as my sworn duty, I shall prosecute these cases to the last breath of my dying body which I am prosecuting only for the sake of justice."

But a far more serious accusation leveled against the language of the law is that it is antiquated, stilted and incomprehensible. There must be something in this charge, since it arises on both sides of the Atlantic. As far back as 1817, Jefferson went on record as disapproving of the "verbose and intricate style of the modern English statutes," which had already gotten to the point where "nobody but we of the craft can untwist the diction, and find out what it means; and that not too plainly but that we may conscientiously divide, half on each side."

Today, the Justice Department inveighs against the legal description of a Post Office killing in Topeka, in which sixteen lines are used to identify the Post Office, seven adverbs to charge premeditation, and nine lines to state the victim died; there is an Elizabethan flavor, however, about the conclusion of the report, to the effect that the mortally wounded Mr. X "thereby did languish, and languishing did die."

The chairman of the American Bar Association Committee on Continuing Education blasted the old-fashioned parlance that means nothing to the clients and little to the lawyers, and advocated a reform of the legal language, at the same time that the House of Lords in Britain called for the shelving of all obsolete words and expressions in statutes that date from 1235 to 1800.

But contemporaneously with these meritorious movements for the abolition of the parties of the first part and the sums in hand paid, there arises a far worse menace to the English language and the comprehensibility thereof. In Britain they prefer to call this dire threat *Officialese,* in America it goes by a name coined by Maury Maverick, *Gobbledegook* (*Gobbledygook* is a variant spelling, and *Bafflegab* has more recently been offered as a synonym).

The language of the bureaucrats and administrators must needs be recognized as an outgrowth of legal parlance. There is no other way to explain its pervading, pervicacious and pernicious meanderings. Lawyers ensconced in administrative bureaus and feeling secure in their new-found castles were undoubtedly the originators of a linguistic form that threatens our language to the same extent that their activities are alleged by some to threaten our liberties. Proof of this statement may be had in the version of *Jack and the Bean-Stalk* jocularly issued by a lawyer's magazine to lampoon the legal language. It begins: "Once on or about a time, there was a minor named John or 'Jack' (as he will hereinafter be designated), other name or names to your relator unknown."

When we compare this with our own Federal Prose, we discover a kinship that cannot be accidental. Take, for instance, this excerpt from a piece of proposed financial legislation: "The semi-annual assessment for each insured bank shall be the amount of the product of one-half the annual assessment rate multiplied by an assessment base which shall be the average for six months of the differences at the end of each calendar month between the total amount of the liability of the bank for deposits and the total of such uncollected items as are included in such deposits and credited subject to final payment."

In Federal Prose (alias Washington Choctaw) a beer-bottle label is said to have "retained a tendency to mislead"; adjustments to new situations are "made interstitially without organic reconstruction of the legal framework"; there is "affirmative facilitation"; estimates are not yet "finalized or maximized." One speaks not of *orders,* but of *directives,* not of *food,* but of *units of nutritional intake,* not of a *year,* but of *twelve calendar months.*

Military Gobbledegook, not content with *survivability, overkill, fallout, manpowerization, defense postures,* and that variety of armament known as *soft hardware,* has gone on to *termination capability* (the power to carry on nuclear warfare to the bitter end) and *forces recyclable in a degraded environment* (survivors of a nuclear attack who can still fight). Originating (probably) with the State Department is an entire series of weasel adjectives descriptive of some of the so-called nations we have taken under our wing: *underdeveloped, emerging* (or *emergent*), *have-not*; even *fledgeling* (but this seems to have been coined by Eleanor Roosevelt); *uncommitted* and *unaligned,* for those that criticize and oppose us while they accept our handouts. Other creations of the bureaus, but of a slangy type, are *teacup gossip, to fuzz up a recommendation* (for the purpose of spreading the responsibility), *to beef up the background* (load a paper with inconsequential comments), even *to bird-dog* (put aside and consider later).

This creeping paralysis of the language knows no boundaries, but is a blight that crosses oceans and contaminates continents. France has *dirigisme,* which is the Planned Economy. Russian has *bumashka* (a pejorative form of *bumaga,* "paper," which means any official document); a Soviet government directive has also been known to speak of the "mobilization of personnel for the removal of dust." In Nationalist China, Chiang Kai-shek has ordered official documents to be drawn up in ordinary Mandarin, not in the highly literary *Wên-Li.* Germany reports that there is a growing chasm between East and West Germany by reason of two different versions of government gobbledegook, and a full-sized book titled *Aus dem Wörterbuch des Untermenschen* ("From the Vocabulary of the Subhuman") describes and satirizes them.

Plain Words, a book written by Sir Ernest Gowers at the request of His Majesty's Government for the purpose of stemming the tide of Officialese, reported: *perpetual interim development, unexpended portion of the day's rations, bottleneck in bottles, ablution facilities.* There are abbreviations which are also euphemisms, such as *A. T.* (= Animal Traction = mule). One English columnist undertook to paraphrase "There's no place like home" as it would sound in Officialese: "It has not come to our notice in the course of exhaustive inquiries, made through appropriate channels, that there is any unit to come within the same residential category as an accommodation unit."

But without having resort to the imagination, here is an authentic order from the Food Ministry: "References in this order to any order shall be construed as referring to that order as amended by any subsequent order whether made before or after the making of this order, and if any order referred to in this order is replaced by any such subsequent order, the references shall be construed as referring to that subsequent order."

Not even the Commonwealth is spared, as witnessed by this New Zealand item: "It is obvious from the difference in elevation with relation to the short depth of the property that the contour is such as to preclude any reasonable development potential for active recreation."

It is no wonder that M. P.'s thunder out in Parliament against the use of Officialese, which a former Treasury Secretary and Civil Servant No. 1 described as a "jargon of fear," born of a desire on the part of officials to "use a language deliberately framed so as to mean as little as possible in the hope that since so little meaning could be attached to them they would not lead to embarrassment."

War is officially declared upon Officialese, Washington Choctaw and similar linguistic diseases. One phase of this crusade covers the designations by which simple objects are known to various government bureaus. It was discovered, for example, that there are 1,100 designations for a cotter pin, 253 for a common nut, 322 for a lock washer, and 262 for a screw. The standardization of these names of government property has so far succeeded in cutting four hundred thousand names down to 334,000. This would seem to indicate that it is not only officials who are at fault for complicating the language, but also industrialists who supply those officials.

Back in October 1951, Paul Porter, Chief of ECA, issued a circular to his employees demanding clear, concise writing, and avoidance of words and near-words like *dichotomy, conceptual, built-in inflation, disincentive, ratiocination.*

The campaign against Officialese may win some important battles, but we may be forgiven for expressing doubt as to the ultimate outcome of the war. Many forms of Gobbledegook are in the nature of linguistic creations of the same species as those which have in the past been adversely criticized, but have nevertheless made the dictionary. According to one British authority, *hospitalization* is said to be "a dreadful word, one of the worst examples of Officialese." Yet *hospitalization* is in full and popular use today in the United States, having been adopted even by labor unions. *Accommodation* for houses, *representative* for salesman, *construction* for building, *global* for world-wide, *recondition* for mend (all expressions criticized by the foes of Officialese) are similarly in general use. So are the numerous words with -*ee* suffix (*draftee*, etc.) which arouse the ire of the anti-gobbledegookians.

A partial list of Gobbledegook expressions that have penetrated the everyday language has been offered. It includes such terms as *computerize, telegenic, disadvantaged, finalize, definitize, space race, space age, population explosion, special interests, nuclear holocaust, American way of life, short of seasonal expectations* (this for a firm whose balance sheet shows a loss instead of a profit). *Creeping Socialism* and *spiraling inflation* are right-wing contributions, while educational psychology gives us *over-achiever* and *fully realized person,* and the world of advertising *planned community, oversized rooms, pre-owned car, young moderns* and *problem skin.*

Those who fear excessively for the future of a language beset by Officialese and Washington Choctaw may take solace in the fact that language has its own sifting machinery whereby a selective process is exercised. The problem posed by Gobbledegook may therefore be viewed as practical and immediate rather than long-range. Gobbledegook is essentially a class jargon with which the layman is occasionally forced to come in contact, to his own confusion worse confounded, but which does not as yet, and probably will not in the future, affect the language's basic structure.

The contributions made by religion to the language are for the most part in the past. Religion is far from static, but it is conservative. The ancient Biblical words, *cherub* and *seraph* and *hallelujah* and *amen,* have been with us without change for centuries. The religious terminology of the Catholic and Episcopalian churches, the simple yet exalted language of the King James and

Douai Bibles form part of the linguistic stock of most of us who speak English.

From time to time the need is felt to revise the language of religion, usually by the expedient of a brand-new translation from the original Biblical languages. Interesting in this connection is the fact that the Catholic Church, most conservative of all in theological doctrine, is not in the least backward when it comes to linguistic revisionism. Typical of this attitude is the new Hartdegen translation of the Old Testament, which eschews *thou* and *behold,* using instead *you* and *see.* The old Douai version has at the beginning of Chapter 12 of Genesis: "Go forth out of thy country, and from thy kindred, and out of thy father's house, and come into the land which I shall shew thee." The new version reads: "Leave your country, your kinsfolk and your father's house for the land which I will show you."

This is a matter of modern vs. antiquated wording. Occasionally we also encounter a linguistic innovation of specifically religious origin, like the term *in-gathering,* adopted in the eighteenth century to indicate the protracted meeting which was the ancestor of the modern revival (itself a religious term). A very recent one is *kneedrills,* used by the Salvation Army to denote the half-hour weekday service. Nor may we overlook the religious use to which certain secular words are put: in parts of Africa cultivated by missionaries, the word for *heaven,* of which the natives still have a somewhat dim concept, is *bingo.*

Chapter Six

ENGLISH AS A CLASS TOOL (2)

The Argot of Finance—Commercialism and Commercialese—The Language of Science and Technology—Pedagogues and Pedageese

At first glance, the language of finance is something that should interest financiers and no one else. But it is estimated that one family out of every four in the United States is in the financier class by reason of ownership of stocks and bonds. A financial writer, in fact, wants the British *shareholder* to be used in the place of the more customary American *stockholder,* because *share* is descriptive of the stake many of us have in the private enterprise system. Furthermore, there is a deliberate drive on the part of what is vaguely known as "Wall Street" to extend such ownership to more and more people. In the words of the representative of a large brokerage house, "brokers can no longer depend on doing business with just a handful of the rich and financially literate; they've got to do business with John Jones and Bill Smith, and that means they'll have to forget financial lingo and talk in language that everybody can understand."

This campaign marches on side by side with another, that has definite political overtones, designed to make us aware of the true meaning of *capitalism* (a word for which euphemisms are perennially sought, not because there is anything intrinsically wrong with it, but because left-wingers have given it a negative semantic charge), *free enterprise, profit,* the *incentive system, inflation, equity capital*— Let's stop right there. How many know the precise meaning of *equity* used in the financial sense?

The language of finance has: 1) a phraseology that is reminiscent of that of the law, from which it definitely stems: 2) a terminology of special words, and expressions used in a special sense; 3) a class jargon all its own.

Typical of the first are expressions like "for the year then ended," supplemented by a few foreign phrases (*ad valorem* for import duties, or *piculs* for tin, the *picul* being a Straits Settlements measure representing 133.5 lbs.), and Graecisms, like *Stochastic method* (just trial and error to you and me; used in opposition to methods based on charts, graphs and theories), along with *monopsony* and *chroma*. But modern languages, too, enter this complicated vocabulary of finance: French with *demurrage, allonge, entrepot, seignioriage,* Spanish with *bienes,* Italian with *agio, del credere* and *tale quale,* German with *bielbrief. (Easement, attorn, ullage* are nondescript.)

For the second, you have the stock market definition of *long, short, futures, hedging, bulls, bears, lambs;* the *debentures* which are neither stocks nor bonds; or that strange real estate usage of *taxpayer* to refer not to the long-suffering John Q. Citizen, but to a temporary building that defrays the taxes on a piece of land otherwise unused.

Lastly come the coinages, combinations and abbreviations that keep the outsider guessing: *blue chips,* solid leading stocks; *cats and dogs,* speculative stocks; *out the window,* used when a new issue is over-subscribed; *keno!,* to indicate that corn has reached the limit for one day's decline; *auditors and attendants,* to refer to an audience or those who attend a stockholder's meeting. *Hot issue* refers to heavy demand when the security is issued; *yo-yo* means high fluctuation; *hung up* means that the customer can't sell without taking a loss; *pups* are low-priced, inactive stocks; *falling out of bed* means a sharp decline.

Most laymen would interpret *recap* as something you do to a worn tire; but to the financier it is an abbreviation for *recapitalization,* itself a term of dubious significance to the layman. On the stock market floor strange initial abbreviations are used, like *B.C.D.* for "best can do," and *K.I.M.* for "keep in mind." Practically every stock has its pet trade nickname, from *McClanahan*

Oil for Standard Oil of Ireland, to *Whoopie* for Worthington Pump.

It is safe to say that the stock market tongue is still a class jargon, but this description can hardly any longer be applied to the tongue which the hucksters of the advertising world are forever foisting upon us. By its repetitious, propagandistic nature, this tongue is designed to reach the masses, make them "conscious" of something or other, induce them to ask for a product by name or slogan or jingle.

The gentle art of display advertising in periodicals has been traced back as far as 1743, so far as America is concerned, though there is evidence that, nearly ten years before, Benjamin Franklin, in his *Pennsylvania Gazette,* had hit upon the expedient of using larger type to draw attention to a "notice." Among early American advertising media, we find reference to tombstones, used in New England to notify the passer-by of the continuance of a business established by the late lamented, billboards on wagons, and handbills dropped from balloons.

It is undeniable that the two major contributions made by the hucksters' language to the general language of all of us are trade names and trade slogans. The successful trade name "must be easy to read, pronounce and remember, have no unpleasant connotation, and be connected with the intrinsic qualities of the product."

Yet some of the most effective trade names seem to escape these qualifications. *Pall Mall,* for instance, confuses speakers by ranging in pronunciation all the way from Britain's *Pel Mel* to the Midwest's *Paul Maul. Peter Pan* has nothing about it that is connected with a product, yet it is successfully used for bakeries, clothing stores, cleaning establishments, peanut butter and soft drinks. Familiarity, the elusive sense of eternal youth, and freedom from copyright are perhaps as important as the qualities named by the researchers.

Popular among trade-name suffixes are *-ize* and *-ex,* the first perhaps because it conveys an active connotation, the latter because of *excellent. Atomic* is a word much used of late, in connection with such widely diversified products as brake fuel, lead pencils, refrigerators, cigarette lighters, golf balls, love seats and tomatoes.

M. M. Mathews' *Dictionary of Americanisms* has given full standing to *Coca-Cola* (first mentioned in print in 1887, and said to be older than nine out of ten Americans), *Coke, Studebaker,* as well as to trade names and general terms like *kodak, vaseline, celluloid, victrola, B.V.D.'s, mimeograph, yo-yo* and *Eskimo Pie.*

Interesting are the shifts in trade names. The *brassière,* or *bra,* was not always so designated; in the first decade of this century, it was styled *debevoise,* after its first American designer, and dealers had a very hard time getting the new name into circulation. It may also be remarked that trade names are not necessarily international: *Uneeda,* in America, is connected with biscuits; in Britain, with cigars. A deodorant named *Veto* in America becomes *Charmis* in Mexico, *Tact* in Australia. *Wildroot* is *Fiajacrema* in Mexico. *Fab* is *Ola* in Italy, *Pax* in France, *Fluffi* in Germany. *Vel* is *Daisy* in Denmark, *Gam* in France, *Coin* in Germany.

The number of active trade marks listed with the Patent Office reaches the incredible total of 330,000. The trade mark aims for short, punchy words, explosive consonants with lots of *b*'s, *t*'s, *d*'s and *k*'s for the hard sell; but *s*'s, *ch*'s, *z*'s, *zh*'s for feminine products (witness *Charm, Supp-hose*). A new name may cost up to $50,000. *Toronado* took a whole year to figure out. *Touch and Glow* was a fortunate choice. *Tab* was found by a computer. Standard Oil used *Engro* for a new fertilizer, then discovered that in French it sounded like *en gros* ("wholesale"), and shifted to *Enagro.* Procter of Procter and Gamble got *Ivory Soap* out of the "ivory palaces" in the 45th Psalm. *Xograph,* the new three-dimensional photograph, gets its *x* from *parallax.* Eastman devised *Kodak* because he liked the letter *k,* but later lost exclusive right to it, just as Bayer lost *aspirin,* Du Pont lost *cellophane,* and Goodrich lost *zipper.* The Gillette people were at one time perturbed over the fact that in foreign countries the name of their product had become synonymous with "safety razor," and inquired whether the language academies of those countries might be able to help by pointing out to the speakers that *Gillette* was a particular brand, not just any old safety razor.

The copycatting of advertising slogans, as well as of trade marks, is attested by a Japanese beer ad: "Put a tiger in your tankard."

Clark claims that the use and abuse of certain words in American English is almost entirely due to hucksterism (*custom-made* and *exclusive* are among his choices). *A-1* might be added, though it comes from the British insurance field (it was originally used by Lloyd's of London for ship rating). The advertising language is not at all above coinage (*contemporama* for a store ad, *centorama* for a centennial celebration); slang (*trip tease* for a travel folder); incorrect usage (*chaise lounge* for *chaise longue*, defended by a Philadelphia store on the ground that "it is preferred by retail advertisers"). Neither is it above violating the canons of traditional grammar ("like a cigarette should"; "Us smokers would rather fight than switch"; "coffee-er coffee"; "Swissiest cheese"; "peanuttiest"; "macaroni-est"; even "egg-noodliest").

Lastly, it is not above legal complications. The Federal Trade Commission commands, under dire penalties, that furs be exactly labeled with the true name of the animal. This means that rabbits may no longer parade as *Baltic leopards, beaverettes,* or *erminettes;* it means that such familiar names as *mink-dyed muskrat, caracul, Australian chinchilla* and *Hudson seal* are henceforth banished from the American vocabulary, and, since the country of origin must be mentioned, it means that we shall have such hyphenates in the fur world as *Tibetan-Persian lamb* and *Russian-Persian lamb.*

The language of the Madison Avenue advertising agencies is reputed to be responsible for an outlay of one billion dollars a year, mainly for words like *white, power, mild, refreshing, relief,* and for slogans like "whiter than white," "stronger than dirt," "refreshes you best," "don't wait to be told," "for those who think young." It is not above coining its own clichés, a few of which eventually become popular and are used in all sorts of extraneous connections ("of course I'm particular!"; "we must be doing something right!"), though occasionally they defeat their own purpose, as when "Mother, I'd rather do it myself!" had to be taken off the air because it aroused too much laughter.

I. S. Hayakawa, the semanticist, while deploring certain

phases of the Madison Avenue language, boldly asserts that the advertisers are the poets of today, creating symbols of pleasant connotations, and using language in new and untried ways. But such creativeness is a double-edged weapon. Even the most poetic creations are occasionally of the tongue-in-cheek variety, witness "gang green," "Freudian gilt," "barrywater gold" and "statutory grape" for colors of men's shirts; "French custard," "ex-blood blue," "Ingrid suntan" for colors of cars. Newspaper critics, after briefly reviewing creations of the type of *dura-drive, vibra-free, foot-o-matic, tiltamatic, cruisomatic* and *quadrapoise,* ironically suggest *moochandizing* for what the agency does, *caloricraniumed, superschmooched zimgrained valves of molybenillium* (hardest substance known to man) for car parts, *dedentalize* for what some toothpastes do, *fractorium* for the finest floor wax.

The Madison Avenue contribution fortunately includes an inside jargon as well as items destined for the consumer: "I don't get through to your switchboard"; "I get no nourishment out of this material"; "He's a vacant lot"; "Let's run the flag up the pole and see who starts saluting"; "This is pure horseback"; verbs like *to premisecize* and *to preliminate; to swivel-chair* and *to popcorn.* They "make a mother-in-law survey" when they take a poll of TV watchers, but they also "get down on our hands and knees and talk to the consumer."

The language of science and technology enjoys the distinction of being by far the most productive of all the class languages. Fully half the words in our tongue (the half less often and less generally used, to be sure) are of scientific or technological origin. In this respect, science outstrips even slang. Furthermore, its creations are more stable. It seldom happens that a scientific word really drops out of the lexicon; even when it becomes outmoded, it stays in the vocabulary, as a marker and milestone of the progress of scientific thought.

This situation is not surprising, when we stop to think of the pervasiveness of science and its tremendous impact upon life, particularly in the course of the last hundred years. Human activity today is largely connected with science and technology, and even those fields which seem least allied with science are discovered, upon closer examination, to have some scientific or technical angle.

The language of science is often described as international. This is partly true, partly exaggerated. While the majority of scientific terms, based upon Latin and Greek roots, are internationally used, there are, in addition to the phonetic differences presented by their use in each tongue, also certain differences in application which the scientists have not yet succeeded in ironing out.

The men of science, being accustomed to dealing with facts, are realistic in their approach to the language problem. They recognize the existence of other languages, something that people in other walks of life are not always inclined to do. Medical and other scientific gatherings generally carry on their proceedings in at least three or four of the world's major languages. A congress of statisticians that met in Washington, for instance, used a simultaneous translation system similar to that of the UN, with English, French and Spanish as the official languages.

Scientific journals frequently appear in several languages. The Journal of the International Congress of Surgeons carries abstracts in French, Spanish, Italian and Russian as well as English. The British Medical Association publishes its studies and quarterly bulletin in English, French and Spanish. But *Excerpta Medica,* a digest of some seven thousand medical journals from every part of the world, appears exclusively in English, on the ground that "English today is the common language of most scientific men in the world," a proposition that is somewhat debatable, though a survey indicates that about fifty per cent of all scientific articles are now published in English, with French, German, Russian and Italian following in that order. The question of Russian scientific production is, of course, partly obscured by the secrecy that prevails behind the Iron Curtain.

For what concerns scientific English, the question often arises whether it should not be made plainer and more accessible to the layman. On the one hand, the inability of scientific men to express their thoughts clearly is deplored; on the other, the jargon of science is lampooned. Engineering students are put through courses in ordinary English at Rensselaer Polytechnic

Institute so that "they may learn to think and write clearly." A noted scientist makes this pronouncement: "Scientists do write poorly. They rarely use three short words to say anything if ten long ones will suffice." There follows an energetic plea to the scientists to "avoid unnecessary hocus-pocus" and make themselves clearly understood, at least by one another. A Topeka doctor claims that the needlessly complicated writing of his fellow-scientists is due to a blend of two factors: an unconscious wish to be different from the crowd, and a sense of insecurity that makes them afraid of unqualified statements.

Another writer finds a painful parallel between Federal Prose and Medicalese. The sample given deals with a patient who "suffered a bilateral digital amputation" (lost two fingers), with a resultant "diminution of digital dexterity, the end product of same being a severe limitation of his preoperative ability" (can't use his hands so well any more). Yet physicians are so concerned with the impact of current general American slang on their foreign colleagues practising in this country that the Philadelphia Medical Society has set up courses in "colloquial English" to acquaint the foreign doctors with the precise meaning of such symptoms as "a stitch in my side," "sick to my stomach," "I've been out boozing and getting loaded and I really feel lousy."

There is also the story of the drop in the price of antibiotics, at which a druggist remarked: "Now if they will only cut them down to words we can pronounce, there won't be so many wrong doses." A bacteriologist suggests that *desoxyribonucleic acid* be cut down to *dorna*. Another scientist complains that some 750 terms in chemistry are obsolete, and even scientists admit that the Einsteinian language is Greek to most of them. The American Medical Association bows to the demand for comprehensibility by changing the title of its monthly from *Hygeia* to *Today's Health*.

There are, of course, two sides to every question. If we take the ordinary dictionary definition of *diplosis,* this is what we find: "The doubling of the chromosome number by the union of the haploid sets in the union of gametes." Granting that this is Choctaw to the layman, the fact remains that if one knows the meaning of *chromosome, haploid* and *gametes* it becomes mean-

ingful. The point might be made that the person who does not
go seriously into a certain branch of science does not need to
know its terminology, and for a great many of the terms of
science there is no layman's substitute, nor need there be. Hence
the newspaper that lampooned the title of a doctorate thesis at
M.I.T. was basically out of order (the title read in part:
"Synthesis of pseudo-pellecterine and its use in an attempted
synthesis of cyclolctatetraene-carbolic acid").

There is much that is fascinating in scientific terminology,
both of the popular and the learned variety. *Antabuse* is a variety
of disulfide guaranteed to cure you of lost weekends. *Tibione*
(TB-1) is a code name for one of tuberculosis' bitterest foes.
Gymnodinium is a simple form of marine plant that causes the
"red tides" of Florida. *Castrix* does away with rats, but if your
pets take it by mistake, use barbiturates as antidotes. *Jobbins*
(origin unknown to this writer) is a new blood group. *Aerosporin*
is the poetic name of a new antibiotic, and *bacteriophage* is any
virus that "eats" bacteria.

Scientists, too, use certain general words in special connotations. *Sequestration* in chemistry is the softening of water without precipitation of the softening agent.

The words of science are for the most part of Greek and Latin
origin. In paleontology, for instance, the names of the great
lizards of the past are Greek: *bauriamorph, phytosaur, tyranno-
saurus,* etc.; in archaeology, we find the Latin *artifact;* in geology,
cryopodology (the study of frozen ground) is Greek, *congelifract*
and *pergelisol* are Latin (but *ice-blink* for pack ice is straight
Saxon). But botany, astronomy and meteorology often surprise
us with names drawn from other languages, including the
Oriental. Among the names of azaleas are the Japanese *hino-
degiri, kurume* and *yodagawa yedoensis,* side by side with Latin
nudiflora, altaclarense and *calendulacea.* Cherry-tree varieties in
particular bear the names of the country of origin; *Shirofugen,
Sekiyama, Ichiyo, Hisakura. Pluie de feu* (shower of fire) is from
the French, *tulip* (literally "turban") from the Turkish, *hepatica*
("liver-shaped") from the Greek, while *camellia, peony* and
poinsettia are named, respectively, after a missionary (Camellus)
who first introduced the camellia to Europe, an ancient Greek

physician (Paeon) who used the juice of the plant to heal wounds, and an American ambassador to Mexico who brought the "fire-flower" to the United States.

The names of stars and constellations are more often Arabic than Greek or Latin (a precise count of 183 star names shows 125 Arabic, 26 Greek, 14 Latin, 9 Arabic-Latin, 3 Persian: *Alshain, Tarazed* and *Alcor*). The Arabian astronomers made full use of the previous lore of the Sumerians and Assyro-Babylonians. Such terms as *zenith, nadir, azimuth* and *almucantar* show our indebtedness to the Arabs. But *asteroid, coma, parallax* are Greek, *albedo, corona, facula, flocculus, nebula, nova, penumbra* Latin. *Trojan group, sarge, scarp* (for a lunar cliff), *red shift, light year, earth-light* are our own coinages, and *quasar* consists of the first and last syllables of *quasi-stellar*. *Influenza* is originally an astronomical (or rather astrological) term, since medieval Italian astrologers thought its incidence was due to the "influence" of the stars.

Meteorologists use the Japanese *tsunami* for an ocean wave caused by a submarine earthquake, and the German *graupel* for soft hail. Popular weather terms like *hurricane* (West Indian for "evil spirit") and *typhoon* (Chinese for "big wind"), along with *blizzard* (origin unknown, but use restricted to snowstorm accompanied by sub-zero temperatures and high winds) are common property. The U. S. Army meteorologists, in addition, use girls' names, in alphabetical order, for each individual hurricane (*Dora* and *Karen* are typical). They also use terms like *Fido* ("Fog, intensive dispersal of": a fog-dispelling apparatus) and *Zerp-Zerp* ("Ceiling zero, visibility zero"). One meteorological term that often baffles the layman when he hears it on the radio is *degree-day;* this is explained as the number of degrees the average daily temperature is below 65 Fahrenheit; if the day's average is thirty-five degrees, the day is a *thirty-degree-day,* and a month of such weather would total nine hundred degree-days.

Atomic fission has contributed a wealth of terms, both to the popular and the scientific vocabulary. *Chain reaction* is by now a familiar expression. *Health Physics* is the name given to medical and biological research in protection against and treatment of atomic radiation. The *millicurie* is the unit of radiation, defined as thirty-seven million atomic disintegrations per second. *Radiologistics* designates the application of the knowledge of radiation to the identification and alteration of matter. A *radiac* set detects radioactivity, and the same *-ac* ending, standing for "analog computer," appears in the quasi-proper names affectionately bestowed by the scientists upon their electronic robots: Eniac, Reac, Binac, Univac. *Electron, isotope, betatron, nuclide* are in fairly general use, though not many of us know their precise meaning.

Mathematical terminology is traditional (among its elegant borrowings from Latin are *abscissa, idempotent, integer, simplex*). But there is a whole "new" mathematics based on the computer's *binit* system, so abstract that the students are encouraged to use nonsense words like *zilch, zumzi, gerf, sloogles* and *quins*. Computerdom itself has its own terminology: *alphameric, bit, cobol, fortran, laser, white noise;* uses such common words as *housekeeping* and *garbage* in its own specialized meanings; and coins such terms as *ruly* (the opposite of *unruly*), *howby* (the mode of proximate cause, such as limping as the result of a fall, or gaining polish from wear), *sli resilrig* (for slightly flexible), *adornblem,* and *attractive-non*.

From space rocketry come such terms as *wedge angle, delta V, posigrade* and *retrograde burn, phasing maneuver, transfer orbit, radiosonde, aerobiology, aeronomy, aeropause, afterbody, lox, gox* and *zero gravity. Translation* is used in connection with a sideways thrust. *Apogee, perigee, giga, mega, micro, pico,* are held in common with other sciences. You don't *destroy* but *destruct* a malfunctioning rocket, and the malfunction itself is slangily known as a *glitch*. Picturesque, often mythological or literary, are the names bestowed on the missiles: *Neptune, Kingfisher, Little Joe, Gorgon, Gargoyle, Bumblebee, Loon.*

The social and psychological scientists, too, are verbose, and their prolixity is less justified, since for the most part their nomenclature deals not with material objects, as does that of the physical scientists, but with entities of their own creation.

Accordingly, the criticism leveled at psycho-sociological parlance is far more bitter than that which meets the physical scientists and technologists. A college president says that "today sociologists are building up a terrible jargon, though I have yet to find in their books an idea that is not capable of being explained in standard English." A prominent book reviewer inveighs against the "fantastic lingo invented by the structural-functional school of sociologists," which he describes as "profundity through obfuscation." A circular by the head of ECA to his subordinates states that the clumsy, obscure and long-winded language they use is often even worse than that found in "the writings of university social science departments, whence has come much of the present-day corruption of style."

What are some samples of this objectionable language? The anthropologists, long in the field, have a traditional terminology which includes *levirate* and *sororate, neoteny* and *couvade, mana, amok* and *tabu, dolicocephalic* and *brachycephalic.* But there is a sociological branch of anthropology which has given us *folkways, value-free, nuclear family* (merely father, mother and children), *peer groups, reference groups, internalization, ethnocentricism, differential association, anomic. Mores* was a vogue-word circulated in the past by this group. Today they favor *charisma,* the quasi-miraculous communicative power which a leader like Kennedy or Castro has for the masses (one might call it *personality* and not be too far off).

The traditional philosophers rest with their *nous* and *noumenon* and *categorical imperative.* Dr. Wiener has given us *cybernetics,* which is simple and descriptive enough if you know that *kybernein* in Greek means "to steer." It is the more psychological sciences that are linguistically creative. *Dianetics* has *engram* and *basic-basic, pre-clear reactive mind, reverie* and *time-track.* Scientology offers *somatic release, enmest, entheta, look scanning, dubins, rock-slams, anal* (or *genital,* or *oral*) *character, cephalocaudal progression, equipotentiality, idiot savant. Gestalt* is an old and established term; so are *synesthesia, sibling rivalry, Einstellung, paranoia, libido, id, ego* and *superego, Oedipus complex* and *schizophrenia.*

The manias and phobias are extraordinarily numerous, including such forms as *anachoresiphobia,* a reluctance to back up when facing adverse conditions. Then we have the *ecto-, endo-*

and *mesomorphs,* into which constitutional psychologists and sociologists would divide all human beings. *Amnesia, aphasia, agraphia* are legitimate terms to describe conditions wherein one loses the power to remember, speak or write, and *endophasia* is obviously speaking to oneself. Lastly come the recent coinages of the psycho-sociologists, both legitimate (*psychotechnics,* to describe the application of psychology in industry) and humorous (*imaginitis, scarecoma, apprehendicitis, fearosis,* to describe the condition of some of the psychologist's patients).

It is more and more the fashion these days to view the entire process of education as a social science, rather than the imparting of factual knowledge. Hence the educationists have developed a full-fledged social-scientific jargon, which the more level-minded among them have labeled *pedageese.* This language is made up of pretentious words like *motivation, integration, frustration, ambivalence,* and equally pretentious expressions like "basic insecurity," "behavior patterns," "parent resentment," "expanding democracy," "changing world," "educating the whole child" and "experiences in social living." More specialized are "negative motives of learning," "need imbalance," "cultural immersion." These are accompanied by quaint and misleading names for various educational activities—*workshop, colloquium course,* and something that sounds like *canine program,* but on investigation turns out to be a human *K-9.* A few deliberately humorous designations appear, like the *slave market* that well describes educational conventions at which young (and sometimes old) aspirants bargain for collegiate jobs. Despite PTA meetings and much drum-beating on the part of "progressive" educators, there seems to be little likelihood that this class jargon will to any great extent infiltrate the general language.

Is there any general conclusion that may be drawn from our survey of language as a class tool? So long as a class language remains a jargon, it is harmless and may be, at least in part, necessary. The danger of class jargons begins when they attempt to spill over into the general language and influence the thought-processes of the community. At this point they assume propagandistic overtones. Whether the lingo is communistic, artistic, political, legal, financial, commercial, scientific or pedagogical, the minute it overflows its bounds it becomes a tool to strengthen the hold of a given class over the population at large, or, in the best of hypotheses, to create a snobbish class superiority which is at variance with the spirit, if not the letter, of democracy.

Reasonable recommendations for the specialists in the various fields would be: 1) to keep their linguistic creations to a minimum, so as not to clutter up the language more than it is already cluttered; 2) to reserve them strictly for the trade and not flourish them for the bedazzlement of the layman.

The layman might correspondingly be advised to guard against semantic overcharges, hidden linguistic propaganda which is as insidious as Congressional lobbying, and too ready acceptance of terms that are not readily understood; and next, to laugh and satirize out of existence, if possible, the pompous and pretentious coinages of those who would like to pose as high priests of new and mystic religions parading under the name of sciences and movements. Discrimination must, of course, be exercised in both these processes. The general warning embodied in the Spanish proverb "Don't drink water you can't see" is in order. Healthy skepticism, like chicken broth, never hurt anybody.

At the same time, linguistic history teaches us that elements from class jargons have at all times filtered into the general speech. The speeding up of this process in modern times is simply due to the multiplication of man's activities. Likewise, there is no discovered cure for human gullibility. The type of language forecast in *1984,* or a reasonable facsimile of it, may yet come to pass if present trends continue unabated.

Chapter Seven

THE ENHANCEMENT AND
DEGRADATION OF THE LANGUAGE

*The Amusement World—The Tongue of Stage and
Screen—The Language of Radio and Video—The
Speech of the Fourth Estate—The Language of Sports*

Stage, screen, radio, television, press—and sports reporting as
included in some of these classifications—are the great diffusers
and transformers of present-day language. Yet they, too, have
special, semi-secret tongues, similar in most respects to the jargons of the trades and professions. But, unlike the latter, the
language of these great media of modern propaganda has an
excellent chance of penetrating everyday speech and influencing
it deeply, far beyond other fields of human activity. A term from
the movies or TV, a choice bit of newspaper parlance, a baseball
expression, which one day are obscure to all save the initiate,
may the next day sweep the land. Far more subtle than individual words, entire linguistic attitudes and processes may pass
from one of these specialized fields into the popular speech. The
great means of mass communication and entertainment are the
fields that particularly bear watching if we want to get a clue to
the significant language movements of the future.

It would not be fair to say that the innovations of stage, screen,
radio, TV, press and sports are the only sources from which the
language receives accretions and is inspired to change. Nevertheless, if our tongue changes drastically within the next fifty years,
the chances that it will change through those instrumentalities
are large. Whether the prospective change will result in an
enhancement or a degradation of the language is best left to the
reader's judgment.

We may now pass on to some of the specific contributions

made by each entertainment field, with the distinct understanding that some of them are mere words, such as might be contributed by any jargon, while others display very specific language trends.

"The stage" is an expression that covers a multitude of activities. There is an operatic stage, a musical stage, a burlesque stage, a legitimate stage, even a night-club and a lecture stage. From each of these an influence is exerted upon the language.

Some of the words of the stage are common property. *Angel* and *Rialto, the road* and *Tin Pan Alley,* the *clique* and the *claque* are well known (concerning the last two, a theatrical critic declares that "a clique is to a claque as a crime of passion is to Murder, Inc.").

Slightly less familiar are *Borscht circuit* (now also *Silo circuit,* or summer stock), *rocking-chair hit,* a song that leaps out of obscurity and sweeps the nation, and a few foreign terms like *succès d'estime. M. C.,* an abbreviation originating in night-clubs, has become one of our most productive examples of functional change (*to emcee, emceeing*), while *Femcee* for "mistress of ceremonies" has sprung from it like Eve from Adam's rib. Then there are the mystery words which still have not gotten across to the great unwashed, words like *to shill, sides* (either the boundary of a stage, or a page of dialogue intended for a single character), *lobby professor* (a lobby critic on the opening night of a road try-out). To the initiate, an *Annie Oakley* is a free pass. Many know that the *Tony* awarded for acting ability goes back to Antoinette Perry, its first recipient. Many words and expressions in common use had their inception on the stage: *deadpan, double take, flashback, heavy, to lay an egg, limelight, punch line, on the road, runway* (at first used in burlesque shows). More slangy are *tin pan, turkey, twofer, upstage, ad lib, boffo* (said to come from *box office*). More elegant, to the point of preserving their original foreign form, are *tableau, vaudeville, soubrette, panorama, melodrama, ingénue, Grand Guignol, ensemble, deus ex machina, dénouement, Commedia dell'Arte, climax, catharsis.* Slightly out of date are *terpery* (dance hall, presumably from Terpsichore, goddess of the dance); *blue stuff* (risqué stage business); *Booners* (talent scouts, from Daniel Boone); *to brody* (to flop, from Steve Brody), *cuffo* (for free, on the cuff). Very modern additions are the *theatre of the absurd* and the Japanese *kabuki*.

The legitimate stage's greatest contribution to language lies perhaps in the field of phonology. It may or may not be true that Shakespeare was instrumental in fixing numerous innovations in English pronunciation, and that David Garrick was responsible for inventing the British broad *ah* in *ask, bath, dance,* etc., but it is undoubted that many countries recognize the stage pronunciation of their language as the official one (the Germans have even devised the term *Bühnenaussprache*). Currently, American reviewers are expressing their dissatisfaction with certain pronunciations they hear or think they hear on the stage: *gawt, certin, markit, subjict, heeyah, hatrid, supportid, prawfits, nawnsense.*

However, there is little doubt that the legitimate stage has dropped into the background so far as its influence upon the spoken language is concerned. Today it is the movie, radio and TV that really influence the masses. But a sufficient number of old stage actors have passed on to those fields to allow us to assert that the dividing line between stage, screen and TV is tenuous indeed.

The world of music is a linguistic world in its own right. It differs from the spoken stage and its ramifications by having a subject-matter which does not seek to ape the world of reality. Correspondingly, its influence upon everyday speech is relatively slight. It has, of course, its own vast terminology, a good deal of which consists of purely foreign words. Many of these have so penetrated the spoken tongue that they are used today without any musical connotation whatsoever (*staccato, falsetto, bravo, impresario*). Others are highly picturesque but little known (*hemidemisemiquaver, mixolydian, passacaglia, voci bianche*). Some lend themselves to misspellings (*a cappella,* "chapel fashion," generally rendered in print as *a capella,* "little goat fashion"); or to misnomers (*alto,* "high," for a "low" feminine voice; the original unabbreviated expression is *contralto,* or "counter-high"). Some of the musical world's coinages verge on slang, like *jazz, swing, hep, gutbucket* (defined as "slow, dirty blues") or Sigmund Romberg's *middlebrow* (half-way between highbrow and lowbrow).

The language of the music critic, like that of the art critic, is normally incomprehensible; take, for instance, this passage: "There is a unity of style in chordal progress and melodic direction that bespeaks a rather individual idiom." That the critics are themselves aware of this is indicated by a two-column article by the late Olin Downes entitled "Down with Neo," in which the critic voiced his strenuous objection to terms like *neo-classic, neo-impressionistic* and *neo-atonalist,* and recalled that Verdi, on being asked whether the score for a tragical moment should be cast as an aria or a recitative, replied, "I'd just write a little music."

But when we sum everything up, it can hardly be said that the terminology of the music world exerts too great an influence on language. There is perhaps one division where such an influence could be exerted, in one of two possible directions. I am referring to the great controversy as to whether opera should be sung in foreign languages or in English. Samuel Johnson once defined the opera as "exotic and irrational entertainment," but this early pronouncement did not hold. Today, the growing popularity of operatic music has led to a demand for translation of the words into English, so that the action may be followed with complete understanding by the audience.

From the standpoint of permanent effect upon the language, the operatic controversy gives the clue to some long-term trends. If opera remains foreign in speech, it may lead to more foreign-language study on the part of Americans and to a healthier attitude toward those languages and their cultures. If the translation tendency wins out, we may expect a permanent clarifying effect upon the phonetics of English, a clearer and more distinct enunciation of a language too often mumbled and jumbled by its speakers, possibly even a regression of our unstressed vowels to the clear-cut quality they once had and lost, with the attendant disappearance of the grunts and snorts that have replaced them in the prosaic mouths of nations too practically inclined to watch their diction. All considered, it would seem that the language cannot lose, whichever way the battle goes.

The screen, older than the radio or TV, has been making contributions to the language since its inception. Everyone knows how the diction of screendom's stars is dictated by dialogue people who are expert phoneticians. They patiently work on stars who say, "I sawr Mayry and spent fi' dollars on the way," or, conversely, train them to say, "Didn' I tell ya?" when the role calls for such pearls of enunciation. When American movie actors prepare for British roles, the phoneticians give them complete courses in the Oxford accent, working the process in reverse when British actors must play American parts. Deliberately or not, our movie phoneticians have long been fostering a new "universal English," equally comprehensible and acceptable in America, Britain and the Commonwealth, and this is evident from the fact that whereas twenty years ago British screen pronunciation was almost totally incomprehensible to Americans and vice versa, today both are readily understood in all parts of the English-speaking world.

This process of linguistic unification has other tools, to be sure. The radio is a powerful auxiliary of the spoken film. So are TV and Telstar. Ease of communications lends a hand. But if, in the year 2000, the differences that grew up in the seventeenth, eighteenth and nineteenth centuries between the King's English and the American Language are fully erased, a great portion of the credit must go to the spoken film, which brings to the masses of one nation the speech-habits of the other so that an unconscious blend may ultimately result.

The language of the radio and TV has, first and foremost, its complicated technological jargon, which is only in part comprehensible to the masses. Among radio's expressions we find *Deejay* (or *pancake turner*) for disk jockey, *gabber* for commentator, *adenoid* for a shrill-voiced or squeaky singer, *bye-bye* for the line "We take you now to—" or "We return you to—." A *cowcatcher* or *hitchhiker* is a commercial given at the end of the program to advertise a secondary product of the sponsor, a *crawk* is a sound-effects man who imitates animals, a *creeper* (or *mike mugger*) is an actor who inches too close to the mike; to *cue-bite* is to begin one's lines before the preceding performer has finished; *dead air* is a period of silence, *fun-in-the-studio* designates lines designed to sound like ad-libbing; an *inherited audience* refers to listeners left over from the previous program, a *razoo* is a Bronx-cheer-producing instrument used to convey a buzzing sound, a *quonk* is a noise made by a person not on the program, *walla walla* are crowd-scene sounds, and *zilch* is a generic name for a person whose name is unknown, like the John Doe of the law.

TV offers *bloom* (light-struck image), *ghost* (secondary image caused by reflection), *rain* (vertical interference patterns), *washtub weeper* (daytime soap opera), *channel swimmer* (a viewer who constantly shifts stations). In television language an *oater* (or *they-went-that-awayer* is a Western. *Fish bowl* is used for observation booth, *arsenic* for a spot announcement of boresome content, *bullfrog* for a deep voice, *lockjaw* for a tired singer, *klinker* for a bad note, *residue director* for the man who fits programs together.

You may have noticed as you read the foregoing that definitions are occasionally given in terms which are themselves radio or TV jargon, but are fully known to the general public (*mike,* with its TV counterpart *ike,* for iconoscope; *commercial, ad-libbing,* an old stage term that has now passed into the radio, *soap opera, disk jockey.* Other such terms within the general domain are *guesting* (appearing as guest on radio or TV) *telegenic* and *videogenic,* based on an earlier *photogenic,* and, in the more scientific division, *sonochrome* (black and white), *polychrome* (color TV), *definition* (distinctness of image), *simulcast* (program on both radio and TV), *linearity.* *Crooner* is generally known, but *boff singer* and *belter* are not (they denote one who sings with an open throat, letting the bad notes fall where they may).

One curious historical note about the term television itself is that it seems to have made its first appearance in 1907, in a magazine entitled *The World Today,* where it was defined as "photographing through a telegraph wire," obviously the process by which distant news photos are received today. "Distant electric vision" was the term used by engineers when TV was still in the blueprint stage, and the battle now is between *video* (Latin for "I see") and the abbreviated TV, with the latter winning out.

What of the more general and enduring effects of radio and TV on the everyday language? First, we have both media confirming their audiences in bad linguistic habits so far as other tongues are concerned. All we have to do is listen to an advertiser's radio rendition of the names of such products as Bon Ami and La France to realize that the new instruments of popular information do not consider it part of their mission to teach their listeners how to pronounce foreign words correctly. Newscasters are only slightly superior to advertisers in their handling of foreign names and words, despite the existence of excellent manuals and guides to radio pronunciation, like Cabell Greet's now famous *World Words*.

But according to some critics, it's the national language that suffers even more than the tongues of other lands from what goes on in radio and TV. One writer objects to cliché puns and their slangy connotations. A second columnist mourns over the displacement of the simple affirmative *yes* by the quiz-bred *that's right*. Another deplores the effect on children of stars who may earn half a million dollars a year but still have not mastered English. Walter Cronkhite's *Febuary* has drawn fire. So has Dean Martin's "Evvabuddy luvzumbuddy zumtime" (at least that's how it sounded to the critic). Others protest the current "Do you read me?" for "Do you hear me?" when airplanes or submarines communicate, but here perhaps the fault lies with the military rather than with the medium.

One metropolitan paper proclaims editorially that if Americans now talk more rapidly and literately than their parents did, they owe it to "the breathlessness of masters of ceremonies, the almost hysterical attempt of commentators to cram as many words as possible into a limited number of minutes, the haste of contestants to blurt out a prize-winning answer before too many seconds elapse." As against the advantageous trend, says the editor, the present generation, despite its larger vocabulary and incredible speed, expresses itself with less precision than did its predecessor, and he concludes that the radio's unseen audience is driven not so much to talk as to double-talk.

One final effect of radio and TV on the language must be noted. There is no doubt that these great media of information have cut down considerably the time that used to be devoted to reading, both of newspapers and of books. This means in turn that while radio and TV may enhance the spoken language (if indeed they do) they also tend to make of us a nation of functional illiterates, absorbing our language through the ear rather than the eye. Some may view this as a return of language to its original form and function; others may consider it a reversal, pure and simple, to the semi-literate Middle Ages.

Next on the list of potent factors that exert their influence on present-day speech is the dread Fourth Estate, wielding its power directly over the written tongue, indirectly but oppressively over the spoken language.

One is sometimes tempted to wonder whether the *Acta Diurna,* the daily official news-bulletin of Republican and imperial Rome, had its part in shaping the Latin of Caesar, Cicero and Virgil. We do know for a fact that since its first modern appearance in the seventeenth century, the daily press has been molding our own English. Charles II's *Intelligencer,* later known as the *Oxford Gazette,* and still later as the *London Gazette,* was one of the earliest mouthpieces for bureaucratic *do*'s and *dont*'s, exceeding in venerability the London *Daily Universal Register* which later became the *London Times.*

Since then, the press has had among its daily duties to collect and propagate bits of linguistic innovation, words and grammatical constructions and figures of speech from all fields of human activity, barring none. The entire world is its arena. It is not trammeled by literary tradition, as books are (or were, until recently). It deliberately seeks out the timely item, the picturesque episode, the witty saying. Slang, jargon, argot, colloquial and substandard language, all find shelter under its mighty wing. It may not create literature, but literature finds itself compelled more and more to borrow from its style if it wishes to live.

It may be objected that in all these multifarious activities, the press plays not a creative, but merely a recording role, and that its written language follows, in an almost literal sense, the spoken tongue of the multitudes. But this is not always or altogether true. The press makes its own innovations, and the spoken tongue often bows to it and follows it. Professor Clark, for instance, attributes to the press the use of such compounds as *Kremlin-inspired, air-minded* and *teen-age,* as well as the current use of verbs like *to brief* and *to screen.*

There are at least three divisions of language in which the press resolutely takes the lead and sets the pace. First and foremost is the matter of snappy headlines, which give tone to the newspaper language, but which also affect, by a process of unconscious imitation, the tongue of the people. "Nab 3 Holdup Teens" crackles a headline. If we analyze this, we find several separate linguistic processes at work. There is the omission of a subject, the use of a verb in "impersonal" fashion; then comes the use of monosyllabic abbreviations for full-length words, *nab* for *arrest, teens* for *teen-agers.* The use of a written numeral for the word *three* is a space-and-time saver. Lastly, the great English process of functional change is reflected and abetted by the use of *holdup* as an adjective; and in this connection let us not forget that *holdup* is technically "incorrect" even as a noun, its original form and function being the verb *to hold up.*

To say that this telegraphic style does not affect the spoken language is nonsense. Full spoken sentences such as (I) "donwannago," (they) "got 'im," (you) "goin' out?" are, if not fostered, at least encouraged by the headline that starts with a verb. The miraculous functional changes of English, whereby *contact* and *crest* become verbs and *boost* and *cut* nouns, find their justification, if any were needed, in newspaper headlines. But the field in which the newspaper language reigns supreme is the creation, resurrection and coddling of three- and four-letter monosyllables (not all of them necessarily of Anglo-Saxon origin, by the way), which tend more and more to oust their polysyllabic synonyms. This process has gone on so long that we are sometimes at a loss to recall the longer equivalents which have been all but banished from the language. What newspaper speaks today of a *salary increase,* when *pay boost* is available, of an *automobile collision* in the face of a *car crash? Ban* for *exile, flay* for *denounce, gems* for *jewels, rap* or *score* for *criticize, kin* for *relatives, sleuth* for *detective, thug* for *criminal, wed* for *marry, mart* for *market,* are only a few of the substitutions that have been made in our journalistic language, some of which are downright anachronisms (*Norse* for *Norwegian*), others inaccuracies (*Nazi* for *German, Red* for *Russian* or *Communist, Dominica* for *Dominican Republic*).

All this makes the language pithy, terse, brief. But there are limits. *Quiz* has to do service for both "examination" and "investigation." "To back" is not quite as accurate as "to support," nor is *jobless* as dignified as *unemployed.* Headline English is a form of pidginization, and results in confusion and misunderstanding. When you see "Million in Gold Flies," can you be sure that it is a million in gold that takes wing, or is it a million in flies made of gold? "New Jersey Jobless Pay Up" might mean that they are getting more money, but it might also mean that they are paying their just debts. "Drunken Mule Driving Charged" makes you wonder whether the mule or the driver was drunk. A collection of headline gems gathered over a period of years includes the following puzzles: "Casualties from Cold Cut" (could cold cuts inflict casualties?); "AMA's Lenin Quote Hit" (since when did Lenin belong to AMA? Conversely, was his quote a hit, or was it hit?); "Death Claims Insurance" (how can death claim insurance?); "Algiers Has Draft Check" (a payment for the draft?); "Dies After Fumigating Plant" (but the plant died first?); "French Official in Leningrad" (the Soviets display good taste in making French co-official with Russian?); "Black Bars Stay for Slayer" (what does that mean? But then you find out that it's Justice Black).

Perhaps the fault lies with a language that permits such constructions even under headline conditions. At any rate, if, in the course of the next thousand years, English becomes a completely monosyllabic, flectionless and positional language, like Chinese, to the press and its headlines must go most of the credit or blame.

Yet, with all the "degrading" influences wielded by the press on the language, we find strange intellectual jewels in our daily newspapers. A columnist, writing in a paper supposed to be popular, speaks of "Weltschmerz and human frailties." A financial writer, describing the state of the stock market, uses, verbatim and untranslated, Villon's famous refrain *"Mais où sont les neiges d'antan?"* And the New Orleans *Times-Picayune* for years opened its financial page with a quotation from Shakespeare appropriate to the operations of the day.

If the press "debases," it also educates and elevates. Sad indeed for the speakers of English will be the day when they and their speech are no longer served by a press that is free to do both!

The last of our chosen divisions, sports, exerts upon the language an influence that is at the same time less obtrusive and more flamboyant than that of other fields. It is more of a creator and less of a carrier. It does not have at its disposal the means of influencing the speakers directly, but in return its innovations are more picturesque and carry a greater imitation-appeal. It can, furthermore, use each and every one of the other media as a diffusion tool.

With sports, it is not so much a question of changing people's phonology, for the phonology of the sporting world is directly derived from the mouths of the people. Morphological innovations are likewise scanty. It may be that some day we shall all be using *slud* as the past of *slide,* after the pattern set by Dizzy Dean, or that Infield Ingersoll's desire to "easify the languish" will lead us to use *swang* and *flang* on the analogy of *sang, plew* for *played* because of *slew* from *slay.* But if these infringements of our verbal system occur, they will be only minor historical repetitions of a phenomenon that has been going on since Anglo-Saxon days, whereby verbs shift from one category to another and back again. In the syntactical field, Dean's "don't fail to miss tomorrow's game" is on a par with the song writer's "them spurs ain't very far from wrong." The very lack of logic of such creations, saying the opposite of what the speaker means, works against their general acceptance.

It is the field of vocabulary that is the true stamping-ground

of sports. *Good-asterous* as the Deanesque opposite of *disastrous*
did not catch, but few people realize how many of the words and
expressions of our common colloquial language stem from sports.
"To play ball," "to play ball with someone," "he's in there pitch-
ing," "hit and run," "to be caught flatfooted," "to get in one's
innings," "to pinch-hit for someone," "to warm up," "to warm
up to," "to be caught napping" are fair samples of what the
American common language gets from baseball. *Crestfallen* comes
from cock-fighting, *neck and neck* from horse-racing, *sidestep* and
straight from the shoulder from prize fighting, *stymied* from golf,
behind the eightball from billiards.

Sports borrow freely from one another's terminology. *Boxer*
is not only a prizefighting term, but also the name of a breed of
dogs who like to spar; in a day of more cruel sports, these dogs
were known as *bull-biters* or *bear-biters. Uppercut,* another fighting term, is also used in bridge to describe the trumping of a partner's high card to force out a high trump from the declarer's hand.

Of course, each sport has its own peculiar jargon, which often
fails to get out to the general public. In basketball circles, an
extra tall player is known as a *goon* or *giraffe. Sudden death* is
used in several sports to indicate that two teams that are tied at
the end of the regular playing period must go on till one scores.
Court tennis uses *love, dedans* and *penthouse,* curling has *kizzle-
kazzle,* wrestling speaks not only of *half Nelsons* and *toe-holds,*
but refers to non-wrestlers as *civilians,* and skiing has *snow-bun-
nies* (novices), *boilerplate* (hard snow), *baskers* (half-trained skiers)
sitzmark (impression left in snow by one who has sat down in it,
with *bathtub* for a large size), *schussboomers* (those who get to
the bottom of a hill with the least possible delay), *langlauf* ("long
run," from the German), and expressions like "no tow, no go."
Horse-racing speaks of *place* and *show* in its own sense. *Spelunk-
ing* is the relatively infrequent sport of exploring caves, and its
addicts are *spelunkers.*

There is little doubt that a certain amount of sporting terminology is coined not by the players but by the press reporters. G. B.
Shaw, in his younger days, composed a news report of a prize-fight
that was a gem of poetic slang; "plush on the boko napped your
footman's left" ran one of the lines, others of which held such

terms as *dicebox* and *ivory;* but these expressions were probably already in use in British sports terminology. We are uncertain about "tall can of corn" for a high fly, but "circus catch," "wild pitch," "twin bill" (double-header) seem to fall under the heading of press rather than sports creations. Definite creations of the writers are *pennantitis* (a strong hankering for the world's series pennant), *nickel series* (a thing of the past; two teams from the same city, normally New York, vying for the pennant, with the fans able to travel to either team's park for a nickel).

Instructive to linguist and layman alike is the attempt of a British reporter to describe a World's Series game in cricket terms: "The pitcher (bowler) stands almost as far away from the batter as in cricket, and it is by no means as easy to hit a homer (one that gets you right around and back to the home plate) as experts at rounders might think," the account reads in part. "Other single terms are catcher (in the wicket-keeper's position) and shortstop, who is a nippy infielder like silly mid-on. It takes years to master the finer points, like one batter making a sacrifice hit for another," he concludes.

Whatever the British may think of it, the great American sport of baseball enjoys the distinction of exerting a mighty influence, not only on our language, but on others. French, Spanish, Japanese are all infiltrated by baseball terms, in all of the language divisions. There is the loan-translation, as when Latin-Americans cry *"Maten al arbitro!"* and French fans *"Tuez l'arbitre!"* (Kill the umpire!"). There is also a bad loan-translation, as when the former Brooklyn Dodgers used to be called *los perezosos* "the shirkers," "the lazy ones") south of the border. There are hybrid words, in which the American-English root is used with a French or Spanish ending (*baseballeur, faulear, el fildeo*). There are straight borrowings with modified spelling (*beisbol, jonrón, jit, tim*), and other borrowings where the spelling is unchanged, but the pronunciation is weird. If English is ever accepted as the international language, it will be due almost as much to our predominance in sports as to our leadership in trade.

Is there any general conclusion to be drawn from this survey of the influence exerted upon the language by the various entertainment industries of the land? Aside from the varied phenomena we have outlined, this fact seems to be self-evident: people learn best what they acquire painlessly. A language habit gained at the theatre or the movies, a form of speech acquired while listening to a favorite program on radio or TV, a phrase or expression picked up from a sport we love to watch or a newspaper we enjoy reading when we are relaxed has a better chance of imprinting itself upon our consciousness than what we have to learn as a chore. Psychologically, this makes our entertainment industry the very highest educational instrument at our disposal, superior even to our schools and colleges, with their pedantic approach and artificial restrictions. Permanent innovations in the language are therefore more likely to come from this source than from any other.

This would seem to be an ideal set-up for a sermon on how we could turn our stage, screen, radio, TV, press and sporting fields into prescriptive educational agencies, at least for what concerns the "purity" of the language. Not at all. The primary mission of these media is to entertain, not to educate. The minute education becomes uppermost in any one of them, they will lose their hold over the masses, which will properly recognize them as propaganda weapons wielded by someone with an axe to grind. The essence of their educational potentialities is that education must be incidental, a by-product of entertainment.

As for the language, we can safely leave it to shift for itself. Language's most inherent characteristic is change. It is not doing the language a favor to put it into a straitjacket and keep it frozen where it is today. By all means let it be "enhanced" or "degraded," as the case may be and as our individual leanings may lead us to view the process. The screen and radio and press and sports innovation of today may become the official language of tomorrow; or it may not, as the public sees fit. It is the users of the language who decide, by a far more thoroughly democratic process than any yet devised by political theorists and statesmen, a process that has gone on since the beginning of speech and will undoubtedly accompany the human race to its grave. There is no stopping the enhancement or degradation of the language.

Chapter Eight

THE WHIMSIES OF THE LANGUAGE

How Words Come Into Being—Linguistic Misconceptions—The Old Curiosity Shop of English—Strange Speakers and Stranger Usages—Believe It or Leave It

There are several related spheres of language which are not too important, either scientifically or practically, but which nevertheless cast a spell over all but the most untutored minds.

Chief and most serious among them is etymology, the lore of word-origins, of which many samples have already appeared. Etymology is a recognized branch of linguistic science, even though it forms the basis of many popularizations. Just as modern scientific chemistry and astronomy had charlatan precursors in alchemy and astrology, so was etymology made the subject of amateurish attempts through the ages. The word-origins suggested by some of the greatest writers and philosophers of Classical times are often such as to make the modern linguist's hair stand on end, but they testify to the everlasting curiosity of the human mind as to where words come from. As late as the sixteenth century, writers of world-wide renown like those of the French Pléïade indulged in overimaginative word-derivations, and were properly satirized for their pains by Rabelais. Today, despite the vast amount of serious scholarship that has gone into the subject, we are still plagued with so-called "folk etymologies," which are a monument to the powers of the misdirected human fancy.

The human being likes not merely to speculate about the origin of his words; he also likes to play with the words themselves. The result is a series of strange linguistic creations—the tongue of crossword puzzles, the secret languages of Gypsies, British tinkers and American teen-agers, the nonsense-language of Spoonerisms, and a form that may have started out as a joke, but is becoming alarmingly widespread—the double-talk that apes a professional jargon incomprehensible to the multitudes and that has already crossed the written-language boundary, aided and abetted, perhaps, by the strange misuses to which the language is subjected by some of our *avant-garde* poets and writers.

There are also the thoroughly useless but ingenious arrangements af letters and words designed to mystify the reader, as when a correspondent points out that there are at least three words with four consecutive vowels (*aqueous, queue, sequoia*) and one which contains all five English vowels (*miaoued*); that the best available series of four very long words making complete sense is *Constantinopolitan maladministration superinduces denationalization*. Another sets out to construct ten-word series of "cats and dogs," and comes out with *cataclysm, catacomb, Catalan, catalepsy, catalogue, catalyst, catamaran, catapult, catastrophe, catechism, category* for the first, and with *doge, doggerel, dogma, dogcart, dogfish, dogged, dog Latin, dogrose, dogear, Dog Star, dogtrot* and *dogvane* for the second. No one in the English-speaking world, however, has ever equaled the *tour de force* of Spanish writer Carlos Ibáñez, who, in each of his twenty-eight novels, completely dispensed with a separate letter of the Spanish alphabet.

Offsetting the deliberate nature of these linguistic malcreations are the "boners" of the language, the Malapropisms, the accidental humor-coinages due to ignorance pure and simple. Their significance (and it is a limited one) lies in the fact that the language lends itself to them. A greater significance, perhaps, embraces them as well as their intentional counterparts. "Language" that does not communicate properly is not truly language, since the essence of language is full semantic transfer, the completion of the circuit that binds both speaker and hearer. Let this principle be kept firmly in mind by all our would-be innovators!

Among picturesque word-origins, the name of the card-game *faro* goes all the way back to the Pharaohs of ancient Egypt, since French playing cards had an Egyptian monarch as one of the kings in the pack. *Sardonic* really means Sardinian, having first been used by Homer to describe sinister laughter because a herb grown on the island of Sardinia was in his day said to cause death by laughing. This word-origin, in turn, calls to mind the popular Australian name for the giant kingfisher or kookaburra, *laughing jackass,* due to the bird's cry. Also connected with laughter is the term *quid* used for a plug of tobacco; it seems that an early plug manufacturer, grown rich, inscribed on his carriage the Latin *Quid rides?* ("What are you laughing at?"); but bystanders failed to recognize the inscription as Latin, read it in English, and figured that since Quid was riding, his product might as well be known by his name.

Then there are ancient words like *lethal,* derived from the waters of the river Lethe, which in Greek mythology ran through the land of the dead, and *dicker,* from Latin *decuria,* a group of ten, and more specifically a bale of ten hides, used by the Romans for barter with frontier tribes. More recent in history is the word *royalty* used in a financial sense; the term was first applied to a perpetual pension granted in 1676 by Charles II to his illegitimate son, the Duke of Richmond, which consisted of a duty of one shilling a ton on all coal exported from the Tyne for consumption in England; this, of course, means that John L. Lewis had greater historical backing for his use of the word than have authors of books or owners of oil wells (one author holds that in view of the decline in the value of book royalties, their name should be changed to *peasantries*). Still more recent is *buffs,* a term applied to volunteer firemen in the last century from the buffalo robes some of them wore.

On the other hand, *termagant* goes all the way back to an apocryphal Moslem deity, Tervagant, first mentioned in the eleventh-century *Chanson de Roland; caterpillar* is the Norman-French *catepelose,* "hairy cat"; and *Jim Crow,* despite its nineteenth-century American appearance, seems to go back to an earlier Worcestershire dialect expression, *Jim Crow and Mary Anne,* used to describe unsettled weather.

Equally fascinating is the story of word-substitutions. How many know that the adjunct to feminine beauty known today as *falsies* existed a century ago, but under the name of *palpitators?* Or that corsets were originally known as *form-compressors?* Or that the phone, when it was being developed by Bell, was known as the *harmonic telegraph,* while the original telephone *hello,* prior to 1880, was *ahoy?*

Word-groups, too, have entrancing histories. *Red herring,* for instance, goes back to early English fox-hunting days, when the smoked, dried, strong-smelling fish would be drawn across the fox's path to set the hounds at fault and thereby give the quarry a sporting chance. *Pork barrel,* that grand old American political institution, goes back to our early southern planters, who used a barrel to distribute part of their pork production to the slaves; but *lame duck* is of British origin, having been first used around 1740 to describe a person who could not meet his financial obligations on the stock market. *Not worth a continental* refers, of course, to the currency issued by the Continental Congress before the days of Federation (it seems that continentals were later redeemed at the rate of ten cents to the dollar, so the term is to some extent a misnomer).

Four terms, each reminiscent of one branch of the armed forces, illustrate the way language grows. *Round robin* is in origin the French *rond ruban,* "round ribbon," being a method of taking grievances to superiors with the remonstrance signed in circular form by the complainants, so that no one name would head the list. *Blue Monday* comes from the eighteenth-century naval practice of noting offenses during the week and arranging floggings for punishments on the following "black and blue Monday." *Horse Marines* is defined by Webster as "a mythical body of marine cavalry, hence, a man out of his element." There is a story to the effect that "Tell it to the Marines" began with Charles II when listening to an account of flying fish given him by an admiral and corroborated by a Marine officer. Lastly, the *Mae West* used by flyers was first so named by the Royal Air Force, with the blessing of Miss West herself, who stated she would be happy to think that a life jacket bearing her name would "supply the woman's touch while the boys are flying around nights."

These are historically attested words and expressions, now fully settled in the language. What of the unstable creations, the nonce-words, the humorous coinages? Why and how do they come into being?

For one thing, there is the matter of ignorance. Lack of knowledge of an object's name is responsible for *gadget, thingumabob, jigger, doohickie, whatyoumaycallit,* and similar words.

Then there are the words that owe their life to the political scene. Internationally, the expression *Unescan* seems to have been created by a secretary of the British Ministry of Education to describe one who owes his allegiance primarily to the United Nations. In the good old days of the Republic of China, someone described Mme. Chiang Kai-shek as the *Missimo,* an evident take-off on her husband's title of *Generalissimo,* or *Gissimo. Stateside* was similarly created in the sense of "pertaining to the United States."

Local and national politics have given rise to such words as *poll-slacker* (one who fails to vote). The series of words coined on the analogy of *democracy* is almost infinite; *mobocracy* is a columnist's version; *squirrelocracy* was created by a consultant to the Bureau of Federal Supply to describe that trend in Federal Bureaus which led them to amass supplies far beyond their current needs. These words, it will be noted, are hybrids, since the *-cracy* suffix is of Greek origin while *mob* is Latin (*mobile vulgus*) and *squirrel* French (*écureuil*). More legitimate is Lancelot Hogben's elegant *chrematocracy,* "the rule of gold." *Menticide* is suggested for the totalitarian crime of killing people's minds, and it is likewise suggested that *electrocute,* which is erroneously based on *execute,* be changed to *electrocide.* Another suffix, put into vogue by President Harding (the *-cy* of *normalcy*), gave rise to such unstable creations as *legalcy, loyalcy, personalcy, fertilcy, majorcy, originalcy, genialcy,* before it petered out. These formations illustrate the process of word-growth and word-decay, for most of them vanish as soon as they are created.

A somewhat greater degree of success attends the creations of advertising agencies, which are in a position to push their linguistic as well as their commercial products. A Florida city decided to introduce a *Tropicanza* festival. Not satisfied with the almost endless crop of *-burgers* (*hamburger, cheeseburger,* etc.), Key West has developed a *turtleburger.*

It would be strange if the professional linguists did not make a few contributions of their own to this list of created words. *Amerind,* for "American Indian," is in the nature of an abbreviation, but it is used by archaeologists as well as to describe the languages of the American aborigines. The term *linguist* itself, backed by such precursors as *chemist* and *physicist,* seemed to some members of the fraternity to lend itself to confusion with *polyglot,* one who speaks many languages but does not necessarily pursue language scientifically; hence they came out with *linguistician,* for which the precedent of *mathematician* was cited; the trouble with this term is that it has been given a faint aura of charlatanism by such other terms as *mortician.*

Last in the line of linguistic creation come the humor-words, deliberately coined with tongue in cheek, of which an outstanding historical example is *tandem,* Latin for "at length," applied to a conveyance drawn by two or more horses strung out in a line. In such cases it is relatively easy to trace the creator, but it is equally easy to perceive that great names do not necessarily assure success. Dickens' *vocular,* Thackeray's *viduous,* Darwin's *gossipaceous,* Carlyle's *dandiacal* are not in very general use today. One humor-word that has survived through four centuries is *blotterature,* invented by John Colet, Dean of St. Paul's Cathedral, to describe the "ffylthynesse and all such abusyon which the later blynde worlde brought in."

The field of humor-coinage is almost equally divided among politicians, literary people and representatives of the Fourth Estate. At one time Churchill, describing the goal of his Labor opponents, exclaimed that "the Socialist dream is no longer of utopia, but *queuetopia.*"

Infracaninophile (lover of the underdog), *anti-fogmatic* (alcoholic drink that counteracts the effects of fog), *ferroequinologist* (railroad, or "iron-horse," lover) are all of literary origin, but *slumberbug* (a foghorn device guaranteed to scramble up your thoughts and put you to sleep) is from the world of science. Gelett Burgess is specifically responsible for *goop, blurb* and *bromide* (in the sense of stale saying).

Consider now the creations of the press. One sheet speaks of the evil doings of *rapesters,* another of an epidemic of *televitis.*

Glamazon and *gamorous* remind you of Lewis Carroll's portmanteaus, as does also *smelodious. Know-how,* already criticized by some, grows into *why-how,* and *whodunit* into *whydonit* and *howdonit.* A columnist who dislikes intellectuals speaks of them individually as *ga-ga cognoscenti* and collectively as *academic nincompoopage.*

One combination-word that threatens to get into the language (I have found it even in the first draft of a Ph.D. thesis) is *irregardless,* in which *irrespective* and *regardless* clash. But for the most part, the nonce-words of the language, deliberate or accidental, remain nonce-words and literary curios. This is fortunate for us, the speakers, who would otherwise be condemned to learn twice as many words and expressions as we have to learn today. *Perish forbid!* ("Perish the thought!" crossed with "Heaven forbid!")

Next to word-etymologies, it is the anomalies of the language that attract: eye-words that are seldom, if ever, spoken, like *anfractuous* and *floccillation, pseudandry* and *nepionic;* unusual plurals like *kine, brethren* and *children* (all of them spurious, in a sense, since they did not have an *-en* plural in Anglo-Saxon, but acquired it by imitation of nouns that did; Middle English had many more analogical plurals in *-n: toon, treen, shoon,* for *teeth, trees, shoes*): or forms like *grief, strife,* with their regular *-s* plurals, derived from the French, as compared with *thief, life,* where the *f* changes to *v* in accordance with an Anglo-Saxon rule.

Why should the feminine of *fox* be *vixen?* It was once *fixen,* but the Southern English dialects, with their predilection for *v,* were responsible for the change.

It is a peculiarity of English that names of animals used collectively in the food sense have a plural that is like the singular ("to catch fish"), but in other connotations the plural is regular ("to feed fishes"). We may also, however, use certain group-names which are relatively little known in America (*covey* of partridge, *bevy* of quail, *school* or *shoal* of fish, *drove* of oxen, *clowder* of cats, *kendle* of kittens). J. Donald Adams, intrigued by the formation, went on to give a further list: *gaggle* of geese, *murmuration* of starlings, *colony* of gulls, *walk* of snipe, *spring* of teal, *exultation* of larks, *siege* of heron, *muster* of peacocks, *watch* of nightingales and, of course, *pride* of lions.

There are semantic curios, too, in the language. *Virtue* is etymologically the quality of a man (Latin *vir*), but one speaks more often today of feminine than of masculine virtue. *Steorfan* in Anglo-Saxon meant "to die"; gradually it gained the more specific connotation that appears in *starve;* but in Yorkshire it took a different semantic turn: first "to die of cold," then "to be cold." To some Scots a *girl* is still the young of either sex.

The term "folk etymology" is used by linguists to describe popular misconceptions concerning the origin or meaning of words. Such misconceptions may or may not lead to new spellings. "Eating humble pie," for instance, should be "eating umble pie," the expression going back to early English days, when all ate at one table, but lowly persons, seated at the foot, were served the intestines of the animal, including the umbilical cord, from which *umble* comes.

There are legends such as that surrounding *sirloin:* a king of England, fond of loin of beef, is supposed to have dubbed the dish *Sir Loin*. In reality, the expression comes from French *sur longe,* "above the loin"; and the chances are that the word would be spelled *surloin* today were it not for the influence of the legend.

Ancient examples of folk etymology are *carry-all,* from *carriole* (French for "small conveyance"); *hang-nail,* which is not a nail that hangs, but comes from Old English *ang,* "pain"; *bridegroom,* where the *groom* has no connection with horses, but comes from Old English *guma,* "man"; *crayfish,* not from *fish,* but from French *écrevisse,* which in turn goes back to Germanic *krebiz,* "crab." *Woodchuck* and *terrapin* have nothing to do with the chucking of wood or the pinning of earth, but go back to American Indian words.

To take some complete expressions, "till death us do part" is in origin "till death us depart"; but centuries of mispronunciation eventually had their way. "The devil to pay" has nothing to do with *devil* or *pay* in their ordinary acceptances; both are nautical meanings, the *devil* being the seam on the inboard side of the outboard plank of a ship's deck, while *pay,* in shipboard parlance, is to cover a seam with hot pitch. The *devil,* because of its size and location, is the hardest seam to *pay,* whence the expression.

Amazing popular etymologies turn up in the names of old English inns. One originally called *Caton Fidèle* turned into *Cat and Fiddle;* another, known as *Bacchanale,* became *Bag o' Nails,* while *God Encompass Us* was metamorphosed into *Goat and Compasses.*

Among famous misnomers perhaps the most familiar is *Indians,* applied to the natives of the Western Hemisphere because the discoverers thought they had reached the Indies. Another is the *Pennsylvania Dutch* title applied to the German settlers from the Palatinate, who correctly called themselves *Deutsch* in their own language.

"Popular" etymology may on occasion be quite learned. *Rime* (from Old English *rim,* "measure") is often spelled *rhyme;* this is only because it is crossed with *rhythm,* where the *rh* and *y* are of legitimate Greek derivation. The Thames, from Latin *Tamesis,* owes its unpronounced *h* to a learned blending with *Thomas. Triphibious,* which we seem unable to shake from our military language, is the creation of Churchill, who should have known that in *amphibious* the *amphi-* means "two" or "both," while *bios* is "life" (*tribious* would have been the "correct" formation). Kipling's "without benefit of clergy" overlooks the fact that the historical expression refers to the privilege of exemption from secular criminal courts claimed by the Church for its clergy. A financial writer says that "labor's rank-and-file rousers may be hoist with their own poniard" (*petard* is what he means; hoisting with a poniard would be a difficult, though not impossible, feat).

Grammatical forms, too, are subject to popular etymology, as when *pea* and *cherry* were incorrectly formed from a collective *pease* and a French singular *cerise,* taken to be plurals, or *Bedouin,* already a plural in the Arabic *Bedawīn,* is repluralized by the addition of *-s.* Then there are all those misleading Greek and Latin neuter plurals so often misinterpreted as singulars: *phenomena, insignia, data, memoranda, opera, stamina, agenda;* and there are the "impossible" plurals of words like *omnibus* and *ignoramus,* for which it is *not* correct to replace *-us* with *-i.* But even native -*s* plurals are occasionally a source of embarrassment, as when we discover that "the wages of sin *is* death," and that *innings* is plural in baseball, but singular in cricket.

Once a newspaper came out with an imaginary conversation that began "Ave, fra, how wends it?" and ended "Tempus, alack, hies on the aten. I must to the agora. Vale. Accept no lignate shekels." ("Hi, chum, how's it going?"—"Well, it's getting late. I'm due at the market. So long. Don't take any wooden nickels.") Yes, you've guessed it. It's the language of cross-word puzzles which, luckily, no one uses in real life.

Later came another piece, stuffed with such words as *cognito, couth, kempt, descript, dain, chalance, veterate, dolent, eptly, becilic, ane, gusting, pudent, dignation, digent, astrous, onymous, traught, gruntled.* All you have to do here is prefix one of the negative prefixes (*in-, un-, non-, dis-,* as the case may be). The point, and it was a good one, is that these and many other words in our language are used only in their negative forms. Still another piece suggested two irregular comparisons: *be utiful, be more utiful, be most utiful;* and *handsome, handmore, handmost.* At the same time, the writer pointed to the glaring contradiction between *ravel* and *unravel,* which mean exactly the same thing, and *cleave to your kind* and *cleave the rock,* where the same verb has diametrically opposite meanings.

Another writer, Winthrop Wadleigh, in more serious vein, produced a study of echo or rhyming words in our language, of which only a sampling can be given here. At the same time, he expressed his doubts as to whether this particular phenomenon ought to be classed under the heading of onomatopoeia, alliteration, anaphora or homophony: *wishy-washy, claptrap, chit-chat, hocus-pocus, fuddy-duddy, harum-scarum, namby-pamby, hanky-panky, willy-nilly, shilly-shally, okeydokey, Humpty Dumpty, Georgie Porgie, Hinky Dinky, fuzzy-wuzzy, tootsy-wootsy, backtrap, boogie-woogie, hubbub, mumbo jumbo, flimflam, knick-knack, helter-skelter, mishmash, hodge-podge, humdrum, riff-raff, hobnob, true blue, superduper, hi fi, bigwig, hoity-toity, hurly-burly, kowtow, heebie-jeebies.* It will be noted that while the majority of these expressions submit to the principle of rhyme, a few favor the device of consonance, where everything is similar except the stressed vowel (*flimflam*). A few come close to rhyme, but don't quite make it (*hillbilly, honky-tonk*); *know-how* has eye-rhyme, but not ear-rhyme; *topsyturvy* subscribes to the unusual principle of similarity at the beginning and end of the words. It will also be noted that while the majority of these formations are either colloquial or downright slang, a few, like *hubbub, knick-knack, hobnob* and *true blue,* have thoroughly penetrated the literary language.

For years, a gentleman who signed himself "Colonel Stoopnagle" produced for the *Saturday Evening Post* brief pieces consisting entirely of Spoonerisms, the sort of accidental or deliberate transposition of sounds that occurs when one says "beery wenches" for "weary benches," or "Dorna Loon" for "Lorna Doone." This kind of nonsense-talk has as its best imaginary sample a remark by a church usher: "Madam, this pie is occupewed; may I sew you to a sheet?"; but an authentic occurrence came within the writer's hearing in a Lowell Thomas newscast, in which Sir Stafford Cripps was referred to as "Sir Stifford Crapps."

According to tradition, the Rev. W. A. Spooner, Warden of New College, Oxford, is said to have started the vogue with "It is kisstomary to cuss the bride," following it up at a later date with "It is most exhilarating to take to the open road on a well-boiled icicle" and "We will now be favored by a selection by the sex brasstette." A Canadian paper reported that a local radio announcer, signing off a speech by Health and Welfare Minister Paul Martin, referred to him as the "Minister of Wealth and Hellfare."

The English Gypsies, in addition to their ancient language originally imported from India, also possess a secret tongue so interspersed with Gypsy words that it is normally incomprehensible to the uninitiate. Similar "languages" are said to be the possession of the English tinkers and other trades. In the Boston suburbs there arose among the teen-agers a linguistic form that almost drove their parents crazy—an *ab*-language of which this is a sample: *Thabis abis aba sabample abof thabe nabew laban-*

guage. It was quickly recognized by the old-timers, however, as merely a revival of something that had been current in their own youth. People often boast of private family "languages," or at least individual words, incomprehensible to all but family members.

But these instances merely lead up to a full-fledged class of strange speakers, whose normal haunt is Broadway, and who have devised a new humorous linguistic form known as double-talk. The original purpose of double-talk seems to have been to dazzle the layman, but according to latest accounts it is paying good dividends on the stage and at conventions, where it is known as *scrambled words* or *drowned English*.

It is a requirement of double-talk that it must start off sensibly, so as to lull the hearer into a state of fancied security. It is reported that this sort of thing can be done in any language (Sid Caesar attempts it in French and Italian). A newspaper photographer who speaks Italian fluently once tried it on the fifteen members of an economic commission from Italy who had just landed here. His Italian, interlarded with nonsense-words like *tradasta, frammi* and *rearadata,* intrigued his listeners no end, and they decided to take it back to Italy with them. Since certain people are in the habit of appropriating everything in the way of inventions that is not nailed down to the floor, this may be as good a time as any to declare that the institution of double-talk is definitely of American English origin, and that we are ready to fight for it. Nevertheless, we must bow to the inspired French and German translations (done, respectively, by Frank L. Warrin and Robert Scott and appearing in Forum Paperbacks' *The Annotated Alice*) of Lewis Carroll's immortal "Jabberwocky":

> *Il brilgue: les tôves lubricilleux*
> *Se gyrent en vrillant dans le guave*
> *Enmimés sont les gougebosqueux,*
> *Et le mômerade horsgrave.*

and

> *Es brillig war; die schlichte Toven*
> *Wirrten und wimmelten in Waben;*
> *Und aller-mümsige Burggoven*
> *Die mohmen Räth' Ausgraben.*

Double-talk is not merely a spoken variety. It gets into print, too. James Thurber in his books has told us all about those famous prehistoric animals, the *queeches,* the *cobble-tufted wahwahs,* the *hippoterranovamus,* the *woan,* and the common *thome.*

One of the double-talk varieties runs as follows: "I thought I'd put my loaf on the weeping and catch a spot of bo" (*loaf of bread* —head; *weeping willow*—pillow; *bo-peep*—sleep). Just the old Cockney rhyming slang moving to new Gotham quarters.

More insidious than traditional double-talk is a new form of corruption known as double-take, as exemplified in the writings of Corey Ford and Robert Sylvester. The first offers such gems as "After all, none of us are human"; "I hope it goes over with a crash"; "Don't miss it if you can"; "From time immoral"; "He tells me something one morning and out the other"; "Everybody in the room was there"; "I never liked you, and I always will"; "We miss you almost as much as if you were here." The second speaks of a character named Joe Hunt, whose wife gave birth to a pair of triplets, has a friend with a sightseeing dog, likes the nylon lights of Broadway, has a heart affected by a Cadillac condition, thinks blood is thicker than mortar, and threatens to sue for definition of character. Double-take leads you into a cliché whose climax is unexpected.

Lastly, there are those misuses of the language which are due to error pure and simple, otherwise known as "boners," as when a letter from Greece to a Columbia professor was addressed to Workingside (instead of Morningside) Heights, or when a student listed under Shakespeare's plays "Anatomy and Cleopatra," while another asked to be enrolled in a class "in the humilities" (instead of the humanities). Out of the *Cumulative Book Index* come such headings as "Baptists, see also Drunkards," "Prince of Whales," "The Teaming Millions of the East," and "The Church of the Early Bathers." There is also the charge, lodged against a theatre owner, of "maintaining illegal marquise" on an avenue.

Then there are people like the secretary who insisted on describing a lady's hat as *bed-raggled,* spoke of the people not inclined to make friends outside their own group as "going around in clichés," and referred to her own optimistic self as "a regular Polly Adler."

For these, *et similia,* it would be unfair to blame the language. Yet the blame cannot be altogether laid on the shoulders of the individual speaker who makes the boner. To the extent that the language lends itself to such anomalies, it may be said to be the accomplice of the boner-maker.

Glossolalia, the practice of praying, singing or speaking in fluent accents whose meaning is not known to the speaker, is a rather serious affair, as it is said to be part of the restoration of charismatic, or spiritual, gifts lost since the beginning of the Christian era. It purports to reproduce the "speaking in tongues" described in the New Testament as one of the nine gifts of the Holy Spirit (the Apostle Paul, in his First Epistle to the Corinthians, says that "one who speaks in a tongue speaks not to men but to God, for no one understands him, but he utters mysteries in the Spirit"). Trained linguists are at present investigating the phenomenon, which has spread to various sections of the United States and even to Europe.

Chapter Nine

ON THE BORDER LINE OF LANGUAGE

The World of Abbreviations—The Alphabet Soup of English—The Tongue of Politeness and Impertinence —The Lost Art of Profanity—The Symbolic and Gestural Part of English

There are certain semantic phenomena, manifestations, tendencies, or call them what you will, which are not easily classifiable, and yet pertain so definitely to the complete picture of present-day language that they cannot properly be dismissed.

Everyone knows, and most persons have been disturbed by, the current tendency to abbreviate words, use initials of long names, and generally turn the language into an alphabet soup. Is this really an ultramodern trend, or does it have its roots in the past? To what extent does it belong to the spoken, or to the written language, or to both? Is it duplicated in other languages, or is it purely an English-language phenomenon?

English speakers in general and Americans in particular are said to be curt, brusk, impolite in their speech. Is this really so? How do polite expressions in English compare with those of other tongues? Does the curtness of English speech, if it really exists, betoken a discourteous natural psychology, a wilful disregard of the rights of others, in short, an intolerant and even imperialistic attitude? Or is it merely the rough tegument that covers a heart of gold?

Are English speakers more impertinent than others? Are they more easily stirred to insult, to profanity, to lewd talk? How do our expletives compare with those heard abroad?

Lastly, there is that unspoken, unwritten part of "language," in the broader semantic sense, which covers symbolism and gesture. Do English speakers make greater or lesser use of this auxiliary of speech, which is probably older than speech itself? It is easy to say that continental Europeans are given to wild gesticulation, but what of an American crowd in a baseball park, or at a football game? Entire picture-volumes could be written about the gesture-language and meaningful facial expressions of the various nations. Do a nation's gestures hinge upon that nation's spoken language, or are the two manifestations entirely distinct?

The complete answer to each of the above questions would probably require a separate book, or at the very least a separate lengthy chapter. We cannot hope to do more than skim the surface for the purpose of conveying some understanding of those vague linguistic, semi-linguistic and paralinguistic processes which constitute an essential part of the English speaker's ethos.

That the use of abbreviations, alphabet soup, formulas of politeness and insult, improprieties, symbolism and gesture tend to enhance or degrade the language (usually the latter) there is very little doubt. The precise measure of enhancement or degradation is difficult if not impossible to establish. Even harder to determine is their probable future course.

The mania for abbreviated language is a world-wide disease. Born only in part of modern pressures, it is an attempt to compress long utterances into briefer spans of space and time. Abbreviations, both spoken and written, are to be found in languages like Russian, where they are logically needed by reason of excessively long words and cumbersome endings, as well as in those that could reasonably dispense with them, like English.

English abbreviations seem to stem primarily from the speakers' innate predilection for monosyllables. This is self-evident in our inherited stock of shortened forms, for many of which the original long form is all but lost from the speakers' memory. Who remembers today that *gin* is from *Geneva, wag* from *waghalter, grog* from *grogram, rum* from *rumbullion, still* from *distillery, cab* from *cabriolet?*

These are all clipped words, with the surviving syllable usually, but not invariably, the stressed one. It comes most often from the beginning of the word, occasionally from the middle (*flu* and *skeet* from *influenza* and *mosquito, vs.* the Tewkesbury, England, use of *meds* and *progs* for *medievalists* and *progressives,* two factions at loggerheads concerning the replacement of a row of antique cottages), or even from the end (*fence* from *defence,* with British spelling). Rarely two syllables survive, as in the British *Cantab* for *Cantabrigian* and *oppo* for *opposite number,* or the American *fotog* for *photographer, ammo* for *ammunition.* More frequently the popular abbreviation is monosyllabic, as when GI's in Vietnam refer to enemy casualty figures as *wegs* (*wild-eyed guesses*), which stems from initial letters.

Frequently enough, a polysyllabic expression is coined from the initial syllables of two or more words. British educators, for instance, have made *corpun* out of *corporal punishment* (something that in America survives only in dictionaries). But Americans are perhaps more imaginative. The Federal National Mortgage Association is known to its intimates as *Fanny May.* The U. S. Navy has developed such code names as *Cinclant* for Commander in Chief, U. S. Atlantic Fleet, *Cominch* for plain Commander in Chief, and *Bupers* for Bureau of Personnel. There is a variety of political talk known as *Rockspeak,* used by Rockefeller and his aides during the 1964 nomination campaign to abbreviate lengthy political clichés (*bomfog* for "brotherhood of man, Fatherhood of God"; *moat* for "mainstream of American thought"; *fisteg* for "fiscal integration"; *goveclop* for "government closest to the people"). The New York Telephone Directory has *bus* for business, *Mad* for Madison, and *Jus Pce* for Justice of the Peace, but these are purely written-language abbreviations. They differ but slightly from the ancient *viz., oz., etc., et al.* and *Dr.* (which can stand for either Doctor or Debtor).

Hybrids among written-language abbreviations are *cwt.* for hundred-weight (Latin *centum* plus English *weight*) and *lbs.* (Latin *libra* plus English plural -*s*). The *d.* used in Britain for pence is entirely foreign, standing for Latin *denarius.* There are on record several cases of written-language abbreviations giving rise to brand-new words. Latin *quando,* "when," abbreviated to *Q.,* served as a script direction to an actor to speak his part; it was read and pronounced *cue. Fad* is said to have been similarly derived from the initials of *for a day*. One curious first-name written abbreviation is *Jno.* for "John."

The term "alphabet soup" is properly reserved for those designations which are made up exclusively of initials. Here again the British, with their *V. C.*'s and *H. M. S.*'s, seem to have been the original offenders. There is even an unsubstantiated story that the word *tip* in the sense of "gratuity" originated with the initials *t.i.p.*, "to insure promptness," placed on offering-boxes in English eighteenth-century coffee-houses. But, as usual, America has gone to far greater lengths than Britain. Our alphabet soup is primarily political, but also commercial and financial.

If the combination of initials is such as to spell out a pronounceable word, there is a strong temptation for the speakers to pronounce it in that fashion, often with ludicrous results, particularly if the abbreviation and the speakers are of different tongues. During the Second World War, *Amgot* had to be avoided in Turkey by reason of its obscene connotation in Turkish. *ECA* in Italy did not work out well, because its initials are also those of an association of licensed houses of ill repute, and was replaced by *ERP*, but then *ERP* itself, which in America was made to rhyme with *burp*, gave rise in Italy to a pun whereby the nations receiving U. S. aid were called *erpivore* (*ERP*-eating), close enough to *erbivore* (grass-eating) to get a laugh. *WRU*, the call letters of some of our Voice of America stations, coincide with Russian *vru*, "I am lying," and arouse laughter behind the Iron Curtain. The British censors issue an *X*-certificate to pictures that are unobjectionable, and this has given rise to a make-believe contest for "the *X*iest film of the year."

Other alphabet-soup combinations are confusing, like *G.O.P.* and *G.P.O.* (General Post-Office), or *G.I.*, which in medical parlance is not a Joe, but "gastro-intestinal" (a G.I. series is what you get when your stomach is x-rayed).

On the other hand, there is the case where the lady elected to the Society of Industrial Realtors managed to add *S.I.R.* to her name. Banking has a pleasant *Lisa* for "life insured savings account." The *C.B.* of the construction battalions led easily to a *sea-bee* that seemed to describe their activities accurately, and from *sea-bee* some one later coined *air-bee*.

"The translation of names into alphabetic symbols," says Paul Porter, "is a fad of our times which we have to endure." It includes, he adds, *shld* and *wld* for *should* and *would,* sticking out like sore thumbs in the midst of five-syllable words. The labor unions join forces with the government agencies, matching the FAO's and CAB's of the latter with their own ILO's, ILA's, CIO's and ILGWU's. But the businessmen who complain of the Federal alphabet soup should remember that their own came first. GM, MGM, SOCONY, KATY, CON ED are among the best known, but the Stock Exchange also knows an RR and RY that are symbols not of railroads, but of Remington Rand and Reo Motors, along with what seem to be good masculine names (REX, RAY, GUY, TOM, ED), and even a lonely SHE (Sheaffer Pen). There is also MONY (Mutual of New York). In the international field, UNRRA, UN, UNESCO, and all other combinations beginning with U and N are condemned by a newspaper correspondent on the ground that U is a "cold" letter and N a "negative" one.

An alphabet soup of a different and practical nature appears in business codes for telegraphic or other communication. These consist of 100 to as many as 400,000 five-letter combinations, cost the subscribers in the neighborhood of $100 (but this can go up to $10,000 to $50,000 if a subscriber wants a really private code to be created for his use); are usable in at least two languages; and are changed every two years to bring them in line with new technologies, laws, boundaries and forms of transportation. Illustrations are: OIQGL, "cannot make sale"; ONAPJ, "will buy from you 700,000 French francs"; JYROG, "that's all."

The origin of some of our abbreviations is mysterious or curious. It took a long time to discover that the *D-Day* of World War II stood for Decision-Day. *VIP*'s was quickly translated as "Very Important Persons," but *posh,* used in the same connection, turned out upon investigation to be "port out, starboard home"; VIP's traveling from Britain to the Orient and back were given port-side and starboard-side cabins that would catch the prevailing winds as their ships traveled through the red-hot Red Sea.

The language of abbreviations, alphabetical and otherwise,

seems to be with us for keeps. It need not preoccupy us over-much. Judging from what has happened in the past, those ab-breviations which strike the popular fancy will develop into fresh words. The others will shrivel and fall away, along with the objects or institutions for which they stand. For the time being, however, it is of interest that the first six volumes of the Odyssey Scientific Library, designed to bring together all signs, symbols and abbreviations from the principal fields of engineering and the physical sciences, contain over 60,000 entries.

Though it is often remarked by foreigners that English is an impolite tongue, other neutral observers praise the straight-forwardness of English on the ground that where personal rela-tions are involved, both English speech and English writing take half the time and number of words to say what they mean and do it far more effectively.

There is very little doubt that the English universal *you,* used in all connections, lends itself to both the purposes of simplicity and those of democracy. In tongues with a double triple and quadruple form of address one must always be on the watch lest his interlocutor take offense, and feelings of personal relationship involving inferiority and superiority are established which are very difficult to break.

On the other hand, one misses in English the little polite touches that add zest to life in countries where such *politesses* are in vogue. One English speaker complains that the direct English "I want" and "Give me" sound arrogant to foreigners with whom we come in contact, and lend themselves to the accusation of imperialism fostered by our foes "I should like" and "would you please let me have" are phrases suggested for our cultivation.

Not all foreign languages, of course, have the superabundance of politeness displayed by some. As against the Malay speaker's horror of the direct command and the infinite circumlocutions of Japanese, there are both East and American Indian languages which cannot even say "Thank you." Not everywhere in the world, let alone in America, do authors get the type of Chinese rejection slip which states that if this book were to be published, it would be impossible for the publisher thereafter to issue books that would not come up to the same standard, and since it is extremely unlikely that the equal can be found within the next ten thousand years, the manuscript must regretfully be returned.

By international standards our letters, both private and commercial, are on the curt and somewhat impolite side. An American standard business letter, translated into standard Spanish, will require at least one-third more words and space. Yet there are some in our midst who deprecate "Dear Sir" and "Yours truly" as a sheer waste of time. It must be confessed in this connection that Americans have gone much farther along the road to simplification than the British; the commercialese deplored by Partridge for the British written language deals primarily with stereotyped, time-wasting formulas which we have largely discarded.

Such expressions as *Sir, Madam, Miss* in direct address are no doubt less often used in English than are their counterparts in other languages. Military practice may be credited with having fostered the use of *Sir* in the place of the incorrect *Mister* not followed by a name. The British have the custom of addressing a princess as *Ma'am,* and this always strikes American visitors to the Court of St. James as an understatement. But the British make up for this simplicity by their *My Lord* and *My Lady,* which extend down the ranks of the nobility as far as baron (for baronets and knights, use *Sir,* but foreign-born knights don't rate even that).

There are historical fluctuations within the same language in the matter of politeness and polite forms of address. The French tried in vain to do away with *Monsieur, Madame,* and *Mademoiselle* at the time of their revolution, and the Russians, who succeeded with their abolition, have restored in their armed forces forms of reply from a soldier to his superior which at least imply special courtesy (*tak tochno,* literally "exactly so," for our "yes, sir"; *nikak nyet,* "by no means," for "no, sir"). A 1964 issue of *Literaturnaya Gazeta* informs us that a poll taken among its readers shows that they are overwhelmingly in favor of the restoration of the old "sir" and "madam" in the place of "comrade," "citizen," "citizeness." Our own use of *master, mistress, mister, Miss* throughout the centuries fluctuates, even semantically.

Differences in politeness within the English-speaking area may be regional. The British are more addicted to the use of titles than we are. The wife of London's Lord Mayor, for instance, is properly referred to as "The Right Honourable the Lady Mayoress," though "Your Ladyship" suffices in direct address.

Formulas of impoliteness and insult, profanity and obscenity leave the experts in doubt as to whether the English language is richer or poorer than its contemporaries. Other languages can point to their long strings of improprieties, but so can we.

To begin with, there is a long list of ancient and obsolete terms: *crawfish-catching, turtle-chasing mudchunker; gyppos, pikies and swing-kettles; inglers, makebates, daw-pluckers, bung-hole sippers; higglers, federal muckworms, scrim-shankers, jimber-jawed politicasters; blanketers and hedgerow campers; don't-know-enough-to-stamp-a-hole-in-a-rathole.* Luckily, these are no longer in use.

On the popular level, it is pointed out that the use of certain animal names to symbolize certain human qualities is international. *Dog* (including *bitch*), *pig* (including *swine* and *hog*), *donkey* (*ass*), *mule, snake, rat, louse* are to be found as terms of insult in many tongues. *Fish* for "sucker" is matched in other languages by *chicken*, which our teen-agers use for "coward." English does not make use of the names of horned animals to refer to deceived husbands, as do many Romance languages. *Wolf* is in some languages a term of endearment, but then so are *little louse* (*kleiner Lausbube*) in German and *little cabbage* (*mon petit chou*) in French. Americans have been known to use as terms of insult the names of certain birds: *old squaw, buffle-head, common loon, ruffed bustard, pied wagtail, green toady, yellow-bellied sapsucker, nuthatch, hoopoe, coot, tufted coquette, ruddy duck.*

The Italians use a whole string of cheese names to describe inept card players (*mozzarella* and *provolone* are among the most popular); we limit ourselves to a generic *hunk of cheese* as a general term of disparagement. *Salame* is to the Italians a little worse than *ham* is to us. They use *torso di broccolo* (broccoli stem) for a chump, *pignolo* (pine nut) for petty, small-minded, *finocchio* (fennel) for homosexual; we use *nut, lemon* and *raspberry* with unpleasant connotations (the last has even yielded a back-formation verb, *to razz*).

Insulting terms to refer to another's race, religion or place of origin are numerous in all languages. Mencken reports *Chicagorilla, Baltimoron* and *Omahog* as typical American coinages. It is curious to note that in the majority of terms of this sort there is no offense meant originally. *Nigger* is simply an illiterate American pronunciation of a foreign word, *Negro;* the Southern *Nigra* seems to be a mere mispronunciation of *Negro.* (Deplorable is the fact that the British, who once criticized our racial relations, came out in a by-election with the slogan: "If you want a Nigger for a neighbour, vote Liberal or Labour"). *Polack* comes closer to the Polish form than does *Pole; Wop* goes back to Spanish *guapo,* "handsome," and *Dago* to the Spanish name Diego, James. This, of course, is not true in all cases (*greaser, sheeny, harp, wetback,* etc.). Side by side with these slurs are common expressions implying ethnic criticism (*German measles, Dutch courage, to welch* or *welsh* on an obligation, etc.).

Unfortunately, what people object to is not the real meaning of words, but the erroneous connotations attached to them. In New Zealand, the aboriginal Maori have succeeded in getting the word *native* out of all acts, regulations, orders and by-laws. They maintain that the word has acquired a derogatory sense, meaning "partly civilized races living on a lower plane." A term applied disparagingly, but with little in the way of race to justify it, is the *indigenous* by which the descendants of Liberians who were once restored to Africa from America by President Monroe after being freed describe their fellow-nationals whose ancestors never left Africa.

Some racial terms seem to have been coined in a spirit of self-defense. Gypsies call non-Gypsies *Gorgios* (origin and meaning unknown). The Koreans call all Westerners *Big Noses,* while the disparaging *Gook,* originating in Korea, but later applied by our service men to Orientals and North Africans indiscriminately, comes, strangely enough, from the Korean *Megook,* which specifically means "American."

On the professional level, J. Edgar Hoover says *cop* is insulting, since it places the law-enforcement officer on a par with *quack* in medicine or *hack* in the professions. A Maryland Court of Appeals, on the other hand, ruled that *screwball* or its New Jersey equivalent, *souphead,* are not to be construed as insults.

One of the fields in which the language of insult is apt to get out of hand is the political. Former Greek Premier Sophoulis once stated: "The right to insult is one of democracy's main features. I'm sure it never happens in America that journalists insult Government leaders as they do here. You can't insult in another language as you can in Greek."

Of this we are not at all sure. With us, the democratic right to insult is the prerogative not only of journalists speaking of or to government leaders, but of government leaders addressing journalists. Both British and Australian parliaments put what amounts to a gag on their members. In Australia, this means specifically that one cannot use such expressions as "jabbering nincompoop," "miserable body snatcher," "sewer rat," "bounder," "cad" or "my winey friend." The British restrictions go back in part to a 1562 pronouncement of Commons that "no reviling or nipping words must be used." Today's guide prescribes rules of "good temper and moderation" for parliamentary debate and is an extension of Sir Thomas Erskine May's 1844 treatise on parliamentary usage. The following epithets are expressly forbidden: *lie, liar, villain, hypocrite, pharisee, criminal, slanderer, traitor, hooligan, blackguard, murderer, cad, dog, swine, stool pigeon, bastard, jackass, puppy* (or its extension, *cheeky young pup*), *ruffian, rat, guttersnipe, member returned by the refuse of a large constituency.* Permitted, on the other hand, are *Parliamentary leper, purveyor of terminological inexactitude, goose* and *halfwit. Tory,* once an expression of ridicule applied first to the Irish Roman Catholic outlaws, then to the supporters of James II, has become enhanced to the point where the Conservatives glory in it. But other *verboten* expressions include *impudence, scurrilous, dishonest, vicious, vulgar, corrupt, blether, cheat* and, surprisingly, the highly literary

Pecksniffian cant. But there are ways of circumventing the prohibitions. Disraeli once remarked that "half the Cabinet members are *not* asses," while Aneurin Bevan, at a later date, used the banned words in quotations from literary sources.

Other expressions disallowed by one or another Commonwealth Parliament include *smart alec, card sharper, non compos mentis, numbskull, stinking clown, brains in a nutshell.* By way of contrast, the Japanese Parliament, which forbids the use of *bakayaro,* best translated as "stupid idiot," permits such gems as "dessiccated calculating machine," "bloodsucker's bulldozer," "high-stepping hearse horse," "monkey and organ grinder," "insect."

Our own Congressional debate is governed by similar rules, but they are rather in the nature of a gentleman's agreement. Still, it has been charged that many Washington whispering campaigns are based on terms which no one really understands. A Senator, for instance, is charged with being a "shameless extrovert." Another is a "former thespian"; or, before he was married, he practised "celibacy." This, coupled with vague accusations of things like "nepotism," very often finds the mark with unwary and uninstructed listeners.

International relations having once been put on the well-known lofty plane exemplified by the gentle repartee of Vishinsky and Austin, it is not surprising to find Russians and westerners slinging epithets across UN floors. Even in more temperate days, however, we had such expressions as *Meddlesome Matty* applied in America to the then mighty British Lion.

Profanity, says the title of a book, is a lost art. The author divides the field into three branches, blasphemy, obscenity and scatology, and gives examples of forgotten soul-stirring imprecations like "Rat me!," "By cocks precious pot-sticks!," "By the foot of Pharaoh!" He also reminds us that offensive persons could once be crushed with appellations like *chuffin head, coof, nornigig* and *yonack,* or, if their gender was feminine, *daffock, lirrox, trashmire* or *wally-draggle.* There are, he claims, fourteen basic ways of using *hell* in American speech, and one of them, "What the hell are you up to?," draws fire, because it ends in two prepositions ("Up to what the hell are you?" is suggested as a more grammatical substitute).

A reviewer cites Mencken to the effect that profanity is not really an American art, and goes on to demonstrate that in comparison with even the most illiterate Oriental we show no proficiency in either anatomical or genealogical vituperation.

It is true that on one hazardous occasion, when traversing the slimy footpaths of the Grottoes of Postumia, this writer heard an emotional companion switching from English to Italian, then to French and Spanish in a search for cuss-words as impassioned as were his attempts to keep his footing. It is likewise true that English lacks the religious obscenity of, say, a language like Italian, which at once rises to lyrical pinnacles and sinks to depths of depravity.

Yet there is a stock of unprinted and unprintable words in a collection of G.I. invectives, culled from an entire company of students working in linguistics under the Veterans' Law, which will never, I hope, see the light, and which rivals anything I have seen or heard in any of our sister-languages of the West. But it is possible that my attitude is too prim and old-fashioned. A colleague who teaches English to what are euphemistically described as the "disadvantaged" not only permits the use of "bad" words in the classroom, but uses them as a partial basis of his teaching, giving the students who utter them their etymology and the "rules" governing their usage.

The movie industry, which has to abide by a code, has devised a most ingenious series of opprobrious epithets which sound authentic, yet get by the censor. Among them are *filth* and *son of a Yorkshire steer*. *Hell* and *damn* are officially banned from TV, along with, presumably, such compound forms as *God damn* or *Goddam* (interestingly, this expletive is turned into a noun by a medieval French writer, Olivier Basselin, and applied indiscriminately to all Englishmen, who are referred to as *ces godons, panches à pois* ("these pea-bellied Goddams").

Without going into the field of the unprintable, have we not expressions so expressive as to give rise to fully popular euphemisms, for which there is no true justification, save that the speaker utters the original words with such emotional content that they seem to him to be the height of impropriety? Why *nerts?* Why not the full-bodied tang of that great word said to have been used in the Battle of the Bulge by the leader of the encircled Americans? Is it not as deathless as the French five-letter word used by Cambronne at Waterloo, and later elaborately paraphrased into "The Old Guard dies, but does not surrender!"?

In the same vein, it is interesting that Webster III, which claims to be squarely based on usage, while it lists and defines practically all four-letter words which had been included in earlier dictionaries, still balks at a couple of the worst but also the most popular ones. The explanation given for this breach of the doctrine of usage is that school children would look them up and gloat over them, to the distress of their teachers and parents. But would not this apply to the ones which are included as well?

There is, last of all, that long list of words which are altogether innocent in our language, but have obscene meanings in others. The previously mentioned *Amgot* is a case in point. Frenchmen have been known to smile as they gaze at our "Con Edison" signs over street repairs (we can, however, return the compliment by laughing at their word for "seal"). The following list of English words should not be used in the presence of a Hungarian speaker: *bus, fuss, pitch, boss, pin, huge, closet, toy.* It is small wonder that when big firms want to launch a new product on the international market, they hire linguistic experts to make sure that the name they have selected for it will have no obscene, offensive or ridiculous connotations in any of the languages of the countries where they want to sell it.

The language of symbols and gestures is generally supposed to be international. In reality, this is far from the truth. Each nation has its own well-developed system of symbolism and gestural language, and these systems differ so much from nation to nation as to arouse confusion rather than understanding. They also differ from epoch to epoch.

An exception must of course be made for those sets of signals which are specifically designed to serve internationally, like the

S.O.S. of ships in distress. A uniform weather code for aviation, based on groups of five figures, was adopted by the International Civil Aviation Organization, of which, miraculously, even the Soviet Union forms a part. The VOR and VHF radio systems are designed for American fliers, but their mechanism is so simple that anyone can learn it. The language of toots and whistles used by ships at sea is also, by its very nature, international.

Auditory symbolism includes such items as the voice print by spectrogram, carried on by Bell Laboratories, by means of which an individual can be identified just as surely as by his fingerprints. It includes the classification of automobile noises as danger signals to the motorist, worked out by General Motors; this sevenfold classification runs: squeak, rattle, thump, grind, knock, scrape, hiss. It includes the representation of natural noises, including those produced by human beings and by animals, which forms a specialty of the Donnell Library Center in New York. Research into their collection of noise symbolism, for instance, reveals that the sound of a sneeze, which is *ker-choo* to an English speaker, is *hah-chee* in Chinese, *ap-chi* in Russian, *a-tchouin* in French, *gu-gu* in Japanese, *wa-hing* in Indonesian. An American dog's *bow-wow* or *woof-woof* is paralleled by a French dog's *oua-oua,* an Italian dog's *bu-bu,* etc. Only the cat's *miaou* seems to be fairly international, if we make allowance for orthographic differences in the various languages.

Another exemplification of auditory symbolism (though compression would perhaps be a better word) is the Eltro Information Rate Changer, which artificially shortens language by recording it on tape, cutting the tape into thousands of little pieces, discarding all blank pieces and splicing the rest into a single tape half as long as the original. This "compressed speech" is claimed to provoke the attention of the listener, and is said to be extremely effective in transmitting orders to planes from control towers, where time is of the essence. Other applications are in the education of the blind, telephone access information, rapid tape library scanning, student review; side benefits are pitch changes for music teaching and deep-sea diver conversation, speech analysis, and even simultaneous interpretation.

One rather weird form of symbolism, involving the sense of touch, is the "Vibratese," or "skin language" reported by Dr. Frank Geldard of Princeton's Department of Psychology. Here a special vibrator is placed in contact with various parts of the recipient's skin to convey different messages. Since the skin discriminates differences not only of position, but also of intensity, frequency and duration, the possibilities of transmitting and receiving different messages by this device are almost endless.

The most elaborate symbolic systems are visual, and while the older ones are quite limited in scope, the more recent developments in this field are such as to lead some to wonder whether an international spoken language will be needed for the communications of the year 2000.

Many symbolical systems that are still used in some English-speaking lands have all but died out from our own midst. There is, for instance, the language of the early English millers (windmill in straight up-and-down position to signify "out to lunch," or mill in X-position to indicate a death in the family). There is the flirting language of the fan, current in Europe (fan wide and held against the face, "wait for me"; fan drawn across cheek, "I love you"; fan held in right hand and rested on right shoulder, "follow me"; fan twirled in left hand, "don't annoy me"). There is the language of flowers, practically forgotten by us (rose between two buds, "keep the secret"; iris, "a message for you"; white roses, "we must part"). Red carnations mean "I am carrying the torch for you," while an orchid says, "I find you beautiful." Sweet peas are equivalent to a thank-you note for a lovely evening. A single red rose means "I love you," while jonquils or daffodils are a request for the return of affection, and gladioli an attestation of sincerity. But other messages conveyed by flowers are less complimentary. Gentians, dropped casually on daddy's or hubby's desk, mean "You need a shave"; johnny-jump-ups, left on a neighbor's doorstep, mean "Keep your dog at a distance." A cactus plant betokens that it's a long time between drinks; and the waving of a bit of ivy, in certain teen-age milieus, implies: "Who let this creep in?"

There is the café language of old Europe (clapping the hands, "waiter, come here"; spoon across water-glass, "I'm coming back to this table"). Many European restaurants have comic drawings accompanying their lists of dishes, so that the foreign tourist may at least be able to tell whether he is ordering soup or bananas. We have developed a wolf-whistle which is almost spoken language, and for which continental Europeans have a far more elaborate system of gestures (pressing forefinger in cheek and rolling eyes, for instance).

There is the practical symbolism of our traffic signals, along with the visual symbolism of low license numbers for status purposes, with USJ for federal judges, NYP for reporters, MD for physicians. But trouble starts with the symbolism of directions for automobile drivers, which are either in the national language or in a system of symbols separately developed by each country. Here there is no uniformity, even among our fifty states, let alone the countries of the world. The UN has produced a series of proposed international road signs, all based on a visual symbolism that seems thoroughly clear and logical, and these are now accepted by most European countries. But when some of these signs, taken from the codes of foreign nations, were tried out in Ohio, there was a storm of protests, with the customary disparaging expressions about anything foreign and extravagant praise of what is "our'n." Yet the critics ought to remember that on a purely numerical basis an international system of signs will benefit the American tourist driving abroad more than the foreigner driving here.

This, however, brings us to what may be the greatest and most important development of visual symbolism, the glyph, as advocated by Margaret Mead, earnestly pushed by the International Committee for Breaking the Language Barrier and its indefatigable Japanese director, Soichi Kato, and widely reported and described in such press organs as the *New York Times,* the *Christian Science Monitor* and the *Washington Post.*

Basically, there is nothing new about the glyph. For years, newspapers and magazines have been using little figures to represent, say, a country's inhabitants (each 人 stands for one million people) or the number of troops in a given area (each 卜 stands for one full army division).

Arthur Rushmore, a production manager for Harper, long retired, had at one time devised for the use of people who write and read works on linguistics and philology a symbol that would precede a word and mark it as either popular or learned: a human ear for the first, an open book for the second.

What is now suggested is that we use glyphs on a hitherto unheard-of scale to symbolize all sorts of things, independent of the language or culture of the viewer. These symbols would serve internationally for "police station," "bus stop," "customs," "public telephone," "wet paint," "exit," "first aid," "no smoking," "ladies' lounge," "danger," "restaurant," "taxi stand," and all the other million things the traveler or even the local resident may look for. A crossed knife and fork can do the trick for "restaurant," a crossed comb and scissors for "barber shop," and so forth.

A few snags have to be disposed of. Differentiating between "men's lounge" and "women's lounge" by human silhouettes wearing pants and a skirt, respectively, might not work out too well for visitors from countries, such as China, where women regularly wear pants and men long robes. The sign of the Red Cross for "first aid" might not be understood by Moslems, who use a crescent-and-star symbol. To serve their avowed purpose, hundreds, perhaps thousands of symbols would have to be devised and individually learned. It might get to be almost as complicated as learning a spoken language for international use.

Gestural systems have been worked out on an international plane by the Boy Scouts, but for the most part each nation has its own characteristic gestures. Despite our vaunted emotional stability, we are no exception, as can be witnessed by any foreigner who has attended one of our World's Series games. When the English speaker really lets himself go, his gestures can be as wild and expressive as anything one may see in the lands of southern Europe.

We are perhaps more practical and utilitarian in our use of gestures. Traffic policemen with their hand signals, baseball umpires indicating balls, strikes, outs and safes, football referees marking the type of penalty by the use of standardized gestures, are indicative of our tendency to put gesture-language to a definite use.

A spectacular sign-language is used by grain traders in the Chicago Pit, with strange identifying signals, such as pointing to one's head and laughing to indicate that he is buying for Wiglaff & Co. There is that strange language of gestural symbols used by baseball players, which includes cap-tugging, kicking up the dust, wiping one's hands on one's shirt, and rubbing one's bat.

The world's strangest gestural language is said to be that of our radio workers, who must be seen but not heard. Touching the nose quizzically means "Is the program on time?" If the man in the control room responds by raising his hands and drawing them apart slowly, it means "Stretch it out." If he wants it speeded up, he will extend a forefinger and revolve it in a clockwise direction. If he wants to tell the speaker how many minutes are left, he raises that number of fingers, but crooks or crosses his fingers for half minutes. If you must stop at once, his gesture is a menacing cut-throat one. But thumb and forefinger forming a circle mean that everything is perfect. In TV, if the control covers his eyes it means, "You have no picture; carry on with audio only"; but if he covers his ears it means, "You have no sound; carry on with picture only."

It is difficult to determine whether there is a basic relationship between a people's emotional gestures (as distinct from planned systems like the ones described above) and their spoken language. The short, nervous, jerky gestures of English speakers, as contrasted with the more numerous, elaborate and leisurely gestures of continental Europeans, would seem perhaps to indicate that the same psychology underlies both gesture and speech. But a thoroughgoing study would be necessary to prove it.

Chapter Ten

ENGLISH AS A SPEAKING TOOL

*The Sinews of English—The Strength of the Language
—Weaknesses of the Spoken Tongue—What its Users
Say—What Foreigners Say*

It is difficult to evaluate a language in terms of that language itself. Its speakers are normally unaware both of its advantages and its drawbacks, which can properly be brought into focus only by comparison with another tongue. And since those acquainted with another tongue are a rather small minority, the majority of speakers go through life in blissful ignorance of what their tongue really represents in the world of language.

As a spoken tongue, the alleged advantages of English as compared with other western languages are many. Jespersen and Robertson, who have devoted considerable attention to the question, bring out the fact that structurally English saves many syllables by expressing plurality only once, since articles, possessives and adjectives are not inflected (compare English *of two good women* with Latin *duarum bonarum mulierum,* or even modern Portuguese *de duas boas mulheres*). Jespersen represents this advantage as an algebraic formula, comparing the arrangement $axyz + bxyz + cxyz$ of Latin with the $(a + b + c)\ xyz$ of English. It may be remarked that the benefits of this arrangement are usually offset by the need of a greater number of shorter words.

The use, mentioned by Robertson, of the noun as an adjective (as in Shakespeare's *Carthage queen, Rome gates, Tiber banks*) is part of the great functional change characteristic of English. This is a doubtful advantage, since it lends itself to a type of confusion that is impossible in other tongues.

English has an extremely large number of words of echoing and symbolic origin, or what the linguists call onomatopoeia (etymologically name-making). In this connection, Jespersen and Robertson assert that we are prone to use the thin vowel *i* to convey the impression of smallness (*little, kid, slim,* and *chit*); diminutive connotations by -*y* and -*ie* endings (*teeny-weeny*); explosive sounds and ideas by initial *bl*- (*blast, blare, blather, blah*); awkward movements by *fl*- (*flounder, flitter*); sudden noises by *p*-, *t*-, *k*- (*pop, tap, crash*); rustling sounds by final -*sh* (*rush, swish*). A full study of onomatopoeic sounds and syllables in many languages would probably be fruitful, but its difficulties would be immense.

One of the most outstanding characteristics of English is its basic monosyllabism, brought about mainly by the fall of old Anglo-Saxon flectional endings. The number of possible English monosyllables was once figured by Herbert Spenser at 108,264, but Jespersen claims as many as 150,000. This, Robertson points out, gives the typical English word a consonant frame-work within which there is a play of vowels (*s-ng,* which can expand to *sing, sang, song, sung; t-p,* leading to *tap, tip, top;* etc.). The basic monosyllabism of the language, according to Jespersen, leads to a rhythm which normally makes us place first the shorter of two words (*bread and butter, cup and saucer, head and shoulders, free and easy, rough and tumble*).

It seems to us that there are more fundamental implications in the preference of English speakers for monosyllables than our authorities have brought out. Consider, first of all, the constant admonition issued to young writers to use short, terse, punch-packed words instead of rippling, mouth-filling polysyllables; a typical one is A. A. Kudner's warning to his son never to fear big, long words, which name only little things, but to learn to use in a big way the little words which name big things—*life, death, peace, war, hope, love, home.* Compare English *fall in love* with Spanish *enamorarse,* keeping in mind that the "long" Spanish word is the only way of expressing the concept in Spanish, and must be used by all the speakers, illiterate as well as cultured. Consider that a radio plug, advising listeners to go to a doctor if headaches "persist or recur frequently" was quickly changed to "if headaches hang on too long or keep coming back." The key to English monosyllabism is that you can, if you wish, express most concepts monosyllabically, and that English speakers normally prefer to do so, although they have at their disposal words every bit as long as those of other languages. Contrariwise, most other western languages have no choice in the matter. Their structure is such as to compel the speaker to use longer words. Historically, this peculiarity of English goes back to the loss of endings, but after a while the process becomes a vicious circle. The English speaker, forced to use monosyllables resulting from that loss, becomes accustomed to monosyllables and impatient of longer words, which makes him say *mike* for *microphone* and *mag* for *magazine*.

We must not, however, view English as a language where the monosyllabic tendency is absolute, as it is in Chinese. After creating monosyllables by all the devices at their command, English speakers often recombine them in compound words every bit as long as the words they displace. We have at least three legitimate ways of describing one who is under age: *adolescent, minor, juvenile*. What happens? All three are overlooked in the scramble for a *teen*, which, without even benefit of apostrophe, represents every number from thirteen to nineteen. Then there is a sudden pang of conscience. Will plain *teen* be understood? Just in case it isn't, we combine it with *-age* or *-ager,* and now have a highly descriptive word which is, however, of two or three syllables. Was it worth the effort? It probably was, because the connotations attached to *teen-ager* vary slightly from those attached to the older words.

English is replete with tough, hardy combination-words which express, economically and precisely, concepts that require anywhere from two to six words in other tongues. Take, for instance, *turnover, overhead, deadline*. As a native speaker of one Romance language and a fair speaker of others, I rack my brain in vain to find suitable single words that will express those three concepts, born, perhaps, of Anglo-Saxon mercantilism and hurry. How pale in comparison are *giro d'affari, spese generali, estremo limite di tempo!* Even a language like Chinese, which in many ways parallels and outstrips English in conciseness, had "Order of Literary, Patriotic, Harmonious Fists" for what the English happily translated by the single word *Boxers*. Expressions like *wishful thinking, hangover, hitchhiker,* even such simple, un-compounded monosyllables as *home* and *pet* cannot be rendered in many languages save by clumsy circumlocutions.

This does not mean that occasionally another language cannot come out with a word that is more concise and expressive than what we have to offer. I am thinking of the French *tiens!,* or the German *ach, so!,* as an exclamation of surprise mixed with belief and disbelief, beside which our English *why! really!, indeed!,* etc. pale into insignificance. But such examples are rare, save in the case of much longer words (Spanish or Italian *antipatico,* for which English *unpleasant, disagreeable,* etc., are vague and im-personal, or French *tourisme,* for which English has not yet really developed an equivalent, or *demi-tasse* and *Gemütlichkeit,* which we have to borrow untranslated).

There are words in English which may be very expressively used in meanings quite different from the original. When Gaye-lord Hauser's *Look Younger, Live Longer* was translated into French, the title came out *Vivez Jeune, Vivez Longtemps* ("Live young, live long"). *Look,* in the sense in which Hauser uses it, has in English an active connotation which cannot be matched by the closest French verbs (*paraître, sembler, avoir l'air,* with their mild meaning of "seem," "appear").

Greatest among the advantages of English is its immense vocabulary, which, having drawn indiscriminately from all sources, permits us to express shades of meaning that other languages cannot fully attain. In UN procedure, *trusteeship* has to be rendered in French by "administrative tutelage," while Spanish cannot distinguish between *president* and *chairman* save by using the English word for the second, and Chinese finds it impossible to separate *commission* from *committee.* But even in popular language we can distinguish between a purely physical *sky* and a half-physical, half-spiritual *heaven* where French, Spanish and Italian cannot (if they have *paradise* as a full theological possibility, so have we). We can go Anglo-Saxon with *shun,* Latin with *avoid,* French with *eschew,* or Germanic with *shift,* Latin with *transpose,* Greek with *metathesize.* We

have synonyms galore, as a trip to Roget's *Thesaurus* will prove
(14 for *sober,* 164 for *drunk,* 6 for *to be born,* 132 for *to die*).

Basic monosyllabism and ease of functional change, the ability
and willingness to create compounds at will and to use the
treasures of an almost boundless vocabulary, drawn from every
source—these constitute the true sinews of English, the strength
of a spoken tongue that is tough and hardy, agile and resilient,
inventive and resourceful, freedom-loving and quite unwilling
to submit to dictation, an ideal tongue for individualists and
lovers of private initiative.

There is, of course, a reverse to the medal we are pinning on
the English language.

Without, for the time being, touching on the spelling issue,
there is, first and foremost, the question of English sounds.
Robertson discusses the loss of musicality in English caused by
the loss and merging of unstressed vowels, as well as the am-
biguity which this brings about. The fall of ending-vowels has
left us with almost unmanageable consonant-combinations at the
end of certain words, particularly when a plural *-s* is added
(*desks, pests*). Where fully unstressed short vowels have survived,
they have assumed, regardless of their antiquated spelling, a
generalized value (as in sen*a*te, part*e*d, at*o*m, loc*u*st), to which
the only exception, not always observed, is the short *i* in words
like *blowing* or *turnip.* Here one linguist suggests that we may
obtain relief through the process known as "coloration of the
shva" (neutral vowel-sound of *the* in "the many") from the
written language, as where a distinction is generally made between the initial sound of *accept* and that of *except;* that this
does not always work is indicated by the widespread pronunciation *presumptious* for *presumptuous.*

In the case of stressed vowels, English has phonemic distinctions which are extremely difficult for speakers of other languages to grasp (*hall-hull, caught-cut, leave-live,* etc.). This is
complicated by regional pronunciations whereby *laugh* comes
out as "larf," "laff" or "loff," *what* as "whut" or "wot," etc. But
in reply to this criticism of the English phonemic pattern, one
may say that a language does not have to apologize for its sounds

to speakers of other languages, provided its own speakers are able to make the necessary distinctions and utter the appropriate sounds.

More pertinent is Robertson's second criticism, to the effect that the loss of flections has led to a stereotyped word-order which lessens the possibility of graceful variations, as illustrated by Latin *astra regunt homines, sed astra regit Deus* ("the stars rule men, but God rules the stars"). Here too, however, the defense can be made that so long as meaningfulness is preserved, it matters little whether it is done by flections or by word-order.

Jespersen brings out the point that the only important flectional ending we have left is *-s*, and that the presence or absence of this *-s* is utilized to distinguish between singular and plural in nouns and verbs; but that while the *-s* indicates plurality in nouns, it indicates singularity in verbs, and its absence likewise works in reverse ("the king speaks," "the kings speak"). That this can lead to confusion there is no doubt, in view of the freedom of functional change in the language. Jespersen might have added the modern English flectionless adjective and its freedom of interchange with the noun to his list, since that lends itself to even worse confusion, particularly in headlines ("June Tires at Peak"—is the month of June wearying just as it reaches its peak, or are tires placed on the market in June reaching their top price? "Chinese Score Gains"—are the Chinese making gains, are they criticizing gains made by others, or is it a body of twenty Chinese that is gaining? "New Class Studies Disturbed Child"— is a new class studying the disturbed child, or was the child disturbed by new class studies? "Soviet Asked for Evidence against Poles"—did the Soviet ask for the evidence, or was the evidence requested of the Soviet?).

Jespersen also brings out the point that in origin the noun is often ingeniously distinguished from the verb in English by the voiceless or voiced quality of the final consonant (*belief, believe; glass, glaze*), or by a difference in the vowel (*bit, bite*); but he deplores the fact that later on the verb was often reused as a noun (*prize* and *bite* are used as nouns).

The fact that English is filled with homophones (words sounded alike but having different meanings, with or without different spellings) is brought out by Craigie, who exemplifies with *him* and *hymn, time* and *thyme, flocks* and *phlox*. It might be argued that the context normally brings out the desired meaning, but contexts, particularly in colloquial language, are often misleading ("customer's always right"; "customers always write"). Deadly are those homophones that make no spelling distinction and often appear in headline form ("Will Names Medical College"—does this refer to a person named Will, or to a last will and testament? "Fare Kills Driver"—was the driver overwhelmed by the amount he received, or is *fare* being used in the sense of *passenger?*).

It is an authentic complaint of the Turkish Information Office in New York that the clipping bureaus regularly send them items about Thanksgiving turkeys and turkey recipes, while the Dutch Office gets everything dealing with Dutch courage, Dutch treats and Dutch uncles.

There are at least two points in spoken English usage which have never been settled and probably never will be: the division of words into syllables, and the proper accentuation of words of more than one syllable. The first perhaps affects the written language more than the spoken, but the second is purely a matter of speech. Why *compáre* and *cómparable, fámous* and *infamous?* If you think you know English, try yourself out on this brief list of words: *grimace, clandestine, formidable, incognito, intrepid, lamentable, acclimate;* then go on to *impious, irreparable, precedence, domicile, consummate.* It is a fact that even radio and TV announcers, literate though they are, have to take stiff tests in speech before they are hired, and frequently have to refer to such guides as N.B.C.'s *Handbook of Pronunciation.* Among the traps are such words as *congeries, triptych, dour, cynosure, eleemosynary, draughty, mischievous, nuance, viscount, thyme, leprechaun, philately.*

The "genius" of the language calls for initial stress, and this applies to the majority of native words. Trouble begins with Latin, Greek and French loan-words (*adult, research, detail, detour, recess, chauffeur, baptize, romance, resource*), and it is here that the speakers, with their initial-stress tendency, have forced even some dictionaries to give way. They also displayed their "genius" in other ways, utilizing both stresses to differentiate between noun and verb (*áddress, addréss*); noun and adjective (*cóntent, contént*); or two different meanings of the same part of speech (*Prótestant, protéstant*), though sometimes without benefit of official sanction.

On the grammatical side, our tendency to use combinations of verbs and prepositions, or verbs and adverbs (*eat up, play down, give out;* Joseph G. Harrison of *Christian Science Monitor* has created the convenient term *by-verb* for these compounds) is at the same time one of the most characteristic, flavorful and disconcerting qualities of English. It forms the backbone of the verb system of Basic English, making the ease of the latter to foreigners a snare and a delusion. Consider, for example, *to see something through* and *to see through something, to go fast* and *to stand fast;* or *to run down,* in the double meaning of *to catch* and *to deprecate,* and *to make up,* in the sense of *to become reconciled* and *to constitute.*

Here is where the so-called "plain and simple language" is most confusing. Professor Lorge informs us that there are 570 words which by their frequent use make up more than two-thirds of all printed language; but these words have about ten thousand meanings (*run* alone has 832). The little adverb-preposition *up* is particularly offensive: you *drink up, clean up, call up* (or *ring up*), *do up, join up, mix up, line up, offer up, play up, tie up, set up, work up, pay up, step up,* and the question comes up, just what does all this "uppishness" contribute to the picture?

But there are other evil consequences of the English by-verb. For one thing, the prepositions are often contradictory. Does it make any difference whether a house burns up or burns down, whether a train slows up or slows down? Despite their vast number, they often carry an excessive semantic load. You *make up* your face, your mind, your bed, a story; you *make up for* and you *kiss and make up.* The single combination *give up* can have the following synonyms: *abandon, abjure, cease, cede, desert, desist, discontinue, forgo, forsake, relinquish, renounce, resign, sacrifice, stop, succumb, surrender, vacate, withdraw, yield.* Lastly, the by-verb lends itself to such excesses as "up with which I will not put" and "Why did you bring that book I don't like to be read to out of up for?"

Others of our disadvantages are purely semantic. *Blunt speech* and *sharp speech* should be opposites, but they are not. *Batter,* on the other hand, is not only the man behind the bat in baseball and what is usually fried in cooking; it is also the backward slope of a stone wall in gardening, and what fire blight does to your quince trees in horticulture. The *diner* and *sleeper* are both the person who dines or sleeps and the place where he performs those functions, generally a railroad car. *Garbage* is not only what you consign to the Department of Sanitation; it is also material ejected from a space-craft in orbit, and undecipherable information included in the output of a computer. In "children shrink from being washed," the meaning of *shrink* is not quite the same as in "shirts shrink from being washed." *Set,* according to the Oxford English Dictionary, has more than 200 meanings. Too many words, and yet too few. The tale is told of a New York ophthalmologist who saved the eyesight of an Indian maharajah, was paid his fee, and then was offered a bagful of diamonds as an extra token of appreciation. These he felt he could not accept, but the ruler insisted that he wanted him to have a personal gift. He suggested a set of golf clubs as a relatively inexpensive present. A month later, he received a cable from the maharajah: "Have bought four golf clubs for you. Regret one in Maine has no swimming pool."

Still others of our troubles are due to mixed sources. Take the prefix *in-*. Often, especially when it comes from Anglo-Saxon, it means *within,* but when it comes from Latin it more often means *not.* This leads to confusion in such words as *inflammable,* for which plain *flammable* is now often used as a replacement, or *inhabitable,* which was used by Shakespeare in the sense of *uninhabitable.* Jespersen and Robertson point out that in a mixed language such as ours the noun and the adjective often do not come from the same source and are unrelated (*son-filial, sun-solar, house-domestic, sea-marine*), and this to some extent outweighs our advantage in having a wealth of synonyms like *male, manly, masculine, virile.*

Despite this wealth, we often show extreme poverty in collo-

quial use. Foreigners are confused when we use *school* for everything from kindergarten to Einstein's supergraduate "school."
Gun is popularly used for revolver, rifle, musket and a giant cannon. Some women resent the expression "all men are created
equal," and advocate the creation of a word that will truly include both sexes. The Civil Aeronautics Administration wants to
find one thousand single-meaning words which cannot be misunderstood when pilots talk to control towers, at the same time deploring the fact that the language seems to be degenerating into
a series of unconnected jargons.

The women's complaint about "all men are created equal"
leads to other considerations of a grammatical nature. It is quite
true that modern English spares us the need of constant agreements whereby gender and often number are repeated in articles,
adjectives and participles after being once stated in the nouns
(Spanish *las malas muchachas han sido castigadas,* with four indications of feminine plural, as against "the bad girls were
punished," with only one). But is this an undiluted blessing?
Consider, particularly if you are a married woman, your husband's non-committal yet perfectly truthful statement that he is
going to "dine with a friend," where Spanish would compel him
to specify the friend's sex (*con un amigo, con una amiga*). Consider the fact that our *they* is genderless, and may refer equally
to males, females or inanimate objects, while other languages
can be more precise without really trying (*ellos, ellas*). And what
about a singular pronoun that will refer to a person whose gender
is as yet undetermined? Lastly, observe what you can do with a
shift of final -*s*, in an expression like *government(s) control(s)
live(s)*, ranging from *governments control lives* to *government
controls live.*

Before we pass final judgment on English as a spoken tongue,
it may be of interest to hear what has been said about it, both
by its own users and by foreigners.

Personal opinions about languages have been voiced since the
beginning of time, both by speakers and non-speakers of whatever
language happened to be under discussion. It is therefore not
surprising that there should be on hand a rather voluminous

body of pronouncements regarding the beauty, effectiveness and durability of English.

Among the earliest of these, the majority frankly leans to the pessimistic side. Bacon, for example, expresses a fear that his writings may not be understood in a few generations, and therefore proposes to translate them into Latin, a stable tongue. Waller says, in his *Of English Verse:*

> Poets that lasting marble seek
> Must carve in Latin or in Greek.
> We write on sand. . . .

Pope, in his *Essay on Criticism,* still avows that "and such as Chaucer is, shall Dryden be."

But in the middle of the seventeenth century a new spirit of optimism comes into being, despite the fact that Swift is still of the opinion that the spoken language does not have to change, but can be arrested, like Greek. Concerning the state of the language in his own day, however, Swift was even more pessimistic than his predecessors. Monosyllabic abbreviations like *rep* and *mob* he described as the "disgrace of our language." He hated the neologisms of his period (*sham, bubble, bully*), and would have consigned to the *Index Expurgatorius* forms like *don't, shan't, uppish, phizz* and *incog.*

The eighteenth century really begins to show a glow of pride in the English language. "Wondrous the English language, language of live men," says Samuel Johnson.

More recently, opinions have been mixed. Walt Whitman claims that "good English is plain, easy and smooth in the mouth of an unaffected Englishman." H. G. Wells, in *Anticipations,* says of English: "It has the start of all other languages—the mechanical advantage—the position. And if only we, who think and write and translate and print and put forth, could make it worth the world's having!"

In this statement, it will be noted, there is more than a hint that English may be considered for the post of world language. There is also more than a hint of that tenacious quality of English speakers described by Professor Krapp in his *Modern English,* which leads them to refuse to learn other languages, thereby spreading their own. A somewhat similar attitude is to be seen in Churchill's wartime speech urging the adoption of Basic English as a world language and, to take a voice from this side of the ocean, in John Kieran's impassioned plea of 1944 for world adoption of standard English. In 1949, Churchill issued another statement when accepting the London *Times* award for literature: "The English language is the language of the English-speaking people, and no such combination, so powerful and so fertile and so living, exists anywhere else on the surface of the globe."

But these writers advance no particular reason for their choice save sentiment, supported by what the Russians would call imperialistic considerations of the extent, distribution and importance of English.

The voices that rise in criticism and opposition are perhaps more detailed in their objections. Leaving out of consideration Shaw's somewhat flippant remark that "the English have no respect for their language, and will not teach their children to speak it," we have a pronouncement made to the House of Commons to the effect that the wording of some treaty clauses is incomprehensible unless we refer to the French text; another, in a London daily, that a White Paper on the economic problems facing Britain proves the Queen's English to be incomprehensible to most of the Queen's subjects, since "there is a wide gap between the ordinary citizen's powers of understanding and the language in which he is addressed"; a third one, by a writer, to the effect that "the decline in the use of decent English is directly connected with the chaos in which the world finds itself today."

Most devastating among the native critics of English is the American linguist Sapir, who charges that the "pseudo-simplicity of English is really masked complexity and bewildering obscurity." From the other side of the ocean, another renowned linguist, Eric Partridge, speaks of English sub-varieties which he labels "Jungle English," "invertebrate English," "elephantine English," "journalese," "commercialese," "officialese," and goes on to utter a prayer for the prompt burial of the public-school standard. An up-to-date criticism comes from Dr. Sherwood Cummings of the University of South Dakota, who simply states the fact that "seven different meanings can be put in the following sentence by successively inserting the modifier *only* before each of the words in the sentence: 'She told me that she loved me.' "

Far greater comfort, on the whole, is to be derived from the statements of people to whom English is not native, beginning with the great German linguist Jakob Grimm, who asserted that "in richness, good sense, and terse convenience, no other of the living languages may be put besides English." Jespersen, a Dane, is probably the greatest champion of the English language. To him English is "methodical, energetic, businesslike, sober, noble, rich, pliant, expressive, interesting, masculine, the language of grown-up men, with very little childish or feminine about it." He cites the conciseness of English in phrases such as *when spoken to, till called for, once at home;* he points out the superiority of English *glad* over French *ravi;* he delights in the fact that there are few diminutives and inversions in our language.

Jespersen, more than any other writer, is singled out by Soviet critics for his straightforward advocacy of English as an international tongue. What the Soviet non-linguists think about our language may be gathered from the apology made by Vishinsky on one of the few occasions when he switched from Russian to English during an address: "I trust you will excuse my barbarous English, but it is well known that English pronunciation often cannot be mastered, not only by Russians, but also by Americans."

What Etiemble thinks of the English language, particularly in its penetration of French, has already been stated. More guardedly, the *Office du vocabulaire français* exhorts French papers and magazines to avoid *snobisme,* which is best defined as the use of overseas (read English) words. But it is strange that in voicing its guarded criticism, the *Office* should make use of precisely one of those words.

On the other hand, Alfredo Todisco, writing in the Milan *Corriere della Sera,* offers a very lengthy list of English words that have come into Italian. He also gives examples in a context: "È un vero playboy, molto sexy, il beniamino dell'international set; industrial design è il suo hobby, e di più è un health fiend; figurati, va dal dottore per un check-up ogni due mesi." ("He's a real playboy, very sexy, the darling of the international set; industrial design is his hobby, and besides, he's a health fiend; imagine, he goes to the doctor for a check-up every two months.") Todisco concludes that there is no cause for worry; English additions to the Italian language make the latter simpler and more modern. "We can swallow our Anglicisms with our minds at ease. The first favorable results are already apparent in the replacement of hypotaxis by paratactic constructions—in everyday language, the abandonment of complicated sentences full of subordinate clauses in favor of simpler, clearer sentences based on co-ordinate structures." This would seem to give English a clean bill of health.

But an Esperantist, nationality undisclosed, composes a satiric piece about the "discovery" of a language with the strange name *Inglish*. "Its supporters make a most fantastic and incredible assertion, that in some parts of the world (e.g., Britain and North America) there are persons who have gone so far as to learn it, and from time to time even try to make themselves understood by means of this strange code." He then goes on to describe the language, mercilessly searching out its deficiencies.

One final evaluation of English deals with its slangy or colloquial reaches. The reaction of a group of foreign students participating in a youth forum was mixed. One complained that Americans talk too fast, another that they talk too much in initials. Most were mystified by such expressions as "twenty bucks," "on the ball," "old hat." One praised the onomatopoeic features of such words as *crack* and *buzz*. A Yugoslav student said that if she were faced with a choice of English or Russian, she would prefer Russian, because "they express things so tender and beautiful" (but her native tongue being close to Russian, this impression may have been purely subjective and due to previous associations of words with meanings). A student from India preferred English on intensely practical grounds, "because it is most widely spoken."

A Spanish proverb says that Spanish is the language for lovers, Italian for singers, French for diplomats, German for horses, English for geese. This disparaging statement perhaps dates back to an earlier day, when Spanish and English were vying for the mastery of the New World.

This cross-section of world opinion is far too brief and incomplete to lead us to any definite conclusion. Most English speakers like their own language, but when they have a basis of comparison with other tongues they do not always agree in feeling that English is the linguistic *summum bonum*. Speakers of other tongues may be expected to favor their own languages over ours, but when they are linguistically trained many of them seem to discover qualities in our language which lie concealed from its own speakers.

Like all other languages, English has its merits and its drawbacks. As a spoken tongue, it suits its own speakers, but so do all others. The real test of a language comes when it is faced with people of different language habits. Here, it would seem, English has proved its worth. It draws to itself immigrants to English-speaking lands and foreigners in their own habitats. When the instinctive preference of the uncultured is matched by the pronouncements of men of the stature of Grimm and Jespersen, it is impossible to deny that there is something about the English language which attracts, and that, if this attraction is properly cultivated, the future of English as a possible world tongue may be a bright one indeed.

Chapter Eleven

ENGLISH AS A WRITING TOOL

From Runes to Roman—Uncials and Minuscules—The Story of Capitalization and Punctuation—The Printer's Way—The Eye and the Ear

It is generally held that the earliest phonetic alphabet, in which written symbols stand for sounds rather than for ideas or objects, appears in inscriptions found in the vicinity of Mount Sinai, dating from approximately the fifteenth century B.C. This early Semitic alphabet, adopted by the Greeks, later gave rise to the Roman, from which our system of writing stems.

It is an interesting fact that the Semitic names of the letters (*aleph, beth, gimel, daleth,* etc.) give a clear clue to the pictographic origin of the phonetic alphabet. *Aleph* is the Semitic word for *ox,* and the earliest form of our letter A is definitely a picture of the head of an ox; the same holds true for *beth,* Semitic for *house; gimel,* Semitic for *camel,* and so on to the end of the character list.

The Greeks, borrowing the Semitic alphabet, borrowed also the names of the letters, but in modified form, to conform with their own language habits. *Aleph* became *alpha, beth* turned into *beta, gimel* into *gamma, daleth* into *delta,* etc. The Romans, on the other hand, knew the letters only by their sounds, as we do. The term *alphabetum* for the complete list of letters, however, was of Roman origin, being first mentioned by Tertullian around A.D. 200, and was only later applied by the Greeks, despite the fact that it was based on their own names for the first and second letters.

The Germanic tribes evolved their own alphabet, called Runic, though whether they borrowed it from the Greeks, the Romans, or other sources is not definitely established. From the third century A.D. on, these Runic writings appear in Scandinavia. The Goths received from Wulfilas a special alphabet, which was a combination of Runic and Greek. The Anglo-Saxons used a Runic alphabet of twenty-four letters in their earliest inscriptions on English soil. They were fond of inscribing it on wooden boards, memorial stones, metal tools and coins. It ran indifferently from right to left or left to right.

These early Germanic letters were supposed to have magic power (the Gothic word *runa* means "secret thing," "mystery"), and were actually divided into "bitter runes," used to work witchcraft, "good runes," used to bring good fortune, and "medicinal runes," used for healing. It was doubtless because of these pagan connotations that the missionaries who Christianized the Anglo-Saxons did their best to replace the Runic alphabet with the Roman, which they brought with them from both Ireland and the continent. But progress in this direction was slow. There is still extant an Anglo-Saxon poem of twenty-nine short stanzas, of the eighth or ninth century, which describes the Runic letters. The first letter of the Runic alphabet, F, is called *Feoh* (wealth), and is described as "a comfort to every man"; yet, the bard goes on, "every man must give of it freely if he wishes to gain glory in the sight of the Lord." This combination of a pagan tradition with Christian teachings is significant of the spirit of the times. Also significant is the fact that each rune is given a word-value; *U* is *Ur*, the aurochs, or wild ox; *TH* is *Thorn*, etc. This parallels the system used by the Semites but discarded by the Romans.

Even after the Runic alphabet was superseded by the Roman, several of the old letters were retained or reintroduced, chief among them the symbol for the *th*-sound (thorn), the one for the w-sound (*wen*), and a ʒ which originally had the value of hard *g*, but later turned into *y* before front vowels.

The so-called insular script of the later Anglo-Saxons was therefore a modified form of the Roman alphabet used also on the continent, but with many divergences which made it perhaps closer to the Irish than to the continental script.

There is little reason to suppose that this system of writing did not coincide fairly closely with the sounds of the language for which it was devised. The coming of the Normans, however, brought confusion, both to the spelling and the script.

France had been strongly influenced in its system of writing by England in the days of Alcuin of York and Charlemagne. The Merovingian script of the seventh and early eighth centuries, derived from the Roman half-uncial, was angular, cramped and difficult to read. The Insular script of England and Ireland, on the contrary, had developed from a half-uncial to a minuscule which was far easier on the eye. Even before Charlemagne summoned Alcuin to head his monastery schools, the Franks seem to have borrowed some of the Anglo-Saxon and Irish writing characteristics, and incorporated them into the scripts that flourished at Luxeuil and Corbie. There is no direct proof that Alcuin was responsible for the graceful Carolingian script that suddenly flowered in the France of his day, but it seems likely that he helped along the good cause of legible writing.

The Carolingian minuscule, clear and simple to the eye, was what the Normans brought with them in 1066, and the merging of the Insular and Carolingian scripts was not too difficult. In the process, however, there occurred certain instances of confusion which continued for centuries. *K*, which had been very seldom used in Anglo-Saxon, was now used to replace *c* before *e* and *i*, since in French the value of *c* was not uniform, as it had been in Old English. The old *cw* was replaced by French *qu*. The Runic *wen*, which had been retained in Insular script, was replaced by *w*; ȝ continued in existence, but was replaced by French *g* whenever the hard *g*-sound was wanted. This restricted ȝ to its new *y*-value before *e* and *i*. Thorn (*þ*) was replaced by *th*. In the North, however, both ȝ and *þ* (the latter often modified in form to *y*) continued in general use; ultimately, with the advent of printing, ȝ was often misconstrued and misprinted as *z* (*zellow*, *ze* for *yellow*, *ye*), while *thorn*, in its modified form so similar to a *y*, often became a *y* in print (*yat*, *yem* for *that*, *them*). This last misconception comes down to the present day in forms like *ye* for *the*.

On top of all this, the Normans were responsible for the introduction of *j* (it is this "long *i*," used in Old French whenever *i* stands alone or is final, that gives rise to the peculiar English

custom of capitalizing the first person pronoun); and for the inser-
tion of silent *u* in words like *tongue* and *guess* (in accordance
with French orthography, the only way to keep *g* hard before *e*
is to insert a silent *u*).

It may therefore be reasonably asserted that our spelling troubles begin with the Norman Conquest, and are due to the original sin of the mingling of two languages and two systems of
writing.

To return to the script, the Carolingian minuscule prevailed
until the end of the thirteenth century, when it was superseded
for nearly three hundred years by the Gothic, to return in modified Humanistic form during the Renaissance and give rise to
the first printed Roman characters.

But the invention of printing would have been of little avail
without another invention of Chinese origin, that of paper. The
clay and wax tablets of the ancients, the tree-bark which gives
rise both to the English *book* (originally synonymous with *beech*)
and the Latin *liber,* the vellum and parchment of the Middle
Ages, would have been unsatisfactory in quality and insufficient
in quantity for the new mode of writing by a mechanical device.
Starting in China around the first century of the Christian era,
paper, made from macerated rags, reached the Arab world in the
eighth century, and became established in the West in the thirteenth. But it was Gutenberg's "invention" which gave paper its
big impulse as a tool of the written language. It would perhaps
be best to call Gutenberg's a "re-invention," for the art of printing on paper had already been discovered by the Chinese in the
ninth century, and movable type had been devised by them in
the eleventh. Thirty-seven years before Gutenberg's Bible, King
Tai Chong of Korea, "Father of Culture," had decreed that all
characters be cast into bronze movable type, and that all laws
and classics be printed for the enduring benefit of posterity.

Punctuation and capitalization, word and syllable division,
paragraphing, which play such an important role in modern
writing, were not too consistently used by the ancients. Several
of our writing devices were slowly and painfully evolved in the
course of the Middle Ages, like the question mark that arose from

the first and last letters of the word *quaestio,* placed one above the other, or the exclamation mark, derived from the Latin *io,* an exclamation of surprise or joy, with its two letters likewise placed one above the other.

Classical Greek and Latin manuscripts usually had no word-separation, but in inscriptions and non-literary works, dots or apostrophes were often used to set off individual words. The custom of separating words by spacing was fitfully used from the seventh century A.D. on, becoming fairly systematic only in the eleventh. The division of a word at the end of a line was almost invariable made after a vowel in Greek, Latin and medieval manuscripts.

Paragraphs had been indicated since pre-Christian days, first by short horizontal strokes or wedge-shaped signs, then, in Latin manuscripts, by a new line. Concurrently with this practice came enlarged letters (some of them almost as long as the page) to mark the beginning of a new paragraph. These were the ancestors of our capitals. As late as the fifteenth century, titles were usually placed at the end rather than at the beginning of manuscripts.

Punctuation was in irregular use since the third century B.C., but unsystematically, with double dots or single dots placed high in the line to indicate the end of a sentence. Some Greek writers used a high dot for a period, a low dot for a semicolon, and a dot placed midway between top and bottom for a comma. Latin seventh-century manuscripts generally show a high dot for a comma, a semicolon in its modern function, and a double dot, or dot and dash, for a full stop. The present-day comma comes in only with the Carolingian period.

The ancestors of our modern quotation marks were arrow-heads in the margin of the manuscript, though these were sometimes dispensed with, and indentation used in their place.

An interesting light on the use of punctuation in early Middle English is cast by a folio of *The Equatorie of the Planetis,* where the *solidus* (/) is used as a comma or semicolon to mark off subsidiary units, the wedge-shaped sign (◁) is used as a period, and a double diagonal (//) appears whose function is not clear.

Accent marks (acute, grave, circumflex) were used by the Greeks, but not by the Romans. The acute accent returns to use, however, in medieval Irish and English manuscripts, where it is used, for no apparent good reason, over monosyllabic words and words consisting of a single letter.

English has always been sparing in its use of diacritic marks, such as accents, the cedilla of Old Spanish, French and Portuguese, or the tilde of Spanish. Most of these superscript and subscript marks originated with the very numerous abbreviation-symbols devised by ancient and medieval copyists to simplify their labors. The cedilla was in origin a small letter *z* placed under a *c* to indicate a palatal instead of the customary guttural value. The tilde was a small *n* written over another *n* to indicate the palatal sound which in the oldest Spanish manuscripts is denoted by *nn* (the spelling *duenna* for *dueña* is a throwback to this older system). Many of these diacritic marks have today become shibboleths or means of identification of individual languages in their written form. A cedilla under a *t,* for instance, or a breve over an *a,* is characteristic of Rumanian; a hook under *a* or *e,* indicating a nasalized value, of Polish; an *o* with a slanting bar through it of Danish and Norwegian; an *i* without a dot of Turkish. English has no such distinctive characters for its written form, which is a blessing for both typists and typesetters.

But English does make use of punctuation, and punctuation problems can still be quite complicated. There is the story, for example, of a package containing a book, which was marked "From Napoleon, to Mussolini." This, thought the mail-clerk, was a rare historical and literary find, a correspondence that could never be matched. But a minute's inspection of the contents revealed that it was simply a case of a comma interpolated in the straightforward title of a volume dealing with recent European history. By an act of 1901, the British monarch was described as "King of the United Kingdom of Great Britain and Ireland and of the British Dominions." After the creation of the Irish Free State in 1926, the title was changed to "King of Great Britain, Ireland and the British Dominions." The comma which replaced *and,* known as the "O'Higgins comma" after the Irish constitutional lawyer who insisted upon the new formula, set Ireland off as a distinct political entity.

Despite the importance of punctuation as witnessed by these examples, there is a great deal of confusion on the subject.

Fowler's seventy pages devoted to punctuation are, to this writer at least, of very little use. Still less useful and more confusing are the directions for the styling of manuscripts issued to authors by different periodicals. No two agree. When should a comma or period be included in quotes, when should it be placed after the closing quote? "Usage varies" is the sole, unsatisfactory answer to a problem which, by reason of its artificial origin, must needs remain a matter of convention. This is not to say we would be better off without punctuation. The example of the written response given by soothsayers to Roman soldiers inquiring whether they would return alive is a classic: *"Ibis et redieris non morieris in bello"* ("You will go and return not die in war"). A comma before or after *non* would give a very clear meaning, which is precisely what the soothsayers wanted to avoid.

Humorous suggestions for the reform of punctuation and capitalization, as well as of spelling, abound. In a *Look* magazine article, Carl Huss suggests "deflation points" (upside-down exclamation points to denote lack of enthusiasm); a "never-mind mark" (¿) for the man who asks questions but never pauses long enough to get the answers; "colosemi" (⁏) for joining two unrelated sentences; and even a "sapostrophe" (-'-'-) for people who can't remember whether the possessive form of his name should read Huss's, Husss' or Huss' (make it Hus's's'). A letter from a prospective (but not effective) contributor to a magazine begins: "i wrote and sent a story to you sometime ago which i see you did not accept i do not no the reason i suppose it is because the desimal points were not placed or story not long enough perhaps not wrote correctly but that did not discourage me rather encouraged therefore i have wrote another which is much better." This system, of course, would place us beyond all need for rules of any kind.

Spelling (that is to say, the written form we give the spoken word) is not a problem that affects only English speakers. Spelling troubles are a matter of degree, not of kind. Short of employing IPA (International Phonetic Alphabet) notation, no system of spelling, in any language, reflects with absolute accuracy the sounds of that language.

One generalization may be made: the more a language is in

widespread written use, the more the spelling tends to crystallize, regardless of changes in pronunciation, unless one does something about it. This is the main reason why languages that have been in widespread written use for many centuries in the course of which they have undergone drastic pronunciation changes (English and French are two excellent examples) have systems of spelling that baffle not only the foreign learner, but also the native. Widespread illiteracy lends itself to easy and frequent spelling reform, as evidenced by the ease with which the Turkish language changed from the Arabic to the Roman alphabet.

Also, it is not at all true that languages more fortunate than our own in the matter of coincidence between sound and symbol do not afford their speakers opportunities for spelling errors. Scratched on walls in Cuba were found such forms as *puevlo* (for *pueblo*) and *venseremo* (for *venceremos*), reflecting the general Spanish phonetic equivalence of *b* and *v*, the peculiarly local equivalence of *s* and *c* before front vowels, and the dropping in speech of final -*s*, which is a general trait of Antillean Spanish.

So far as English is concerned, this reflection of present-day local pronunciation in the spelling of the semi-literate is betokened by the widespread American use of *of* for *have* in such written phrases as "I should of done it," and in the British notice "Trespassers will B percecuted to the full extent of 2 dogs which neve was sochible to strangers."

In addition, English is plagued by written-language rules whereby the plural of *lady* is spelled *ladies* rather than *ladys,* as it very well could be without disturbing the pronunciation, and the plural of *bus,* which bothers nobody in speech, creates serious doubts in writing (*busses,* where the conventional double consonant, which would give you the proper value for the *u,* runs into the noun and verb *buss,* which is more or less a synonym for *kiss; buses,* which gets away from semantic confusion, tends to provoke in the reader the *u*-sound of *abuses*).

The question of spelling reform for English is sufficient to warrant special and lengthy discussion in a later chapter. Suffice it here to say that in a language once variously spelled as *Englisc, Englysshe* and *Englisch,* belonging to a country variously known

as *Englaland, Englelond, Englond* and *England,* the eye affects
the ear and the ear affects the eye in what might be described as
a vicious circle. How else to account for such eye-ear-eye spellings
as *Californ-eye-aye* and *Eye-talian?* Scholars deplore the fact that
one cannot distinguish in writing between *I read* (present) and
I read (past); that only the capital saves us from pronouncing
Polish as *polish,* and *vice versa;* that there is no way of distinguishing in writing between "Boy!" issued as a call to a waiter
and "Boy!" voiced as an exclamation; or of uniformly distinguishing in speech between "he lives in the White House" and
"he lives in the white house," or "lighthouse keeper" and "light
housekeeper."

Printing, which at first cast spelling into confusion, gradually
led to standardization, though not to regularity. The printers
were less educated than the scribes, and more prone to make mistakes; but the scribes were lawless individualists who followed
their own whim, whereas the printers were compelled by pure
economic necessity to create a spelling that could be automatically used each time the word recurred, instead of following copy
and reproducing variant spellings. Nevertheless, it was a very
long time before full standardization took place. In a printed
seventeenth-century document of Maryland, for instance, we find
pson for "person" *vppon* for "upon," *heritick* for "heretic," *Pres-
piterian, prest* and *Se'patist* (Separatist). We further find half the
common nouns capitalized, modern German fashion, but *papist*
and *puritan* beginning with small letters. The printing "errors"
occurring in early Bibles include the "Adulterous" Bible, where
"not" is omitted in the Seventh Commandment, the "Vinegar"
Bible, where *vineyard* is replaced by *vinegar,* and the Bible where
David is made to say, with some justification (Psalms 119:161):
"Printers [instead of *princes*] have persecuted me without cause."
Today, misprints are generally kept to a minimum, but the frequent and Celtic-looking inscription *etaoin shrdlu,* appearing in
newspapers where one would least expect it, is due to the fact that
these characters are the easiest combination to run off on the lino-
type machine, consisting of the first two vertical rows of letters
to the left. Also, *The Pleasures of Publishing* complains about

authentic cases whereby *sectaries* is invariably converted to *secretaries*, "a visit to Grasmere" becomes "a visit to Gasmere," "didactic aims" turns into "diabetic aims," "buffo arias" into "buffalo arias," and "The Story of the Three Bears" appears as "The Story of the Three Beats." My own latest set of galley proofs had *conversions* changed to *conversations*. One magazine editor, apologizing for typographical errors, says: "They are most unfortunate, but strictly according to Freud." He goes on to admit that "when we criticize adversely anything that has to do with words, there will always be errors to show that we aren't as smart as we editors think we are."

One by-product of early printed works, with their cramped, angular characters, was a rapid improvement in spectacles, designed to relieve the eye-strain induced by the type. Ear-hooks for eye-glasses were finally devised at the beginning of the seventeenth century.

Printing and kindred mechanical appliances, like the typewriter, have almost done away with the fine art of handwriting, much cultivated by our forefathers. The British postal system reports that over three million pieces of postal matter remain undelivered each year because of illegible handwriting, combined with crude phonetic attempts, such as *Arijaba* for "Harwich Harbor" and *11 zoom* for "Levenshulme." In America, some schools, in desperation, have given up trying to teach cursive and concentrate on so-called "manuscript writing."

The seventeenth-century invention of shorthand, or stenography, by Timothy Bright, was no doubt due to the desire for writing speed equal to the speed of utterance. Many people, however, resort to shorthand to get away from the inconsistencies of English spelling (Shaw was a notable example of this), and even to escape from handwriting difficulties and illegible cursives. Today it is claimed that the Gregg system has been extended to cover thirteen languages, and is used by eighteen million people throughout the world. But the word "invention" used in connection with modern stenography, as with Gutenberg's printing press, is an exaggeration, since ancient Rome developed the first system of shorthand, with *subrostrani* (reporters who stood under the speaker's rostrum) taking down accounts in Tironian shorthand notes of the *Acta Populi Romani Diurna* (Daily Doings of the Roman People).

Shorthand itself is rapidly giving way to stenotyping, which had an ancestor in eighteenth-century "logographic" or word-printing, in which a single type appeared for words in common use, like *the, and, as,* etc. Stenotyping, in turn, is yielding to tape and wire recording, which skips the writing stage in any of its forms and registers the human voice directly, with all its emotional content. Authors like Daphne du Maurier, John Hersey, Laura Hobson and John Steinbeck are among those who dictate their "writings" into a soundscriber. The schools of the not too remote future may abolish the teaching of handwriting altogether (save perhaps for signatures), replacing it with courses in typewriting or stenotyping.

Neither is it too surprising to find some claiming that the art of writing, like that of reading, is fast disappearing in the face of such mechanical encroachments. The death-knell of the written language is seriously sounded on many sides. In a review of *Life's Picture History of Western Man,* the *New York Times Book Review* suggests that as time goes on we may more and more lapse into pictures accompanied by mere brief captions, in substitution for the descriptive books and articles of the past and present.

Others go even further. Andrew Kucher, head of Ford Motors Scientific Laboratories, presents a "rosy" picture of the future which includes the elimination of letter-writing and mail service by the introduction of complete voice and visual communication. H. M. McLuhan, Professor of English at the University of Toronto, has stated that "literary culture is through, at least temporarily."

And there you have it. The written language finally supplanted by auditory records and visual picture devices, some sort of combination pocket-size phonograph-and-motion-picture gadget that will replace the books, newspapers, letters and other written-language devices of today!

The comic books, which reduce to a minimum words (usually of the *crash, bang, zip, oooww, whammo, awrk* and *uggh* type) and present a story largely in pictures, are said to be symptomatic of the trend. They lead the London *New Statesman and Nation* to assert that "the printed word is on its way out."

Some ultramodernists among our educators defend this movement on the grounds that the written language is, after all, only an auxiliary of and a substitute for oral speech, and the veriest of parvenus in the field of communications; that it presents vast difficulties of learning, particularly in the case of languages like English, in which the spelling is not phonetic; that the present-day tendency is to seek and find mechanical short-cuts and time-and-labor-saving devices. If the problem of human communications and instruction, they say, can be satisfactorily solved by the elimination of the institution of writing, which for so many centuries has been at once man's slave and man's master, should we view this possible development with undisguised horror, or with something akin to pleasant anticipation? They remind us that the day may not be too far distant when we shall regretfully but firmly bid farewell to the railroad, automobile and steamer, as we previously did to the stagecoach, post-horse and sailing vessel, and do all our traveling by airplane and helicopter, which save time and intermediate steps. And they inquire: "If the problem of human communications receives a similar solution, so that man can dispense with the reading and writing machinery that has served him through his past centuries of progress, and devote the time now spent on acquiring the reading-writing art to the acquisition of vital factual knowledge, of which there is always more and more to acquire, need we be utterly horrified at the prospect?"

But there is an altogether different side to this picture. In the course of many centuries, the written language has ceased to be a mere expedient, and has become an art. The power of words, particularly written words, runs far beyond that of visual or auditory records. We are at once made aware of this when we compare the phonograph recording of a speech with a printed version of the same, or a microfilm with a printed book. The written, printed language gives you time to reflect, ponder, absorb, criticize. It permits you to exercise the truly human powers of the mind. How often do we not find ourselves stopping at a given point in our reading in order to extract its content and use our characteristically human faculties of logic and ratiocination? How often do we not halt merely to enjoy the beauty of a particular written passage? It is a generally recognized fact that the word-picture of a landscape, a scene, an event, often has far greater evocative powers than the object or scene itself, and when it comes to portraying states of mind—that portion of human behavior which is subtle and elusive because it is not material but psychological—there is no substitute for the descriptive force of language, particularly written, permanent language, endowed with its rich wealth of semantic and symbolical content.

Human progress has been accompanied, step by step, by a progression in the symbolism of expression. Mankind began this tedious, difficult process by rough portrayals of external objects, then went on to combine its early pictographs into ideographs, just as spoken language had previously evolved words symbolic of complex, unpicturable concepts out of original onomatopoeias, or sounds created in imitation of the material sounds in nature.

Today we are accustomed to the symbolism of written language just as we are accustomed to the symbolism of such words as *liberty* and *democracy* in our spoken tongue, or to the symbolism of flags and insignia in our national and international dealings, or that of paper currency and checks in our economic exchanges. Would it really be progress, or would it not rather be a historical regression, to go back to the pictures out of which our written language once sprang?

At no time has such widespread use been made of the written language as appears today. The man who indulges in comic strips must nevertheless read some words. His counterpart, in days gone by, was a complete illiterate. Better by far to have him read comic strips than nothing at all.

On a purely quantitative basis, the activities of the human race today are such as to absorb and utilize to the full all the modes of communication we have developed—motion pictures and TV, the radio and the auditory records, the spoken tongue and the written tongue, which has never been quite so much in evidence as it is at the present time. We would therefore subscribe to the thesis that English as a writing tool (and this applies to all written languages) shows no sign whatsoever of being on its way out.

Whatever comparison is to be made between English and other languages as writing tools hinges largely on the question of spelling, or the relationship between the spoken and the written form. In this respect, we must regretfully acknowledge, English stands very low on the list.

There are systems of writing, like the Chinese, which are completely or almost completely pictographic and ideographic. In these systems there is utter divorcement between the sounds of the spoken tongue and the symbols used in writing. The latter stand not for sounds, but for objects, ideas and concepts (our $10 is a good illustration). The tremendous disadvantage of this system is that as objects, ideas and concepts multiply, so do written symbols. A Chinese student cannot consider himself literate until he has mastered at the very least four thousand such symbols. The advantages of the system are that it is potentially international, since it does not depend upon any particular spoken tongue (speakers of mutually incomprehensible Chinese dialects can understand one another perfectly in writing, and there is even limited comprehension in writing between speakers of such dissimilar tongues as Chinese and Japanese); and that it is everlasting, since changes in the sounds of the spoken tongue do not have to be recorded by the writing system.

At the other end of the line are systems in which every effort is made to record in writing the sounds of the spoken tongue. Languages like Finnish and Esperanto are well-nigh perfect in this respect. Each letter of the alphabet can have but one sound and one only, the rules of stress, vowel-length, etc., are fixed, and one can read the language with phonetical correctness after a few hours' instruction, even if he does not understand what he reads.

Most of our western languages started out this way, but as the sounds of the languages changed, corresponding changes were not always made in the writing-system. The result is that today we have all gradations of correspondence between spelling and pronunciation. Some languages which have been conservative in their sound-transformations, like Spanish or Italian, have a relatively simple system of spelling, with few possibilities of confusion. Others, like French and English, have made vast changes in their sound-structure, but have not modified their orthography to keep pace with these changes. The result is that the relationship between sound and spelling is anarchical, or nearly so. It is safe to assert that there is no language on earth more anarchical than English in this respect.

This places English as a writing tool at a distinct disadvantage, both for what concerns foreigners trying to use the language and native speakers who have to learn to read and write it. The former must learn the hard way how to spell each word they assimilate in spoken form, or how to pronounce each word they assimilate in written form. The latter, who acquire the spoken language by natural processes, must start to learn spelling in grade school, continue its study through grammar school, high school, college and the university, and after they emerge with Ph.D. degrees still find themselves making an occasional error in spelling.

This is a time-wasting and irritating situation, and one that places the English language at the very bottom of the scale among languages using a phonetic or semi-phonetic system of writing. There is no use mincing words, or pointing to the fact that our literacy average is fairly high, and that foreigners manage to learn our language when they set out to do so. Were it not for the spelling of English, with the educational means at our command our literacy average would be perfect; far more factual knowledge could be assimilated by our people in the time it now takes them to learn to spell; a far greater number of foreigners would turn to the learning of English, and learn it in half the time and with half the effort it takes them now.

The full history of the problem and its attempted solutions will be presented later. For the present, let us register and face the fact that English, as a writing tool, is like an Anglo-Saxon plow, not like a modern American tractor.

Chapter Twelve

THE GENIUS OF THE LANGUAGE

The Spirit of English Speakers—Attitude Toward Their Own Language—Attitude Toward Other Languages—Opera in English—Linguistic Realism—The Proof of the Pudding

In most respects, the attitude of English speakers toward language is perfectly normal; that is to say, it is wholesomely unconscious. Spoken language is automatically learned and used, by the English or American child as by the Zulu or Russian child. Language-consciousness arises in school, primarily in connection with the written form. Here English speakers are made painfully aware of the differences between their spoken and their written language by a process of learning to spell that is not duplicated in most other languages. Grammar, and the distinction between "correct" and "incorrect" forms of speech, come into play in the schools, but the English-speaking student is normally less bothered by the problems they pose than is the student of other nationalities. Nine-tenths of English grammar is syntax and word-order, and only one-tenth morphology and endings, and syntax is far better learned by direct practice than out of normative books.

Later (much later, in fact; as a rule, only in college) the English speaker is made aware of "language" in general and its more delicate structural and semantic problems. The fact that few English speakers have at their immediate disposal a basis of direct comparison, such as another language, tends to blunt their sensitivity to the problems of language in general, and to aid and abet them in their normal inclination to handle their own language functionally rather than intellectively. True, popular newspapers and magazines often go to great lengths to point out the importance of "language" in connection with clear thinking and expression, and even with the problem of earning a living. Psychologists and educators admit that they are severely handicapped when they have to deal with persons of limited vocabulary, and tend to establish a correlation between the individual's linguistic stock and his supply of ideas. To ease their own dismay at their findings, and bring about a measure of logical understanding of language, they set up courses in what they call "communications arts" and "semantics." Few of them, however, realize that this is merely beating about the bush, and that the only true and tried method whereby language ability and its correlated clear thinking may be developed is the ancient one of establishing a comparative basis by imparting another language. As a result, we have the twin phenomena of the dropping away of foreign-language requirements in schools and colleges, coupled with the rise of inconclusive courses that serve only to leave the student more confused.

It is quite possible that this is a phase of that mental attitude which a writer has happily labeled "Anglocentricism," the ramifications of which extend far beyond the boundaries of language, and whose manifestations include such peculiar expressions as "Times Square, crossroads of the world," "Boston, Hub of the Universe," "World Series" and "World Champion" to describe something that only the United States is interested in, or "nine out of every ten people do something or other," with the implication that the situation is world-wide, when actually it is restricted to our own country or, at the most, the English-speaking nations.

This spirit is characteristic of the Anglo-Saxon world. It is not that the speakers of other languages do not consider their own tongues and cultures to be the best, just as we do; but they are invariably aware of other tongues and cultures. We are not. We like to forget them, put them into the background of our consciousness, pretend they don't exist. If an English speaker and a foreigner get together on a linguistic compromise, in nine cases out of ten they will compromise by using English. If there is clash of customs or habits, it is usually the foreigner who has to give way. This perhaps is what the Russians mean when they accuse us of being imperialists.

Linguistically, this spirit has its advantages and its disadvantages. Krapp may or may not be correct when he asserts that the spreading of the English language is due primarily to the obstinacy of its speakers in insisting on using their own tongue, but surely we have forced more people to learn English in order to have anything to do with us than has been the opposite. On the other hand, we have more often revealed ourselves to be boorish and pig-headed in matters of language than any other race under the sun, and when we find ourselves faced with a situation where English will not work, we are far more helpless than any other nationality, which has also contributed to the international legend (and it is only a legend) that we are stupid and ignorant. Also, we are not able to carry off our linguistic intransigence with a measure of easy grace, as do the French. They are somehow able to arouse in others who do not speak their language a sense of regretful, apologetic inferiority; we seem able to arouse only antagonism and resentment.

With respect to our own language, the general feeling of English speakers is that it is by far the best in the world, one that others would do very well to adopt, for their own good as well as ours.

An analysis of this mental attitude shows that it has many different facets. One of these is undoubtedly racial. There is, for instance, the oft-repeated plea, voiced to our own speakers and writers, to use the "hardy Saxon monosyllables" in the place of the longer words of non-English origin. No less experts than the Fowlers, in *The King's English,* tell us in one breath to "prefer the Saxon word to the Roman," and in the next to prefer *preface* to *foreword.* Another language expert urges that we use brief Anglo-Saxon monosyllables like *pay* (which happens to be of French-Latin origin) rather than the longer words contributed by Latin and Greek to our language. All this, to our mind, is arrant nonsense. The English language is a vast treasure-house, and its speakers should be not merely allowed, but encouraged to make use of all its wealth. If a word fits, what difference does it make whether it is of one or of four syllables, whether it has its roots in ancient, honorable Anglo-Saxon or in the even more ancient and honorable languages of Classical antiquity?

Next come pronouncements like Churchill's war statement about the effectiveness of the collaboration between British and American forces by reason of linguistic understanding, with the corollary that such advantages could be extended to other nations by the adoption of Basic English. But linguistic understanding does not always breed union and collaboration, as proved by the fact that in the earlier years of our Republic we found ourselves allied with the French against the English. Secondly, is it for us to advocate the use of our language as an international medium, or ought not this candidacy to be left to others to propose?

Another interesting facet of our linguistic naïveté is presented by our constantly offered lists of the most "beautiful" words in the language, such as the one composed by Wilfred Funk in 1932 (*dawn, hush, lullaby, murmuring, tranquil, mist, luminous, chimes, golden, melody*), to which the National Association of Teachers of Speech countered with the ten "ugliest" words (*phlegmatic, crunch, flatulent, cacophony, treachery, sap, jazz, plutocrat, gripe, plump*). (Funk's own list of "overworked" words included *okay, terrific, lousy, definitely, gal, racket, certainly, darling, swell* and *contact*). A British novelist had previously submitted *carnation, azure, peril, moon, forlorn, heart, silence, shadow, April, apricot*. Henry James had at one time suggested *summer afternoon* as the two most beautiful words in the English language, while George Ade had countered with such sweet-sound expressions as "dinner is served," "all is forgiven," "sleep until noon," "here's that ten," "check is enclosed" and "O.K., I'll buy." J. Donald Adams, in a *New York Times* literary column devoted to hideousness in words, after discussing the relative merits of *intelligentsia* (which does not really qualify as an English word), *funeral home, housewife* and *galluses*, finally fixed on *polygamous, pneumococcus, mortician, snaggle-toothed, pulchritudinous, adumbrate, pococurantism*. But in all these lists the evidence is overwhelming that the reference is to meaning, not to sound. The only way to compose lists that would make sense would be to have them done by foreigners with no previous knowledge of the language, who would be guided by sound alone. For those of my readers who do not know Russian, Japanese and Swahili, how about *skazka, ptitsa, izba, yuki, kumbembeleza?*

A nation's attitude toward its own language is often to be gathered indirectly from the way that nation reacts to other languages. Here the material for observation is abundant. There are pronouncements, both humorous and serious; there are significant errors made in the use of foreign languages when they are used; there is the reaction to translations, both into and from the foreign languages; there are the cases of downright linguistic intolerance. Conversely, there is the amount of study and use of foreign languages that go on within the nation in all fields, indicating either a broad spirit of tolerance and intellectual curiosity or the slavish acceptance of existing conditions.

The proof that English speakers are fundamentally tolerant of other tongues is to be gathered not only from historical records, but from the present-day state of the language. Had narrow provincialism prevailed in the past, we would certainly not be possessed today of a tongue whose vocabulary is at least seventy-five per cent borrowed. On the other hand, it may be remarked that the English language today is fairly fixed and stable, its processes of growth, whether originally native or foreign, are fully determined. There is therefore a legitimate comparison with the attitude of present-day Americans, of very mixed racial origins, to "immigrants." The English language has in the past admitted all newcomers, but has forced the naturalization of the vast majority of them. Today, English is a conglomerate, but for this very reason, perhaps, its speakers shrug their shoulders at foreign tongues. French, Latin, Greek, Italian? Don't we have enough elements from all those tongues in our own, the speakers unconsciously seem to say; and since we do, what is the use of studying them?

But a psychologist goes deeper into the interrelation of cause and effect. He speaks of the great American "language block," and analyzes its causes, chief among which is the unconscious association, built up by long decades of economically motivated immigration, between foreign languages on the one hand, and poverty, low living standards and an inferior standing in the community on the other. Italian, he says, generally recalls to the American, even of Italian ancestry, not Dante, but the shoemaker on the other side of the tracks; Polish is not a reminder of Sienkiewicz and Paderewski, but of untutored miners and railroad workers. Hence, aptitude in a foreign language is not an achievement, but a stigma. Stress on Americanization and the acquisition of faultless English leads, deplorably but inevitably, to scorn for foreign languages and those who speak them. Let us not forget that one of our greatest Presidents, Theodore Roosevelt, spoke out strongly against the "foreign boarding-house" concept of America and in favor of a rigidly unilingual nation.

Exemplifications of this basically intolerant attitude are still many. Some years ago, much was made of the fact that in a section of New York where Italians are numerous two traffic signs in Italian were put up to prevent accidents. But have we yet reached the heights of courtesy presented by those same Italians to our tourists in their own city of Rome? Their traffic policemen are all required to speak English, while in pre-war Budapest all policemen wore armbands indicating the foreign tongue they spoke in addition to Hungarian.

Our travelers abroad normally distinguish themselves by their uncouthness, which is at least in part linguistic. Seldom does an American make an attempt to speak the language of the country in which he finds himself, and where he is the "foreigner." Yet we expect all foreigners in our midst to speak and understand English and, remarkably enough, they usually do. As far back as 1953, Eleanor Roosevelt, describing a dinner at the American embassy in Tokyo, reported in her column that her daughter-in-law had remarked: "How easy it is when everybody speaks English," adding that this proved the need for a single language that all would learn from childhood on, and in which all could communicate freely. The reference, however, was to English. At the other end of the line, so to speak, is the highly insulting "Speak white!" occasionally used by English-speaking Canadians to their French-speaking fellow-nationals.

There is, indeed, a new spirit afoot, born of our new-found tolerance and internationalism, but the indications are still mixed, and we have a very long way to go before we achieve what may even remotely be described as a civilized attitude toward other nations and their tongues. Meanwhile, here are a few good signs.

A poll conducted among housewives several years ago indicated that seventy-eight per cent favored the study of foreign languages in the high schools, and fifty per cent would even have liked to see them taught in elementary schools. This shows that the average American woman was even then far more tolerant and intelligent than the average American educationist, who in his desire to make room for courses in "democracy," "tolerance" and "good citizenship" idiotically favored dropping foreign languages from the so-called "core curriculum." That the housewives eventually won out is indicated by the fact that as against 2,000 elementary-school pupils studying foreign languages in 1939, there were over 700,000, or 7 per cent of the total enrollment, in 1961.

The National Academy of Broadcasting advises people in radio work to study at least two foreign languages, so as to have a background for handling scripts with musical and geographical terms. Our geographers and map-makers now often present foreign place-names in their original forms, along with an English adaptation. Even Churchill, indefatigable advocate of the English language, stated in his *Painting as a Pastime* that there is nothing that will refresh and enliven the mind as much as reading for pleasure in another tongue.

The reverse of the medal appears in flippant statements by columnists to the effect that in Rome, surprisingly, even the little children speak Italian, that sign language is more effective than French in France, that there is nothing like living in a country seventy-two hours to become really familiar with the language, and that all you need to get around in Europe is the foreign-language equivalent of *please, you're welcome, what did you say?, I beg your pardon, of course, no doubt,* and *perhaps,* all accompanied by appropriate gestures.

There are joking references to French culinary terms (*paté of phooie grass* and *rag-out de boof,* for instance) and wilful commercial mispronunciations of foreign place-names (*Stromboli* and *Capri,* which should be stressed on the first syllable, are samples). There are the well-known military approaches to language summarized by the universal "Aw, let 'em speak English!").

More serious are such terms as "unpronounceable" affixed to names of foreign statesmen, the slaughter of innocent Greek roots in coinages of the type of *photomat* and *drinkomat,* the protest, voiced in intellectual quarters, against the use of untranslated quotations, which are said to "embarrass the reader with the author's learning and the reader's own ignorance." All these are manifestations of what Stuart Chase calls "the spirit of the In-Group," directed against the Out-Group, "those foreigners, speaking gibberish."

By far the best observatory for the working of language attitudes is that of operatic and other vocal music. Here the issues are clearly drawn. The contestants are members of an intellectual elite, not lowly G.I.'s or segments of the great unwashed. The question hinges not on mere translation values, but on the suitability of the linguistic medium for a clear-cut purpose. Should opera on the American stage be sung in the languages for which it was originally composed, or in English, for the delectation and better understanding of those operagoers who know no other language?

This controversy extends to the translation and transposition of plays. One interesting experiment in this sphere was the transplanting of Russian plays to locales in the U. S. South, with Ivans, Nikitas and Akulinas becoming Peters, Rosas and Marthas, and such names as Dmitri Prokovitch Razoumikhin and Casimir Stanislavovitch Lushinsky completely eliminated. What one loses in flavor, it is claimed, one gains in understanding. But one opponent wonders why playgoers who have to bone up on Shakespeare, whose tongue is their own, should object to studying some of the sparkling foreign lines outside the theater.

A sympathetic attitude toward foreign languages is displayed by the motion picture industry and the broadcasting media. This is probably an outgrowth of the relentless search for realism in the movies, a realism that can never be quite achieved (true realism, after all, would require *Quo Vadis* to be spoken in Latin, and *David and Bathsheba* in Hebrew). But within reason, a great deal is done by Hollywood and TV to create the ap-

propriate atmosphere. When foreign spoken films first came to
these shores they were given new English sound-tracks. Now they
are generally left undisturbed, save for English subtitles. Courses
in foreign languages are imparted by the industry itself, with
expert instructors. Multilingual offerings, like *The Last Bridge*
and *Combat!*, are fairly common. In the first, the Yugoslav
partisans speak and sing their own tongue, while the German
forces of occupation are linguistically equated to American GI's
and speak the English in which most of the significant action is
carried on. In the latter, the German troops speak German, the
French peasants speak French, and the American soldiers use
GI English.

There are three fields in which even insular Americans realize
that foreign tongues cannot be dispensed with. They are the
governmental, the military and the commercial.

It is by now a commonplace that foreign-language experts
staff the Voice of America and the monitoring services of the
State Department. Interpreters and translators are scorned
neither by our Immigration and Naturalization authorities nor by
our courts. Georgetown University's Institute of Languages has
now been functioning smoothly for years as a training school for
present and future diplomats, who carry on their studies under
conditions closely resembling those of the UN Assembly. One of
the major discoveries stemming from the intensive study of
foreign languages carried on by our State Department is that
from the study of the language it is easy to move on into consideration of the psychology and social patterns of the speakers.
This conclusion, which should have been reached long ago, is
referred to the attention of educational experts interested in
"tolerance."

On the military side, it was quickly recognized that the North
Atlantic Pact forces could not be run exclusively in English.
Accordingly, American officers were given mandatory courses in
French, while it was unofficially decided that English, French
and German would become the official tongues of the armies
whose mission it might be to defend western Europe. It was
nevertheless signifcant that while about 75 per cent of non-

American personnel spoke English on arrival, only about 25 per cent of the American officers could be described as bilingual. The situation is now described as vastly improved so far as the Americans are concerned. Both English and French are official languages for the NATO naval forces in the Mediterranean, though what the status of French may be after France withdraws from NATO is a matter of conjecture at the present writing.

At the same time, the U. S. Army Language School at Monterey, now expanded into the Defense Language Institute, with an East Coast branch at Anacostia, works overtime to produce speakers of dozens of European, Asian and African languages, while the Air Force receives similar instruction in Colorado and, occasionally, at various civilian institutions. It is quite obvious that the lessons of World War II were not lost on the high brass, even if they made no dent in the tegument of high school and college administrators.

Our major industrial and business concerns, including import and export houses, airlines, and giant organizations like General Motors and Standard Oil, have long since discarded linguistic isolationism and turned the attention of their staffs to the study of languages. To cite a few scattered examples from this field, the Arabian-American Oil Company set up a school in Arabic for some one hundred of its staff. World Airways requires French, German, Portuguese, Italian or a Scandinavian language from all its stewards and stewardesses. The American Society for Metals sponsors a multi-language journal in which all articles appear in the original tongue with English abstracts. The American Type Founders Exhibit in Chicago provides personnel able to converse in German, French, Spanish, Portuguese, Norwegian, Dutch and Hebrew for the benefit of its foreign visitors.

Most encouraging is the display of foreign-language advertising that goes on both in the press and on radio and TV, and which can no longer be attributed purely to snob appeal, or to a desire to attract that part of our reading, listening and viewing population which has foreign backgrounds. Entire newspaper and magazine ads, or large portions thereof, now appear in foreign tongues ranging from Classical Latin, through French, Italian and Spanish, to Swahili and Hawaiian. Toothpastes and beers are publicized in sketches where all of the conversation is carried on in foreign languages, and only the voice of the announcer reminds you that in New York, where there are more Hungarians than in Eger and Mohács put together, more of something or other is sold than of any kindred brand.

The ultimate evaluation of our attitudes toward other languages hinges on registration figures in high schools and colleges. Here the picture, while more encouraging than it was fifteen years ago, is still far from flattering, and the fault lies not with the students or their parents, but with the reformers of our educational system, who at one time had all but driven foreign languages out of our schools to make room for every fad and fancy under the sun, from courses on courtship and marriage to courses in garbage disposal.

The language enrollment figures are high, but not in proportion to our total high-school and college population. Nearly five million of the fifteen million high-school students in the country are learning one or more languages. For the colleges, nearly a million are engaged in language study, out of nearly four million. This means that barely one out of three eligible American students has the time, inclination or opportunity to learn something about another language, and this compares very unfavorably with most foreign countries, where practically the totality of students beyond elementary school receives linguistic training.

A spectacular indication of how far we are behind other nations in the practical aspects of language learning is offered by figures for the study of Russian. Not too much Russian is taught in high schools, and even in the colleges it still lags far behind Spanish, French and German (1963 figures, latest available to us, show 34,000 for Russian to 302,000 for French, 246,000 for Spanish, 183,000 for German). Yet Russian will be a vital language if the clash comes, or even if it does not. The Russians are much more farsighted; English is a required subject in their high schools and colleges. Chinese, another strategic language, has fewer than 5,000 students throughout the land.

But the most distressing fact about our language teaching is the incredibly short time devoted to the subject. A two-year course, at the rate of three to five hours a week for thirty-two weeks, is normally considered sufficient. Only occasionally do we find a student proceeding to a three- or four-year course. In contrast, the average length of time devoted to foreign language study in European and Asiatic countries often goes up to ten and even twelve years.

This gloomy picture is somewhat relieved by the fervor of language studies in private institutions like the Berlitz School, along with self-instruction by means of Linguaphone and other language records. The Asia Institute in New York offers exotic languages like Chinese, Arabic, Persian, Tibetan, Korean, Vietnamese and Thai. Our major universities offer very elaborate language programs. A survey made by the Berlitz School indicates that where one American studied a foreign language a decade ago, five are doing it today, and one of the more surprising features of this popular interest in languages is that in the San Quentin Prison School Russian is one of the most popular courses.

This would seem to indicate that the hearts of the American people are in the right place, and that with any encouragement on the part of the school authorities our standards could rise to high levels indeed. But there will have to be a more complete change of heart on the part of administrators on school boards and in colleges before this comes to pass.

On the other hand, it cannot be denied that because of or in spite of our attitude toward foreign languages, English has been spreading apace throughout the world, to the point where it may be regarded as a satisfactory international language in vast areas of the earth. What are the chances that it may spread still further, thereby eliminating the need for foreign-language learning on the part of English speakers? Is such an eventuality to be regarded as desirable, or with misgivings? What are the major factors that favor it? What are the highest stumbling-blocks in its path?

The answers lie in the realm of the largely unpredictable future. Yet the future is not altogether unpredictable, and it is altogether fascinating. Shall we look into the omens?

PART THREE

The Future

Chapter One

ENGLISH ON THE WEIGHING-SCALES

The International Language Problem—Weaknesses of the Constructed Languages—English as an International Tongue—Suitability, Adaptability and Popularity—Modified English—The Opposition

Next to the problem of world peace, the issue of a world language is paramount in international affairs. Many there are who envisage a link between the two, and suggest that if we can once achieve a single language for the world, peace will naturally follow in its wake. This view ignores the lessons of history, which present bloody wars among people of the same speech. It nevertheless has a foundation of justification in the fact that a common tongue at least tends to eliminate that segment of conflict which is due to sheer misunderstanding, and that portion of mutual antipathy which has its roots in contempt and aversion for those who cannot speak our language.

These factors are perhaps more powerful than we realize. It is quite possible for individuals who speak the same tongue and understand one another perfectly to entertain a cordial reciprocal hatred, and this fact is often advanced by those who claim that an international language will not prevent wars. Groups, however, differ somewhat from individuals. The behavior of a group is the sum total of the tendencies of the individuals who constitute it, which means that the more moderate, intelligent and unselfish elements in the group may do something to offset the behavior of the more extreme and unreasoning. It would probably be more difficult for, say, an Argentinian dictator to convince his people that the people of Uruguay, with whom they have perfect linguistic understanding, are monsters in human form than it would be for Mao Tse Tung to persuade his Chinese that the Americans, whom they don't understand, are blood-thirsty warmongers.

There is more. Psychologists and sociologists are agreed that the psychological processes of individuals and groups depend at least in part on the language they speak. Stuart Chase, in his *Tyranny of Words,* points to the rigid time-sense built into the western mind by the tense-system of the western languages, and describes the tendency of these languages to divide things into two and only two categories (possibly an outgrowth of our grammatical gender-system), so that we "feel obliged to judge events as right or wrong, good or bad, black or white, with no allowance for shades of gray." This language-derived tendency, he concludes, creates one of the most powerful blocks to agreement in personal, social and international relations.

H. C. J. Duyker, writing in *Acta Psychologica,* points out that science depends on language, that psychology is handicapped by the fact that the language in which its findings are stated is not consistently agreed on, that an experiment based on the words of one language may be quite a different matter in another. "Everyone's inner experience" he concludes "can best be expressed in his own language, and cannot be translated without change of meaning."

If all this is true, it means that a common language would cause the people of the world to think somewhat alike and share approximately the same reactions. This, in turn, would lead to somewhat identical patterns of behavior, a logical corollary of which would be a decrease in the points of friction and the sources of possible conflict. History, which registers numerous civil wars and wars among peoples of the same language, also offers bright examples of nations living in peace across international boundaries when their languages and customs are not too unlike.

It is perfectly true that in order to establish the hypothetical gain envisaged by this unifying process we would have not only to establish an international language, but to make it predominant to the practical obliteration of existing national tongues. But this would be a fairly natural end-product of the international language, once it had been in existence for several decades or centuries.

Even if we totally reject the possibility that an international language would lead to a decrease in international conflict, the desirability of such a language at this stage of the world's affairs is nevertheless undeniable. It is not only diplomacy that would benefit from it, it is also commerce, tourism, the enjoyment of life, education, science, religion, the arts, and, paradoxically, war. That language differences interfere with the smooth functioning of international gatherings is a commonplace. That they interfere with everything else when speakers of one tongue come in contact with speakers of another is equally obvious, as our former GI's in Europe, Asia and Africa can testify. The international language therefore justifies itself on purely practical grounds. That it has not yet been put into operation is one of the amazing paradoxes of a twentieth century which looses the airplane, atomic energy and the space rocket without devising the means of controlling them so they will serve for the preservation and not the destruction of mankind.

In principle, a large majority of the earth's people agree that there should be an international language. A 1961 Gallup Poll taken in the United States, one of the most isolationistic and linguistically balky nations in the world, reveals no less than eighty-four per cent of Americans in favor of such an innovation, with ten per cent against and six per cent undecided; sixty per cent of the voters also believed that it would increase the chances of maintaining world peace, while only twenty-three per cent thought otherwise. Had this poll been taken in almost any other country, the figures in favor of the international language and its peace-preserving function would probably have risen higher.

What is it, then, that prevents our taking the fateful step in the direction of a world tongue? Nothing but the question of what that tongue shall be. Here there is no majority, nor even a Gallup Poll, to help us. (The poll mentioned above did indeed reveal that twenty-three per cent of the voters favored French and another twenty-six per cent Spanish, but only if English were left out of the running.) Other nations are as confused as we, with their leaders, as a rule, quite vociferous on behalf of their own national language, which under the circumstances becomes a shibboleth of nationalism.

It is primarily this nationalistic bias that has led many serious thinkers on the subject to eschew all national tongues and devise an entire series of artificial, constructed languages, said to be "neutral" to the extent that they are not the language of any one national group. If an existing national tongue were adopted for the world, say these interlinguists, the speakers of that tongue would enjoy a position of cultural and even psychological supremacy over the other peoples, who would have to force their own speech- and thought-ways into the mold and pattern of the dominant language. But with Esperanto or Interlingua this danger is minimized. No one would feel superior or inferior, because those languages do not belong to anyone in particular.

Yet the charge of cultural imperialism is difficult to avoid, even for languages artificially and deliberately constructed. Esperanto is simple in its sounds and structure, thoroughly logical, and reasonably international, provided we restrict our views of what constitutes internationality to the western world, the world of Latin-Romance, Germanic and Greek. But these are days when Slavic and Oriental nations are forging ahead rapidly and demanding their place in the sun side by side with the countries of the West. To the speech-habits of the Russian, the Chinese, the Japanese, Esperanto makes practically no concession. Interlingua, the highly publicized product of a group of New York linguists who labored over this problem for decades, is even less satisfactory from a truly international point of view, since it is merely a compromise of Latin-Romance and English. The late Waldemar Kaempffert of the *New York Times* had this to say about it: "Familiarity of word material counts for more than spelling and pronunciation—the reverse of the principle on which Esperanto is based." But the question then arises—familiarity for whom? A language that is thoroughly familiar to any Romance speaker will be less familiar to a German, still less to a Slav, and not at all to an East Indian or Chinese. On the other hand, if we give proportional representation to all of the world's speaking groups, or even the major ones, we shall have a hodge-podge largely unrecognizable to all and sundry.

There seems to be, furthermore, some definite psychological block to the adoption of an artificial language. Some say that a language like Esperanto, which is not the vehicle of an established culture, is unsuited for world use, forgetting that so long as we reason along that line, no language, national or non-national, can ever be adopted, since the rest of the established cultures are unwilling to be submerged. Others doubt that a constructed language can be made capable of carrying literary values; these people forget that Esperanto has already produced an imposing body of literature, both original and in translation. Still others claim that a constructed language, once adopted, would quickly break up into dialectal forms based on the previous language-habits of the speakers; here it is forgotten that modern means of education and communication are such as to make this type of dialectalization extremely unlikely. The real obstacles to the adoption of a constructed language seem to be the covert opposition of the world's major governments, which find it expedient to keep their citizens isolated behind linguistic iron curtains for purposes of internal control and propaganda (this charge, unfortunately, applies in part to the democracies as well as to the dictatorships); and the general indifference of the world's masses, not yet sufficiently alerted to the shortcomings of their governments.

The alternative to the adoption of an international language by deliberate common consent of peoples, expressed through their governments, is the gradual imposition of a national language by reason of commercial and cultural superiority of one nation over the others, or the relatively sudden emergence of such a language by reason of military and political predominance. These are, after all, the historical processes by which national languages have been formed out of diverging dialects. Latin arose in this fashion to overspread the ancient western world, and the predominance of Latin as a language for all remained undisputed from the late Republic to the fall of the Empire, and as a language for scholars to the end of the Renaissance. Castilian in Spain, Francien in France, Tuscan in Italy, all became the national tongues of large areas by a mixture of these processes. If nature is allowed to take its course, in accordance with historical conditions, what likelihood is there that one national language will take the lead throughout the world at this time? Or will the development rather follow the lines once suggested by Stalin in the famous Russian linguistic controversy, to the effect that the world's major areas may be expected to develop each its own predominant language of common intercourse (Russian for the Soviet Union and its European satellites, Chinese for eastern and southeastern Asia, Spanish for Latin America, English for the Atlantic nations, etc.)?

The second hypothesis comes close to being a statement of the *status quo,* and is about what might have been expected from a realist of Stalin's type. It really is no solution of the world's language problems, save that it would present a limited number of languages for study in the place of the almost unlimited array that faces us today. There would undoubtedly be some advantage to knowing that Russian would save us the trouble of having to learn Polish, Hungarian, Czech and Rumanian, and that Chinese would do in the place of Burmese, Thai and Korean; but we would still have to learn at least half a dozen difficult and widely dissimilar languages to achieve satisfactory world communications.

We may remark in passing that it is quite amazing to see how many people in the West follow Stalin's linguistic leadership, even where they would recoil in horror from his political philosophy. France, to cite but one instance, swarms with movements designed to establish French and English, or French, English and Spanish, as compulsory world languages to be taught in all of the world's schools. But what of the speakers of German? What of the Slavs and Orientals? We can, of course, leave them to their own devices and concentrate on the two or three chosen languages of the West, which the others will enthusiastically reject. To the extent we do that, we shall be playing Stalin's linguistic-political game.

What of the first hypothesis, the emergence of a single world tongue of the national variety, by reason of military-political predominance or of cultural-commercial penetration? The first half of this dilemma lies in the future, perhaps the imminent future. The second may be studied in the present. The position of English as a world tongue of common intercourse is particularly patent. Unlike French, its roots do not lie largely in the past. Unlike Chinese and Russian, they do not climb like Jack's beanstalk into the realms of the invisible to come. If there is one language today which may be said to offer its world candidacy in unmistakable terms of the present, that language is English.

From the standpoint of suitability and adaptability, English has thoroughly proven itself. It is precise and concise for commercial use at the same time that it is capable of infinite distinction of shades of meaning for literary purposes. Its vocabulary is not only the most abundant in the world, but also the most international of all existing major national languages—more international, in fact, than that of Esperanto. Its speakers are more numerous than those of any other tongue save Chinese, and widely and strategically distributed over the earth's surface. It is *par excellence* the language of science and technological progress. Its popularity among non-English speakers is such that if it came to a vote today it would undoubtedly gather more second-choice votes than any other national language.

Since this last statement may be hotly disputed, let us look into a few statistics and related facts, culled from a variety of countries and fields. An earlier Gallup Poll, taken in 1950, which extended to certain smaller European countries (Norway, the Netherlands, Finland), where English, not being the national language, was not out of the running, revealed an approximately sixty per cent preference for our tongue in the international role over all others. A poll of the Gallup type, conducted by a Japanese organization among students at the University of Tokyo and foreign tourists to Japan in 1960, showed practically the same percentage in favor of English. Another Gallup Poll conducted in Sweden to determine foreign-language preferences, without reference to official international use, indicated that eighty-five per cent of all Swedes wanted to learn English. The English-language *Scandinavian Times,* published in Copenhagen, expanded its circulation from twenty thousand to forty thousand readers in the course of a few years. Almost ten per cent of the population in small continental nations such as Norway, Switzerland, the Netherlands and Denmark speak English.

In Italy there are towns where English is the popular language (Ricigliano, near Salerno, and the island of Ponza, in the vicinity of Naples, are typical; over half their populations have spent long years in the United States). Finland reads English almost as readily as Finnish; seventy per cent of all foreign-language fiction on sale in that country is in English, despite the proximity of Germany and Russia and the close cultural ties with Sweden.

The progress of English on British soil is indicated by the latest figures for Wales, which show that out of two and a half million people over one and a half million speak only English, and over 800,000 both English and Welsh. Ireland, which has been trying rather desperately to undo its English cultural bonds, puts up signs that say: "Cut the last tie with England, the language! Use Irish!" But the signs are in English.

The languages of continental Europe are studded with English words. A French poster warning the people not to hoard said, *"Ne stockez pas."* France's feminine TV announcer in the Eiffel Tower is known as *la téléspeakerine.* Greece and Turkey use *nylon* in the sense of "superfine." Both countries are now definitely out of the French and in the English cultural orbit, as evidenced by their school curricula and reading habits.

The Yugoslav weekly *Republika,* beginning some years ago a series of English lessons at the request of its readers, stated that "660 million people (or one-third of mankind) speak English, or can make themselves understood in English," an assertion that even Britishers and Americans would hesitate to support.

In Africa, English is the second European language, running half a million behind the nearly five million speakers of French; but out of 600 African newspapers and periodicals, 250 are in English, and only 175 in French. English is the leading foreign tongue of Ethiopia, being taught in all the schools. "Both French and English are still used in the administration, but there is a gradual shifting over to English alone," says a Guggenheim scholar who recently spent a year in that country.

In the schools of Israel, three languages are taught—Ivrit (modern Hebrew), Arabic and English, and English is by far the most popular with the reading public.

India claims through one of its official press releases to be, next to the United States and Great Britain, the most important of the English-speaking nations, with at least ten million speakers of English and 150 English-language newspapers and periodicals. When the Indians wanted a slogan for their anti-polio campaign, they called it the "March of Annas," in direct imitation of our "March of Dimes." The University of Lucknow, which had endeavored to shift to Hindi as the language of instruction, was forced to revert to an Anglo-Hindi jargon by reason of the far too numerous technical words and expressions that have not yet been translated into Hindi. The Middle East Technical University at Ankara, in Turkey, after a long controversy concerning the language of instruction, finally settled on English because of its widespread use and the ready availability of textbooks and laboratory manuals.

English is already a sort of *lingua franca* of the Philippine archipelago. English, more or less pidginized, is also, in the words of the *New York Times,* "the *lingua franca* of the common man from the African coasts to India, Malaya, China and the islands of the Pacific." Japan, not content with teaching English in all its high schools and colleges, also broadcasts English lessons to its millions via radio, with "Uncle Come-Come" Hirakawa, a teacher of twenty years' American background, at the microphone. Words like *mishin* ("machine"), used in Japan only for a sewing machine (*kikai* is the regular native word for "machine"), and *tomato,* in the name of a firm like *Aichi Tomato Kabushiki Kaisha,* bear witness to the cultural penetration of English.

A remarkable item attests the power of English in Latin America. The *Reader's Digest,* though it puts out Spanish- and Portuguese-language editions, now issues also a special English-language edition for its Latin-American readers.

Even behind the Iron Curtain, no less than sixty per cent of college students go on studying English, while the Russian language continues to become studded with English technical terms, like *tractor, incubator, disk, separator* and *silo.*

But there is much more. The Soviet cultural office competes with the British and American, in underdeveloped countries, in offering *English* courses. No fewer than thirty million volumes in English have been shipped by the Soviets to Afro-Asian countries, including such children's books as *Goldilocks and the Three Bears,* claimed to have been authored by Leo Tolstoi. Freight shipments from the Soviet Union to eastern countries are stamped with the English-language inscription "Made in USSR." Broadcasts of a propaganda nature are made from Moscow to Afro-Asian countries in English. (Also in English, by the way, are the majority of international propaganda broadcasts that issue from Peking.) A Ceylonese mission to the Soviets was greeted in English on its arrival. One of Moscow's best selling books is an English grammar, and English is taught even in the elementary schools of Tashkent, in Uzbekistan.

Beatles songs and movies, in English, are raptly listened to in such Communist countries as Poland and Czechoslovakia. The study of Russian in Communist China is outstripped by that of English, as well as that of German and Japanese. In Singapore, where English, Chinese, Malay and Tamil are all co-official, over fifty-five per cent of both elementary and higher instruction is in English.

The growing use of English at international gatherings is well known. Not only was the 1955 Bandung Conference of twenty-nine Afro-Asian nations conducted in English, but cultural treaties among these nations, such as the one signed by Egypt and Indonesia, are drawn up in English. Even the conversational exchange between Nehru and the Dalai Lama, when the latter reached India after his escape from the Chinese Communist invaders of Tibet, took place in English.

English is the language of international aviation. For this there is said to be a practical reason in the brevity of our language as compared with others, notably French. It is easier, it is claimed, to use *jet, flap, fin* and *stick* than *avion à réaction, volet de flexion, empennage arrière* and *manche à balai.* French-speaking pilots are given such aids to English pronunciation as *menreunvei* (main runway) and *claoud-beise* (cloud base), and German-speaking pilots have developed a jargon of their own, such as *off-getakt* for "taken off."

The international scientific aspects of English may be gathered from the single fact that out of all chemical abstracts published in recent years, nearly fifty per cent were in English (Russian had twelve per cent, French eleven per cent, Italian six per cent, German and Spanish five per cent each).

The spreading of English abroad, particularly in under-developed countries, has a double impulse from our State Department, with its Peace Corps and cultural centers, and the British Foreign Office, which matches us school for school and program for program. Our USIS had, at latest reading, nearly 400 cultural centers in 80 nations, used by over twenty-eight million persons in one year. Over a million people attend English-language seminars scattered throughout the world, and it is estimated that among them there are at least 5,000 local teachers of English, who in turn give English-language instruction to over two million pupils of their own.

Included in this linguistic and cultural drive whose end product is the spreading of English are not only schools and USIS libraries, but also radio and TV programs, motion pictures, recordings of songs, mobile libraries, exchange fellowships, and even our American comic strips, which go out to ninety foreign countries in thirty-two languages, from African to Siamese (Popeye has been known to double the circulation of a Japanese newspaper). India buys ten million American paperbacks each year. The same paperbacks reach practically all countries, both Western and Communist. They appear on the stands in Cairo, Belgrade, Budapest and Bangkok.

The further spreading of English, despite the language's obvious advantages, is impeded by precisely the same psychological factors that obstruct the increase of foreign-language learning among English speakers. Children learn languages easily and naturally, but adults do not. The learning of another language at the grown-up stage is fraught with heart-breaking difficulties, as anyone who has taken up a language in high school or college can testify. The difficulties of English are twofold. The foreign adult learner is faced not merely with a grammatical structure and vocabulary unfamiliar to him, but also with a divergence between speech and writing which is far greater than in any other western tongue.

332 THE STORY OF THE ENGLISH LANGUAGE

Hence, various modifications of English have been proposed to facilitate its acceptance for international use. Some of these are mere makeshifts of limited application to serve a specific purpose, like the ILA (International Language for Aviation) devised by the Civil Aviation Organization. Others are in the nature of blueprints for spelling and grammar reform, like the Anglic invented by Zachrisson in the earlier part of this century, or the Model English of Stuart Dodd of the University of Washington, which ingeniously combined a measure of spelling reform with a complete regularization of English grammar. In accordance with Dr. Dodd's system, all forms of *to be* become *bi,* distinguished only by the subject pronoun; the past tense is always indicated by *did;* irregular plurals, like *children* and *these,* become regular (*childs, thises*).

The modified English form which has met with greatest popular success and enjoys limited use (it had Churchill's favor) is the Basic English devised by Ogden and Richards. The guiding principle of Basic is not one of change, but of selectivity. English words are not modified in their spelling, pronunciation, meaning, or grammatical use; but instead of the entire range of the English vocabulary, about one thousand words are selected as basic and made to do the work of all the others by a replacement process. This means that "The Lord is my shepherd" becomes "The Lord takes care of me as his sheep." Basic English is far harder on the English speaker than on the foreigner, since the former must learn to restrict himself, cut himself away from his linguistic heritage, and adapt himself to clumsy circumlocutions to say what he has already learned to say easily and directly. It is nevertheless argued that Basic English forms an ideal stepping-stone to ordinary English for foreign learners, and Basic is employed in imparting our language to foreigners in the armed services and in various schools and colleges abroad.

One need not be inspired by an overly critical spirit to voice the hope that too much may not come of Basic English, or any other modification of English that is of a restrictive nature. As a teaching device, we have no quarrel with it. As a permanent transformation of the language, its merits seem to parallel those of economic measures whereby the abundant American living standards would be brought down to the level of the majority of other countries in order that some sort of universal social justice may be achieved. We would favor instead raising the standards of other nations to our own levels, and if English is to be conferred as a boon upon the world's masses, we would likewise favor that it be the rich, full-blooded language we have evolved out of centuries of accretion, rather than a subsistence handout.

Reference has already been made to the advocacy of two or more international languages, either to serve different areas of the world, or to live side by side as joint universal languages. These systems amount to little more than a codification of an existing state of affairs. Early advocates were Comenius, who suggested Russian for eastern Europe and English, or French, or both for the West, and de Lansac, who urged that all seventeenth-century ambassadors know Spanish, Latin, French and Italian. The French, who feel that their language is steadily losing ground as an international language of diplomacy and common intercourse, are particularly favorable to the sort of solution that would crystallize the status quo. They point to the fact that in many countries of the Middle East French and English live side by side in a state of harmonious symbiosis, and that the two languages are the favorite ones at UN gatherings.

Some go further, and propose that English and Russian, the predominant languages of the two great political groupings vying for the domination of the world, be excluded precisely because they are the leading contenders. It is doubtful, however, that the dark horse principle, which occasionally works out in American political conventions, can be made to prevail in international affairs. The resurrection of Latin as an international tongue is occasionally put forward, and even Classical Greek has been suggested as a "neutral" tongue. Spanish and Italian are often suggested on grounds of phonetic ease, and as often rejected on grounds of grammatical complexity.

French, with its formidable background of international use, finds supporters not only among native French speakers, but also among the cultured millions who have been brought up in the French tradition. In fact, French, the great military and political tongue of the Middle Ages, the diplomatic and cultural tongue of the three centuries that preceded our own, still has impressive chances. Despite its losses, it is official or co-official in about as many countries as English, and is the favorite school language in as many more. In its international role, it would be foolhardy to write it off, as so many English-language enthusiasts are inclined to do. Nor should we forget that leader among constructed languages, Esperanto, which makes its appeal through its neutrality of forms and sources, its absolute regularity of grammar, its absolute coincidence of spoken sounds and written symbols, its absolute standardization. In the 1950 Gallup Poll which showed English in the lead in such small European countries as Norway, Holland and Finland, the runner-up in popular favor was neither French, nor German, nor Russian, nor Spanish, nor Italian, nor Chinese; it was the constructed, "neutral" tongue, Esperanto, making its powerful appeal to speakers of "small" languages who are tired of forever having to defer to the big, powerful tongues.

All these manifestations of a negative nature, coupled with the positive hostility of the Communist world, point to the barriers that English must overthrow or encircle if it wishes to march on to what many of its speakers consider to be its manifest destiny. There are also positive symptoms of opposition, and they come from numerous and sometimes unexpected quarters. That these symptoms are often connected with political states of mind is beside the point, unless one chooses to believe, quite erroneously, that there is no connection between political attitudes and linguistic history.

In Ireland, where English is still the popular spoken language, theatrical companies are nevertheless required to give occasional performances in Gaelic. It may take the actors five years to learn the ancestral Irish tongue, but this eventual mastery has a chance of being passed on to the audiences. Another spot where Gaelic strives to rival English is, surprisingly, Nova Scotia, where the descendants of Highland Scots have at St. Ann, on Cape Breton, the only Gaelic college in America, conduct most of their church services in Gaelic, and hold an annual Gaelic *mod,* or gathering of the clans. This is altogether separate from that other Canadian phenomenon whereby the French speakers of Quebec react rather violently to the use of English and insist on *cirage, casse-croûte, cabaret, estaminet* and *auto-buffet* in the place of *shoeshine, quick lunch, cocktail lounge, bar* and *curb service.*

The Israeli cabinet has plans to present a bill abolishing the use of English as one of the nation's official languages, leaving only Hebrew and Arabic. So far, not too much seems to have been done about it.

Although Negro Africa seems in general content to retain the old colonial languages, there is a movement in Zambia to change the name of the world-famous Victoria Falls to Mosiuatunya, "smoke that thunders." But this may be difficult, in view of the fact that white-ruled Rhodesia owns the opposite bank.

The constitution of the Philippines aims specifically at the abolition of both English and Spanish and at their eventual replacement as tongues of common intercourse for the Commonwealth by a "common national language based on one of the existing national languages," which has since turned out to be Tagalog.

In some Latin-American countries, bans on English signs and firm names are demanded, in the name of the "defense of the Spanish language." Puerto Rico, where English replaced Spanish as the official language in 1898, has gone back to Spanish in the elementary and high schools. It is distressing but true that precisely those Spanish speakers who are most subject to American influence are the ones who most resent our political-linguistic penetration.

The situation of India is at present a curious one. Claiming to be the third English-speaking nation in the world, with possibly as many as 25 million of its nearly 500 million inhabitants speaking English in one fashion or another, it had planned, during Nehru's lifetime, to implant Hindi as the national tongue, with fourteen other regional languages co-official in their respective regions. The cut-off date had been set for 1965, but as it approached there were such violent protests from the Dravidian-speaking areas of the south that Premier Shastri was compelled to postpone the abolition of English until some indefinite future date, with the result that the Indian schools now teach three languages, Hindi, English and the regional tongue.

Ceylon abolished English as an official language several years ago, but has now realized that neither Singhalese nor Tamil are adequate for growing international contacts, and is planning to reestablish English in all its schools, with UN aid for teacher training.

Under the circumstances, one is forced to do some mighty wondering. Is the future of English on the international scale quite as bright as some of its advocates would like to paint it? Does English have a world-wide mission to which it must perforce go on? Or has it reached its astonishing peak, and is it destined henceforward to recede from some of the positions it has conquered, like the Imperial Latin of Rome in the centuries that immediately preceded and followed the barbarian invasions? The omens are indeed mixed, and the man who would be a soothsayer would be extending his neck to an inconceivable degree.

It would perhaps be wise, at this point, to leave the question of international English in abeyance, reserving the right to reexamine the omens for the immediate future at a later point, and to concentrate instead upon the probable internal developments of the language, in the hope that they may shed some light upon the broader world scene.

Chapter Two

THE PROBLEM OF SPELLING REFORM

Why Spelling?—First Perception of the Problem—
Half-Way Measures vs. Complete Phonetization—Ob-
stacles—Can It Be Accomplished?—What Will It Do
to Us?—What Will It Do for Us?

English spelling is the world's most awesome mess. The
Chinese system of ideographs is quite logical, once you accept
the premise that writing is to be divorced from sound and made
to coincide with thought-concepts. The other languages of the
West have, in varying degrees, coincidence between spoken
sounds and written symbols. But the spelling of English reminds
one of the crazy quilt of ancient, narrow, winding streets in
some of the world's major cities, through which modern automobile traffic must nevertheless in some way circulate.

In no other language is it possible to get seven different
sounds out of a combination of written letters like *ough* (*dough,*
bought, bough, rough, through, thorough, hiccough), or conversely, spell a sound like that ordinarily represented by *sh* in
fourteen different ways (*shoe, sugar, issue, mansion, mission,*
nation, suspicion, ocean, nauseous, conscious, chaperon, schist,
fuchsia, pshaw). In no other language would it be possible to
write *phtholognyrrh* for *Turner* by using the *phth* of *phthisic,*
the *olo* of *colonel,* the *gn* of *gnat* and the *yrrh* of *myrrh,* or to
spell, plausibly, *kaughphy* for *coffee.* In no other language could
a Hollander write, for the instruction of his fellow-countrymen
wishing to learn English:

> I will teach you in my verse
> Sounds like corpse, corps, horse and worse. . . .
> Beard and heard, and lord and word;

Gear and tear, but wear and tear. . . .
Meat and peat, but sweat and great
(The last word rhymes with freight and weight);
Quite different again is height
Which sounds like bite, indict and light. . . .
Crew and blew and few, but sew,
Cow and row, but sow and row. . . .

and so on for many, many lines.

In no other language could a native poet write:

A pretty deer is dear to me,
A hare with downy hair;
A hart I love with all my heart,
But barely bear a bear.

In no other language could a foreigner be tricked into pronouncing *manslaughter* as *man's laughter*. Concerning no other language could Nazi Propaganda Minister Goebbels threaten his German listeners with a new allied atrocity if they failed to win the war, warning them they would be forced to learn English, and that English spelling is very, very difficult. It is possible, but not likely, that we could find another language where semantic opposites, like *reckless* and *wreckless,* are distinguished only by their spelling.

It is quite simple to say that the *p* of *pneumonia* and the silent *k*'s of *knickknack* were sounded when Caxton's printers began to codify the written language, and offer that as an excuse for their presence today. We can even point with pride to the abandonment of medieval spellings like *housbonde, mynde* and *ygone,* and account for the irrational spelling of *delight* (once *delite*) by saying that it became confused with *night* and *light.* The fact remains that our spelling is more than irrational—it is inhuman, and forms the bane not merely of foreigners, but of our own younger generations, compelled to devote interminable hours to learning a system which is the soul and essence of anarchy. It is hardly surprising that one of America's leading linguists suggests that we stop teaching spelling altogether for a few years, at the end of which time a new system based on the sounds of the spoken language will have perforce evolved.

A glaring example of the inadequacies of English spelling appeared in a test given to sixty-four graduate students of journalism at Columbia University. The average was twenty-five misspellings out of seventy-eight words. Typical words used in the test were *analogous, dissension, harassed, siege, canoeist, ecstasy, restaurateur, vilification, dietitian, guerrilla, supersede,* and appropriately, *misspell.* Foreign students did better than the native-born, pointing up the advantages of bilingualism. Another series of spellings so ghastly as to be almost unbelievable is submitted by Professor Arnold Hartoch of the Chicago Navy Pier branch of the University of Illinois: *dumnb, middnite, lieutendent, wisch, rifel, cowtch, natly* (naturally), *tyered, youniform, sodiers, speach, aliet* (alight), *theirfour, theorhea* (theory).

It is somewhat surprising, on the other hand, that a high-school survey should reveal that the words most frequently misspelled are not the hard ones one would suspect. Instead, they are relatively simple and much in use, like *develop, cordially, proceed, meant, absence, decide, receive, athletic, sincerely, practical, volume, argument, finally.* The list also includes *February, whether* and *secretary,* but here it is probably the ear that deceives the eye (pronunciations like *Febuary, wether* and *seketary* are current). *Principal* is confused with *principle, scene* with *seen,* while *foreign* has a *gn* that is in conflict with our high-frequency *ng.*

Another school test revealed eighteen spellings for *Appalachian,* including *Appelation, Appleachean* and *Appliciation. Alleghany* was much misspelled also, but in extenuation of this it must be remarked that there are correct local variants, such as *Allegheny* and *Allegany.* Variant spellings, so common in the days of the early printers, are often permissible today (*comptroller* and *controller,* or *gray* and *grey.* Historically, we find *segar* as a current mid-nineteenth-century spelling for *cigar, travail* used for *travel* in British railroad instruction books of a century ago and, if we go further back, the spelling *parliament* for Medieval Latin *parliamentum* while the pronunciation stems from Old French *parlement,* as well as the *h* of *Magna Charta,* recently abolished, from a late Latin *chartula* probably already influenced by French *charte.*

Yet, surprisingly, one good word may be spoken for English

spelling conventions which no one seems to have spoken hitherto. English transcriptions seem slightly superior to those used by other languages to transcribe words, and particularly names, from still other tongues. Compare, for example, English *Kosygin* with French *Kossyguine;* English *Surabaya* with Dutch *Soerabaja.* Had English speakers gotten to South America first instead of Spanish speakers, we would have *Atawalpa* and *Kechwa* instead of *Atahualpa* and *Quechua.* The Japanese words for November and husband appear in English transcription as *jūichigatsu* and *shujin,* in Italian transcription as *giuiccigazzu* and *sciugin.* Our transcriptions are more phonetic, even if our spelling of native words is not.

When did spelling first become a conscious problem with English speakers? The *Ormulum,* composed about 1200, shows a doubling of consonants after short vowels, which would indicate an attempt to reflect pronunciation. There are rumors of an early thirteenth-century attempt to regularize spelling, but the details are vague. The sixteenth century marks the real beginning of the reform movement. This was the period when a gardening treatise uses indifferently *Zodiac, Zodiack* and *Zodyacke,* and places an *-yng* ending on *tillyng* and *sowyng, -ynge* on *speakynge,* and *-ying* on *buyldying.* The problem of "right writing" was uppermost in the minds of the sixteenth-century grammarians, one of whom is rumored to have devised a phonetic alphabet of no less than 450 characters. Cheke, Hart, Bullokar and Mulcaster vied in "improving" the quality of the written language, and if we are tempted to belittle their efforts, let us at least give thanks that they left us generally with a single irrational spelling for words that had previously had half a dozen equally irrational variants.

Samuel Johnson, who endeavored to put a premium on "correct" spelling, was himself torn asunder by the conflicting forces of analogy, etymology and pronunciation. To him and his followers we owe in large part the inconsistency of *deceit* vs. *receipt, design* vs. *disdain,* the *b* of *debt* and *doubt,* the progression of *gn* from *reign* to *sovereign* to *foreign,* one of the words, be it noted, that disturb our present-day high school spellers. He suggested a *k* for *critick* and *musick,* on the ground that "truly English spelling should always have a Saxon *k,*" and this, remarks Robertson with tongue in cheek, is Johnson's own personal contribution to the Anglo-Saxon alphabet.

Benjamin Franklin and Noah Webster were America's pioneers in the realm of spelling reform, but while the former limited himself to the vague advocacy of a new alphabet, the latter made distinct contributions that color the written American language of today. To his *American Dictionary* of 1828 we owe the use of *-or* vs. the British *-our* (*labor, labour*), *-er,* vs. *-re* (*theater, theatre*), the single *l* of *traveled,* the *k* of *mask* (*masque*), the *ck* of *check* (*cheque*), the *f* of *draft* (*draught*), the *-se* of *defense* (*defence*), the *w* of *plow* (*plough*), though he pulled his punches on several of the drastic reforms he had advocated in 1789 (*helth, breth, frend, beleeve, receeve, yeer, rong, ritten, tung, munth, iz, lauf, touf, korus, mashine, wimmen*).

It was Webster also who gave a fillip to the spelling bee, which he said was "good for the articulation," and for which Franklin had laid down the rules in 1750. For over a century the spelling bee cast a magnetic spell over America (four thousand people crowded the Philadelphia Academy of Music in 1875 to see eighty competitors spelled down), and the vogue is far from dead. The spelling bee proved fairly conclusively that women are better spellers than men, possibly because they are more conscious of appearance, in words as well as clothes.

In 1837 Isaac Pitman devised his method of stenography, which opened the eyes of many scholars to the deficiencies of English spelling and the advantages of phonetization. Coupled with the filtration into learned milieus of the earlier versions of the International Phonetic Alphabet, this led to the first serious attempts at phonetic spelling reform. In England, G. B. Shaw fought for a standard phonetic alphabet that would enable him to transfer to the printed page the full tang of "coster English," the "grave music of good Scotch," and the "exquisite diphthong with which a New Yorker pronounces such words as *world* and *bird.*"

On this side of the ocean, we have had a Simplified Spelling Board since 1906; but even the support of Theodore Roosevelt could not arouse the American people to the importance of the problem. Senator Robert Owen's attempt to create a "Global Alphabet" elicited from a distinguished kinswoman of the reform-loving Theodore, Mrs. Eleanor Roosevelt, the comment that "it seems quite difficult to learn."

And there the matter rests. With the exception of some popular innovations, mostly of commercial origin (*thru, tho, alright, Starlite, nite* and *nitery, donut, burlesk, thanx, sox*), the great spelling problem of the English language is still unsolved.

It is not that there are no organizations and individuals interested in spelling reform. Quite the contrary. On both sides of the Atlantic we find swarms of would-be reformers. There are the Simplified Spelling Society of England and the Simpler Spelling Association of America, which advance a composite method whereby *may* is spelled *mai* or *mae, who* becomes *huu* or *hoo, there* appears as *dhaer* or *thair*. There is an American Phonetic League, which would bring in new symbols and suprascripts (*bilō* for *below, fØlz* for *falls, sum* for *some*). There is a Georgia organization which seems to stem directly from the Websterian tradition (*agen, hipnosis, wurld, gras, enuf, vois, vizit, stopt*).

As early as 1883, a physician from Hunterdon County in New Jersey, Cornelius Larison by name, mindful of the trouble he had had with spelling in his boyhood, produced a book called *The Fonic Speler and Sylabater,* further described as "desind as an Ad in Acqwiring a Noleg ov the Fundamental Principls ov the English Langwag." The 1964 article describing his life and times is entitled "Wurds and Wurks ov a Dunz Hoo Becam a Fizzishun." There were no permanent results. As late as 1965, Representative Harlan Hagen of California offered a bill to create a "U. S. official dictionary," to be prepared by a five-man commission that would be authorized to "wring superfluous silent letters out of American words."

Britain is at present toying with a 44-letter so-called "Initial Teaching Alphabet," which is used in the schools to give children their initial instruction in reading and writing. The alphabet can only be described as semi-phonetic, and is not designed to be permanent, but only transitional; after learning the basic arts of literacy, the students are shifted over to conventional spelling. Advocates of the system claim that it works wonders in speeding up the learning process, but since anything even remotely resembling a phonetic alphabet would be bound to do that, the question remains open whether ITA represents the best solution to the problem of teaching Johnny to read. A somewhat similar system has been devised in America by a Chicago economist, John Malone, who calls his 40-symbol alphabet Unifon. This, too, is being experimentally tried in some schools.

In view of the fact that the greatest objection to spelling reform seems to involve any deviation from our conventional 26-letter Roman alphabet (printing and typing become very much involved with anything that diverges), I have myself proposed a reform involving the use of a certain number of digraphs (two-letter combinations) with single-sound invariable values, fuller utilization of such seldom-used letters as *x* and *q,* and the possible use of the apostrophe to represent the most frequent of our spoken vowel sounds, unstressed *e* of *the* and unstressed *a* of *a.* A sample runs as follows: "Dh' rifohrm av Inglix speling iz ' prabl'm dhaet haez lohng aejiteyt'd spihk'rz aend rayt'rz an bowth saydz av dhi 'tlaentik."

With all due respect for the hard labors and excellent intentions of the reformers, there are two major criticisms of their efforts that may be advanced at this point. One is purely technical and deals with their procedure. If we are to go through the throes of a major linguistic transformation, why not do a complete job? The sounds of spoken English, whether British or American, are limited in number; for each of them there exists a precise symbol in the International Phonetic Alphabet. Adoption of these IPA symbols, or a modification of them to simplify the printing problem, is perfectly possible, and thereafter we should have a completely phonetic written language.

The other criticism is concerned with the praiseworthy but erroneous ideology displayed by the majority of the reformers. For some incomprehensible reason, they choose to link their activities with the two largely unrelated problems of the adoption of English as an international language and the preservation of world peace. "Simplify English spelling," many of them say, "and you will abolish the major obstacle to the adoption of English as a world tongue; then, when we have an international language, and this language is English, there will be no more quarrels among the nations, and no more wars." One spelling reformer goes so far as to assert that we could make several major political concessions to the Soviet Union in return for their acceptance of phonetized English.

One might say that this logical sequence is so illogical that one should take no notice of it. The three desiderata (phonetization of English, adoption of a universal tongue, and world peace) are each of them such worthy causes that it is a pity to see them thrown together into a stew-pot of confusion. It goes without saying that the adoption of an international language will not, all by itself, halt wars. It also remains to be proved (and no foreign government has been heard from on this score) that if we reform our evil spelling ways other nations will adopt our tongue. The reform of English spelling is such an urgent internal problem that it can and should be discussed on a purely internal basis rather than on an international one. Is it a worth-while project so far as we, the speakers of English, are concerned? If it is, let us proceed to discuss it, in our own selfish interests and without too much regard for what foreign nations may think or do about it. Other countries never asked our permission in connection with their own language changes. The Turks switched from the Arabic to the Roman alphabet, the Russians revised their Cyrillic spelling, the speakers of Portuguese and Norwegian go through periodic spelling revisions, and all without consulting anyone outside their own countries. Surely our children and children's children, who have to go through the drastic spelling-learning process we went through, should be enough of a consideration with us to warrant our careful study of the question, regardless of the possible and very hypothetical future actions and reactions of other nations.

It is often asserted that the only thing that keeps us from reforming our spelling and going over to a simpler system is the dead hand of tradition, or, to put it another way, our national perversity. Clark, for example, states: "English-speaking peoples, particularly Americans, take a perverted pride in the intricate and mysterious anomalies of the spelling of their language; it makes them feel superior to foreigners." This is a splendid wise-crack, but it hardly corresponds to the linguistic reality. Robertson has neatly summarized the advantages and disadvantages of spelling reform. The former, according to him, are: a saving in education, printing, typing, an improvement in pronunciation, an aid in the Americanization of foreigners and a contribution to the acceptance of English as an international language. The disadvantages (and we should note them carefully) are: the loss of etymological values, the falling together of homophones, the impossibility of keeping related words together in the dictionary, and a loss in the esthetic quality of the language. An additional difficulty, cited from Samuel Johnson, is that the reformers would be taking "that for a model which is changing while they apply it," which means in effect that the process of phonetization would have to be repeated every fifty or a hundred years to keep pace with spoken-language changes.

To each of these arguments there is a reply, to be sure. The "loss of etymological values" means that whereas a few of us now know at a glance what the derivation of *phthisic* is, we would no longer know once the word was spelled *tisic* or something similar. Other languages have been through this particular mill, with no apparent ill effects. Italian *tisico* has no trace of Greek *phth,* but the Italians seem to be able to struggle along. Homophones like *pear, pair, pare* would fall together in spelling if the reform were adopted; this would not be a new situation; we already have it in *Pole* and *pole,* and, without even benefit of capitals, in words like *post, toll* and *bat.* There are even corresponding advantages in the distinction that would arise between *tear* [ti:r] and *tear* [te:r], *read* [ri:d] and *read* [red]. Context and word-order, as Chinese teaches us, are great aids to comprehension. More serious is the dictionary divorcement of *zeal* and *zealous, nation* and *national,* but cross-references could be created by titillating the ingenuity of our lexicographers. As for the esthetic factor, that seems to coincide largely with traditionalism. We think that is beautiful which is familiar. The changing phonetics of the English language could be taken care of by a periodical revision, as in Portuguese, and we ought not to forget that a truly phonetic writing-system would act as a powerful deterrent to pronunciation changes which are now largely arbitrary because the pronunciation is not supported by the writing.

Robertson, it would seem, has overlooked what is undoubtedly the principal valid objection to spelling reform, an objection that was dramatically brought into the limelight when a commission of American educators urged the Japanese to use Roman characters instead of their ideographs and *kanas*. "What shall we do with all our present printed works?" asked the Japanese. "Scrap them and reprint them in Roman, at infinite cost of money, time and labor? Or allow them to remain in our libraries, side by side with the new works in Roman alphabet, which will mean that our growing generations will have to learn both systems, the old and the new?"

Orthographic reform is relatively simple where the majority of the population is illiterate, as was the case in Kemal's Turkey. It becomes a terrific problems where the majority is literate, as in Japan, Britain or America. The older generations must learn all over again, while the younger cannot be separated at one blow from the previous tradition, save by the well-nigh impossible expedient of burning all past records and creating them anew.

Robertson makes the observation that phonetic spelling is not necessary if only the letters are associated by habit with the word. It is not the sole function of writing, he holds, to symbolize the spoken language's sounds. We too have ideographic elements in our capitals and punctuation, not to mention our spelling of homophones like *so, sow, sew*. But then ought we not to go over to a frankly ideographic system, like the Chinese? What is galling about our English spelling is that it is neither phonetic nor ideographic, but attempts to combine both elements.

In an impassioned and lengthy letter to the *New York Times* Charles Funk once protested against the full phonetization of English. His major argument was the difference between British and American pronunciation, which he claimed was such as to

compel both British and Americans to use glossaries to read phonetic transcriptions of each other's spoken tongue.

This, of course, is another major stumbling-block in the path
of spelling reform. It seems to point, indeed, to a need for reform
in speech rather than writing, and is hence best reserved for the
following chapter.

Before leaving this question of spelling reform, however, let us
summarize what a phonetic spelling could do for us, not on the
international plane, by making our language easier for foreigners
to swallow, but on the isolationistic, national level.

English spelling is at times confusing to those who know it well,
and leads to frequent trips to the dictionary to discover not the
meaning, but the form of words. But to our younger native
learners of English, those descendants concerning whom so many
fine words flow, it is distressing and difficult. How much of the
school child's time is spent on the purely mechanical memoriza-
tion of spelling? If all those hours were added up and multiplied
by the number of learners, the sum-product would be astronomical. If those hours were devoted, as they are in most other western
countries, to the acquision of factual knowledge, what might we
not expect in the way of educational improvement?

This consideration alone ought to give us pause and make us
reflect on what might be the advantages and disadvantages of a
true phonetization of our written language. The body of material
knowledge at our disposal is increasing at an astounding rate.
Already it is difficult, not to say impossible, to achieve that well-
rounded education that used to be the boast of earlier centuries,
and this is not because we have become intellectually duller, but
simply because there is so much more to learn, so many fields of
which our ancestors, even our parents, had no conception, but
with which the educated man of today must have some familiarity. If, under the circumstances, we were to unburden ourselves
of one of the unnecessary burdens our grandparents carried so
easily in their stride, would we not be doing the intelligent thing?
Must a twentieth-century soldier, in addition to his modern
equipment, continue to carry a nineteenth-century knapsack and
a twenty-pound musket?

Chapter Three

THE PROBLEM OF SPEAKING REFORM

A National or an International Standard?—King's English vs. American Language—Is Standardization Desirable?—Is It Attainable?—Speak as You Write, or Write as You Speak!

The primary problem that faces any would-be reformer of spoken English is that of the unity of the language. Shall English be allowed to degenerate into a series of regional dialects, each supreme and official in its own sphere? Or shall there be a single, international standard for all speakers of good English?

Linguists are at pains to tell us that no two localities (indeed, no two individuals) speak exactly alike. Dialectalization, carried to its logical linguistic conclusion, implies that there are as many speech-varieties as there are speakers.

Freedom of the individual, carried to its ultimate conclusion, leads to anarchy. By a system of fairly reasonable checks and balances, however, we manage to make individuals live together under one law, while at the same time preserving for them a modicum of personal freedom. In like manner, the linguists group the speech-forms of individuals and localities into larger units, corresponding to the governments, local and national, of the political world, and say that two people whose individual speech may differ considerably nevertheless speak the same dialect or language. The infinite speech-varieties of Britain, the United States and the Commonwealth are thus placed under subheadings, the sum total of which is that somewhat vague entity known as the English language.

The two largest and most inclusive units of English are the British and the American. It is needless to add that each is subdivided. The point is that there is something which comes close to being a British standard to which most cultivated Britishers subscribe. Its American equivalent is more vague and difficult to define, but nevertheless exists.

Either these two predominant forms of English must live side by side, in which case each will become a separate national standard; or they must merge into a form of international English acceptable to both major groupings. It is noteworthy in this connection that in 1922 a proposal was made to create an *International* Council for English, something that would have come fairly close to an English-language academy, had it gone through.

Without going once more into the many differences that distinguish the British from the American standard, it may be well to emphasize at this point that a difference in pronunciation is noticeable in about one-fourth of all words which the two languages hold in common. American is said to be generally understood by the British, thanks particularly to the movies, but the reverse is somewhat hesitantly denied. Robertson claims that the differences between the two languages are often overstressed, but Webster conceived of American as eventually differing as much from British as Danish does from German. In addition, Vachel Lindsay presents the case for two American languages, which he labels "U. S." and "American"; one of these is said to be colloquial, the other formal. Actually, a similar distinction could be established not only in British English, but in the majority of languages. Robertson is probably closer to the truth when he asserts that American is more uniform than British, with no standard dialect, and with less spread between the language of the educated and that of the uneducated, something which may stem from what James Truslow Adams calls the American tendency to "mucker pose," the affectation by educated men of the language of uneducated half-wits. But here again we are treading on thin ice.

Since the first objections to American were voiced by eighteenth- and nineteenth-century Englishmen of renown, it has been fashionable in Britain to criticize the American speech. The Fowlers, in *The King's English,* sum up the British learned opinion of the turn of the century when they say, "Americanisms are foreign words, and should be so treated" (they remind us, however, that many reputed American traits go back to the British dialects). They come to the attack again when they pronounce: "The English and the American language and literature are both good things; but they are better apart than mixed."

Few reputable critics agree with this pronouncement. Partridge, for instance, asserts that the Public School Standard of Britain is the most slovenly of all ways of speaking English, and accuses it of a "sword-swallowing manipulation of consonants"; he goes on to quote Greig to the effect that "thousands of English speakers all over the world utter prayers for its early demise." Robertson, for his part, accuses the Public School Standard of being really a class dialect in disguise, and Mencken suggests that while American may have started out as a dialect of English, the latter may, if it continues to borrow, turn out to be a dialect of American. Abroad, some years ago, a Japanese newspaper agency significantly advised Japanese students of English to pay more attention to the language of Truman and less to that of Thackeray.

If the two languages are to merge into a single standard, what shall be the direction of the merger? Interesting experiments have been carried out by the film industry to produce a type of language that will be equally acceptable to all English speakers. British attempts to duplicate American gangster films have been described as linguistically ludicrous by American movie critics. The British, on the other hand, resented American actresses in the role of Victoria Regina, and the idiomatic American spoken by GI characters in various war films proved hard on London audiences. Scottish audiences, however, prefer the "clear, distinct" enunciation of American players to that of Englishmen, particularly when the latter use Cockney. In the screen adaptation of *Alice in Wonderland,* Columbia University's ace phonetician, Cabell Greet, was called in to determine a phonetic speech-pattern of universal acceptance, with seeming success.

Non-English-speaking nations continue to make much of the spread between American and British English. The French especially, perhaps because they have an axe to grind, label books as *traduit de l'américain.* Individual Americans and Britishers perversely, or perhaps naïvely, perpetuate the tradition of two different languages. Sir Herbert Broadley, addressing the Washington Landladies, a group interested in land and all it produces, began by saying: "Unfamiliar with your language, I assumed this meant a gathering of proprietresses of boarding-houses," a pardonable error even for an American. On the other hand, the American-born small daughter of an Englishwoman confided to her mother's friend: "I do wish mommy would talk American, like you and me; don't you think she sounds just like a foreigner?"

Despite all this, a fairly obvious conclusion seems to emerge from the varied episodes of British-American linguistic conflict. We are becoming more familiar with each other's speech-forms all the time. This is due primarily to new mechanical means of communication, like the radio, TV, and the spoken film, and to increased, easier, faster travel. The modern trend is definitely toward standardization and away from dialects, even such outstanding ones as British and American. The emergence of an international English standard may be only a question of time and, very fortunately, it does not hinge on governmental approval, but only on the continuance and enhancement of existing conditions.

The fact that both British and American are subdivided into numerous dialects is no deterrent, since those dialects themselves are in the process of being absorbed by their respective national standards. The innovations of both Britain and America tend to become nation-wide as they are spread by rapid and abundant means of communication. There is, furthermore, a spirit of tolerance in the air that was not present in the days of crusty British superiority and arrogant American nationalism. Both sides are eager to listen to and borrow from each other.

This does not mean that absolute uniformity will ever be achieved, even within one country. Localisms and regionalisms will always exist. But they will be pushed farther and farther into the background. Granted a continuation of present historical conditions and social-economic trends, the eventual appearance of a single standard of general cultured acceptance, without benefit of Academy or governmental constraint, is almost a certainty. The details, we may add, are unimportant. If it is true, as Clark states, that science and democracy are less restrained in America than in Britain, and that in consequence there is more change in American than in British English, we may expect the British to accept the majority of our innovations. We, on our part, show little hesitancy in adopting theirs, jokingly perhaps at first, then seriously. For what concerns pronunciation standards, it would not hurt Americans to adopt some of the graceful refinement and rhythm of enunciation that distinguish cultivated British speakers, nor would it hurt the British to adopt some of our clearness, minus our nasality and lack of tone. Disputed and controversial pronunciations and accentuations appear at present within both languages; the addition of a few variants will hurt no one, and the essence of such variants is common recognition rather than common use. The English language, in short, is big enough to receive both British and American under its wing. Grammatical structure and syntactical arrangement, which constitute the essence and backbone of language, are already fundamentally one.

Let us therefore broaden our already broad linguistic tolerance, and bring into play all the resources of our spirit of compromise. Hard days lie ahead, and in union there is strength.

The question of the double standard (British and American) is perhaps the most glaring, but it is not the only one agitating English speakers. As you run your eye over a page of the dictionary, you will find many, indeed far too many, points of disputed and double pronunciation. Should one say *Paris* or *Paree*, *ballet* or *ballay*, *préstige* or *prestíge*, *foyer* or *fwayay*, *pasturized* or *pasteurized?* Without going into recent French loan-words, should it be *apricot*, with *a* of *bat*, or *āpricot*, with *a* of *lady?* *Pumpkin* to rhyme with *bumpkin*, or *pungkin? Herb* or *erb? An historic* or *a historic occasion? An humble* or *a humble servant?* Should we, as a writer suggests, start with *tomaytoes* in the garden and wind up with cream of *tomahto* soup in the kitchen?

A list of most frequently mispronounced words includes *orgy, human, forte, genuine, acumen, admirable, mischievous, radiator, grimace, impious, finis, naïveté* and *integral.* Some of these words supply much food for thought on language-processes. *Forte* is *fort* when it means "the strong point" (in which case it comes from French), but *fortay* when it is a musical direction and comes from

Italian. *Genuine,* with influence of *wine, line* and *dine,* is a mispronunciation due to the same eye-deception that causes *Eyetalian; admīrable* is erroneously influenced by *admire; rad-iator* is probably due to a wrong syllabic division, with, perhaps, some influence from *sad* and *mad.* But why should we have to violate our initial-stress tendencies in order to preserve the original French accentuation in *grim-ACE,* while we wilfully disregard the correct Latin pronunciation of *finis* and the correct French version of *demise?*

The question spontaneously arises: "Who decreed that these words should be pronounced thus and so, anyway?," and a partial and inconclusive answer appears in the next chapter. But in view of the lack of an Academy or other governing body of the language, in view also of the absolutely insufficient support that the spoken English tongue derives from the written, is it any wonder that native speakers of English mispronounce as they do? Is it even any wonder that a few extremists among the linguisticians advocate that you should talk as you please, and let the chips fall where they may?

Recourse to "good usage" in the case of the pronunciation of unusual or even usual words is begging the question so far as English is concerned. Who are the arbiters of good usage, and by what authority and according to what standards do they pontificate? If we are to follow the well-known democratic procedure of the rule of the majority, there is little doubt that *mis-CHIEVous* and *GRIM-ace* will be the standard forms, along with *I ast 'im, I'd a seen 'im, ain't, who did you see?, I laid on the bed,* and other gems of the substandard.

The "genius" of the substandard speaker, as brought out by many complainants, runs to a sloppy, careless form of diction miscalled "Americanese": "Waddya Know?"; "Watcha have?", "Doncha see?", "Joo see 'em?" and similar forms, which unfortunately are not confined to the illiterate and uneducated, but seep upward into the ranks of business executives, professional people, and even actors and actresses who have devoted years of study to proper diction. This is a phenomenon that strikes all languages at given historical periods. Many linguists surmise that it was precisely this sort of slipshod speech that caused classical Latin to degenerate into the forms of which the documents and inscriptions of the period that immediately preceded and followed the collapse of the Roman Empire give abundant attestation. This "degeneration" of Latin ultimately led to the rise of Romance languages which are in all respects the equals of the Roman tongue in beauty, expressiveness and utility. Ought we to expect a similar outcome for the current "degeneration" of the English tongue?

It may be remarked in passing that the phenomenon in question is powerfully aided and abetted both by educators of the permissive school and by linguists who hold that language is what people speak, not what purists think they should speak. One manual for the guidance of teachers urges them to learn and cultivate such forms as "Cha doon?" (for the uninitiate, this stands for "What are you doing?" in substandard speech). Another piece composed by a linguistic scientist claims that "Them dogs is us'uns" (Ozarkian for "Those dogs are ours") is good, meaningful American language, however restricted as to area. It is the claim of this school that the native speaker can do no wrong, and that only foreign learners can make true mistakes in the use of the language.

Among the numerous opponents of this *laissez-faire* doctrine applied to language, various authoritative voices have arisen. One Ohio State University professor, stationed at Bolling Air Force Base, claims that for communication between pilots and control towers, where there is much interfering noise, a stuttered pronunciation helps to clarify the muddled sounds and meanings. A so-called "bounce block" stutter such as *wuh-one, tuh-two* makes for intelligibility. The professor and his team are now investigating the applicability of this principle to ordinary speech in the interests of sound communication. The basic philosophy underlying this point of view is that language fails in its basic purpose if it is so condensed and telescoped that it is not understood.

All this serves to bring up a point which is usually hush-hush among the linguists, though Clark and a few other brave souls screw up the courage to mention it. Much is said of writing as you speak, or phonetizing the spelling of the language to conform with the pronunciation. What would be the chances of deliberately changing the pronunciation to harmonize with the spelling, or in other words, of having us speak as we write?

The obstacles would probably be insurmountable. On the practical side, it would be argued that you cannot shake the speakers out of their normal speech-habits and make them retrace their steps over a thousand years. Charlemagne's noble eighth-century experiment, in the course of which he tried to make people who were definitely on the French side of the linguistic divide go back to grammatical Latin, stands as a mighty monument to the proposition that history, linguistic and otherwise, does not march backwards.

Yet there would be a peculiar charm about an English language spoken as it is written, as, say, an Italian who has learned it out of a grammar pronounces it, or as an Anglo-Saxon would probably pronounce it if he came back to life. There would also be an esthetic improvement in the sounds of such a hypothetical language—vowels coming out in full and with their pure sounds, consonants completely and authentically uttered. The language would have far more of a majestic flow, and the speakers would finally be compelled to open their mouths wide, instead of grunting, snorting, wheezing, puffing and whining.

But this is little more than an idle dream, and one impossible of fulfilment. All that can reasonably be asked of a language such as English is that it give up a small part of its eighteenth- and nineteenth-century rugged individualism and submit to a very minor amount of regularization, both in its sounds and in its orthography—not the kind of iron-bound regularization that French, Italian and Spanish academicians have endeavored, with varying measures of success, to fasten upon their tongues, but the sort of thing that would enable us to eliminate some of the too numerous variant spellings and pronunciations that appear in our dictionaries today.

This could perhaps be accomplished, almost painlessly, through a closer collaboration among British, American and Commonwealth lexicographers, whose dictates at present are not greatly heeded because they are too divergent and confusing. Between the rigid Romance tradition that says, "This is right, and everything else is wrong," and the ultraliberal Anglo-Saxon custom of accepting and recording as of equal value everything that happens along in the linguistic line, there must be an *aurea mediocritas,* a golden mean. Can we discover and apply it?

Chapter Four

THE VOICE OF AUTHORITY

The Question of Usage and Taste—The Drawbacks of Dictionaries—Origin and History of Grammars—A Language Academy?—Guides to Good Usage, and How to Use Them

Since the days of Sumerian Nippur, from which there comes to us a tablet that is probably the earliest sample of a combination grammar and dictionary, it has been the self-appointed mission of learned men to exercise a watchdog function over the language. Panini, who codified the rules for the use of good Sanskrit, the numerous Greek and Latin grammarians who have left us excellent prescriptive accounts of their languages, the early medieval scholars who toiled at the court of Charlemagne, all played the role of the Voice of Authority. Since language is almost invariably in a fluid state, while the product of the labors of grammarians and lexicographers is necessarily static, there is an inherent and perpetual conflict between the scholars' ideal and the language as it actually is.

The earliest work of the kind in English is Bede's "Grammar," consisting of imaginary dialogues on linguistic and other liberal studies between Alcuin and his pupils, and particularly between a young Frank and a young Saxon. A typical pronouncement is that "vowels are the souls, consonants the bodies of words." The all-inclusive nature of the work is to be gathered from the fact that the Alcuinian parts of grammar comprise "words, letters, syllables, clauses, sayings, speeches, definitions, feet, accents, punctuation marks, critical marks, orthographies, analogies, etymologies, glosses, distinctions, barbarisms, solecisms, faults, metaplasms, figurations, tropes, prose, metres, fables and histories."

English grammar as a codified subject of study seems to have first arisen in the sixteenth century, and among its contributors were Milton and Ben Jonson; but its function in those days was primarily to instruct foreigners. The early seventeenth century brought the first English dictionary (Henry Cockeram's), and the latter part of the century saw a chair of Anglo-Saxon at Oxford, a first grammar of Anglo-Saxon, and the advocacy of a "universal grammar" based on Latin and Greek. It was the function of the eighteenth century to produce English grammars for Englishmen, notably those of Priestley and Lowth, which enjoyed great vogue. Lowth, in particular, settled at one fell swoop the disputed question of the double negative by pronouncing that two negatives destroy each other, or are equivalent to an affirmative. But individual points of grammar had been "settled" even earlier. Wallis, for instance, had pronounced on the uses of *shall* and *will* in 1653. At least twenty English dictionaries appeared in the seventeenth century and the first half of the eighteenth.

Along with the rise and spread of grammars and dictionaries, the eighteenth century was notable for the controversy that arose between the Voice of Authority and the doctrine of usage. The former was based largely on Classical models. The latter, first timidly advanced by Hughes in 1698, was taken up by Johnson and Chesterfield, who turned the Classical norms against their own supporters by citing Horace's *jus et norma loquendi*. Priestley, in his 1761 *Rudiments of English Grammar,* says that custom is supreme, and the only authority is the body of the people. Campbell, in his 1776 *Philosophy of Rhetoric,* describes language as "purely a species of fashion," and insists that the only business of the grammarian is to note, collect and methodize the laws of language from usage, present, national and reputable. These remarkably modern points of view are only in part vitiated by the fact that their promulgators did not always practise what they preached. Johnson, for instance, objected to the use of *who* for *whom* and of *whose* for *of which,* and to locutions like *between you and I, it is me, the largest of two, more perfect, this here, that there, you was, taller than me, had rather, had better,* despite the fact that some of these "errors" were justified by very ancient usage, as was later sustained by Webster. There is also in the grammatical philosophy of some of these writers a curious tendency to reason by analogy rather than by usage (*written,* for example, is said to be preferable to *wrote* as a past participle because it differentiates the two parts of the verb).

Meanwhile, the rise of the Italian Accademia della Crusca, in existence since 1582, and of the French Academy, created by Richelieu in 1635, had given the English grammarians something to think about. The English lexicographers could hardly fail to be impressed by the six-volume edition of the Italian Academy vocabulary, of which four editions had appeared by 1738, or the French Academy's vocabulary of 1694. Dryden, Defoe, Swift and Addison began the agitation for an English academy, but the opposition of Johnson, Sheridan and Priestley, combined with the natural reluctance of English speakers to extend too comprehensive powers even to the most learned scholars, proved too strong. English continued to "muddle through" with grammars and dictionaries none of which bore the stamp of official sanction. That the going for the Voice of Authority was not altogether smooth even in the Romance countries is shown by Vico's satirization of Aristotle's logical categories in language, and his insistence upon the poetic, creative, and therefore illogical elements in linguistic development, a theory of which the outstanding modern exponent is Croce, also a native of the land that created the first language academy.

Authority by appeal to Latin grammar, the demand for the kind of permanence in the language that an academy would carry in its wake, Johnson's desire for "ascertainment" (defined by him as settled rule and established standard, and somewhat at variance with his expressed purpose not to embalm the language and destroy liberty), all gradually fell by the wayside, and the English language marched on to its new freedom, or stumbled along to its present state of anarchy, according to your viewpoint, without balls and chains, and without an official standard.

American attempts to create something resembling a language academy were, as might be expected, even less successful. In 1780 John Adams proposed to Congress that an academy be set up on American soil for the purpose of "refining, correcting, improving, and ascertaining the English language." This, the proposal continued, would have a happy effect, for English was destined to be a world language. Despite its prophetic aspects, the suggestion fell on deaf ears.

It may be true, as many linguists hold, that the English-speakers' unwillingness to accept authority has led to the great change in the language. It is definitely true that an undoubted parallel can be established between the linguistic and the legal institutions of the Anglo-Saxon peoples (our common law, based on precedent, it is in direct opposition to the Roman law of the Romance countries, based on code, just as our "good" language, based on "usage," contrasts with theirs, founded on the rulings of academies). In France, you can even address inquiries about disputed French grammatical points to an *Office de la langue française* and receive a final pronouncement, while the mere suggestion of such an institution would cause Britishers to explode with wrath and Americans to laugh it out of existence.

Yet it would be ingenuous to deny that there is in modern English a "Voice of Authority." The respect and awe with which that vague entity known as the King's English is viewed in Britain are matched, if not surpassed, by the American's reverence for the dictionary, which in effect means Webster, in one of a dozen variants.

The British are in the habit of ridiculing Americans for their respect for the dictionary, yet it was, as Robertson points out, their own middle-class preoccupation with "correctness" in the eighteenth century that led to the importance of the dictionary. "Dictionary making," says a reviewer, "is an art, a science and a marathon. A lexicographer needs the precision of a poet, the patience of a saint, and the perseverance of a cross-country runner." The English themselves, who have contributed such monumental works as the *New English Dictionary*, far more comprehensive than anything attempted in America, ought not to decry the respect that is shown such works, even while maintaining an open mind about questions of good usage.

When we come to grammar, syntax and pronunciation, we find that the English are far greater respecters of the Voice of Authority than we are. Baugh says that grammarians want to fix rules, which are often arbitrary, and that they make it a business to point out "errors," even in the greatest writers. This obnoxious characteristic is startlingly displayed by the Fowlers, stuffiest of English grammarians, in *The King's English*. Not content with telling us that *I would like* is not English, that only southern Englishmen know instinctively how to use *shall* and *will*, that *write to someone* is utterly incorrect, these English academicians go on to give us an extremely long list of "right" and "wrong" uses of *that, who* and *which,* on grounds of defining and non-defining clauses, with the "wrong" examples deliberately picked from some of the best writers of the language (Thackeray, De Quincey, Macaulay, Meredith, Poe, Scott, Emerson and Dickens among them). Not yet satisfied, they proceed to object to various uses of *individual, mutual, unique, aggravate, extemporaneously, partially,* and regale us with a distinction between *specially* and *especially* worthy of a medieval theologian (use the former for what is opposed to the general, the latter for what is opposed to the ordinary). After completing a perusal of this masterpiece, one feels like borrowing from the language of the teen-agers and inquiring: "How puristic can you get?"

However, it is only fair to point out that the strictures contained in this work of joint authorship, which first saw the light in 1906, and of which the third and latest available edition appeared in 1930, tend largely to disappear in the far better known *Dictionary of Modern English Usage,* composed by Henry W. Fowler alone (first edition 1927), and are practically out so far as the 1965 revision by Ernest Gowers is concerned. This, presumably, is an indication of the march of time and the progressive change in the thinking of even a single individual. There is no question that the doctrine of usage and permissiveness plays a greater and greater role as we go on. The *Dictionary of Contemporary American Usage* of Bergen and Cornelia Evans, published in 1957, stands almost at the opposite pole from *The King's English*. Reasonable compromises between tradition and usage are achieved by Margaret Nicholson's *Dictionary of American-English Usage* of 1957, Charlton Laird's *Writer's Handbook* of 1964, and Theodore Bernstein's *The Careful Writer* of 1965.

Without actually going out of his way, Shaw was probably one of the greatest debunkers of the Voice of Authority on his side of the Atlantic. Not content with being "in favor of dividing up the income of the country equally *between* everybody," he split his infinitives defiantly. Once he invited the London *Times* to get rid of a busybody who spent his time chasing split infinitives, it being "of no consequence whether he decides to go quickly or quickly to go or to quickly go."

On our own shores, the general attitude of grammarians is laudably liberal. Baugh sustains that no region holds a monopoly of good English. Robertson points out that the unsplit infinitive is often ambiguous, and asks several pointed questions of the purists. What is "good usage"? Who are the "speakers"? Shall we assume the artificial and divergent pronunciations of the stage, radio and talkie to be our authority? "Standard," he logically concludes, does not mean "uniform."

At times non-specialists get into the fray. Two Los Angeles judges, after a long debate on the split infinitive, compromised with the following Solomonic decision: "To always split an infinitive would be to sadly torture the English language. But it probably is all right to now and then split one."

Our leading educators assume reasonable middle-of-the-road positions. Dean Pollock of N.Y.U., addressing the National Council of Teachers of English some time ago, held that it was "not a crime to sometimes split an infinitive," and that a preposition might be "a useful word to end a sentence with." There are, he added, "various levels of good usage" and "social penalties attached to slips in good usage and social rewards for excellent usage," which reminds us of the half jocular assertion of a linguist that if you don't conform to linguistic superstitions you won't be invited to tea again.

Norman Lewis, who believes in what he calls the "Kinsey approach to language," suggests that the codified rules of grammar often limp a number of years behind common idiomatic usage. His surveys indicate that four primary grammatical categories are responsible for the majority of "errors": the use of personal pronouns (*between you and I, it is me*); forms of *lay* and *lie* (*he laid on the bed*); uses of *who* and *whom* (*who did you see?*; jocularly, a highbrow is defined as one who can use *whom* without self-consciousness); plural and singular verbs (*one of those men who never says die*). He holds, rightly or wrongly, that many errors stem from over-correction in the schools, and stresses the absurdity of punishing a child for saying, "It's me," and then having him hear Churchill use precisely that locution in some of his recorded speeches.

Despite this liberality, there are several things our American educators still decidedly frown on. *I seen, ain't, hadn't ought, whom are you?*, they say, are not merely below the standards of "proper-proper," but even of "colloquial-proper." Robertson, prince of liberalism that he is, yet looks askance upon *between each bed, like he does, these kind of apples, none are, had rather.* A reviewer declares flatly that he is not "in sympathy with the school which insists that if you say something wrong often enough it becomes right." Another American judge thunders against the use of *contact* as a verb, and calls *and/or* a "hieroglyphical hybrid."

Conflicting trends appear in the business world. *National Sales Executive,* for instance, proclaims: "Increase your vocabulary constantly with words of not too many syllables, especially verbs of action, and respect the rules of grammar"; but the financial commentator who reports this adds: "Who in 1962 particularly wants to respect rules of grammar when there are shorter and less cumbersome ways of saying things, and with more precise meaning? . . . The trend in speech and writing is away from the blue print of correct English that sometimes seems as though it arrived with the Pilgrims. . . . The President in a formal speech says 'I'll buy that' in lieu of 'accept.' "

The Soviet Union had its great linguistic controversy back in the days of Stalin and N. Y. Marr. The United States may be said to have had its great Battle of the Dictionary in 1961, when the third edition of the big Merriam-Webster dictionary came out. Noah Webster's original *American Dictionary of the English Language* had appeared in 1828. A vastly revised edition, brought out by the Merriam firm, and done with the collaboration of William G. Webster, Noah's son, and Professor Chauncey A. Goodrich of Yale, had appeared in 1847. Successive editions were brought out in 1864, 1890 and 1909. The so-called Second Edition of 1934 had reigned supreme for nearly three decades, and had assumed, in practically all respects, the function of the Voice of Authority in our land. Specialized works such as Mencken's *American Language* or Mitford M. Mathews' *Dictionary of Americanisms* of 1951 had supplemented, but in no sense superseded it.

Dr. Philip Gove, who headed the large and impressive staff charged with the compilation of Webster III, was and is a firm believer in the doctrine of usage. His guiding principle was that if a word, or a word-combination, is in use, no matter in what layer of society, the fact should be recorded in a comprehensive dictionary. To this principle there would not have been too much opposition, for earlier editions of Webster had operated under that general directive. But earlier editions had been careful to label all words that were not in educated usage as "slang," "dialect," "vulgar," "substandard," or, at the very least, "colloquial." Gove worked largely on the principle that these labels were unnecessary, and that the fact that the word was in use was the word's only needed justification. This, of course, tended to undermine the dictionary's unofficial but widespread function as the Voice of Authority. Where people had been in the habit of consulting Webster's to find out whether the word or expression they wanted to use was in accordance with the *best* usage, they now found themselves thwarted at every step, and robbed of the guidance they sought. In addition, where earlier dictionaries had given quotations taken only from literary writers and orators, Gove now gave them a sprinkling of quotes from people prominent in the news—but hardly by reason of literary or rhetorical merits— such as baseball players and keepers of houses of ill repute. The explosion that resulted had something atomic about it. Reviewers thundered out against the new version. Professional linguists came to Dr. Gove's defense. But Gove was perfectly capable of marshaling his own defense. In a lengthy article that appeared in the pages of the *New York Times,* he firmly asserted that a dictionary is not to be taken as a tool of prescription or a Voice of Authority, but merely as a record of usage, high, low and middle. This is the crux of the matter, and here the controversy rests. If Dr. Gove's views ultimately prevail, America will have lost its one and only Voice of Authority as to what constitutes acceptable language, and what is to be interpreted as substandard and consequently to be avoided by Bernstein's "Careful Writer," or, we may add, Careful Speaker.

By and large, we subscribe to the view that a language is what its speakers choose to make it. This is particularly true of English, with its system of functional change, its dearth of inflectional endings, its borrowing propensities, its lack of correlation between pronunciation and spelling and, above all, the mood of its speakers. A tongue that has flatly rejected for itself the services of a language academy, and that has announced through the mouths of its greatest writers its firm intention to remain free, is not and has never been a tongue that will bow to the dictates of the early Fowler-type grammarian.

Yet there are dangers in excessive linguistic liberalism. The dangers lie not so much in the innovations themselves as in their implications. If it is true, as even the most liberal among our grammarians inform us, that language reflects social and class usage, is it quite the thing to do to encourage our most illiterate and uneducated classes in the belief that they can set the linguistic pattern and pace? Will not this inbred confidence in their own mass superiority then be transferred to other fields, far more factual than language, with possible dire results? If we proceed to settle a question like the use of *who* or *whom did you see* by a nose-counting procedure, may it then not strike the untutored mind that the answer to how much is two and two should also be derived from a "one man one vote" popular poll? Rejection of authority in the field of language may conceivably lead to rejection of authority in other fields, where the issue is not one of fashion, or good usage, or individual preference, but of cold facts and figures. The signs of this disturbing trend are already quite visible, particularly in the political and economic spheres, and they occasionally crop up in other even more factual fields. Language unconsciously colors all our thinking, and a devil-may-care attitude in matters linguistic is bound to be reflected elsewhere. The value of linguistic discipline may have been overstressed in the past, but the evils of excessive discipline can hardly be cured by running to the other extreme.

Another danger that bids fair to arise from our lack of respect for the Voice of Authority is that we may run into some sort of unofficial linguistic Gestapo based on popular usage, that the man who uses good traditional English may be laughed to scorn because he refuses to subscribe to popular innovations and the fads of the moment. I once had occasion to use the term *hard-boiled eggs* in a manuscript submitted to a food editor; it came back "corrected" to *hard-cooked eggs*. "No one uses *hard-boiled* any more; it is passé" was the dictum; yet *hard-boiled* is the good old term I have known since I first acquired English. Another similar "correction" was *to point up* for *to emphasize*. So far as I am aware (and I am open to correction) *point up* is one of the veriest newcomers to our linguistic scene; *emphasize, stress, point to the importance of* are all old, respected, established utterances. Yet one is old hat, it seems, if he does not discard them for the parvenus.

One field in which the Voice of Authority tends to make itself felt more and more is that of written-language styling. The Secretary of the Modern Language Association recently took a poll of seventy-eight scholarly journals and thirty-three university presses to determine the stylistic rules prevailing in the matter of manuscripts. These were combined into a thirty-two-page booklet which is the *dernier cri* for manuscript styling, and which was forthwith adopted by the majority of the periodicals and presses consulted. If this movement gains headway, we shall eventually be faced with a regularization in our writing and printing styles which will come dangerously close to the pronouncement of a language academy. It will mean fewer doubts and headaches for writers, editors and publishers. It will also mean a partial regimentation of our written language.

For the spoken tongue, we have numerous proposals which go back to the days of Thomas Cooke, who in 1729 suggested that all verbs be made weak, all plurals be formed in -s, and the comparative and superlative of adjectives be invariably formed with *more* and *most* instead of -er and -est. Greig, in the twentieth century, advances practically the self-same proposals, which would turn English into a semblance of Esperanto.

It is conceivable that one day, for international or other reasons, some of these proposals may be translated into action. For the time being, there is very little chance of this, and the very fact that we have no language academy or other body qualified to do more than record established usage works against their acceptance.

The foreseeable future does not hold out the prospect of any major changes in our language, written or spoken, beyond the numerous vocabulary innovations that are contributed to us day by day from the most varied sources. If there is to be a spelling reform, the chances are it will occur very gradually. The sounds of the language will probably remain what they are, save for a gradual *rapprochement* between British and American pronunciation, and a gradual obliteration of extreme dialect features in both varieties. The grammar seems to have reached the point of crystallization, and is unlikely to undergo further simplification, save in the eventuality of cataclysmic occurrences. The syntax has achieved a working pattern within whose framework there is room for all reasonable innovations and combinations of words. The vocabulary, of course, is in a state of transformation and evolution, as it has always been, and the present-day Englishman or American would probably need a comprehensive glossary to understand all the words of the English of the year 2067.

Grammars, dictionaries, and the Voice of Authority will always be with us, tending, as they have tended since their inception, to become less normative and prescriptive, more objective and descriptive. They are to be used, like all works of reference, not blindly, but with a measure of critical spirit. There is, after all, only one Book directly inspired by God. All other guides to human conduct are man-made and therefore fallible. Let us accept and use them for what they are, not for what they cannot be expected to be.

Chapter Five

THE TEACHING OF ENGLISH

Problems of Literacy—English to Foreigners—Spelling and Grammar vs. Style and Literature—The Value of English Classes—Abolishing the Study of English—A Saner Way

Occasionally, and surprisingly, a voice is raised to inform us of the distressing "illiteracy and ignorance" that prevailed in the ancient Roman Empire. Actually, the standards of literacy of Rome were as high, or higher, than those that existed in the western world until the dawn of the nineteenth century. When we became a nation, barely twenty per cent of the people knew how to read and write. As late as 1840, when our first census was taken, only forty per cent of the population of the United States was literate, and the situation in the countries of western Europe was, if anything, worse. Distinctive signboards over stores and other places of business, symbolic devices like our cigar-store Indian and the red-and-white barber pole were not decorations; they were necessities. Carved Chinese images indicated tea stores, and pictured Beau Brummels directed attention to tailors' establishments in the days of our largely illiterate great-great-grandparents.

What has brought about the change in the literacy situation is the spreading of public, free, universal, compulsory education —the same device, incidentally, barring the feature of compulsion, that the Romans developed in the later centuries of their Empire, when state-endowed *grammatici* were planted in every town and hamlet of Italy and the provinces.

In the United States, according to recent studies, there are about ten million "sheer or near illiterates," people without the equivalent of a fourth-grade education, who either cannot read or are unable to understand what they read well enough for the purposes of good citizenship. 4,200,000 are said to be native-born whites, 3,200,000 foreign-born whites, and 2,700,000 Negroes. One million of these people live in New York State, nearly half a million in Illinois, nearly four hundred thousand in California. Louisiana, with an estimated thirty-six per cent of its population illiterate, has the poorest showing among our states, Iowa, with only four per cent, the best. The illiterates outnumber our college graduates nearly three to one, which is appalling.

The fourth grade as a dividing line between literacy and illiteracy is based on the Army's wartime experience, when it was discovered that as a rule people with less than fourth-grade schooling could not read or obey simple orders. This leaves a little leeway, and we may, if we choose, console ourselves with the thought that many people with less than four years of formal education are intelligent, and manage to make their way and add to their education in their spare time. Yet, when we compare our showing with that of countries like England, Germany, Switzerland, Norway or Japan, where fully ninety-nine per cent of the population is literate, we realize that this is one field where we cannot boast of being the best. Even Samoa, where ninety-four per cent of the population over ten years of age is under educational supervision, outstrips us.

Numerous projects are under way to wipe out the disgrace of illiteracy from our midst. Foremost among them is one carried on under the joint auspices of the Carnegie Foundation, the American Association for Adult Education, and the National Conference on Adult Education and the Negro. Headed by John W. Studebaker, former U. S. Commissioner of Education, this project is thoroughly streamlined and employs the Army methodology to teach our illiterates to throw off their shackles. Even our surviving American Indians participate in the crusade, with the Cherokees of Oklahoma holding out for full literacy in both English and their own language, for which Sequoya devised a syllabic system of writing.

The Rev. Frank Laubach, who has helped countless backward nations to overcome the curse of illiteracy, and has devised alphabets for 312 languages previously unwritten, has set up, in con-

nection with the War on Poverty, literacy centers all over the
United States, and particularly in areas with heavy Negro and
foreign populations. In such states as Arizona and New Mexico,
illiterate Spanish speakers are first taught to read and write in
Spanish, then in English.

So far as we of the United States are concerned, literacy means
primarily the ability to read and write the English language.
This means that the problem of literacy is intimately bound up
with the teaching of English, not to foreigners, but to our own
people, and not as a literary, stylistic or esthetic pursuit, but as
a functional, practical, bread-and-butter topic.

Since, however, much may be learned from the experience of
teaching our language to foreigners, both child and adult, it may
be well to survey what goes on in that field before reverting to
the broader and more pressing problem of how best to impart
our language to ourselves.

The man who does not know the language of the country in
which he happens to be may rightfully be compared to a functional illiterate. Keenly aware of this fact, our Federal, State and
local authorities, often with the help of private organizations and
individuals, carry on a constant campaign for the imparting of
English to the foreigners in our midst. Ironically, these "foreigners" are sometimes full-fledged American citizens, as is the
case with New York City's large and growing Puerto Rican community.

Here the problem of teaching English to both children and
adults is a mass enterprise. The children are subject to local education laws, but filling a classroom with children who speak
nothing but Spanish and placing them under the supervision of
a teacher who speaks nothing but English is hardly a solution.
The solution that has been found satisfactory by the New York
educational authorities is to endeavor to limit the size of classes to
between fifteen and twenty-five, select teachers who are acquainted
with the Spanish language and the customs of Spanish-speaking
lands, and, in general, to try to meet the students half-way. This
is a vast improvement over the old methodology of the days of
unrestricted immigration from Europe, when the newcomers were

thrown into a classroom and left to adjust themselves as best they could to an English-speaking environment. Classes for adults are also offered, but here the methodology is somewhat different, because the adults have various linguistic backgrounds and a mature incentive for learning which is lacking in children. By and large, the school system of New York is doing a splendid job in the teaching of English to foreigners at all stages of development.

Cultured foreigners are often put through intensive English language courses that last only two months. Here a combination of Basic English and Army audio-visual methodology, devised by I. A. Richards of Harvard, is put into play, with films and phonograph records used on an extensive scale. Similar systems are in vogue at New York University and at Columbia, where a six-week course at the American Language Center often permits the foreigner to carry on his business in the United States with a minimum of language difficulties. The YMCA and YWCA offer intensive courses for foreigners. Professor Fries of the University of Michigan has devised a course for foreigners which is based on the latest findings of linguistic science; here it is the phonemic pattern of English that is stressed—the significant differences in sound which are reflected in meaning, as, for instance, the distinction between *live* and *leave,* which foreign speakers often interchange with ludicrous results.

In the teaching of English to our American Indian survivors, it has been found expedient to use two instructors at once, a regular teacher and a native "teacher-interpreter." This is largely a duplication of the Army method for imparting foreign languages to the soldiers.

While these experiments in the teaching of English as a foreign language have cast a great deal of light upon problems of foreign-language teaching methodology, a few of their features have been reflected in our teaching of English to natives. If it is possible, for instance, to get the foreigner to distinguish between *live* and *leave* by repeatedly calling his attention to the semantically significant phonemes of the two words, is it not also possible to correct by the same process such native-speaker mispronunciations as *sing-ger* and *boid?* If we can impart the fundamentals of English grammar to a foreigner in a speed-up six-week course, can we not also do something about improving in a hurry the grammatical habits of our native population? If we can quickly broaden the foreigner's vocabulary by a careful selection of true key words, why not extend the methodology to our own school population?

Of growing importance is the teaching of English to foreigners abroad. There are American Language Centers at such institutions as Columbia and the University of Michigan, where foreign students perfect the English which they will presumably carry back with them to their own countries when they leave us. But the really big work in this field is carried on abroad, by our USIS offices, schools and libraries, and by the English Speaking Union and British Council of Britain, which are in collaboration, but also in competition with each other. Robert Hutchins, in a syndicated column that appeared in August of 1964, gave us the pessimistic news that we were losing the Battle of the English Language to the British, whose British Institute schools are imparting British English to the populations of Europe, Asia and Africa more effectively than our own USIS schools impart American English. This may be true, but the USIS record is nevertheless impressive. In one single year, 77 American-language seminars were given for the benefit of over 6,000 native teachers, whose own native student bodies summed up to well over a million. The British Institute Schools are flanked by private organizations such as English Language Services, which undertakes to set up English teaching facilities anywhere in the world at the request of the local government, and has so far set them up in such Afro-Asian countries as Somalia, Iran, Libya, Tunisia, Cameroon, and Guinea. It would seem that our own giant corporations which are endeavoring to do business in underdeveloped countries might follow this highly practical lead.

This duality in the spreading of English has its own peculiar disadvantages. While Hutchins claims that the brand of English spoken in Rome is almost incomprehensible to Americans, and that in Lisbon every taxi driver and waiter says *shop-assistant* and *lift* and fails to respond to *clerk* and *elevator,* another writer, who spent two years in Nigeria, suggests that the British and we get together and create an English Language Institute with merged forms and vocabularies, at least for purposes of international propagation of our perhaps common language.

The present-day teacher of English is a far cry from the old-time schoolmaster who taught by parsing and diagramming sentences on the board and by reading to the class pieces of abstruse poetry that the class could not understand and appreciate. He (or she) is today a very practical-minded person, who is fully aware of the pitfalls of the language and the latest scientific and educational devices for circumventing them. He seldom tries to teach English in a vacuum, but relates the subject to all of life's manifold activities, as well as to the other subjects of the curriculum. Above all, he is no longer a stuffy grammarian of the prescriptive school, but a broadminded person who realizes that language is perpetually changing, and that allowances must be made for this fact.

Despite the generally high quality and modern directives of our English instruction for native speakers, there are frequently voiced complaints that all is not well. It is not only Churchill who has demanded that the language be "not unduly damaged by modern slang adaptations and intruders," and expressed horror at the *quantify* used by the Chancellor of the Exchequer; it is also foreign students in America who protest against the way the language is misused by its native speakers—instructors who don't pronounce words distinctly and leave many of them unfinished, fellow-students whose tongue is "barbarous," "atrocious," "boorish."

Professor Stanley Weintraub, of Pennsylvania State University, suggests that students of both sexes mind their language with the utmost care and make every effort to improve it, not as an academic exercise, but in their own economic self-interest. The type of English you use can aid or block you in the achievement of your ambitions. Ability to communicate quickly and clearly is more important than ever before, and competition for room at the top of the business world is keener. His suggestions: avoid lazy, slipshod habits, both in speech and in writing; revise what you write; when in doubt, ask; speak up, share your ideas, in the best language you can muster; read what is written by those who have authority in the use of words; study how words are used; don't skip words you don't understand or you may lose the sense of the whole passage; check meanings in the dictionary, and use the library.

Occasionally, the blame for poor English standards is placed not upon the students and their desire to conform to sloppy teen-age standards, but squarely upon their teachers. Dean Pollock of N. Y. U., who also happens to be a professor of English, addressing an assembly of the New York State English Council, told the teachers that they were naturally to blame for the fact that students misspell from twenty-five to fifty per cent of words in their themes, and that it was no use passing the buck from one educational level to another, or blaming the home or society. Indifference, fostered by newer teaching practices and ultraprogressive, ultrapermissive methodology, were largely responsible, in his opinion. The thing to do was to give the students, at whatever level, some good old-fashioned drilling in the spelling of such words as *their, receive, too, writing, all right, separate, until, privilege, definite, believe.* An even stronger stand was taken by the editor of the campus paper at Marshall College in Huntington, West Virginia. He accused the teachers of being themselves deficient in both oral and written English, saying *assept* for *accept,* using *don't* where *doesn't* was called for, and using double negatives like "don't make no mistake about it."

There are, however, some hopeful signs. One is supplied by certain new techniques for teaching English in the elementary grades. This involves what is known as programmed reading, where the child, having learned to print the alphabet, is faced with a series of pictures, many of them humorous, and asked to circle the right answer to such printed questions as "Am I an ant?" or "Am I thin?" As an ever-greater written vocabulary is acquired, the child goes on to forms of reading which are more and more complex, at the same time that he acquires his grammar inductively, by pictures and examples.

The other prong of the new teaching has to do with a much higher level of instruction. Here all the resources of modern science are poured into the educational mold—TV with feed-back devices; Visible Speech, where you "see" your voice on a screen; computers, which may be used for literary research and which can save the student untold time in such chores as index-ing and verifying. "We are using the computer," says Professor Stephen Parrish of Cornell, "to do what we have been ac-customed to doing ourselves, only more slowly, more clumsily, and less accurately."

The picture is one of confusion. Perhaps the confusion is no greater than it was in previous centuries, when the battles be-tween the purists and the innovators raged. Yet, in the face of growing literacy and more widespread education, we have a lowering of the standards. In the face of the greatest crop of books, newspapers and magazines the world has ever known, we have one-tenth of our population that never reads a newspaper, and one-third that never reads a book. In the face of more higher education than any country has ever seen, there is less ability to express our thoughts clearly and concisely in our own native tongue, either in speech or in writing.

The crisis in our civilization is one of both thought and lan-guage. It is possible that complex thought may be crystallized in non-linguistic terms, but the evidence is all against it. Language is only a symbol of thoughts, but the symbol is essential and, to the best of our knowledge, indispensable. Our culture has grown up around language in the same fashion that our economic life has grown up around money, the symbol of exchange. Can we go back to direct barter in our economics without wrecking the very basis of our civilization? Can we revert to abstract thought, and its exchange by means of picture-symbols, disregarding and discarding the linguistic medium that has acted as the conveyor of thought since the dawn of culture?

If we do not want this to happen, ought we not to "mind our language," so that it will be as precise a thought-transmitter as possible?

Minding our language means not necessarily keeping it static, but keeping it sufficiently stable and unified, so that it may at all times mean approximately the same thing to all its users. It is in this connection that the teachers of English are called upon to exercise their prerogative and their function, to act not as dictatorial arbiters, but as democratic moderators, recalling to order the most unruly among their disciples, pointing out the very real pitfalls that line the way of those who would march ahead too rapidly, and at the same time gently prodding the laggards, who would lie down and sleep in the cool shade of the past.

"Make way for yesterday!" shout the worshipers of the traditional. "Usher in tomorrow—today!" reply those to whom all change is improvement. But the English language has a present as well as a past and a future. The enjoyment and utilization of that present, the seizing of the day in which we live is essential, if we would make our own contribution to the fleeting historical picture.

It is not one of the functions of the teacher of English to abolish his own subject. The English language, as at present constituted, has a spelling and a grammar as well as a syntax and a literature. English classes are of practical value in apprising the native speaker of the current standards of the language. The study of English should be neither abolished nor curtailed. It should be modernized, but not futurized. Above all, it should be humanized, so that all may grasp its intimate connection with life, liberty and the pursuit of happiness.

Chapter Six

LOOKING AHEAD

What We May Expect in the Next Hundred Years—
The International Predominance of English—Its Most
Fearsome Rival—Can We Impose Our Language?—
After English, What?

The next hundred years do not seem to hold forth any prospect of major internal changes for the language. Stabilization and even standardization of sounds and grammatical forms appear indicated, along with minor syntactical modifications and vast vocabulary accretion. English as a tongue for English speakers seems here to stay.

Accordingly, we may shift the spotlight back to the language's world role. In the light of what has gone before, may we forecast a global function for English, or at least an extension of its present far-flung positions?

We, the English speakers, do not always seem too eager to press the point. Since history has favored us in the past, our attitude is that we should allow history to continue its course. What we generally do is to point out to the other nations of the world our economic, technological and other material blessings. We do not invariably say that they have been achieved through the instrumentality of the English language. We often merely imply it.

But others have been quick to pick up the vaguely proffered gauntlet. A professor of Slavic languages at one of our major universities calls it highly impractical to think of English, Basic or otherwise, as a world tongue. There are too many renascent nationalisms in the world, too many different cultural backgrounds, he asserts. Many fellow-educators agree with him.

Ever since history began, it has been customary for conquerors to impose their languages upon conquered peoples. One major exception to this process was the Germanic wave that engulfed the Roman Empire, and the causes for this exception lie in the fact that the invaders accepted the religion of the invaded realms along with the Roman tradition of universality. Since both these factors converged upon Latin as their established tongue, it was little more than natural for the invaders to relinquish their own tongues in favor of the already universal tongue they found.

The Soviet Union, in its career of ideological and material conquest, is no respecter of established patterns, whether economic, political, religious or cultural. The Soviet oligarchy deems itself the repository and spreader of a brand-new form of civilization, which owes very little to the western past, and which is bound, in due course of time, to submerge and supplant all others. It is therefore only natural that the Russians should wish to impose the vehicle of their culture and to destroy, or at least limit, the positions held by other tongues.

The reports that reach us from behind the Iron Curtain, if they are to be believed, all point in the direction of progressive Russification not merely of the Soviet Union itself, but of the satellite countries. In most of these, Russian is a compulsory subject in the schools, and students who flunk it cannot be promoted. The armies of Poland, Czechoslovakia, Hungary, Rumania, Bulgaria, East Germany, are being given Russian courses. The ratio of translation from the Russian among books published in those lands has been steadily on the rise since 1945.

The Soviet Union itself is a land of many races and tongues (as many as 175 different nationalities and 150 languages have been counted). But Russian, with closely related Ukrainian and White Russian, is the native tongue of over three-fourths of the Soviet Union's population of 230 millions or more. The Russians can afford to be generous to the minority languages and permit their cultural survival, since Russian is the "binding" language of the Union and, above all, the language that pays dividends in terms of political and economic preferment. Getting along without Russian in the Soviet Union is somewhat on a par with getting along without English in the United States; it can be done, but you won't get very far. Persecution of minority languages is unnecessary, and even undesirable, where one language dominates the scene so completely.

A study of the languages of the Soviet Union published in Moscow in 1961 indicates that most non-Russian nationalities in the Union have shifted from the Latin, Arabic, or other alphabets to the Russian Cyrillic. Only Lithuanian, Latvian, Estonian, Finnish, Armenian, Georgian and Yiddish continue to be written in their traditional alphabets. The Moldavian Rumanian of Bessarabia has been Cyrillized as to its written form, although in Rumania proper the language continues to use Roman characters. Languages of the Turkic family, which once appeared in Arabic characters, are now written in Cyrillic.

Efforts are being made to encourage non-Russian tongues to adopt words from Russian rather than from other sources. Speakers of such languages as Polish, Czech, Hungarian, Bulgarian, living abroad, often comment on the progressive Russification of the vocabularies of those languages, a process perhaps as natural as that whereby Japanese, French, Italian and German become studded with English loan-words and loan-translations. As for Russian itself, a member of the Soviet Academy of Sciences once described as "intolerable" a Russian scientific terminology cluttered with foreign words. The fact of the matter is, however, that scientific terminology is largely international in nature, and the Latin and Greek roots that overwhelmingly dominate it are just as "foreign" to English as they are to Russian.

The Soviet linguistic controversy which resulted in the triumph of the rather mild views of Stalin in the matter of the composition of the Russian vocabulary also brought out his prediction that before a world language is achieved there will arise a series of "area languages," each predominant in its own sphere; these zonal languages, he continued, will ultimately merge into one world tongue which will be "not German or Russian or English, but a new language, expressing the best elements." If Russian practice were in line with Stalin's pronouncements, there is little doubt that reasonable compromises in linguistic matters could be reached. (More recent, and presumably uninfluenced by Stalin's views, is the prediction by Gen. David Sarnoff of RCA that as communications become more and more unified, one result will be the emergence of a universal language that will derive largely from English, while another result will be some form of universal culture.)

A language that is official from the Elbe to the Amur, and that holds a measure of ideological sway over some 800 million people, cannot be for a moment disregarded. Nor can it be denied that Russian as a vehicle of scientific thought has made considerable progress in recent years. It is only recently that we were informed that the number of scientific papers published in Russian is now second only to those in English, and the science faculty of Union College urges that we study Russian for scientific purposes, as our fathers and grandfathers studied German, if we wish to keep abreast of Soviet scientific developments.

There is little doubt that if and when the question of a world language comes up for official discussion, the Russians will nominate their own tongue for the post. While the rivalry of Russian is immediate, that of Chinese, the world's most widely spoken tongue, is equally serious, though more remote. The Chinese Communists have already initiated the job of unifying and simplifying the Chinese language and imparting it to the speakers of more than seventy local dialects. The Chinese are also preparing a new phonetic alphabet, and if this development ever comes to fruition we may expect to see a very large drop in China's illiteracy, followed by the probable candidacy of the language for an international role. Meanwhile, Chinese-language textbooks are replacing English texts in the Chinese universities.

In view of all this, the international predominance of English becomes more problematical than ever. English has to a certain extent displaced its most formidable western rivals, French, German and Spanish, but only to see two new and even more fearsome contenders arise in the East.

History has a way of solving its own problems, even linguistic ones, on an inexorable and non-esthetic basis. In the past, the predominance of one or another language has been largely the result of the power factor, almost entirely divorced from esthetic, cultural, or other non-material considerations. Latin became a polished, refined language after, not before, it had spread by force of arms. French achieved its greatest international triumphs in consequence of France's dominant military position on the European continent. Esthetically and culturally Greek surpassed Latin, and Italian was at least on a par with French; but Greek and Italian did not enjoy the long international vogue of their stronger rivals. We need therefore be under no illusions that the present somewhat precarious cultural superiority of English over Russian and Chinese will save our tongue from being submerged as an internationad medium of exchange in case of a military defeat.

Still less should we delude ourselves on the basis of any hypothetical superiority in the grammatical structure of our language, its supposed greater "ease" for foreigners. Languages are not inherently easy or difficult to those who learn them from childhood, or have to learn them out of dire necessity. The complex inflectional endings of Russian, the (to us) bewildering tones and strange syntax of Chinese will be assimilated with the same ease with which Iberians and Gauls absorbed the Latin declensions and conjugations, if history dictates that people who want to travel, trade or hold government posts must know Russian or Chinese.

We must guard ourselves against the illusion that nations and languages are everlasting, or that a predominance once acquired may not be lost. To history, nothing is sacred.

A victorious British-American combination may impose its language over the world. So may a victorious Soviet bloc, and probably by a more drastic process. So may, in the not too distant future, a mighty, united, industrialized China. And, since historical come-backs have been known to take place, there is really nothing to prevent French, or German, or Spanish, or half a dozen major languages from hoping that a lucky cast of the historical die may place them in the running.

There are some today who are of the opinion that history in

the past has been allowed too much freedom to run its course, with patent disadvantage to the victims of its march, comprising the entire human race.

Perhaps these people are thinking far in advance of their time; or perhaps they are mere impractical dreamers whose dreams will never come true.

Yet other human dreams have been realized—the dream of flight through the air that began with the legend of Icarus and ended in actuality with the Wright brothers; the dream of man's triumph over disease and pestilence, and over the blind forces of nature; the dream of conquest over matter that began with the alchemist's retort and ended with the atomic pile.

Two dreams, more persistent than the rest, still trouble the human sleeper. One is the desire to overcome another of the four dread Horsemen of the Apocalypse, War. The other is the ambition to end the confusion of the Tower of Babel, that keeps man apart from full and untrammeled communication with his fellow-man.

Our survey of the English language, brief and incomplete though it is, has carried us far, in time and space. We have seen our tongue rise from the mists of prehistory, undergo the vicissitudes to which every living language is a prey, and march on to regal pomp and imperial grandeur. We have seen it develop from the crude linguistic tool of the Anglo-Saxon tribes to the polished instrument of literary and cultural refinement it is today. We have watched it as it spread across the globe, changing and diversifying as it went.

The streams and tributaries that contribute to the mighty, flowing river of today's English are amazingly numerous and varied. A few of them we have attempted to trace, along a small portion of their course.

Comparisons among the world's great languages are, in a sense, as futile as comparisons among the world's great rivers. Who shall say if the Amazon or the Mississippi, the Volga or the Yang-tze or the Nile, is most beautiful, and most useful to those who dwell along its banks?

Whether English is to continue to play the role of one of the world's major tongues, or whether events will call upon it to perform a more widespread international function, is something for history to decide. In either eventuality, it is for speakers of English to see to it that the language, passed down to them by countless generations that welded and polished it into a remarkable tool of semantic transfer, shall not suffer by their own handling of it.

List of Works
Most Frequently Consulted

List of Works Most Frequently Consulted

Adams, J. Donald, *The Magic and Mystery of Words*, Holt, Rinehart & Winston, New York, 1963

Alexander, Henry, *The Story of Our Language*, Dolphin, Garden City, N.Y., 1962

Anderson, George K., *The Literature of the Anglo-Saxons*, Princeton University Press, Princeton, 1949

Barnett, Lincoln, *The Treasury of Our Tongue*, Knopf, New York, 1964

Baugh, Albert C., *History of the English Language*, 2nd ed., Appleton-Century-Crofts, New York, 1957

Bernstein, Theodore M., *The Careful Writer*, Atheneum, New York, 1965

Berrey, Lester, and Van den Bark, Melvin, *American Thesaurus of Slang*, Crowell Co., New York, 1942

Bradley, Henry, *The Making of English*, Macmillan Co., London, 1904

Bronstein, Arthur, *The Pronunciation of American English*, Appleton-Century-Crofts, New York, 1960

Brown, Charles E., *Flower Lore*, The Author, Madison, Wis., 1938

Brown, Ivor, *I Give You My Word and Say the Word*, Dutton & Co., New York, 1948

Brown, Ivor, *A Word in your Ear and Just Another Word*, Dutton & Co., New York, 1945

Carr, Charles T., *German Influence on the English Vocabulary*, Society for Pure English, Tract XLII, Clarendon Press, Oxford, 1934

Chase, Stuart, *The Power of Words*, Harcourt, Brace & Co., New York, 1954

Chase, Stuart, *The Tyranny of Words*, Harcourt, Brace & Co., New York, 1953

Clark, G. N. *Dutch Influence on the English Vocabulary*, Society for Pure English, Tract XLIV, Clarendon Press, Oxford, 1934

Colville, Derek, and Koerner, J. D., *The Craft of Writing*, Harper, New York, 1961

Craigie, William A., and Hulbert, James R., *Dictionary of American English on Historical Principles,* University of Chicago Press, Chicago, 1936–1944

Craigie, William A., *The Growth of American English I-II,* Society for Pure English, Tracts LVI-LVII, Clarendon Press, Oxford, 1940

Craigie, William A., *The Irregularities of English,* Society for Pure English, Tract XLVIII, Clarendon Press, Oxford, 1934

Craigie, William A., *Northern Words in Modern English,* Society for Pure English, Tract L, Clarendon Press, Oxford, 1934

Craigie, William A., *Problems of Spelling Reform,* Society for Pure English, Tract LXIII, Clarendon Press, Oxford, 1944

Craigie, William A., *Some Anomalies of Spelling,* Society for Pure English, Tract LIX, Clarendon Press, Oxford, 1942

Cummings, Parke, *Dictionary of Sports,* Barnes & Co., New York, 1949

Daryush, A. A., *Persian Words in English,* Society for Pure English, Tract XLI, Clarendon Press, Oxford, 1934

Duckett, Eleanor S., *Alcuin, Friend of Charlemagne,* Macmillan Co., New York, 1951

Ekwall, Eilert, *Concise Oxford Dictionary of English Place-Names,* Clarendon Press, Oxford, 1947

Evans, Bergen, and Evans, E. Cornelia, *Dictionary of Contemporary American Usage,* Random House, New York, 1957

Flesch, Rudolph, *The Art of Readable Writing,* Harper & Bros., New York, 1949

Follett, Wilson, *Modern American Usage* (edited and completed by Jacques Barzun and others), Hill and Wang, New York, 1966

Fowler, Henry W., *Concise Oxford Dictionary of Current English,* Clarendon Press, Oxford, 1951

Fowler, Henry W., *Dictionary of Modern English Usage,* Oxford University Press, London, 1947

Fowler, Henry W., *Dictionary of Modern English Usage,* 2nd ed. (ed. Ernest Gowers), Oxford University Press, London, 1965

Fowler, H. W., and Fowler, F. G., *The King's English,* Clarendon Press, Oxford, 1931

Fries, Charles, *American and English Grammar,* Appleton, New York, 1940

Funk & Wagnalls New Standard Dictionary of the English Language, Funk & Wagnalls, New York, 1963

Gordon, G. S., *Shakespeare's English,* Society for Pure English, Tract XXIX, Clarendon Press, Oxford, 1928

Gowers, Ernest, *Plain Words,* H. M. Stationery Office, London, 1948

Gray, Jack C., *Words, Words and Words About Dictionaries,* Chandler, San Francisco, 1963

Green, Abel, and Laurie, Joe, Jr., *Show Biz,* Holt & Co., New York, 1951

Greet, W. Cabell, *World Words,* Columbia University Press, New York, 1948

Greig, J. Y. T., *Breaking Priscian's Head,* K. Paul, Trench, Trubner & Co., London, 1928

Groom, Bernard, *Formation and Use of Compound Epithets in English Poetry,* Clarendon Press, Oxford, 1937

Groom, Bernard, *Short History of English Words,* Macmillan Co., London, 1934

Hall, Robert A., Jr., *Melanesian Pidgin Grammar,* Linguistic Society of America, Baltimore, 1943

Hayakawa, Samuel I., *Language in Action,* Harcourt, Brace & Co., New York, 1942

Hayakawa, Samuel I., *Language and Thought in Action,* Harcourt, Brace & Co., New York, 1949

Hayakawa, Samuel I., *The Use and Misuse of Language,* Harper, New York, 1962

Herbert, Alan, *What A Word!,* Doubleday, Doran & Co., New York, 1936

Horwill, H. W., *American Variations,* Society for Pure English, Tract XLV, Clarendon Press, Oxford, 1934

Horwill, H. W., *An Anglo-American Interpreter,* Clarendon Press, Oxford, 1939

Horwill, H. W., *Dictionary of Modern American Usage,* Oxford University Press, New York, 1944

Hubbell, Allan F., *The Pronunciation of English in New York City,* King's Crown Press, New York, 1950

Jagger, J. Hubert, *English in the Future,* Nelson & Sons, London, 1940

Jespersen, Otto, *Growth and Structure of the English Language,* 9th Ed., Blackwell, Oxford, 1948

Jespersen, Otto, *Language,* Allen & Unwin, London, 1949

Jespersen, Otto, *Modern English Grammar on Historical Principles,* Winter, Heidelberg, 1927–1949

Johnson, Burges, *The Lost Art of Profanity,* Bobbs-Merrill Co., Indianapolis, 1948

Jones, Daniel, *English Pronouncing Dictionary,* Dent & Sons, London, 1948

Jones, Daniel, *Outline of English Phonetics,* Dutton & Co., New York, 1939

Jones, Daniel, *The Pronunciation of English,* Cambridge University Press, Cambridge, 1950

Kennedy, Arthur G., *Bibliography of Writings on the English Language,* Harvard University Press, Cambridge, 1927

Kennedy, Arthur G., *Concise Bibliography for Students of English,* Stanford University Press, 1945

Kennedy, Arthur G., *Current English,* Ginn & Co., Boston, 1935

Kenyon, John S., and Knott, Thomas A., *Pronouncing Dictionary of American English,* Merriam Co., Springfield, Mass., 1944

Krapp, George P., *Comprehensive Guide to Good English,* Rand McNally & Co., Chicago, 1928

Krapp, George P., *The English Language in America,* Century Co., New York, 1925

Kurath, Hans, and associates, *Linguistic Atlas of the United States and Canada,* Brown University, Providence, R. I., 1939–1941

Kurath, Hans, *Word Geography of the Eastern United States,* University of Michigan Press, Ann Arbor, 1949

Laird, Charlton, *A Writer's Handbook,* Ginn & Co., New York, 1964

Lambert, Eloise, *Our Language,* Lothrop, Lee & Shepard, New York, 1955

Lee, Donald W., *Functional Change in Early English,* Banta Pub. Co., Menasha, Wis., 1948

Lewis, Norman, *How to Speak Better English,* Crowell & Co., New York, 1951

Lorge, Irving, and Thorndike, Edward, *Semantic Count of English Words,* Institute of Educational Research, Teachers' College, Columbia University, New York, 1938

Lorge, Irving, and Thorndike, Edward, *Teacher's Word Book of 30,000 Words,* Teachers' College, Columbia University, New York, 1944

Manual of Style, A, University of Chicago Press, Chicago, 1949–1963

Marckwardt, A. H., *American English,* Oxford University Press, New York, 1958

Masterson, James R., and Phillips, Wendell B., *Federal Prose,* University of North Carolina Press, Chapel Hill, 1948

Mathews, M. M., *Beginnings of American English,* University of Chicago Press, Chicago, 1931

Mathews, M. M., *Dictionary of Americanisms on Historical Principles,* University of Chicago Press, Chicago, 1951

Mathews, M. M., *Some Sources of Southernisms,* University of Alabama Press, University, Ala., 1948

Mathews, M. M., *Survey of English Dictionaries,* Oxford University Press, London, 1933

Matsell, G. W., *Vocabulum, or Rogues' Lexicon,* Matsel, New York, 1859

Mawson, C. O. Sylvester, *Dictionary of Foreign Terms,* Thos. Y. Crowell, New York, 1934

May, Thomas Erskine, *Treatise on the Laws, Privileges, Proceedings and Usage of Parliament,* Butterworth & Co., London, 1946

McKnight, George H., *English Words and their Background,* Appleton Co., New York, 1923

McKnight, G. H., and Emsley, B., *Modern English in the Making,* Appleton Co., New York, 1928

Mencken, Henry L., *The American Language,* 4th ed., Knopf, New York, 1946 (Supplement I, 1945; Supplement II, 1948)

Miriam Joseph, Sister, C.S.R., *Shakespeare's Use of the Arts of Language,* Columbia University Press, New York, 1947

New English Dictionary on Historical Principles, Clarendon Press, Oxford, 1884–1933

Newmark, Maxim, *Dictionary of Foreign Words,* Philosophical Library, New York, 1957

Nicholson, Margaret, *Dictionary of American English Usage,* Oxford University Press, New York, 1957

Nist, John, *A Structural History of English,* St. Martin's Press, New York, 1966

Ogden, C. K., *Basic English,* K. Paul, Trench, Trubner & Co., London, 1940

Ogden, C. K., and Richards, I. A., *The Meaning of Meaning,* Harcourt, Brace & Co., New York, 1952

O'Leary, Frank, *Dictionary of American Underworld Lingo,* Twayne, New York, 1951

Ormsbee, Thomas H., *Field Guide to Early American Furniture,* Little, Brown & Co., Boston, 1951

Partridge, Eric, *Dictionary of Clichés,* Routledge & Kegan Paul, London, 1950

Partridge, Eric, *Dictionary of Slang and Unconventional English,* Routledge & Kegan Paul, London, 1949

Partridge, Eric, *Dictionary of the Underworld,* Routledge & Sons, London, 1950

Partridge, Eric, *English: a Course for Human Beings,* Macdonald Pub., London, 1949

Partridge, Eric, *Here, There and Everywhere,* Hamish Hamilton, London, 1950

Partridge, Eric, *Name This Child,* Hamish Hamilton, London, 1951

Partridge, Eric, *Origins: a short etymological dictionary of modern English,* Macmillan, New York, 1958

Partridge, Eric, *Slang, To-day and Yesterday,* Routledge & Kegan Paul, London, 1933

Partridge, Eric, *Usage and Abusage,* Hamish Hamilton, London, 1948

Partridge, Eric, *Words at War, Words at Peace,* Muller, London, 1948

Partridge, Eric, *World of Words,* Hamish Hamilton, London, 1948

Partridge, Eric, and Clark, John W., *British and American English Since 1900,* Philosophical Library, New York, 1951

Pei, Mario (ed.), *Language of the Specialists,* Funk & Wagnalls, New York, 1966

Pei, Mario, *The Families of Words,* Harper, New York, 1962

Potter, Simeon, *Our Language,* Pelican, London, 1950

Random House Dictionary of the English Language, Random House, New York, 1966

Reddall, Henry F., *Fact, Fancy and Fable,* McClurg, Chicago, 1892

Reifer, M., *Dictionary of New Words, Philosophical Library,* New York, 1955

Richards, I. A., *Basic English and Its Uses,* Norton & Co., New York, 1943

Roberts, Arthur, *Fifty Years of Spoof,* Lane, London, 1927

Robertson, Stuart, *Development of Modern English,* 2nd ed., Prentice-Hall, New York, 1954

Sapir, Edward, *Language,* Harcourt, Brace & Co., New York, 1921

Sayer, Edgar S., *Pidgin English,* The Author, Toronto, 1943

Scott, George R., editor, *Swan's Anglo-American Dictionary,* Library Publishers, New York, 1952

Serjeantson, Mary, *History of Foreign Words in English,* Routledge & Sons, London, 1935

Shaw, Arnold, *The Lingo of Tin Pan Alley,* Broadcast Music, New York, 1949

Shipley, Joseph T., *Dictionary of Early English,* Philosophical Library, New York, 1956

Shipley, Joseph, *Dictionary of Word Origins,* Philosophical Library, New York, 1945

Skeat, Walter W., *English Dialects from the Eighth Century to the Present Day,* Cambridge University Press, 1911

Sledd, James, and Ebbitt, Wilma R.. *Dictionaries and THAT Dictionary,* Scott, Foresmann & Co., Chicago, 1962

Starnes, De Witt, and Noyes, Gertrude, *The English Dictionary from Cawdrey to Johnson,* University of North Carolina Press, Chapel Hill, 1946

Stevenson, Leonard A., *The Ill-Spoken Word,* McGraw-Hill, New York, 1966

Sweet, Henry, *New English Grammar, Logical and Historical,* Clarendon Press, Oxford, 1931

Tauber, Abraham, *Shaw on Language,* Philosophical Library, New York, 1963

Thorndike, Edward L., *Comprehensive Desk Dictionary* (edited by Clarence Barnhart), Doubleday & Co., New York, 1951

Trevelyan, George M., *History of the English,* Longmans, Green & Co., New York. 1937

Turner, Lorenzo D., *Africanisms in the Gullah Dialect,* University of Chicago Press, Chicago, 1949

Ullmann, Stephen, *Language and Style,* Barnes & Noble, New York, 1964

Ullmann, Stephen, *Words and Their Use,* Philosophical Library, New York, 1951

Vaux, James Hardy, *A New and Comprehensive Vocabulary of the Flash Language in Memoirs. Written by Himself,* London, 1819

Waldhorn, Arthur, *Concise Dictionary of the American Language,* Philosophical Library, New York, 1956

Watkins, Julian L., *The 100 Greatest Ads,* Moore Pub. Co., New York, 1950

Webster's Third New International Dictionary, unabridged, Merriam Co., Springfield, Mass., 1961

Weekley, Ernest, *The English Language* (with chapter on American English by John W. Clark), Andre Deutsch, London, 1952

Weekley, Ernest, *Jack and Jill,* Dutton & Co., New York, 1940

Weekley, Ernest, *Romance of Words,* Murray, London, 1927

Weekley, Ernest, *Surnames,* Murray, London, 1936

Wells, H. G., *Anticipations of the Reaction of Mechanical and Scientific Progress upon Human Life and Thought,* Harper, London, 1902

Wentworth, Harold, *American Dialect Dictionary,* Crowell & Co., New York, 1944

392 THE STORY OF THE ENGLISH LANGUAGE

Wentworth, Harold, and Flexner, Stuart B., *Dictionary of American Slang*, Crowell, New York, 1960

Whitford, R. C., and Foster, J. R., *Concise Dictionary of American Grammar*, Philosophical Library, New York, 1955

Williams, Margaret, *Glee-Wood*, Sheed & Ward, New York, 1949

Williams, Margaret, *Word-Hoard*, Sheed & Ward, New York, 1940

Wrenn, Charles L., *The English Language*, Methuen & Co., London, 1949

Zachrisson, R. E., *English in Easy Spelling*, Almqvist, Uppsala, 1929

A Selected List
of Words and Expressions

A Selected List of Words and Expressions

guest, 57
guesting, 235
guilt, 30
gullion, 198
gun, 285
gutbucket, 233
Gymnodinium, 224

hail, 22
hale, 27
half room, 210
Haligonian, 130
hall, 22
hamburger, 184, 248
hand, 41
handbook, 25, 49, 95
hanger-on, 23
hang-nail, 251
hangover, 279
hankie, 192
happening, 120
happy, 27
hard, 21
hard-boiled, 366
Harlem, 128
harlot, 117
harp, 22
harry, 22
hat, 28
have, 92
he, 21
head, 94
heart, 41, 78
hearth, 94
heather, 24
heister, 197
hell, 268 f.
help, 40, 84
hepatica, 224
her, 21
here, 96

highbrow, 73
high-minded, 118
hight, 21
him, 21
his, 46, 83
hit, 27
hitchhiker, 234, 279
hoagy, 171
Hohokus, 128
holdup, 238
holy, 20, 25
Holy Ghost, 25
home, 94, 279
hooch, 168
hookers, 195
hoosegow, 106
Hoosier, 131
horn, 22
Horse Marines, 247
hose, 22
hospitalization, 214
hot issue, 217
hot rod, 112
house, 22, 94
housekeeping, 226
how, 20, 78, 96
howby, 226
howdonit, 250
hubbub, 109
humble pie, 251
humiture, 115
humorous, 61
hundred, 8
hundreder, 25
hung up, 217
hurricane, 66, 225
husband, 27
hussy, 23, 89
hybrid, 104, 260

I, 21, 49, 92 f.

Index

Index

Laird, Charlton, 361
Langland, William, 48, 141
Language academy, 359, 365
Language block, 310
Language learning, 316
Language of flowers and the fan, 272
Larison, Cornelius, 342
Latin, 6, 8 f., 17, 23 ff., 31, 34 ff., 44,
    49 ff., 54, 56, 67, 80, 87 f., 92 ff.,
    100 ff., 104, 111, 125, 127, 208, 222,
    224 ff., 237, 248 f., 251 f., 276, 279,
    281 f., 284, 294 f., 308, 325, 333,
    336, 339, 353 ff., 357 ff., 378 f., 381
Latin America, 329
Latin-Greek, 29
Latin-Romance, 324
Latini, Brunetto, 37
Latinisms, 67
Latvian, 379
Laubach, Frank, 369
"Law French," 40
Layamon, 41, 141
Learned words, 49, 88
Legal terms, 208
Legal texts, 72
Leibniz, Gottfried, 102
-less, 88
Levels of speech usage, 189
Lewis, Norman, 362
Lexicographers, 67, 355, 360
Liberia, 266
Libraries, 331
Libya, 372
-like, 21
Lindsay, Vachel, 349
Lingo of Tin Pan Alley, 193
Lingua Franca, 329
Linguaphone Institute and record-
    ings, 169, 171 f., 317
Linguistic Atlas of the United States,
    169 f.
Linguistic controversy, 363, 379
Linguistic nationalism, 165
Linguists, 354
Literacy, 35, 52, 58, 68, 123, 149, 178,
    305, 369, 375
Literary language, 40, 77, 105, 138
Literature, 18 f., 75, 162, 237, 376
Literaturnaya Gazeta, 264
Lithuanian, 7 f., 379

Loan-translations, 48, 73, 101, 104,
    107, 128, 131, 145 f., 163 f., 167,
    180, 183 f., 242, 379
Loan-words, 10, 22 ff., 32, 88, 282, 352,
    379
Localisms, 351
-lock, 88
Logical gender, 81
London, 17, 46, 52, 157 f.
London Gazette, 237
London Times, 237, 287
Londonese, 72
Longobards, 11
Longsword, William, 32
Long vowels, 78
Lord's Prayer, 29
Lorge, Irving, 118, 283
Loss of flectional endings, 278, 281
Louisiana, 72
Low German, 12 (see also German,
    Germanic languages)
Low Latin, 116
Lowlands of Scotland, 28, 45
Lowth, Robert, 358
Luce, Clare Boothe, 115
Luther, Martin, 107
-ly, 21, 82
Lydgate, John, 50
Lyly, John, 66

Mac-, 133
Mc-, 133
Macauley, Thomas, 361
Macdonald, Dwight, 114
McLuhan, H. M., 301
Madison Avenue language, 221
Mafia, 196
Malapropisms, 245
Malay, 109, 176, 263, 330
Malaya, 174, 329
Malay-Indonesian, 153
Malone, John, 343
Malory, Thomas, 50
Mandarin, 212
Manias, 227
Mannus, 7
Manuscripts, 295
Manuscript styling, 366
Maori, 165, 266
Marie de France, 35

Studebaker, John W., 369
Style, 64
Styling, 297
Subrostrani, 300
Substandard language, 139, 192, 237, 353, 364
Suffixes, 82, 84, 88 f., 95, 98 f., 125 f.
Sumerians, 225
Superlative, 82, 366
Superscripts, 296
Surinam, 176
Sussex, 12, 157
Sweden, 327
Swedes, 72
Swedish, 7, 10, 185
Swift, Jonathan, 65, 286, 359
Switzerland, 327, 369
Syllable division, 294, 353
Sylvester, Robert, 256
Symbolism, 258 f., 263, 270, 272, 274, 277, 303, 375
Synonyms, 41, 99, 103, 280, 283
Syntax, 15, 19, 60, 64, 76 f., 86 f., 174, 306, 352, 360, 367, 376 f., 381

Taboos, 145 ff.
Tacitus, 6 f., 55
Tagalog, 335
Tahiti, 175
Talkie-talkie, 176
Tamil, 330, 336
Technical terms, 93, 329
Technology, 221
Teen-agers' language, 192, 195, 198, 245, 254
-*tel*, 114
Television, 75, 230 (*see also* TV)
Telstar, 162, 234
Tennyson, Alfred, 93, 141
Tense-system, 322
Tenses, 8, 21, 83 f.
Tertullian, 291
Teutones, 6
Teutonic, 21, 31, 94 (*see also* Germanic languages)
Tewkesbury, 260
th, 78
th-, 180, 292 f.
-*th*, 95
Thackeray, William, 249, 361

Theatrical terms, 194
Thomas, Lowell, 254
-*thorpe*, 27, 126
Thurber, James, 256
-*thwaite*, 27, 126
Tilde, 296
Times-Picayune, 140, 240
Titles, 265
Todisco, Alfredo, 288
-*toft*, 27, 126
Tolstoi, Leo, 330
-*ton*, 126
Tones, 381
Toponymy, 127, 131 (*see also* Place-names)
Trade jargon, 195, 204
Trade marks, 219 f.
Trade names, 133, 218 f.
Traffic signals, 273 f.
Transcriptions, 340
Transferred place-names, 133
Transitive verbs, 85
Translation, 18, 55, 233, 264, 313, 378
Transportation, 75
Trevelyan, George M., 36
Trinidad, 177
Tristan and Iseut, 35
Trollope, Mrs., 73
Trucking terms, 201
Truman, Harry S., 134, 144
-*try*, 126
Tuisco, 7
Tunisia, 372
Turkey, 328 f., 346
Turkish, 108, 186, 296, 379
Turoldus of Peterborough, 35
Tuscan, 325
Tuscanisms, 56
TV, 232, 234, 237, 269, 275, 282, 313, 315, 331, 351, 375 (*see also* Television)
Twain, Mark, 29
Tyndale, William, 63, 141
Tyranny of Words, 322

Udall, Rep., 112
"Ugly" words, 192, 309
Ukrainian, 378
Ulster, 157
Umlaut plurals, 80

About the Author

Mario Pei is a linguist, teacher, and author of numerous articles and books on language. He has a knowledge of the world's 2,796 languages, and is recognized as one of the foremost contemporary authorities on languages. George Bernard Shaw once commented that Professor Pei's "prodigious memory and knowledge remind me of Isaac Newton." He has been a professor of Romance Languages at Columbia University since 1937.

The Story of English, of which *The Story of the English Language* is a revised edition, first appeared in 1952.